Praise for *Spoilt*

'Elections are serious business. They are th[...] of a democracy, deciding power and leade[...]. [...] levity and meticulous research, Nick Dall and Matthew Blackman have told the stories of South Africa's long history at the polls in a compelling and entertaining way, bringing narratives to life through the protagonists and the juicy sideshows. From the mother of all elections in 1854 to our journey over the rainbow and the chaos of the ANC internal battles, you will learn way more than you expect between these covers. Crucially, *Spoilt Ballots* will make you value being enfranchised in the face of growing voter apathy.'

– Mandy Wiener, journalist and author

'*Spoilt Ballots* is constructed around the extraordinarily simple but important idea of examining "Elections that Shaped South Africa". So often today, there is so an assumption that the only elections in South Africa that have seriously mattered have been those of 1924, 1948 and 1994, but as Matthew Blackman and Nick Dall demonstrate, there is need to dig much deeper for us to understand the present political impasse. All those who want to understand the country's trajectory over the long run of history will enjoy this lively and well-written text.'

– Roger Southall, Emeritus Professor of Sociology, University of the Witwatersrand

'A superbly researched deep dive into critical inflection points in South Africa's electoral history.'

– Nickolaus Bauer, journalist

Praise for *Rogues' Gallery*

'One of the most entertaining books I've read in recent times... It's a fabulous piece of work, it really is. If it didn't matter so much, it would be hilarious. But it does matter, and that's the point that you make.'

– Bruce Whitfield, The Money Show, 702

'This is one of the most engaging accounts that I have read in a long, long time... If it were up to me, this book would be in every school in the country!... A very important and timeous book; read it and have fun.'

– Marianne Thamm, Daily Maverick webinar

About the authors

Matthew Blackman has written as a journalist on corruption in South Africa, as well as on art, literature and history. He has a PhD in Creative and Critical Writing from the University of East Anglia. He lives in Cape Town with a dog of nameless breed.

Nick Dall has an MA in Creative Writing from the University of Cape Town. His work as a journalist has taken him from Jesuit ruins in Paraguay to the limestone caves of Vietnam, but he now does most of his travelling in history books. He lives in Cape Town with his family.

This book is dedicated to all those who suffered at the
hands of the undemocratic forces that have plagued our country.

SPOILT BALLOTS

The Elections that Shaped
South Africa, from Shaka to Cyril

MATTHEW BLACKMAN and NICK DALL

PENGUIN BOOKS

Spoilt Ballots

Published by Penguin Books
an imprint of Penguin Random House South Africa (Pty) Ltd
Reg. No. 1953/000441/07
The Estuaries No. 4, Oxbow Crescent, Century Avenue, Century City, 7441
PO Box 1144, Cape Town, 8000, South Africa
www.penguinrandomhouse.co.za

Penguin
Random House
South Africa

First published 2022

1 3 5 7 9 10 8 6 4 2

Publication © Penguin Random House 2022
Text © Matthew Blackman and Nick Dall 2022

PUBLISHER: Marlene Fryer
MANAGING EDITOR: Robert Plummer
EDITOR: Alice Inggs
PROOFREADER: Dane Wallace
COVER DESIGNER: Monique Cleghorn
TEXT DESIGNER: Ryan Africa
TYPESETTER: Monique van den Berg
INDEXER: Sanet le Roux

Set in 11 pt on 15 pt Minion

Printed by **novus print**, a division of Novus Holdings

ISBN 978 1 77609 637 4 (print)
ISBN 978 1 77609 638 1 (ePub)

CONTENTS

ABBREVIATIONS

AAC: All-African Convention
ANC: African National Congress
ANCYL: African National Congress Youth League
AP: Afrikaner Party
APO: African Political Organisation
AWB: Afrikaner Weerstandsbeweging
AZAPO: Azanian People's Organisation
BSAC: British South Africa Company
CODESA: Convention for a Democratic South Africa
COPE: Congress of the People
COSATU: Congress of South African Trade Unions
CP: Conservative Party
CPSA: Communist Party of South Africa
DA: Democratic Alliance
DMI: Department of Military Intelligence
DP: Democratic Party
EFF: Economic Freedom Fighters
FF+: Freedom Front Plus
HNP: Herenigde Nasionale Party
ICU: Industrial and Commercial Workers' Union of Africa
IEC: Independent Electoral Commission
IFP: Inkatha Freedom Party
MK: Umkhonto we Sizwe
MPNP: Multiparty Negotiation Process
NP: National Party
NPA: National Prosecuting Authority
NPP: National People's Party
NRC: Native Representative Council
NUM: National Union of Mineworkers
OB: Ossewabrandwag
PAC: Pan Africanist Congress
PFP: Progressive Federal Party
SADF: South African Defence Force
SANC: South African Native Congress
SAP: South African Party
SASO: South African Students' Organisation
SDUs: 'self-defence units'
UDF: United Democratic Front
UP: United Party
ZAR: Zuid-Afrikaansche Republiek

INTRODUCTION

'I have cherished the ideal of a democratic and free society in which all persons live together in harmony and with equal opportunities. It is an ideal which I hope to live for and to achieve. But if needs be, it is an ideal for which I am prepared to die.' – **Nelson Mandela**

Few countries have had a longer or harder-fought battle to achieve 'a democratic and free society' than South Africa. Wars have been waged, moral stands made, murders committed, imprisonments enforced, people tortured, ballots cast (and ballots denied) and gross acts of corruption carried out.

As those who have taken even a cursory interest in South Africa's politics will know, nothing has ever been simple south of the Limpopo. In almost every decade of our recorded history, we have been visited by hate, discrimination and power-hungry politicians. But among these pestilences we have witnessed dramatic and principled stands, made by some of the most fascinating characters in world history.

While it is tempting to blame our past on the actions of a few particularly nasty pieces of work, it is seldom acknowledged that these once-revered leaders drew their power from the (mostly white) people who voted for them. As a survey in *The Star* in 1975 revealed, 87 per cent of the white population believed that Nazi sympathiser President B.J. Vorster was doing a 'good' or 'excellent' job.

It's common to hear people say that we shouldn't judge history by modern standards – 'those were different times' is a common refrain. By quoting at length from contemporary letters, diaries, speeches and newspapers, we show that there have always been some in Mzansi who have felt that black votes matter.

Spoilt Ballots begins by outlining how, after the assassination of Shaka Zulu, collective decision-making about a change of leadership shaped the new Zulu nation. We then trace the first non-racial, democratic constitution of the Cape Colony (men of all races could vote in 1854!) and its slow disintegration in the hands of venal politicians like Cecil John Rhodes.

Taking a detour to Oom Paul Kruger's ZAR, we reveal that despite a franchise banning all blacks and many whites from voting, there was a group of people who longed for something a little more progressive. In fact, Kruger was once very nearly voted out of office by his own *volk*.

Of course, these were simply the precursors to what would become the fantastically badly thought-out Union of South Africa. In Part Two, we follow what happens when politicians with totally opposing views – like John X. Merriman and Louis Botha (1910) and Jan Smuts and J.B.M. Hertzog (1933) – try to get into bed with each other. Continually conceding ground to firebrands and *verkramptes*, rather than listening to moderate oppositional voices (many of which were black and/or female), can take you swiftly down the ox-wagon track to apartheid.

Apartheid itself is often thought to have been an entirely Afrikaner nationalist project, which it was at first. But without a popular majority of white voters, the system would never have taken hold. *Spoilt Ballots* proves that the two great exponents of 'grand apartheid', H.F. Verwoerd and B.J. Vorster, knew all too well they would have to go *hoed in hand* to the English-speaking electorate. And that they did – with considerable success.

For decades, white voters and politicians conveniently ignored the fact that excluding the majority from any form of representational democracy would only end in disaster. Eventually, despite their deeply racist inclinations, P.W. Botha and F.W. de Klerk clicked that concessions were required. As sanctions and political violence heated up in the 1980s, P.W. placed his crocodile toe in the waters of the Rubicon and found them not to his liking. His attempts to rejig apartheid were scuppered when coloured and Indian South Africans stayed away from the polls.

A few years later, with the country in a state of collapse and the moral force of Nelson Mandela weighing on his shoulders, F.W. took the democratic plunge. The ideal for which Madiba had been prepared to die was suddenly one for which he could live. On 27 April 1994, millions of black South Africans voted for the first time, ushering in the supposed pot of egalitarian gold at the end of the rainbow.

But as our newly baptised – and nearly drowned – nation emerged from those elected waters, a new (but entirely familiar) politics of confusion and corruption surfaced under the ANC. Not for the first time in our history, the ruling party's internal squabbles and elections took precedence over the will of the people, and the country's politics are currently as confused as ever.

Spoilt Ballots tells the story of the long road to democracy and how it has repeatedly forked off. First stop, the Zulu kingdom in the winter of 1828...

PART ONE
EARLY DAYS

Before 1910, South Africa was a jumbled collection of kingdoms, colonies and republics with zero consensus on how leaders should be elected – or who should elect them.

CHAPTER I

DINGANE HAS HIS DAY
1828

*'The killing of people is a proper practice, for if
no killing is done there will be no fear.' – **Nzobo kaSobadli**[1]*

'Dingane in Ordinary and Dancing Dresses'
depicted by Captain Allen Francis Gardiner in 1836

IN JUNE 1828, AFTER THE devastating failures of the *iHlambo impi* (the Zulu campaign against the Mpondo people in the eastern Cape), Shaka's warriors were in desperate need of some rest and recuperation at home. Instead, the King of the Zulus immediately called up an even larger force, which included, according to the testimony of Jantshi, whose father had been close to Shaka, 'all the riff-raff... even old men with bad knees'.[2] The *Bhalule impi*, as this hastily organised campaign became known, was to be a long-range mission that would see the Zulu army attempt to bring to heel the Gaza people in the southern fringes of what is now the Kruger National Park.

The combination of tired men and unfamiliar, disease-ridden territory made the second campaign even more disastrous than the one before. In fact, the *Bhalule impi* was later given as evidence of Shaka having gone mad. But in one way at least it was proof that he was still of sound mind. Shaka had hastily convened the *Bhalule impi* because he was worried that his half-brothers Dingane and Mhlangana were, once again, plotting to kill him. The brothers certainly had plenty to be aggrieved about. Since the death of Shaka's mother, Nandi, in August 1827, the king had been even more cruel and torturous than usual, to friends and foes alike. This reign of terror would have been hard enough to bear if Nandi had died of natural causes. But the brothers had reason to believe that Shaka was behind her death and was exploiting it for political reasons.

As historian and Shaka expert John Laband puts it,

> Shaka did what so many other rulers have done when confronted by treacherous but high-born conspirators. He sent them away on a dangerous military campaign to give himself breathing space, and with the hope that they would perish... They in turn would have understood his motives and must have feared that he would execute them if they survived the campaign.[3]

While this might seem like a fairly short-sighted way of dealing with a potential *coup d'état*, there was method in Shaka's supposed madness. He was hopeful that by the time his army returned from the *Bhalule impi*, he would have secured an important alliance with the man he called Mjojo (you may know him as King George IV). Instead, on 26 August, the first Zulu embassy to the British-ruled Cape Colony returned to Zululand with their tails firmly between their legs. Forget London! They hadn't even made it as far as Cape Town, having been fobbed off on the low-ranking officials of the insignificant settlements of Port

Elizabeth and Grahamstown. Shaka wasn't just incensed, he was mortifyingly embarrassed.

The making of the image of a monster

The further one goes back in Zulu history, the less anything can be said for certain. We'll likely never work out when Shaka was born, let alone the finer details of his life and death. But still he looms over our national history like a colossus who has meant many different things to many different people.

Historian Carolyn Hamilton has closely examined depictions of Shaka from the 1820s onwards, with some surprising results. During Shaka's lifetime he was, almost without fail, portrayed by both the Port Natal traders and the press at the Cape as a 'benign patron'. An 1826 newspaper article described him as 'obliging, charming and pleasant, stern in public but good-humoured in private, benevolent and hospitable'.

The European image of Shaka as a despot and madman only started to take shape after his death, writes Hamilton: 'at this point, precisely because the Zulu king was dead, the traders could malign Shaka to provide an "alibi" for their own actions'. (The traders, who had been – correctly – accused of fighting on Shaka's side in various wars, suddenly claimed that they had only done so on pain of death.) Interestingly, '[in] their case against Shaka they drew on a stock of stories … garnered from African informants'.

At the risk of generalisation, these African images of Shaka-the-despot came from two broad camps. First, it suited Shaka – who presided over a vast and barely consolidated kingdom – to be seen as ruling with an iron fist. As Hamilton notes:

the Zulu authorities fostered this image through carefully managed displays of despotism and brutal justice at the court, using terror as a basis for absolute rule across a huge kingdom. The displays were not designed only to inspire obedience from their subjects, they were also meant to strike fear into the heart of their enemies and to impress the traders with Zulu power.

This despotism was justified by the other component of Shaka's image, that of a leader of tremendous abilities, the great unifier and the hero in battle. Both components of this image are present in his izibongo … Nongila claimed that Shaka fed people to the vultures but linked such acts to the maintenance of authority and discipline in the Zulu kingdom. He related how Shaka would cut off a man's ears if he did not listen … and that he would pick out anyone wounded in battle and kill him for being a coward.

And second, once he was dead, the many African peoples who had suffered under Shaka were able to freely express their opinions on his reign. 'Qwabe accounts of Shaka vilify him as a tyrant, *lala* accounts depict him as a marauder, a destroyer and a "madman" *sans caveats* about the maintenance of discipline.'[4] (The Qwabe were one of the dominant clans in Zululand before Shaka's rise, and the *amalala* comprised 'multiple groups of people like the Cele and Thuli.'[5])

In the two centuries since, Shaka's image has undergone frequent reinventions. For decades he was demonised as the 'motor' behind the Mfecane, and apartheid historians even went so far as to suggest that, in the words of vehemently anti-apartheid Rhodes University academic Julian Cobbing, black societies 'self-sequestered themselves into proto-Bantustans in the time of Shaka'. On the flip side, notes Hamilton, Shaka has also become the 'hero of Zulu nationalism, the centerpiece of Inkatha ideology ... the namesake of a South African theme park, even the subject of a major TV [series]'.[6]

Despite the lack of modern communications, news of the failed embassy to the Cape Colony soon reached the men of the *Bhalule impi*. Emboldened by this news, the *abantwana* (princes of the royal house) Dingane and Mhlangana conspired to return to Shaka's capital at KwaDukuza to finish off their increasingly cruel and unpredictable brother while his army was away. Not for nothing do Dingane's *izibongo* celebrate him as 'Restless one, one who left his regiment'.[7] But which of the brothers would replace Shaka after he had been dispensed with? Well, that could wait till later. Let the deed first be done ...

Apart from the exact location of the crime scene, which has been pinpointed to within a few metres, the 'circumstances surrounding Shaka's assassination are difficult to reconstruct with any unambiguous precision,'[8] notes Laband. Depending on who you believe, the killing took place on 21, 23 or 24 September 1828, at a time that was either early in the day, towards sunset or late at night. Current consensus among historians seems to be that it most likely occurred just before sunset on 23 September.

Shaka, together with a few preferred concubines and important members of his court, was watching his immense herds of cattle being brought homewards for the night. On this evening he was also entertaining a group of about ten men who were probably bringing him crane feathers for his ceremonial garb.

None of this was at all unusual, nor was the fact that Shaka was loudly berating the feather-bearers for their tardy arrival. As Laband tells it, 'during this hubbub Dingane and Mhlangana approached the king and greeted him, pretending they had just returned from the hunt … Their intention had been to kill Shaka on the spot, but finding him so surrounded, they withdrew to confer anxiously' with the third member of the hit squad, Mbopha – Shaka's most trusted advisor and the only person allowed to carry a spear in the king's presence.[9]

Mbopha, it seems, ran up to the feather-bearers and, brandishing a spear, began telling them off even more stridently than Shaka. Having lived under Shaka's bloody reign for over a decade, the feather-bearers assumed that Mbopha was acting on royal orders and that the sign had been given for their execution. They scattered, running for their lives into the dusky hills.

As with every aspect of the story, what happened next is the subject of much conjecture. But, because the exact detail of who stabbed Shaka and who did not would have more bearing on the eventual outcome of the succession struggle than any other aspect of the tale, we should probably examine the sources more closely.

A note on sources

Henry Francis Fynn
—

The earliest contemporary written records about this episode date back to the founding of the rudimentary European settlement of Port Natal in 1824. While written by people who had lived during Shaka's reign, the traders' journals were generally only published decades after the events they had described. The journals of Nathaniel Isaacs and Henry Francis Fynn tend to portray the 'Zooloos' as barbaric savages and the money-grabbing British traders as benevolent saviours. The one European eyewitness source that paints Shaka and his people in a more sympathetic light was written by Charles Rawden Maclean aka John Ross, a young English boy who spent several years in Shaka's court. (The 1980s TV series *John Ross* is worth a watch on YouTube.) Reading Maclean, who was only ten years old when he arrived in Natal in 1825, is a breath of fresh air. The following passage, where he debunks the myth that Shaka ordered 'seventy or eighty children to be massacred' because one cheeky kid had peeped into his hut, exposes British attempts to rewrite history:

My intentions are far from vindicating cruelties, with many of which Shaka can be justly charged ... [But] the atrocity of Shaka's barbarity in the above statement is only equalled by the falsehood of the whole tale! ... [A]ny knowledge we have of the Zulus as a nation and of Shaka as their chief, and his slaughter of children, is a portion of that history which was never heard of at Natal up to the death of him who is represented to have perpetrated that atrocity![10]

African sources are also problematic. By far the most important collection of Zulu oral testimonies of Shaka's and Dingane's reigns is to be found in the six (at last count) volumes of the *James Stuart Archive of Recorded Oral Evidence Relating to the History of the Zulu and Neighbouring Peoples*, which records some two hundred conversations between Stuart (a rural magistrate who was fluent in Zulu) and local interlocutors between 1890 and 1920. By speaking to such a wide range of informants, Stuart encountered people who both revered and despised the Zulu king, and as such his archive presents many different viewpoints. But we should also note that the conversations took place between sixty and ninety years after Shaka's death and so must be clouded by both memory and the prevailing views of Shaka at the time.

Two of the European sources, not to mention a number of Zulu testimonies, were convinced that, as Maclean put it, 'the cringing and cowardly scoundrel named Mbopha' had stabbed first.[11] Other sources say that Mhlangana stabbed first because 'Dingane was sickened of killing after witnessing Shaka's constant executions'.[12] It is likely no coincidence that Dingane is never fingered as the primary culprit: some accounts have him simply restraining Shaka as the others stabbed, but many sources say he *did* join in the stabbing. The most truthful utterance came from Jantshi, who told Stuart he could not 'speak accurately on this matter'.[13]

On the subject of Shaka's final words, there is, once again, plenty of conjecture. While some have him begging for mercy from the 'sons of my father' and pleading to be their 'menial', this hardly seems like the kind of thing the great warrior would have said. Equally implausible – if only for the fact that philosophising doesn't tend to come naturally to someone with spears sticking out of them – are the sources who have him conveniently predicting the ills that would come from colonialism. These sources make frequent mention of the white 'swallows' that would come up from the ocean with their houses of mud and 'overrun the land'.[14]

It seems likely, writes Laband, that Shaka's actual last words – like most last words – were more mundane: 'The accounts closest to the time of his death are in agreement that Shaka only had time to gasp incredulously, "What is the matter my father's children?" before choking on his blood and collapsing to the ground as he tried to break free.'[15]

'The nations he hath all destroyed'

While Shaka did eventually fall spectacularly from the tightrope that all military dictators walk, he deserves plenty of credit for his efforts in taking the Zulu nation from also-ran to omnipotent – as these famous lines from his *izibongo* attest:

> The nations he hath all destroyed
> Whither shall he now attack?
> He! Wither shall he now attack?
> He defeats kings[16]

In little over a decade, Shaka went from being pretender to an obscure and largely irrelevant throne (or rather, an *umqulu* or rolled-up mat) to lord of all the people north of the Thukela. This incredible rise was wrapped up in the so-called Mfecane. If you took high-school history at any time in the past century, chances are your teacher taught you about an event that used to be translated as 'The Crushing'. According to this telling, the rise of Shaka caused scores of black African peoples to scatter across the interior of South Africa, leaving it largely unpopulated.

In a series of papers written in the 1980s, Julian Cobbing set the jackal among the pigeons by claiming that 'The Time of Troubles' (an alternative translation of 'Mfecane') had actually been caused by the arrival of white settlers at the Cape and in present-day Maputo. The myth of Shaka's brutal displacement had, he argued, been used as an 'alibi' by generations of white historians who wanted to justify seizing the land.

The truth lies somewhere between these two extremes. These days, it is generally accepted that from the 1750s onwards, there was a period of great turmoil among the people in north-eastern South Africa. The reasons for the upheaval were many (drought, increasing populations, the arrival of Europeans, the Delagoa Bay slave trade), but the net result was that lots of small fry were replaced by a few bigger and increasingly more powerful fish. Shaka's *izibongo* gives a feel for how he took power in those turbulent times:

The voracious one ...
Spear that is red even on the handle ...
The young viper grows as it sits,
Always in a great rage,
With a shield on its knees.[17]

Born sometime in the 1780s, Shaka was one of (it seems) eighteen sons of Senzangakhona kaJama, head of the 'unremarkable Zulu chiefdom in the valley of the White Mfolozi River'.[18] The bones lay against him from the start. Not only was Shaka *not* the 'great son' of Senzangakhona,* but there remains to this day a very strong suspicion that he was born out of wedlock and thus not remotely entitled to the throne. Several sources suggest that the name Shaka is derived from *itshaka*, an intestinal beetle that causes the stomach to swell. The connection being, according to Jantshi, that the beetle's name 'was used to describe a girl who became pregnant before marriage, and the illegitimate child she bore was also spoken of as *itshaka*'.[19]

Unsurprisingly, this is not the only explanation for Shaka's name. Pioneering Zulu historian Magema Fuze reckoned that it referred to the fact that Shaka would 'violently disturb [*shakazisa*] all the tribes'. Yet another source explains that Shaka was an additional praise name given to him by none other than Dingane and meant 'He who beats but is not beaten'.[20]

As a youngster, Shaka was taken in by Dingiswayo, chief of the stronger Mthethwa people. Impressed by Shaka's military nous, not to mention his incredible prowess on the battlefield, Dingiswayo supported his young protégé in usurping Shaka's father. Shaka is said to have played an active role in the bewitching of his dad, with one version describing him actually climbing onto the roof of Senzangakhona's hut while he slept and washing himself with a potion that contained his father's *insila* (toenail clippings, hair, urine or even semen). The evil brew is then said to have dripped fatally through the thatch and onto the sleeping king.[21]

---

* As John Laband explains, the great son or heir (*inkosana*) is the king's eldest son by his great wife (as designated by him) and not necessarily his eldest son, who might have been born to a lesser wife. This 'rule' did not make for a peaceful or easy succession, and both Shaka and Dingane did away with those who were their genealogical superiors. Today, the ongoing succession battle in the Zulu royal house has some familiar features: since the death of King Goodwill Zwelithini in March 2021, conflict has escalated between two factions, one supporting King Misuzulu kaZwelithini, the other supporting the claim of Prince Simakade, who, although born out of wedlock, is the former king's eldest son.

No (Macassar) oil painting

This sketch by Capt. King is the only contemporary depiction of Shaka – but even King seems to have taken a lot of poetic licence

What did Shaka look like? Popular historian Stephen Taylor hazards as good a guess as anyone:

> Zulu sources agree that he was powerfully made, with the heavy haunches ... and that his skin had an especially dark tint. He was extremely strong and, it was said, could lift a cow off the ground by its back legs. But there his resemblance to the perfect physical specimen ... ended. He was not unusually tall, and he was ugly [a fact he admitted to himself]. In what way his features were unattractive is unclear, but he is said by some sources to have had a protruding forehead and buck teeth. Perhaps because of this slight deformity, his speech was impeded.[22]

What's more, one of Shaka's rivals claimed that the great king wore 'as a penis cover the [tiny] fruit-shell used for snuffboxes',[23] while Maclean (aka John Ross) reveals another vulnerable side to the great warrior:

> While closely surveying his person in this mirror for the first time in his life he detected some grey hairs in his beard, which caused him a great uneasiness ... He anxiously enquired of Capt. King [another of the first European settlers] if the Mlungus [whites] had any medicine that could prevent such effects of increasing years. The captain replied in the affirmative, that the Mlungus could do such things, which pleased his majesty so much that he declared when his vessel was finished [King was building a ship] he should send it to his friend King George for the valuable preparation.[24]

And so began a lifelong obsession with obtaining Rowland's Macassar Hair Oil, which played at least a minor role in Shaka's demise – his desire for the stuff was a driving force behind his failed embassies to the Cape.

Then, with the backing of Senzangakhona's conniving sister Mnkabayi kaJama, Shaka conspired to have his brother Sigujana drowned while bathing (a recurring theme) and thus seize the (then inauspicious) Zulu throne. Shaka's star would continue to rise after Zwide, chief of the Ndwandwe, killed Dingiswayo and Shaka became the de facto leader of the wider Zulu–Mthethwa grouping. In the years that followed, his shrewd generalship saw him defeat first Zwide and then anyone else who got in his way.

While he was usurping or displacing all the local ethnic groups, Shaka also agreed to allow the establishment of the first European settlement, in May 1824, on the wild stretch of coastline that had been christened Natal (i.e. Christmas) by Vasco da Gama on 25 December 1497. The trading post at Port Natal (renamed Durban in 1835) was the brainchild of James King and Francis Farewell, who, after riding out a storm in the natural harbour there, had become convinced, according to Maclean, of

the position and advantages offered by Natal for commercial enterprise – the forest abounding in elephants and the rivers with hippopotami, and that friendly disposition evinced by the natives towards Europeans, by which a very profitable traffic might be carried on for ivory.[25]

A group of thirty-five pioneers set off in two vessels, the first captained by Henry Francis Fynn (who would marry a Zulu woman and live out the rest of his days in Natal) and the second by Farewell. The project – like most start-ups – got off to a very rocky beginning, with twenty-nine of the original party calling it quits before the year was out. But, bolstered by consequential reinforcements, including King, Isaacs and Maclean who all arrived in 1825, the six who remained set in motion a process that forever changed the history of the region.

Despite hoisting the Union Jack almost as soon as they arrived, the original settlers were there very much on Shaka's terms, and British officials at the Cape refused to recognise or support them. In August 1828, Fynn and Farewell were summoned to make their case in person at Shaka's capital at kwaBulawayo (between Eshowe and Richards Bay), where

[t]heir outlandish garb, incomprehensible speech, light skin colour, extra-ordinary hair – likened to maize tassels or cattle tails – unfamiliar horses and terrifying firearms threw ordinary people and even the *amabutho* [age-grade

regiments] into consternation and astonished Shaka himself ... It is to Shaka's credit that he decided to make use of them instead of rejecting them.[26]

Shaka realised that he'd have more control over these traders than he would over the Portuguese in Delagoa Bay, and he was also hopeful that they'd be able to foster relations with the British authorities at the Cape. (He was not to know that Farewell and Fynn were nothing more than private traders looking to make a quick buck.) He also saw the value their firearms could bring to his army.

This sketch of Farewell's camp by J.P. Hoffman, one of the
original settling party, shows just how basic things were

Shaka soon put his mark on a document that purportedly gave Farewell and co. the right to occupy a swathe of coastline that extended roughly from Umhlanga in the north to Amanzimtoti in the south, and as far inland as present-day Pietermaritzburg. Tembeka Ngcukaitobi, who has written two books on the history of land in South Africa, points out that there are many problematic aspects to the agreement, not least that 'Shaka had no right to grant land outside of the main Zulu polity'.[27]

As with many other documents in Africa's history, the agreement meant very different things to each side. The traders, who were really only in it for the money, were keen to secure both protection and access to ivory. Shaka, meanwhile, saw the white settlers as just another set of subjects who had to pay tribute and render him military assistance.[28] The fact that Shaka was illiterate might have been used to pull the wool over his eyes (we don't know whether any of his interpreters could read, but we can be fairly certain that none would have been highly fluent in English). But with the Zulu king holding all the trump cards, it was, initially at least, his interpretation that held sway.

Stabbed while dancing

The sheer scale and speed of his ascent to power meant that Shaka's reign was not equally accepted in all corners of his kingdom. Consequently, he had to rely very heavily on force to maintain control of his subjects. Both of these factors were likely behind the first attempt on his life, which Fynn witnessed during the splendid annual *umkhosi wokweshwama* (first fruits ceremony) in 1825:

> As it was dark when I entered the kraal where the dancing was going on, the King ordered a number of people to hold up lighted bundles of dried reeds to give light to the scene ... I had not been there many minutes when I heard a shriek and the lights were immediately extinguished. Then followed a general bustle and crying ... At length I found out that Shaka, while dancing, had been stabbed.[29]

The combination of hysterical crowds and total darkness meant that the would-be killers were not even glimpsed. But this would not stop Shaka – and others – from hypothesising. Shaka's subjects were convinced that the assassins had been sent by Shaka's great rival Zwide, ruler of the Ndwandwe, and they even went so far as to kill several supposed culprits.

Shaka himself was not as easily swayed. And like a true politician, he publicly blamed one faction (the Qwabe people) while secretly suspecting another: his half-brothers Dingane and Mhlangana.[30]

Throughout his life Shaka cited the fact that he'd only ever killed one of his brothers (Sigujana) as evidence of his magnanimous leadership (no matter that he'd had thousands of innocent subjects executed). But was it really magnanimity or just plain foolishness? It's hard to fathom why he didn't act upon his hunch and get rid of his brothers after the 1825 assassination attempt. Shaka, of all people, should have known that the greatest benefit of execution is its finality.

A tale of two holidays

The memorial to Shaka in KwaDukuza

Next 24 September, while you're patriotically sizzling your *wors* and *tjops*, take a moment to remind yourself that Heritage Day started off as a commemoration of the anniversary of Shaka's death. First observed by Zulu nationalists (why they didn't go with the more likely date of 23 September is anyone's guess), it was made a national holiday in 1994 as a way of placating Prince Mangosuthu Buthelezi and his many followers. Now, Jan Braai seems to have claimed it for himself.

The Day of Reconciliation on 16 December, meanwhile, isn't just the day that every second South African wedding takes place. It actually commemorates the resounding defeat of Dingane's forces by the Boers at the Battle of Blood River (aka Ncome) in 1838. '"Dingaan's Day" gradually became a platform for overtly racist political speeches by white supremacists,' writes Sifiso Ndlovu, and in 1952 the apartheid government officially renamed it the Day of the Covenant.[31] At the same time, a rise in Zulu nationalism led to the 'counter commemoration' of the day 'as an act of defiance.'[32] The Communist Party organised anti-pass demonstrations on 16 December 1929, 1930 and 1934. After 1994, it was decided to keep the holiday with the aim of promoting 'national unity' and 'social cohesion.'[33] Falling nine days before Christmas had nothing to do with it.

'Stealthy-mover like a water snake'[34]

Perhaps, as he lay dying on that September evening in 1828, Shaka asked himself why he had not had his brothers killed all those years before.

No sooner had Shaka breathed his last than the electioneering began. Somewhat ironically, considering they had removed Shaka because of the brutal nature of his rule, the first thing the *abantwana* did was to execute several of Shaka's closest advisors. They then performed a sacred ballad honouring the great deeds of their ancestors and sacrificed a black ox in Senzangakhona's honour. The crowds, who had fled as soon as the killers set upon Shaka, now returned to participate in the ceremony.

But the celebrations were short-lived, and, writes Laband, Dingane and Mhlangana 'soon became involved in a dispute that laid bare the smouldering rivalry they had succeeded in damping down while Shaka still lived'.[35] After those who had performed the sacrifice had drunk the ox's gall, it was Zulu custom for the instigator of the sacrifice to wear the empty gall bladder on their arm. Predictably, both Dingane and Mhlangana insisted that they deserved this privilege. Before the brothers could come to blows, Mbopha, simpering third wheel that he was, stepped in and offered to wear the gall bladder on *his* arm (i.e. act as king) until the army returned from the *Bhalule impi* and made their choice of successor clear.

Shaka's corpse was left outside overnight as it was believed hyenas would never disturb the body of a king. But come daybreak, the stiff and mutilated body of 'the voracious one of Senzangakhona' could be ignored no longer.[36] In what might well be another case of history being dictated by the victors, Mhlangana apparently suggested feeding Shaka to the crocs, but the more level-headed Dingane insisted on a proper burial – a process that involved the body sitting in state (tied to the central pole of a dedicated funeral hut and kept company night and day) until everything the king had ever worn or used had been gathered 'from across the kingdom to join him in his grave'. The only thing he would not be buried with were his spears – lest he come back from the spirit world to avenge his killing. Shaka was eventually buried, accompanied by his most elite advisors (talk about taking one for the team) and, according to Fynn, gagged with a piece of his own buttock covering to prevent his malevolent spirit from escaping.[37]

Worried that the Zulu nation might descend into civil war, the Port Natal traders decided to sit out the succession battle in Port Elizabeth. But, much like their white descendants who fled South Africa in the lead-up to the 1994 elections, they had underestimated the Zulus' ability to resolve issues politically.

With the men of the *Bhalule impi* still away on campaign, Dingane and Mhlangana took up residence in separate *ikhanda*, and Mbopha continued his role as acting king. While the once-inseparable brothers succeeded in being outwardly civil to one another, notes Laband, what lay beneath was anything but: 'while they nervously trod water, the two princes eyed each other with increasing distrust and antagonism, their old intimacy shrivelling in the heat of mutual suspicion and intensifying ambition.'[38]

The conflict between the brothers assumed centre stage once they'd put aside their differences to exterminate Ngwadi (a pesky upstart whom Shaka had allowed to assemble his own army). In late November, some two months after Shaka's killing, 'the senior members of the royal house and the great nobles of the realm were summoned to meet and discuss the succession.'[39]

Then as now, the rules were bent by the senior backroom strategists in order to achieve the desired outcome. And none was more senior or influential than Mnkabayi, Shaka's unmarried aunt who was said to 'place' (choose/anoint) Zulu kings. In the kind of absurd debate that could easily take place in most modern parliaments, Mhlangana insisted that he should assume the throne because he had played the greater role in Shaka's killing and only he had ritually jumped over the corpse.

Mnkabayi countered that this was precisely the reason why Mhlangana was unfit to rule. As she put it, 'The one with the red assegai shall not rule.'[40] Her preferred candidate was Dingane. To justify this decision, Mnkabayi called into question Mhlangana's genealogical claim to the throne by celebrating the senior status of Dingane's mother, Mphikase. Conveniently, Dingane's own role in the murder was downplayed, with Mnkabayi decreeing that he was fit to rule as he had only held Shaka while the others stabbed him.

The one with the
red assegai shall not rule

'Opener of all main gates so that all people may enter'

Without the blessing of their aunt Mnkabayi kaJama, neither Shaka nor Dingane would have become king (it was even said that when Shaka was an infant, she prevented Senzangakhona from killing his bastard son), and she remained an important advisor well into the rule of Dingane's brother and successor, Mpande.

As Sifiso Ndlovu points out, 'the king could not exercise his patriarchal power without invoking Mnkabayi's spiritual powers'. In his testimony to Stuart, Ngidi went so far as to say: 'uMnkabayi was the king of KwaZulu who called the army to prepare for war, Zulu kings were crowned by her.'[41] It is a mark of her immense status that Mnkabayi's *izibongo* celebrates her as both male and female:

> Father of guile
> ... Morass of Menzi ...
> Who shoots down birds for her people,
> As they catch them she is simply watching on.
> The opener of all main gates so that all people may enter.[42]

To repay this trust, both Shaka and Dingane gave Mnkabayi control of the most important *amakhanda* (royal military homesteads) in the nation. She was also given the singular honour of being the guardian of the *Inkatha* – the sacred coil described by royal insider Nomguqo (Paulina) Dlamini as

> [t]he magic coil ... so big and so wide that the king could squat on it. It was intertwined with grass and wrapped round with some new cloth. Its contents symbolised the unity of the nation and all the values associated with the king's ancestors. The properties and magic powers of wild animals embodied in this coil were transferred through it to the people. Shaka greatly strengthened the power of the *Inkatha*. He subjected a large number of tribes but formed them into a united people by collecting bits from the *izinkatha* of vanquished tribes and particles from the bodies of slain chiefs and embodying them in his own coil.[43]

The British destroyed the *Inkatha* during the Anglo-Zulu War in 1879, but it remains strongly associated with Zulu nationalism. Mnkabayi, meanwhile, lived to the ripe old age of eighty, dying of natural causes in about 1840 – a privilege not afforded to many of her male counterparts.

Once Dingane had performed a spontaneous victory dance (he wasn't yet king, but he now knew he would be), Mnkabayi moved to the next item on her string-pulling agenda: what to do with Mhlangana. While she was convinced that he must be killed, she was equally certain that his death must be made to appear if not accidental then at least provoked.

With the help of the ever-scheming Mbopha, she convinced Dingane and Mhlangana respectively that their death was being plotted by the other. 'Egged on and assisted by his aunt', in a supposed show of reconciliation, Dingane invited Mhlangana to bathe with him in the nearby Mavivane River, where Mnkabayi's hitmen lurked. While the words below come from Dingane's *izibongo*, they would probably be more appropriate in Mnkabayi's praises:

> Deep river pool at Mavivane, Dingana,
> The pool is silent and overpowering,
> It drowned someone intending to wash
> And he vanished headring and all.[44]

While receiving Mnkabayi's blessing was as big a deal as Zuma or Ramaphosa being elected leader of the ANC, Dingane did – like them – still have to tick the final box by appealing to the majority of the populace.

Around a week after Mhlangana's death, the vanquished regiments of the *Bhalule impi* began to arrive home in dribs and drabs. So disastrous had the campaign been that many of the survivors had been forced to soak their cowhide shields in water and eat them, while others took to gnawing on the sinew that bound the blades of their spears.

Suffice to say that Dingane, like all ANC presidential candidates since 1994, had a pretty easy time winning the 'general election'. Styling himself as uMalamulela, meaning 'saviour [from the] "tyranny" of King Shaka',[45] he went on to make a number of legislative changes that were guaranteed to win over the people, most notably lifting Shaka's ban on unmarried warriors having premarital sex and allowing older regiments to marry. As the famous Zulu scholar Sibusiso Nyembezi explains:

> Young men and women ... could not marry until Shaka had given his sanction.
> He would release a certain regiment of old men to marry and would also release
> a regiment from which the men could choose their wives ... so girls found

themselves compelled to marry men they did not love. Again, all the beautiful girls were for the king and for him alone ... It was from this life that Dingana freed the people and was thus hailed as a rescuer.[46]

With both Shaka and Mhlangana out of the way, and with the all-important backing of aunt Mnkabayi, the stage was finally set for Dingane's *ukubuzana*. And who better to describe what this ceremony was all about than future Zulu king Cetshwayo?

> On the days of *Ukubuzana*, i.e. questioning one another, when the kingship of the country is being transferred from the deceased to the son, all the great men of the country assemble and talk to one another about the heir, whom they look on as king already ... They say, 'That man is king as appointed by the past king, and how are you going to treat him? You have killed some of your former kings, and how do you intend treating this one? You must take care of this king and not act out of an evil heart against him.' They simply talk in this manner to advise one another; they do not talk in anger to one another ... The heir then goes up from his kraal, where he has been staying as prince, to the former chief king's kraal as king.[47]

Of course, once Dingane had assumed the throne, many of the election promises could be thrown out the window. Indeed, his *izibongo* describes him as a 'Stealthy-mover like a damsel going to her lover; Stealthy-mover like a water snake'.[48]

That said, there is little doubt that for the average Zulu subject life under Dingane was much more pleasant than it had been during Shaka's reign. We've already seen why he was praised as 'saviour of wives and husbands, spinsters and their suitors' and, more generally, writes Ndlovu, his '*izibongo* provide evidence highlighting Dingane's good heart, generosity and liberality with cattle and food for his needy subjects. His praise-names include ... "Giver of cows with full udders".'[49]

But Dingane also quickly realised that violence was an occupational hazard of leading the Zulu nation. As his trusted advisor Nzobo kaSobadli put it, 'the killing of people is a proper practice, for if no killing is done there will be no fear'. It didn't take long for Dingane to wheel out his best Shaka impersonation, declaring to anyone who would listen that the king's vultures must be fed.

Gardiner's sketch of Dingane resting at home, surrounded by some of his wives

And Dingane didn't just feed his vultures any old human flesh. Whereas Shaka prided himself on only ever killing one of his brothers, the supposedly gentler Dingane bumped off no fewer than seven of his male siblings, not to mention around seventy other senior members of the royal house, including the deceitful Mbopha (why Dingane spared Mpande, who would later seize the throne from him, is anyone's guess). This section of his *izibongo* certainly doesn't describe a pacifist:

> Elephant whose sleep is fitful,
> While others sleep happily;
> Black arouser of the house of Sikakha,
> Who aroused people to attend their own slaughter,
> Beast that bellowed among the ashes at Nhlapho's place,
> With its mouth turned towards Zululand[50]

What next?

1830–36: Dingane engages in several successful campaigns against neighbouring African kingdoms. His first embassy to the Cape – like Shaka's before him – is a failure.

1837–38: After the Boer invasion of Zululand, Dingane initially cedes territory to the Boers, but then, on 6 February 1838, he executes Piet Retief and the Boer delegation at uMgungundlovu after what Ngcukaitobi terms 'a land deal gone sour'.[51] This leads to all-out war in which the Zulus do the early running, but the Boers ultimately emerge victorious, most notably at the Battle of Ncome (Blood River) on 16 December 1838.

1839–40: Mpande (the only brother Dingane didn't execute) sides with the Boers. With their help, Mpande defeats Dingane in the Zulu Civil War and is recognised as king by both the Zulu people and the Boers. A Swazi and Nyawo patrol surprises and kills the fugitive Dingane.

King Mpande

1840–72: Ruling alongside first the Boers and then the British, Mpande goes on to be the longest-serving (but arguably least impressive) Zulu king of the colonial era.

1872–79: After Mpande's death, the far less amenable Cetshwayo assumes the crown. When, in 1879, the British invade Zululand, Cetshwayo fights fire with fire, resulting in the rout of the British at Isandlwana. Like Dingane before him, the first few battles are his, but the war is ultimately won by the British.

Sell-out or freedom fighter?

In his 1998 paper 'He Did What Any Other Person in his Position Would Have Done to Fight the Forces of Invasion and Disruption', Ndlovu tackles the fact that Dingane's role as 'one of the pivotal figures in the history of South African race relations' has been 'relatively neglected'.[52] Dingane's othering by the Afrikaner people is fairly easy to understand (it's even explained in his *izibongo*: 'He devoured two bearded men of the Boers, Piet [Retief] and [Andries] Pretorius').[53]

But his reputation among his own people is more complex, with African images of Dingane presenting the 'king as a complex and multidimensional individual. His images range from the highly positive to the extremely negative.'[54]

As Ndlovu explains, because conservative twentieth-century African intellectuals like John Dube and R.R.R. Dhlomo 'revered and worshipped' Shaka,

> it became impossible for them to support those who were perceived to be against King Shaka's rule … According to them King Dingane was a 'culprit' who … was tainted with King Shaka's blood. These writers allege that King Dingane together with his paternal aunt, Mnkabayi, was part of the driving force and conspiracy that led to the assassination of King Shaka.[55]

Even today, this narrow perspective of Dingane persists among a large segment of the Zulu populace. But it must, Ndlovu continues, be contrasted with the much broader understanding of Dingane's place in our nation's history propagated by 'radical African intellectuals' like Selope Thema and H.I.E. Dhlomo (not to mention Ndlovu himself). These thinkers

> view King Dingane in 'global' terms by comparing him to contemporaries like Napoleon – and therefore outside the confines of the Zulu kingdom and the history of amaZulu. They also go back further into history by retrieving the past of 'European' leaders like Julius Caesar, William the Conqueror and Philip [II of Spain]. In short, they argue that when compared to these 'great European' leaders, King Dingane should be viewed as a 'patriot', 'martyr', a 'nationalist' and 'great leader' who was trying to defend his people and sovereign kingdom.[56]

They do have a point. Shaka has somehow gone down as arguably the most revered figure in our nation's history, despite being cruel to his own people and doing little to resist European encroachment. Meanwhile, Dingane, who was the first Zulu king to take a stand against the white man, is remembered by many as 'the one who let the side down'[57] for the simple fact that he was ultimately defeated by the Boers.

'Would Shaka have done anything differently when the Voortrekkers arrived?' asks Laband, somewhat rhetorically. 'They had the same generals, so it's doubtful … Being assassinated let Shaka off the hook.' He adds, 'It's always best for a great leader if you die before the end.'[58]

Same same, but different

The Zulu kingdom may seem a far cry from modern politics. But once you've accepted that ritual executions were the ultimate version of cancel culture and that cowhide garments could just as easily be Armani suits, it becomes pretty clear that humans will be humans...

- Even in a one-party state, there will always be factions. Where the ANC has the Radical Economic Transformation and Ramaphosa camps, the Zulu kingdom had *amantungwa* (insiders) and *amalala* (menials), who were said, according to some of Stuart's informants, to 'sleep with their fingers up their anuses' and to have 'farted on the mimosa tree and it dried up'.[59] As with political alliances today, exactly who was an insider and who was a menial changed as quickly as the Drakensberg weather.
- Members of the Zulu royal house, like modern politicians, understood the importance of neutering one's rivals and keeping succession plans a secret to the very last. Most obviously they did this by way of execution or assassination, but Zulu kings also made a point of not bearing any male heirs – either by practising *ukuhlobonga* (external sex) or by simply not acknowledging patrimony.
- If this chapter has left you feeling that Shaka and his cronies engaged in senseless and barbaric killing, you might do well to read about what happened when the Europeans took over...

CHAPTER 2

THE MOTHER OF ALL ELECTIONS
1854

'I would rather meet the Hottentot at the hustings voting for his representative, than meet the Hottentot in the wilds with his gun on his shoulder.'
– William Porter[1]

White men chasing rainbows: The Cape Parliament, 1854

SOUTH AFRICA'S FIRST, TENTATIVE VENTURE into liberal democracy in the Cape Colony came off the back of an almost Boston Tea Party–style rejection of British rule. And it is one of the most unusual stories in our history. If we told you that it came about due to a gay Irishman, a Scotsman and the great-grandson of a slave, you might think that this was the opening line to a potentially problematic joke. Add to this the revelation that the Cape's first democratic constitution was the most liberal and inclusive ever granted to a British colony, and you might well believe that we're simply *charfing* you. But these are the plain and simple facts ...

Seeds of discontent

By the 1830s, at least two men in the Cape Colony were thirsting for representative government and non-racial social justice. Their names were John Fairbairn and Andries Stockenström. As historian of the Cape Parliament Ralph Kilpin puts it, Fairbairn's name 'was to become a byword in the constitutional development at the Cape',[2] while Stockenström was perhaps the one man to steadfastly hold to the principle of justice for all during the first half of the nineteenth century.

It was Fairbairn, and his friend Thomas Pringle, editors of the first truly independent newspaper – the *South African Commercial Advertiser* – who helped end the corrupt and venal rule of Lord Charles Somerset in the Cape in 1826 by publishing all the details of his misdeeds. As Kirsten McKenzie writes, the 'triumph of the *Advertiser* over Somerset was a portent of a wider victory at the Cape of a new vision of political life'.[3]

It might be surprising, considering our racial history, that there were people in the Cape Colony such as Fairbairn whose liberal beliefs would drive the Colony towards a qualified non-racial democracy. What might not surprise you is that, as Andrew Bank puts it, 'liberal policy proposals and attitudes towards Africans also met with deep hostility from land-hungry British settlers on the eastern frontier locked in conflict with the neighbouring Xhosa'.[4]

Fairbairn, slavery and 'Moral Bob'

Influenced by a mix of Scottish Enlightenment and Romanticism, Fairbairn travelled across the South African interior in 1830. On crossing the Cape frontier and engaging with several Xhosa chiefs, he wrote:

> With regard to this people as a nation, or as individuals and their susceptibility of Improvement and Civilisation, as it is called, we would say, without hesitation, that we know of nothing of which an Englishman is capable, of which they are not capable. They have the same powers of mind, the same passions, the same virtues, the same views.[5]

Fairbairn stands up against racism, slavery and autocratic rule

Fairbairn, along with his father-in-law, the missionary Dr John Philip, was at the forefront of the anti-slavery movement in the Colony. He worked on the committee of the local Antislavery Society in the Cape, an organisation that helped free slaves and agitated for their emancipation. Both Dr Philip and Fairbairn would also regularly claim that the history of the Cape Colony was one of 'violent dispossession', 'hopeless bondage' and 'wrongs and outrages inflicted on the innocent and defenceless'.[6] 'I am all alone,' Fairbairn's wife complained to her

'Moral Bob' Godlonton:
Holder of the moral low ground

sister, 'Mr F does nothing but go to sleep when he comes home or sigh & groan over the sins of mankind.'[7]

One of the most prominent anti-Fairbairn voices in the Cape was a man by the name of Robert Godlonton. Godlonton was the editor of the *Grahamstown Journal*, the conservative antithesis to Fairbairn's *South African Commercial Advertiser*. Rather curiously nicknamed 'Moral Bob', Godlonton was a major exponent of colonial expansion on the frontier and a land-grabbing racist of the first water. Bank writes that 'it was Godlonton who was the first to claim that the Xhosa had no more prior land rights in the Eastern Cape than British settlers' and that he would go on to perpetuate the colonial 'empty land' mythology.[8] This myth was taught from history textbooks throughout the twentieth century and reified by Nationalist Party politicians throughout the apartheid era.

Not such a good council

The first tentative nod towards representative government in the Cape came with the arrival of Sir Benjamin D'Urban in 1834. Governor D'Urban had been authorised to create a legislative council that would include five officials of the Cape government and five to seven 'unofficial' members of the public. The council met behind the very untransparent doors of the Slave Lodge near the Company's Garden.

On 25 October 1834, Fairbairn, who had for many years called for representative institutions, officially began his agitation against the council under the headline 'Open Council'. The article detailed the events of three days before, when several Cape citizens rapped on the door of the Slave Lodge demanding 'admittance in the name of the public'.[9]

Governor D'Urban, perhaps aware of the damage Fairbairn had wrought on Lord Somerset, quickly approved a motion to allow each councillor to admit one member of the public and for all newspapers to send a reporter. The council was nevertheless still dominated by the presence of the governor, and was in reality a rubber stamp for Britain's colonial desires. However, it did implement a democratic Municipal Boards Ordinance that allowed ratepayers to form and vote for municipal boards – an early form of local government.

Another significant step forward for the constitutional movement in the Cape was the arrival in 1839 of a new attorney-general by the name of William Porter. Porter was to become the foremost figure in parliamentary life in the Cape. He cut a tall, broad-shouldered figure, and as Kilpin tells us,

> [s]omeone who saw him on his arrival wrote that he had the face of a Greek god, and another on meeting him vowed that he was a prince among gentlemen. He was the lion of society, and when it was heard that his eloquence surpassed anything that had been heard in the Cape, a new interest was given to the debates in the Legislative Council.[10]

Dearly beloved

Porter with a lion's mane

Porter was an Irishman born into the colonial situation that was Ulster in 1805. After training as a lawyer, he was appointed attorney-general to the Cape Colony at the age of thirty-four. When he arrived to take up his position, he did so with a man by the name of Hugh Lynar.

Lynar worked as Porter's clerk, although he certainly could have found a higher-paid job in Cape Town. Porter claimed it suited him and Lynar better because it meant that they could be perpetually together. As J.L. McCracken says, '[F]or many years they worked not only in the same office but on the opposite sides of the same table.'[11]

The *Cape Argus* at the time of Lynar's death said that their relationship was 'all but unprecedented in the annals of friendship'.[12] Several of the letters Porter wrote to Lynar were addressed to 'Dearly Beloved', and the two seemed, from the outside, to display all the signs of marriage. They were often seen out together, with Lynar carrying a lunch basket. And when Lynar, who was by all accounts at times disagreeable, got into arguments with the likes of the station master over trifles, the amiable Porter 'came along and quietly settled the matter'.[13] When Lynar died, Porter, unable to face life in Cape Town without him, left the Colony a mere three weeks later, never to return.

Although Porter was said to be amiable in his personal life, when it came to politics he was, as Kilpin puts it, 'a lion'. In the Legislative Council, he made it quite clear to Governor Sir George Napier on his arrival that he was not going to be simply a rubber stamp. Napier, like D'Urban before him, had got used to getting his own way. But this would end with Porter, who

[t]o the amazement of the onlookers … quietly rose and said that with profound respect to His Excellency he would follow the dictates of his own mind … and roundly declared that if he ever found that his office precluded him from giving utterance to his own sentiments, he would look out for the first vessel that was to leave Table Bay and bid adieu to the colony.[14]

Representation with frustration

By the early 1840s, political frustration was growing in the Cape with regard to representative government. It was fast becoming apparent that the Legislative Council could not service the diverse needs of the Colony. And when Sir Harry Smith was appointed governor in December 1847, he took the early view that 'the Legislative Council is regarded in this colony as a failure'.[15] Smith duly directed Porter to prepare 'such a general plan as would appear to secure the greatest number of the advantages, and shun the greatest number of inconveniences, incidental to the contemplated change of system'.[16]

Harry Smith's murderous Cape record

Hurry Charge Wackalong Smite

Harry Smith had been D'Urban's military chief of staff from 1828 to 1836. Smith was famous for his quick temper and foul mouth; as Noël Mostert tells us, 'those who sought to record Sir Harry Smith's language conveyed its unprintable vigour merely with "--------"'.[17] Much of this behaviour was said to have resulted from a sense of social inferiority that came with his 'lowly birth'.

But whatever his personality, he was widely regarded at the time as a talented soldier of the charge-and-shoot-first variety. This would earn him the nickname 'Hurry Charge Wackalong Smite' (his full name was Henry George Wakelyn Smith). He had fought with Wellington, both in the Peninsular War and at Waterloo, and was a veteran of the 1812 war against the United States, during which he turned up at the burning and sacking of the White House in Washington in 1814.

This kind of military behaviour would be replicated and amplified in his actions in the Cape Colony. In the Sixth Frontier War (1834–1836), he was at the centre of one of the most controversial murders in the Cape's history. Although Paramount Chief Hintsa had had nothing to do with the war, D'Urban and Smith crossed the Kei River and demanded that he appear before them. When he arrived at their camp, they proceeded to hold him against his will.

When Hintsa attempted to escape on horseback, Smith charged after him and knocked him off his horse. Despite having been shot several times, Hintsa made it to a river, where he was caught by Smith's men. On the riverbank, Hintsa was stabbed to death and his body horrifically mutilated by a soldier named George Southey. Hintsa's ears, testicles and penis were cut off, and it is believed that they were later sold in Grahamstown as souvenirs.

Harry smites Hintsa

Dr Philip, Fairbairn's father-in-law, heard the story and learnt that Smith's guide and interpreter during the war, a Khoekhoe soldier by the name of Klaas who had been present at the murder, was willing to testify that Hintsa had been killed in cold blood and his body mutilated. Philip then put considerable pressure on the colonial officials in Britain for a commission of inquiry to be held.

When the commission began its proceedings on 29 August 1836 at Fort Willshire, it soon found itself, as John Milton puts it, 'immersed in a welter of contradictions, evasions, fabrications and lies'.[18] Smith's own testimony was filled with so many inconsistencies as to be completely unbelievable, and the commission found it to be untrue.

But the commission only put Smith's career on hold temporarily. He is said to have turned to the bottle for a while. And as we have just seen, in 1847 he returned to the Cape – this time as governor. Between 1850 and 1853 Smith would again be at the centre of another British instalment of displacement, raiding, cattle theft and murder, otherwise known as the Eighth Frontier War.

In 1848, Porter, having received instruction from Smith, drafted an outline of a constitution that would, if agreed, create a lower representative house of assembly and an upper legislative assembly not unlike the House of Lords. More importantly, in this draft constitution he placed his faith in a colour-blind franchise. As he would write,

> I deem it to be just and expedient to place suffrage within the reach of the more industrious or intelligent men of colour, because it is a privilege which they would prize and a privilege which they deserve, and because by showing to all classes, those above and those below them, that no man's station is, in a free country, determined by the accident of his colour, all ranks of men are stimulated to improve or maintain their relative positions.[19]

And in order to ensure the inclusion of all races and certain lower economic classes such as the Dutch-speaking farmers, Porter proposed to the colonial secretary in Britain, Earl Grey, that the franchise be based on the 'almost nominal qualification' for all males over the age of twenty-one who occupied a tenement valued at £25.

A crisis of convicts

By 1849 there seemed to be every possibility that the Cape would finally settle down and gain a representative government. The Seventh Frontier War had ended and peace seemingly prevailed. There appeared to be no reason to hinder the draft proposals Porter had sent to Earl Grey from becoming the basis of the Cape Colony's constitution. But the residents of the Cape had not reckoned on the British imperial government throwing a spanner in the works. Britain and Ireland (in many ways the former's first colony) had been going through a period of social and political upheaval, and the question of what Britain was to do with its colonial convicts from Ireland, both criminal and political, had become a hot potato.

Earl Grey was determined to make the Cape into a penal colony. Without real warning, in 1849 he announced to Governor Smith that 'a ship had accordingly been taken up and a set of convicts are going to the Cape'. Grey had previously stated that he was aware that this 'would be very unacceptable to the colonists' but Smith was told that he would just have to deal with it.[20]

> ## Not the Colony's cup of tea
> Earl Grey was widely disliked in the Cape, as demonstrated by this epigram
> devised for him in the Colony:
>
> > This point was long disputed at the Cape,
> > What was the devil's colour and his shape,
> > The Hottentots of course, declared him white,
> > The Englishmen declared him black as night,
> > But now they split the difference and say,
> > Beyond all question that Old Nick is Grey.[21]

On 8 February 1849, a ship named the *Neptune* was sent to pick up 286 mainly Irish prisoners in Bermuda. Having supposedly 'benefited morally as well as socially by the sojourn and industry' in the West Indian paradise, these men were herded onto the *Neptune* for transportation.[22] The captain then set sail for Simon's Bay on the Cape Peninsula. When the news reached Cape Town of the *Neptune's* destination and its cargo, it began what Kilpin would call an 'unarmed rebellion'.[23]

Possible penal penetration of the Colony

The idea of the Cape becoming a penal colony was an issue that had all races speaking with one voice. From Cape Town to Port Elizabeth, Grahamstown and the Khoekhoe Kat River Settlement, the idea that the Colony would become a dumping ground for Britain's criminals was met with hostility. In a meeting held at Blinkwater in Kat River, a Khoekhoe man, Mr V. Jacobs, was recorded to have said that if the British *rooibaadjies* (redcoats) – whom Jacobs considered worse than savages – were anything to go by, these white convicts would 'destroy all moral and religious sentiment within the Colony'. It would mean, Jacobs went on, that his community would be forced to distrust all travellers and the inhabitants of Kat River would be obliged to shut their doors to all Englishmen.[24] As historian Susan Blackbeard reveals in her PhD thesis, a group of Kat River women also compiled a memorial expressing their displeasure with the convict idea and sent it to Smith.[25]

Along with Mr Jacobs and the women of Kat River, another person deeply disturbed by the potential dumping of criminals on the Cape's shores was John Fairbairn, who became one of the main organisers of the Anti-Convict Association. In a series of meetings in early July 1849, the association set out their stall. In what

Fairbairn called 'a meeting of the people', a 7 000-strong crowd gathered in Cape Town on 4 July outside the Commercial Exchange on Heerengracht Street (now Adderley Street). Braving strong gales and rain, the crowd listened as Fairbairn demanded 'free institutions, self-government, perfect liberty and the open field for virtue, industry and talent'.[26] At this and other meetings a pledge was taken by huge swathes of the population:

> We hereby solemnly declare and pledge our faith to each other that we will not employ or knowingly admit into our establishments or houses, work with or for, or associate with any convict felon sent into this Colony under sentence of transportation and that we will discountenance and drop connection with any person who may assist in landing, supporting or employing such convicted felons.[27]

This effectively placed a sanction on the Cape government and the British administration. Very few – in fact hardly any – merchants, tradesmen or farmers broke the pledge, as it meant they would be 'held in public odium'.[28] Smith was himself threatened by the Anti-Convict Association with 'starvation' – it claimed it would attempt to stop people selling him food.

Braving the gales: Thomas Bowler captures the anti-convict gathering

In the days that followed these meetings, crowds began to gather on the streets in Cape Town, hooting and hissing at government officials as they went about their business. And as fate would have it, during this period the death of one member of the Legislative Council and the resignations 'due to ill health' of two more left the body without its decision-making quorum. Three new members were needed for it to function legally. Fairbairn, who had now become the moving spirit of the anti-convict movement, would proclaim: 'Will any colonist venture to accept the vacant seat? To offer it at this moment to any gentleman would be an insult. To accept it would be eternal degradation.'[29]

With the *Neptune* on its way to Simon's Town, the council scheduled its next meeting for 10 July 1849. On hearing the news of the meeting, the people of Cape Town downed tools and gathered around the council's building, some forcing their way in. To their shock, they discovered that three new members had been sworn in. When the large angry crowd outside caught wind of this, they began calling for the three new members' heads. Let us 'testify our "respect" for the new members' somebody was heard to cry and the crowd began to press towards the doors.

When Smith left the building supported by his aide-de-camp, he was met with stony silence. The same could not be said for two of the new members who followed Smith out of the door, a Mr Cloete (a wealthy Stellenbosch farmer) and Mr de Smidt (owner of Groote Schuur). 'Down with them – shame on them – traitors – let them have it,' the crowd began to yell, and with this verbal downpour came a shower of rotten eggs and rubbish from the street.[30]

Cloete managed to escape to his brother's offices nearby, but De Smidt was left to his own devices, which were few and insufficient for defending himself against the angry crowd. In short, he received a swift beating before taking shelter in the offices of the Road Board, where he managed to lock the door behind him.

Mr Jacob Letterstedt, the third new member and owner of the Newlands Brewery, had seemingly been more sensible than Cloete and De Smidt. On seeing the unruly crowd gathered at the doors of the legislature, he waited before leaving. Mistakenly believing the crowd had settled down, he finally strode out. As historian Sir George Cory puts it, he left 'under the protection of the great man's wig', but 'in this however Mr Letterstedt miscalculated'.[31] Like the others, he was assailed with sticks and stones and harmful words. He managed to find refuge in the South African Club House on Plein Street, however, and there he waited until mounted police came to scatter those still intent on furthering their 'discussions' with him.

During the night a large crowd of protestors gathered on the Grand Parade, where they burnt effigies of the three new councillors. They were said to have danced around the fires 'with savage glee' while others 'amused themselves by destroying property belonging to the members of Cape Town'.[32] The crowd was finally broken up by another charge by mounted police.

But they had not finished with Letterstedt. Crowds gathered at his various properties across the city and destroyed one of his general stores as well as his large brewery in Newlands. In the coming weeks when he tried to have these repaired, he learnt that his 'great man's wig' was no influence against the Anti-Convict Association's pledge: no tradesman, carpenter or glazer would fix any of the damage done to his property.

Seven days later, with all of this going on and the Colony baying for their blood, 'Messrs Cloete, Letterstedt and de Smidt found it expedient to resign their seats in the Legislative Council'.[33] And when the *Neptune* came to anchor in Simon's Bay on 19 September, a vigilance committee was set up to closely monitor the ship. This was how it was discovered that Captain Robert Stanford and Mr Letterstedt (rather predictably) broke the boycott and profited off the *Neptune*'s presence in the bay by selling produce to the ship's captain. The vigilance committee did, however, make sure that no convict reached Cape soil.

While the *Neptune* was docked in a form of purgatory in Simon's Town, violence began to spread through Cape Town, and Governor Smith declared martial law. As more protests were called, Fairbairn was attacked and beaten in his home in Green Point by a group of 'coloured inhabitants, but also a few Whites in disguise'.[34] These men were seemingly in somebody's pay, and rumours abounded of a plot to murder Fairbairn.

Harry Smith was, like the *Neptune*, now tethered to unwelcoming shores and unable to perform his duties. Eventually, going against the British demands, he refused the *Neptune* permission to release its cargo into the Colony. Due to pressure from the likes of Fairbairn, Smith had stated that he was 'profoundly opposed to the Cape of Good Hope being made into a Penal Colony for ordinary felons'.[35] Finally, with the Anti-Convict Association refusing to give up their protest, Earl Grey gave instructions for the *Neptune* to weigh anchor and head for Van Diemen's Land (modern-day Tasmania).

A stirred, not shaken, political consciousness

The anti-convict campaign had showed what collective and steadfast protest could achieve. As McCracken puts it, Fairbairn's crusade 'had stirred political consciousness as never before and evoked an unprecedented unity'.[36] Once the *Neptune* finally set sail, Smith had to think pretty carefully about just how he was going to fill the vacant 'unofficial' seats of the Legislative Council without reawakening the wrath of the Colony.

Of course, it was not true that everybody in the Cape supported the Anti-Convict Association. The English elite like William Cock (who was an 'unofficial' member of the Legislative Council) and 'Moral Bob' Godlonton had always backed the government's position.

But Smith knew that he would have to offer the Anti-Convict Association a political olive branch. On 6 May 1850, in the first real move towards broader democracy, Smith invited the democratically elected Road Boards and municipal bodies of the Colony to make recommendations for five people to fill the seats in the Legislative Council. A notice was drafted by Smith's right-hand man, Secretary to Government John Montagu, stating that these men would represent 'the sentiments of the Colony'[37] until proper, fully representative institutions were established.

Over the next two months a list of twenty-three candidates was completed by the municipalities. From this list Governor Smith duly appointed five new 'unofficial' members: C.J. Brand, Stockenström, F.W. Reitz, Fairbairn and Godlonton. Also on the council was Cock, Godlonton's political ally, who had been there since before the anti-convict troubles began, and the five official government members.

With these five new members appointed and sworn in, the Legislative Council once again gained legal status. But no sooner had the council convened than an argument broke out. The dispute arose because the five new members were uncertain whether they had in fact won the election of the Road Boards and municipal bodies or whether Smith had simply selected them from the list of twenty-three that the boards had provided.

When the new council met for the first time on 6 September 1850, Stockenström stood up and declared: '[E]very man in the colony should look upon me as a representative of the people, and not as your Excellency's nominee ... I do not intend to sit here in any other capacity than as a representative of the people. If I am sixth on that list, I shall forthwith walk out that door.'[38] Stockenström then demanded that the numbers of votes from the municipalities and the Road Boards be laid on the table in front of them to be inspected.

Sir Andries Stockenström

Stockenström: Head and shoulders
above the Cape's greed and corruption

Born in the Cape in 1792, Stockenström was the great-grandson of slaves from Guinea and the son of a Swedish adventurer, Anders Stockenström, who had been a relatively level-headed administrator for the Dutch and later the British in Graaff-Reinet. As an adolescent, Andries started 'off along a troubled life of public service that took him swiftly to the storm centre of racial politics'.[39] Despite the fact that his father was killed by the Xhosa after what seems to have been a misunderstanding, Stockenström developed a great respect for the Xhosa people, saying that they were as civilised as any European he'd ever met.

Whatever Stockenström's flaws as a man, and many people remarked on his excessive pride and his oversensitivity to criticism, he was an extremely gifted leader and administrator. Despite clashing with almost every British administrator he came across, he nevertheless became an indispensable (and, when he kicked up one of his stinks, very dispensable) figure to the British as a commissioner-general, a lieutenant-governor and a soldier. The British would even give him a knighthood. As Mostert puts it, 'central to the universal respect for him was the fact that his obstinate sense of moral principle set him head and shoulders above the greed, corruption and malicious connivance that were so familiar in [the Cape]'.[40]

Stockenström would spend his life attempting to affect a peace settlement on the eastern frontier. This was despite the fact that British governors like Smith and Grahamstown elites like Godlonton had no desire to do so. It was always Stockenström's contention that the Frontier Wars were encouraged by corrupt profit-seekers and that these people, Boer and Brit alike, had no real desire for peace. When Stockenström ran the Eastern Province, he created the Kat River Settlement, which gave the displaced Khoekhoe people land with full and equal rights in the Colony.

Stockenström was, however, a military man, and he participated in the Seventh Frontier War (1846–47) against the Xhosa. After initial Xhosa successes in the war, he drove his forces to Sarhili kaHintsa's capital over the Kei. Sarhili and Stockenström, whose fathers had both been killed while negotiating, sat down and agreed on a peace settlement.

Unsurprisingly, Stockenström always retained a large popular following among non-whites in the Colony. This was something many of his political opponents, to whom 'his liberal policies had become intolerable', deeply resented and they often referred to him derogatorily as a 'Hottentot'.[41]

When the government finally agreed to show the council the municipalities' votes, it was uncovered that C.J. Brand had received twenty-five votes, Stockenström twenty-three, F.W. Reitz twenty-one, Fairbairn nineteen and J.H. Wicht nine. Despite having come fifth, Wicht had been replaced by Godlonton, whose name appeared way down the list at number twelve, with only three votes.

Godlonton had always been a strong supporter of Harry Smith's frontier policies and had backed the government throughout the convict crisis. As historian Robert Ross notes, Godlonton was also 'the power behind the attempt to exclude the Khoekhoe from the franchise'.[42] The members of the government claimed that they had placed 'Moral Bob' ahead of Wicht in order to give the eastern section of the Colony some representation. But Fairburn rose and pointed out the government's deception: even if this were true, the sixth person on the list, Mr J.J. Meintjies, should have taken Wicht's place, as he was from the eastern Cape.

Brand, Stockenström, Fairbairn and Reitz soon became known as the 'popular members', forming a strong alliance. Porter, although broadly speaking liberal in outlook, supported the inclusion of Godlonton to keep the government in control and had agreed with Smith and Montagu that it was best to keep power away from the four 'popular members'.

Porter's proposal

Although Porter did support Smith and Montagu's Cape government on most matters, their paths diverged with regard to the Cape's constitution. Montagu had, in 1848, proposed a franchise that would allow only occupiers or owners of property worth over £50 to vote. Porter proposed a much lower qualification, to be based on the annual value of land or property occupied. In his proposal, owners of property would gain the franchise if their property was valued at £10. Tenants who leased for at least twelve months could obtain the franchise if the land or property they occupied was valued at £25. When the council sat to discuss the franchise on 11 September, it was Porter's lower franchise proposal that was agreed upon. But this was not the end of the discussion.

On 13 September, the council met to discuss what the qualification should be for members of the upper house. In Britain you had to be a lord, but as there weren't many of these at the Cape, an equally highfalutin status had to be decided. As Cory puts it, 'opinion was divided between personal worth and personal possession'. Godlonton, Cock and the government were as one in agreeing that all candidates for the upper house would have to possess £2000. Porter in fact stated that the qualification would ensure that the Colony would not be susceptible to 'communism, socialism and red republicanism'.[43]

Stockenström, however, stood up and stated that the high qualification for members meant that the upper house may well become an oligarchy of the worst variety. It was then Fairbairn's turn to speak his mind. He argued that the upper house should indeed have a high qualification, but instead of a member's wealth being the measure, it should be his 'integrity, character and ability'.[44]

Fairbairn then played his best hand, pointing out that the government, from Smith to Montagu and Porter, had all been selected on ability, not wealth. But Montagu would not be flattered, deriding Fairbairn for his 'high opinions of human nature'.[45] Porter, too, refused to take the bait. But Fairbairn stuck to his guns, putting forward the amendment to the council that integrity and ability be the measure required.

Fairbairn's motion then was put to the vote. Rather predictably, Stockenström, Brand, Reitz and Fairbairn voted for the motion, while the five government members, plus Cock and Godlonton, voted against it. At this point the 'popular members' were beginning to realise that their work on the Legislative Council was like a broken pencil – pointless. And when Governor Smith began addressing the ordinary legislative business of the council, which was supposed to be decided by the fully representative government that they were meant to be forming, the four realised they were being taken for a bunch of fools.

Eleven reasons for dissent

On 20 September the four popular members went to the council with some very serious intentions. The gallery was packed to capacity, and as Stockenström stood up a thunderous cacophony of shouts and applause broke out. Smith rose and began to try to silence the crowd. 'I will not have applause,' he cried out.[46] The crowd quietened as Stockenström began to put his case to the council. If he had known that the council was to address the ordinary business of the Colony rather than the framing of the constitution, he argued, he would not have agreed to be a member. The council was supposed to be an organ for the transformation of the Colony into a democracy, he continued, and any legislation being undertaken by the council was simply an act of autocracy and against the will of the people. He then put forward a motion that the council give priority to constitutional matters. But this was duly defeated by the usual seven votes to four.

Stockenström then crossed the room to have a whispered discussion with Fairbairn, who was seen to shrug his shoulders. Upon returning to his seat, he produced a document titled 'Eleven Reasons for Dissent' and raised it above his head. It was a summary of the complaints that the 'popular members' had with the council's formation and its legislative focus. As a representative of the people, Stockenström said, he refused to be part of 'an impotent minority packed together merely to complete an otherwise defective machinery'.[47] 'These your excellency,' he concluded, 'are the grounds upon which I differ from the resolution just adopted and I respectfully tender them to Your Excellency together with my resignation.'[48] He then signed the document, calling out: 'I am no longer a member of the Council!' With this, a burst of applause broke out from the gallery and the three other popular members got up, signed the document and followed Stockenström out the door. With their resignations, the council once again had no quorum and ceased to function.

On 21 September, in an address to the municipalities that had voted them in, the four offered a statement saying that the government had been using them for its own purposes. It had, they argued, given them their positions on the council in an attempt to give the council legitimacy but little else. Furthermore, with the aid of Godlonton and Cock, the government had a fixed majority, which the four were powerless to act against. They were, they said,

utterly powerless to check any proceeding which in their consciences they might deem destructive to the liberty and welfare of their constituents. It is

The point of resignation: Stockenström stands on principle

self-evident that such a majority, voting black or white at the bidding of a chief acting under the instruction of the Colonial Minister [in Britain], might concoct a constitution which under the name of self-government would be a mere mask for irresponsibility and despotism. And to this possibility we could not but be accessory. From such a degradation we deemed it our duty to rescue both you and ourselves.[49]

The four were roundly supported by the Cape Town Municipality, which 'did not entertain any cordial feelings towards the government'.[50] And it was at the municipality's request that the four, together with Wicht (the man who was fifth on the list and whom Smith chose to exclude), drew up a draft constitution of their own. This document would become known as the 'Sixteen Articles' and Fairbairn would take it to London, where he was later joined by Stockenström. Unfortunately, nothing came of their attempt to get the British government to support them: Governor Smith sent Earl Grey a communication stating that Fairbairn and Stockenström were not supported by reputable persons and that their petitions were essentially faked and signed by made-up people and the lower classes.

With Fairbairn and Stockenström in London, and while Smith gleefully headed off to engage in his favourite activity of fighting and murdering on the frontier, the conservative Montagu set about undoing all Porter's work. Before departing for war, Smith had set up a commission to take the place of the Legislative Council, headed by Montagu and containing Cock and Godlonton. Porter had already clashed with Montagu and Godlonton over his proposed constitution, and the two conservatives now attempted to push back Porter's constitutional proposals even further.

Porter's point of view

Whatever differences Porter and the now resigned 'popular members' may have had in the Legislative Council, they were of one mind when it came to the non-racial £25 franchise. Porter certainly understood that the £25 franchise would not allow the coloured and Khoekhoe to vote in a member of Parliament on their own steam. However, he did argue in several speeches that 'the coloured vote would lead to the election of more moderate men, and thereby temper extremism'.[51] As he noted when rebellion spread to the coloured and Khoekhoe of Kat River Settlement during the Eighth Frontier War, 'I would rather meet the Hottentot at the hustings voting for his representative, than meet the Hottentot in the wilds with his gun on his shoulder.'[52]

Kangaroo council

The Cape government moved to form a new Legislative Council and appointed, undemocratically, four new English-speaking members: two Cape Town merchants, a wealthy businessman, and the owner of significant properties in the western Cape. Montagu, Cock, Godlonton and the merchant nominees then began working on raising the franchise qualification. As historian Stanley Trapido puts it, 'their reasons for this were unambiguously stated by Montagu. The £25 franchise was too low because it would allow "a body of ignorant coloured persons whose numbers would swamp the wealthy and educated portion of the community".'[53]

This new kangaroo council would also raise the membership qualification for the upper house. As Godlonton would state, 'We are bound to secure the rights of property providing that proper men be elected to make laws by which those rights will be protected.'[54] Godlonton and Cock also demanded that the constitution provide a separate and independent government for the Eastern Province – a federal government they believed they could control.

Who vs. who?

What is interesting about these constitutional debates is that it was never a case of English vs. Dutch. Instead, the rich merchants of Cape Town and Grahamstown, led by Godlonton and supported by Smith and Montagu, set up their stall against a truly diverse group of democrats. These democrats were in many ways strange bedfellows, and they certainly had distinctly different reasons for supporting the low franchise. The Dutch-speaking group, as Trapido says, 'were adherents of a low franchise because they were opposed to the ruling clique of executives and merchants, and it was only the latter who would have benefited from a high qualification,'[55] while Stockenström and Fairbairn aspired to non-racialism.

Fairbairn saw debate over the constitution as the glue that had bound the Dutch, English and non-European communities together, and he believed the constitution would bind them in the future. Almost prophetically, Fairbairn stated that a non-racial constitution 'will reconcile all classes if anything can. If not there will be insurrection and massacres. Indeed, it is wonderful that a mixed population like ours have kept together so long under the absurd treatment [of the colonial British government].'[56]

A fake news media

Montagu, Godlonton and Cock were, however, no shrinking violets. They were determined to subvert the democratic sensibilities that were gaining traction in the Colony. Together they helped to create a Cape Town newspaper with a similar conservative editorial stance to Godlonton's *Grahamstown Journal*.

The *Cape Monitor* was set up by Montagu to rival Fairbairn's liberal *South African Commercial Advertiser*. According to H.C. Botha, 'Montagu controlled the administration and editing and also supplied additional financial backing by means of Government Advertisements and Notices'.[57] From the outset, the Cape government's mouthpiece would do its level best to discredit Fairbairn and Stockenström. When Fairbairn left for London with a draft constitution in 1850, the *Cape Monitor* reported that the crowd that gathered to see him off was mainly of 'coloured persons, and most of them drunk'.[58] In reality the crowd, totalling around 3 000 people, was mixed, and Fairbairn was sent off with a twenty-one-gun salute while a band played popular military music.

Throughout the lead-up to the establishment of the constitution, the *Cape Monitor* continued to push the fake news that Fairbairn, Stockenström and what would become known as the 'Town House Party' were 'a clique of *self-appointed dictators*'.[59] It went on to say that 'instead of self-government for the Colony, we are about to have a Town House oligarchy; and instead of acquiring British freedom and Constitutional liberty, we are in danger of subjecting ourselves and the entire Colony to the despotism of a contemptible faction'.[60]

The beginning of the beginning

While Montagu and colonial secretary Earl Grey were believed to be delaying as well as significantly altering Porter's proposed constitution, a large public meeting was held on 8 October 1852 in Cape Town to discuss the constitutional delays.

A committee was then formed of the usual suspects: Stockenström, Fairbairn, Brand and Wicht. This was followed by a period of general agitation throughout the Colony. Meetings were held across the Cape, resolutions were passed and petitions drawn up. These demanded the immediate adoption of the constitution as proposed by Porter. They also went further, demanding that Montagu, who was on sick leave in Britain, must never be allowed to return to the Colony.

Despite the fact that Harry Smith was fighting another endless and unjust war on the frontier, on hearing about the agitation sweeping across the Colony he ordered troops to be sent from the frontier to Cape Town. They were under orders to supress any potential protests, such as those that had occurred during the anti-convict agitation.

As tensions in the Colony mounted, the Cape was abruptly delivered from more civil strife by a change of government in Britain. At the end of 1852, the Duke of Newcastle joined the Colonial Office; he was a new, liberal breath of fresh air who saw just what was holding back progress in the Cape. And as Trapido puts it, Porter's position was upheld 'because the most important supporters of the high-franchise policy, Smith and Montagu, were both withdrawn from South Africa'.[61]

With Montagu and Smith now relieved of their positions, the Duke of Newcastle announced in March 1853 that on 1 July the new constitution in the Cape would become operative. Although few knew it at the time, the Colonial Office had decided on Porter's lower franchise. As the good Duke would write:

> [I]n conferring upon the colony the boon of a representative constitution it would be exceedingly inadvisable that the franchise should be restricted as to leave those of the coloured classes who in the point of intelligence were qualified for the exercise of political power practically unrepresented ... it was the earnest desire of her Majesty's government that all her subjects at the Cape, without distinction of the class or colour, should be united by the bond of loyalty and a common interest ... [and that] the exercise of political rights enjoyed by all alike would prove one of the best methods of obtaining this object.[62]

Another major decision taken in Britain was *not* to divide the Colony into two provinces with their own legislatures, thus dashing Godlonton and Cock's dream.

Lady Jocelyn

On 21 April 1853, the mail steamer *Lady Jocelyn* put into port at Cape Town carrying with it the Duke of Newcastle's order confirming the constitution. On 3 May the constitution was published. The *Cape Monitor*, which was on its last legs, immediately claimed that Fairbairn and Stockenström (whom the *Monitor* saw as anti-British) would attempt a democratic coup and that they would 'usurp and sway all authority in our future parliament'.[63] As Botha states, 'Fairbairn did not reply to this propaganda in similar vein but limited himself [in his own paper] to discussing aspects of the Constitution. Where necessary he explained procedure and emphasized the newly-gained freedom, which he described as an important milestone in the development of the colony'.[64]

The constitutional ordinance brought by the *Lady Jocelyn* established a Parliament in the Cape Colony that would consist of the governor, an upper legislative house, and a lower House of Assembly. The upper legislative house would consist of fifteen members: eight from the western division of the Colony and seven from the eastern. Members of this house had to be over the age of thirty and owners of unencumbered property worth at least £2 000 or with movables of at least £4 000 above all debts. The lower House of Assembly would have forty-six members. Both houses would be elected by men over the age of twenty-one who had occupation for one year of premises worth £25 or were in receipt of an annual salary of £50. Voting was not secret and was to be done by word of mouth so, as Cory puts it, 'the absence of even so little education as would enable a man to write his own name was excused'.[65] As George McCall Theal writes, 'such were the provisions of the most liberal constitution that had ever been granted to a British colony'.[66]

Registration begins

With the announcement of the constitution, work began on registering voters. Instead of political parties, small committees were set up to campaign for various candidates. Interestingly, Fairbairn and Porter finally joined forces to support Howson Edward Rutherfoord for the upper house. Rutherfoord was a wealthy Cape businessman who had a long history of supporting Fairbairn's democratic and anti-slavery agitation.

Due to the vastness of the Colony and the sparseness of the population, registration of voters took nearly five months. Naomi Parkinson gives us a good account of the process: 'In 1853, during the first period of registration, all such registration officers had been reminded via a circular that the franchise was intended to "benefit and embrace" the "poorer class of voters". Officers were instructed to afford non-European mission residents "every facility for registering their names."' On election days, a regimental band was set up in the Company's Garden for the enjoyment of both the middle and working classes.

Carts were also sent off to the coloured and Malay districts in order to collect those eligible to vote.[67]

Over 15 000 men voted, which was about one-third of the male population over the age of twenty-one. In the election for the upper legislative council, a total of 115 648 votes were recorded: 82 220 in the western division and 33 428 in the eastern. Voters in the western district got eight votes and those in the eastern Cape got seven to us as they pleased.

Happily for the liberals, the results recorded a devastating defeat for Godlonton, Cock and their conservative 'English group'. The pro-democracy supporters in the west took seven of the eight seats of the upper house, with Rutherfoord, Reitz, Wicht and four others being swept into office. Only a Mr H. Vigne of the 'English group' snuck in, in eighth place.

In the eastern division, the great-grandson of a slave, Sir Andries Stockenström, won a staggering victory over all the other candidates, receiving 1 781 votes more than his closest rival, 'Moral Bob' Godlonton. As the conservative historian Cory sourly points out in a hidden-away footnote, 'as unpopular and disliked as Sir Andries Stockenström was by many in high places, it would seem that this unpopularity did not extend to the majority of the general public. For in the Eastern Province he polled the greatest number of votes, viz., 6,315; Mr Godlonton was far behind with 4,534.'[68] This despite the fact that Godlonton hired carts to bring his supporters to the polls. In later elections in the Cape, 'Moral Bob' is said to have paid large amounts of money in order to assure his election and engaged in what many called 'vote-buying'.

Along with Godlonton in the Eastern Province, the conservative 'English group' managed to get two more candidates elected, while the democratic movement gained the rest. Out of the fifteen seats of the Legislative Assembly, the conservatives would only manage four, while the pro-democracy alliance of Dutch- and English-speakers known as the 'Town House Party' gained eleven.

The election of the lower house of assembly would see similar results, with only seventeen of the forty-six elected members belonging to the 'English Party'. Fairbairn had been persuaded by Reitz to run for the Swellendam constituency. And even though he was not a resident of Swellendam, he was still voted in, receiving among the highest number of votes of any candidate. In contrast, despite riding seemingly the length and breadth of the Eastern Cape in order to garner support, William Cock was, as Parkinson puts it, 'nonetheless ultimately unsuccessful'.[69]

The coloured, Khoekhoe and black vote

Historians differ on the effect that non-white voters had on the result. According to Eric Walker, outside Cape Town, in villages and mission stations, there were hardly any non-whites who were eligible to vote. In fact, even among those who were, very few managed to get on the voters' roll – some due to ignorance of the process, others due to apathy. However, in more recent research, Parkinson has shown that, at the very least, by 1859 the numbers of registered voters at the mission stations of Caledon, Clanwilliam and Swellendam, most of whom would have been coloured or Khoekhoe, were significant enough to seriously influence an election. And in 1864 W.R. Thomson won his constituency in the area of Balfour and Hertzog 'with 189 out of the 190 votes he received coming from coloured voters'.[70]

Of course, the Cape's non-racial £25 franchise was far from representative in a modern sense. As McKenzie states, 'women and a mostly black underclass remained disenfranchised'.[71] But as for the people elected, they were a diverse group of English- and Afrikaans-speakers whose beliefs were relatively liberal and inclusive for their time and place. To be sure, they were all white men of their age and their liberalism may not, in modern terms, be particularly remarkable or genuinely inclusive. But considering the history of South Africa and what happened to its franchise in later years, as a start it wasn't at all bad. In fact, you'd have to fast-forward almost exactly 140 years to find anything better.

CHAPTER 3

THE BATTLE
OF THE BEARDS
1893

*'It proved the most violent electoral struggle
through which the Republic ever passed.'* – **Paul Kruger**[1]

Face-off: Paul Kruger and Piet Joubert

THE 1893 ELECTION IN THE Zuid-Afrikaansche Republiek (also known as the Transvaal) was the third time 'Slim Piet' Joubert and 'Oom Paul' Kruger had gone beard to beard. But while Kruger had won the 1883 and 1888 elections easily, by 1893 the political climate had changed dramatically and there was a real sense that it might prove third time lucky for Slim Piet. As Kruger himself wrote, the 1893 contest

> proved the most violent electoral struggle through which the Republic ever passed. I was accused by the Opposition of being autocratic, of squandering the national money, of giving away all rights and privileges in the form of concessions and of awarding all the offices of state to the Hollanders. Reproaches upon reproaches were also hurled against the Opposition. It is far from pleasant to carry back one's thoughts to that time, when the two chief men in the Republic were painted so black that, if only the tenth part of the accusations flung at us had been based upon truth, neither of us would have been worthy to enjoy the confidence of the people for another hour.[2]

The 1893 election also marked the birth of party politics in the ZAR. Before then, notes history buff Herman van Niekerk, 'most elections of leaders in the ZAR were made purely on a personal basis: "I like him and I trust him."'[3] This changed in 1893, as Joubert's candidacy was more about the Progressive cause than it was about the lustre of his beard.

Another notable feature of 1893 was that it was the first time the press was used extensively in South African politics. This chapter will open your eyes to the (hilarious) efforts of *Land en Volk*, a newspaper funded by Uitlander mining bosses, to throw shade on the Kruger administration. And it will show that Kruger also manipulated the messaging that appeared in pro-government papers by sending government advertising their way and dangling lucrative concessions as carrots.

In hindsight it seems that the newspapermen probably didn't realise how much power they wielded; they certainly couldn't have foreseen that a very similar scenario would play out in the next century when papers like the *Rand Daily Mail* (funded by English-speaking mining bosses) would go toe to toe with the government rags of Naspers and Perskor. But we digress...

The proverbial third wheel

'The Race for the Presidential Cup of the South African Republic':
W.H. Schröder's contemporary cartoon shows Oom Paul and
Slim Piet in a mad dash for the finish, with Kotzé bringing up the rear

Kruger's and Joubert's names were not the only ones on the presidential ballot. As C.T. Gordon deadpanned, 'The presence of a third participant in the struggle, Chief Justice Kotzé, who based his candidature on what was probably the most clearly thought out – and therefore the least popular – political platform of the three, was never felt to be a serious threat to the other two candidates, an opinion which the final result of the poll amply bore out.'[4]

'A potentially fatal disjuncture'

The Cape Colony was not the only part of nineteenth-century South Africa grappling with who should and should not be eligible to vote. The ZAR, which had its roots in the 1830s when 6 000-odd Voortrekkers 'who had grown sick and tired of British rule and the decision to ban slavery in the Colony' headed north to their Promised Land, had franchise problems of its own.[5] The issue facing the republic, however, was not about extending voting rights but restricting them: the ZAR's 'guiding principle'[6] was that only *white males* were eligible to vote – but which ones?

Chicken or beef? The complexities of becoming a burgher

If you thought getting a new ID from Home Affairs was tricky, you obviously don't know much about the ZAR. We asked Carel van der Merwe – who has written biographies of Eugène Marais and Anglo-Boer War hero Ben Viljoen – to make sense of the fine print. At the time of the 1893 election:

1. (White, male) foreigners (aka Uitlanders) could be naturalised as ZAR burghers two years after having their names put on the Field Cornet's ward list. This also made them eligible for military call-up – something many foreigners weren't too keen on.

2. After two years on the list you could become a second-class ZAR burgher, provided that you renounced your foreign citizenship. You were then entitled to vote for representatives on the Second Volksraad, a diluted parliament not dissimilar to the farcical tricameral system the Nats would try in the 1980s (see Chapter 11).

3. Twelve years later you could apply for full citizenship, including the right to vote for representatives in the First Volksraad and in the presidential election. But this was only the best-case scenario – you also had to be at least forty years old to achieve ~~nirvana~~ full burgher-hood.

4. There were, however, some exceptions:
    *   Anyone who had done military duty was granted full citizenship. Quite a few Uitlanders obtained full citizenship this way after the Jameson Raid, but the period before 1893 was largely peaceful.
    *   *Kapenaars* and Hollanders (more about them later) who were brought to the ZAR to serve in the civil service or on the judiciary could be fast-tracked.

To understand why the ZAR was so protective of the vote, we have to go back to the origins of the fledgling nation. While the independence of the ZAR meant much to Kruger and his *volk* (Blighty first recognised the republic's independence in 1852, but it was briefly returned to Britain in 1877 before gaining a second independence in 1881), it did nothing to improve their financial lot. As historian Charles van Onselen writes,

By the mid-19th century, economic growth was starting to deliver unprecedented benefits to the urban middle classes on either side of the North Atlantic. By contrast, the semi-arid interior of southern Africa was still an agricultural backwater, barely able to sustain farmer-hunters of European descent, let alone nurture a tiny white middle class.[7]

This all changed dramatically with the discovery of the main Witwatersrand gold reef in July 1886 and the establishment of the township of Johannesburg (known to the burghers as Duiwelstad) five months later. By January 1890 said 'township' boasted 26 303 inhabitants, 772 shops and 261 hotels and bars. Six years later Joburg was home to a hodgepodge of over 102 000 inhabitants (80 per cent of whom were men), comprising

Europeans	50 907	49.9%
Natives	42 533	41.7%
Asiatics	4 807	4.7%
Mixed race	2 879	2.8%
Malays	952	0.9%[8]

Due to the ZAR's complex citizenship rules, all non-whites and the vast majority of Johannesburg's white male residents would have been unable to vote in the 1893 election. This may seem unfair, but try putting your feet in the Boers' *veldskoene* for a moment. While experts are divided on the exact ratio of burgher to Uitlander, the general consensus is that adult male Uitlanders who had arrived because of the gold rush outnumbered burghers in 1893, some say by as much as 2:1.[9] Would *you* want the fate of your country decided by gold-diggers who were in town for one reason only and who might bugger off at any time?[10]

As Van Onselen explains,

After 1886 there was a potentially fatal disjuncture in the state between land-hungry, vernacular-speaking, Afrikaner-Dutch Nationalists drawn from farming backgrounds and entrenched in Pretoria and more middle-class, cosmopolitan, English-speaking, quasi-liberal elements, devoted to commerce and industry in Johannesburg... Given imperfect connections in the wiring system linking political to economic power, and the strong charges emanating from the positive and negative terminals, there was a constant short-circuiting and the danger of an even bigger explosion.[11]

Van Onselen adds that the question 'was not so much as to whether or not there would be a revolution in the South African Republic – there almost certainly would be one – but *when* it might occur and *who* might best seize control of it'.[12]

A clever man?

General Petrus Jacobus 'Slim Piet' Joubert was by no means the first Afrikaner to dream of transforming the ZAR into a modern state. After the disastrous presidency of Marthinus Wessel Pretorius (1866–1871), which had left the ZAR perilously close to bankruptcy, the burghers decided that, in Hermann Giliomee's words, they needed 'a clever man as president'.[13]

With this in mind, a group of influential citizens asked Thomas François Burgers to stand for election. While Burgers was unquestionably 'a clever man', the fact that he'd been suspended as a minister in the Reformed Church in the

Cape for 'heresy' should have been a warning sign that he was not an ideal fit for the ultra-conservative republic. Nevertheless, Burgers waltzed to victory in the 1872 ZAR election, claiming 2 964 votes to William Robinson's 388. (Despite having British parents, Robinson was as Boer as they come – he'd lived in the ZAR since 1845 and was a deacon in the Reformed Church.)[14]

Relying on expensive loans from Cape banks, Burgers attempted to thoroughly modernise the state. While he succeeded in setting up the ZAR's first education system, supreme court, permanent army and currency, his fiscal policy left a lot to be desired. His dream of establishing a railway

Thomas François Burgers

link to the port at Delagoa Bay (Maputo) to avoid being dictated to by the British would cost the ZAR hundreds of thousands of pounds. (In the 1880s and '90s, this railway line, the Oosterspoor, was a constant source of derailment for Kruger's government.)

Perhaps most controversial of all was Burgers's (failed) attempt to ban religious instruction in schools because 'school was the place where science had to be taught'. So scandalised was his electorate that several hundred Boers set off – yet again – in search of the Promised Land, which they now believed lay somewhere beyond the Kalahari Desert. Paul Kruger was sorely tempted to join them, but he eventually chose to stay behind and fight the system from within. While this was clearly a wise move on his part (around 230 people perished on the Dorsland Trek), one can only wonder how different our history might have been had he gone along for the ride.

Burgers's rule came to an abrupt halt when Sir Theophilus Shepstone annexed the ZAR for the British in 1877. This caused much resentment among the Boers, and they eventually rose up in revolt in 1880 in what would become known as the First Anglo-Boer War. After the Boers' dramatic victory at Majuba in 1881, Kruger 'emerged as a national hero, which paved the way for his election as President' a couple of years later.[15]

'n Boer maak 'n (Progressive) plan

Given what was to follow with the Jameson Raid and the Anglo-Boer War, it's easy to fall into the trap of thinking that the revolution Van Onselen suggests was on the cards would be military in nature and Uitlander in origin. But the truth is more complicated.

As C.T. Gordon explains in painstaking (and often hilarious) detail in *The Growth of Boer Opposition to Kruger*, there was, for a few heady months in the summer of 1892–93, a good chance that the revolution would be delivered both peacefully and internally by Boers going to the polls. Gordon details 'the emergence of an active opposition among the burghers of the [ZAR] towards the policies pursued by the Kruger government' and explains that

[i]n the course of this opposition there emerged a self-styled Progressive party, under the nominal leadership of Kruger's chief rival, Commandant-General P.J. Joubert. In the presidential elections of 1893, Joubert came within

an ace of defeating Kruger. Indeed, in the eyes of his followers, he did virtually do so; they regarded the election as illegal and demanded, in vain, a new election.[16]

Before we get to know Joubert the reluctant hero and his overzealous campaign committee, we should look at what Gordon terms 'the issues around which opposition crystallized' against Kruger:

1. **Financial policy.** As is almost always the case in the lead-up to an election, the issue on everyone's lips was the economy. In 1893 Kruger had the misfortune of being at the helm during a severe economic crash. The government had responded to plummeting state revenues (between 1890 and 1891 total income dropped from £526 602 to £333 472) by introducing an unpopular toll on load-bearing ox wagons – the nineteenth-century equivalent of the e-toll scandal. The home-grown opposition, meanwhile, demanded a reduction in the salaries of civil servants, including Kruger himself, who earned a very healthy £8 000 per annum.[17] Eugène Marais was only half joking when he said: 'At present things are so ridiculous in this Republic that it would serve the country better to pay Mnr. Kruger £16 000 per year on condition that he resigns as President, rather than to pay him £8 000 per year to continue with his services.'[18]

2. **Concessions and monopolies.** Much of the criticism of Kruger's government centred on the concessions policy he had introduced in 1881 in an attempt to grow the economy of his impoverished agrarian backwater. (*Rogues' Gallery*, our book about corruption in South Africa, provides sordid detail about the close relationships a small clique of foreign concessionaires – the so-called 'Third Volksraad' – enjoyed with Kruger and his government.) The granting of concessions was always open to corruption, but the stakes were much higher after the discovery of gold. This was particularly true of the various railway concessions, which cost the government untold billions (in today's money), and the highly contentious dynamite monopoly.

3. **Inefficiency and corruption of the administration.** Kruger presided over an administration that was, in the opinion of his opponents, based on patronage – from the president all the way down to the police. (Now where have we heard that before?) Of course, it worked both ways: Gordon's analysis of Joubert's papers unearthed 'endless examples' of letters

asking Slim Piet to use his influence to wangle jobs for cash-strapped individuals.[19]

4. **Education and language policy.** There was, interestingly, considerable opposition, even among the Boers, to the decision of Superintendent N.E. Mansvelt (a Hollander who'd been poached from a Stellenbosch high school by Kruger) in 1891 to ban the use of English in all higher standards at schools. This highly emotive topic was, writes Gordon, 'a confused issue in which the pioneer suspicion of education ... fought with the growing realization of the demands of new times, and growing resentment at seeing the "zonen des lands" [sons of the land] excluded because of their inferior education, from posts perforce filled by Hollanders, Germans and Cape Afrikaners.'[20] Many burghers realised that their social upliftment was directly related to competency in English, even if it pained them to speak the language of their foe.

5. **Hollander policy.** Easier to understand was the widespread objection to the number of Hollanders who occupied important positions. No Hollander was despised more than W.J. Leyds, who had been appointed state attorney in 1884 at the age of only twenty-five. In Gordon's estimation these men played 'a most valuable part in raising beyond all recognition the efficiency, co-ordination and general standards of the Transvaal's government.'[21] However, as J.S. Marais puts it, 'their efficiency probably roused at least as much resentment as their shortcomings, since the Boers were not accustomed to methodical and impersonal administration.'[22] The Hollanders were, to put it bluntly, not well liked by the general populace. They were in many ways as foreign to the Boers as the English Uitlanders.

6. **The franchise question.** But the issue towering over all others was the question of the Uitlander vote. As Gordon writes, 'it was natural that this issue should become the fundamental one, for [it threatened] everything that the old conservative Boer population held most dear ... their tenuous and hard won freedom, their stubborn and exclusive racial pride, their language, morals and whole way of life'.[23]

The Oom says *voetsek* to the Uitlanders

Leyds and the *Kapenaars*

W.J. Leyds – Kruger's Hollander

On paper, W.J. Leyds was hated because he was a Hollander. But closer examination of his behaviour suggests that the real reason might simply have been that he was a snob (a rhyming word beginning with a silent 'k' also comes to mind). The truth is that after the discovery of gold, the ZAR's inept and backward administration needed a foreign skills injection. But where would it come from?

The Cape, with its long history of Dutch settlement, might have seemed like the obvious choice. But almost a hundred years of British rule meant that despite having Dutch heritage, many middle-class *Kapenaars* actually spoke English at home. These men were entirely different animals to the Voortrekkers who had settled in the Transvaal. The ZAR's other option was the Netherlands, where news of their African brethren's victory at Majuba had inspired the formation of the Nederlandsch Zuid-Afrikaansche Vereeniging and the belief that true Nederlanders could 'play an important part in the cultural, economic, and political development' of the ZAR.[24]

Both *Kapenaars* and Hollanders had a tendency to look down on the burghers and their emerging vernacular *taal* (Afrikaans). Leyds did a particularly poor job of disguising his contempt for his adopted homeland, referring to Volksraad debates as 'chatter' and its members as 'those gentry who have learned nothing, including no virtue'. What was more, notes J.S. Marais, 'it is doubtful whether either he or his wife made a single Boer or Afrikaner friend'.[25]

'The *Kapenaars* and our young Boers,' wrote Leyds, 'hate the Hollanders, hate them more than the English ... the *Kapenaars* consider that they have a right to this country, look on this country as their prey ... According to them it is the Hollanders who are the intruders. But the opposite would be nearer the truth.'[26]

The three musketeers

Now that we've got all the heavy lifting out of the way, it's high time we met a few of the personalities involved in this home-grown revolution.

Slim Piet Joubert made for a curious talisman. On paper he had everything going for him. Like Kruger, he had grown up on an ox wagon as a child of the first wave of Voortrekkers in the 1830s. As the long-time leader of the Boer army, his military CV was impeccable, not least for the way in which he had stuck it to the *rooinekke* in the First Anglo-Boer War. While Kruger had sought to resolve his gripes at the negotiating table, Joubert favoured a military solution. And his victories at Ingogo, Laing's Nek and Majuba Hill would forever etch him into Boer folklore. He was rich too: his sharp entrepreneurial bent had helped him to amass

Slim Piet

no fewer than twenty-nine farms and stakes in several gold mines. And he had arguably the best beard in the Republiek.

But for all these formidable traits, Joubert the politician was 'half-hearted' (Gordon), 'cautious, pietistic and reflexive' (Van Onselen) and 'no match for Kruger' (J.S. Marais).[27] As Van Onselen puts it,

> Joubert's earthly success ... was tempered by his belief that access to the highest office in the land was wholly dependent on, first, the will of God and, second, on that of the people. He genuflected in the presence of both; while God may have been approving of the posture, the people were less convinced of his ability to offer firm leadership other than in times of war against African tribes.[28]

Percy FitzPatrick, secretary of the Reform Committee (a group of Uitlanders agitating for change in the ZAR), put it thus:

> The difference between the two men is remarkable. Mr. Kruger, to his credit be it said, has not the remotest conception of the meaning of fear, and would not know how to begin to give in. Mr. Joubert, 'Slim (sly) Piet,' as he is called, possessing a considerable share of the real Africander cunning, is yet no match for his rival in diplomacy, and has none of his grit and courage.[29]

Joubert himself told it slightly differently, explaining that the problem lay not with his personality but Kruger's. As he once explained to General Nicolaas Smit, the hero of Majuba:

Old friend it is like this: I *do* stand up against him [Kruger], I know he is wrong and I tell him so; but first he argues with me, and if that is no good, he gets into a rage and jumps around the room roaring at me like a wild beast ... and if I do not give in then he fetches out the Bible and ... he even quotes that to help him out. And if all that fails, he takes my hand and cries like a child and begs and prays me to give in. Say, old friend, who can resist a man like that?

Either way, a letter written by Joubert to a friend on the eve of the election campaign does not exactly inspire confidence:

That the state of affairs is reprehensible and that a change is highly desirable, indeed essential, [I fully agree] ... But now the question arises to me of how should and how must, such a change take place ... On this point many will reply to me – 'another President'. Well, I will keep silence on that matter. But will the majority say this? Will not the great majority still choose the present President? To me it seems certain that the President with his influential Press and his many supporters will know how to manage matters so that he will once again get the majority.[30]

The consensus seems to be that Joubert's 'reticence, at times of almost mystical proportions, meant that [he] had to be pushed to stand for election and then led from behind'.[31] The backroom strategists doing most of the pushing were two young, liberal, middle-class Afrikaners, Ewald Esselen and Eugène Marais, who had great ideas for how the republic should be run but bugger-all chance of persuading landowning Boers to vote for their urban mugs. Esselen and Marais would probably have liked a more forceful figurehead than Joubert, but he was the best they had. And besides, they fatally told themselves, the *volk* were so *gatvol* with Kruger's backward policies that Joubert simply couldn't lose.

ZAR delegates to the London Convention (1884), which amended the terms of the ZAR's suzerainty from Britain. In those days Ewald Esselen (back right) and Oom Paul (front left) were still batting for the same team

Before washing up on the ZAR's landlocked shores, Joubert's charming young campaign manager Esselen had grown up in the Cape Colony and had briefly studied medicine in Edinburgh and then law in London. On returning to the Cape he entered politics and was quickly on good enough terms with one Cecil John Rhodes to secure a personal loan from him. (Rhodes's chequebook was far more liberal than his politics!)

But Esselen's sojourn at the Cape would be brief. When, aged only twenty-eight, the upwardly mobile young advocate was offered a position as a judge in the ZAR's criminal court (a position that also gave him a fast track to citizenship), he jumped at the opportunity to make his mark on the republic. And make his mark he would: 'Mr. Esselen, from being the closest personal adherent of Mr. Kruger, became for a time his most formidable opponent and his most dreaded critic,' wrote FitzPatrick.[32]

Esselen played a central role in what was arguably the most controversial event of the campaign when he showed his moustachioed face at a meeting of the

National Union, 'a powerful organization ... influentially backed by mining and commercial interests, as well as by many thousands of uitlanders'. At the meeting Esselen didn't just bear silent witness, notes Gordon, 'he declared himself to be "in full agreement with the aims of the movement"' – aims that included granting the franchise to Uitlanders after two years' residence in the ZAR, overhauling the liquor laws (the so-called 'native drink problem' was proving costly to mine owners) and granting greater powers to the Johannesburg municipality. After the meeting, the National Union sent 'an anti-Kruger manifesto to every farmstead in the Republic'.[33] The whole affair was so scandalous that Joubert was forced to take out a full-page advert in *Land en Volk* distancing himself from the actions of his campaign manager.

Which brings us to our third musketeer, Eugène Marais, editor of said newspaper and arguably the most fascinating character in this story. Described by J.M. Coetzee as the closest South Africa has yet come 'to producing a genius', Marais was so much more than a muckraker. He was also a poet, advocate, writer and scientific visionary (the years he spent observing a baboon troop in the Waterberg have seen him hailed as an early Jane Goodall, and he is credited with being the first to suggest that a colony of social insects should be seen as a single organism).[34] On the flipside he was a long-time morphine addict and – full disclosure – his uncle, 'Lang Piet' Marais, was one of the richest mining bosses in the country.

Land en Volk and the 'Hou-jou-bek-wet'[35]

The ZAR was blessed with a thriving and very vocal print media, although 1893 was the first year in which the press seriously impacted the outcome of an election. In general, the loudest Progressive voices could be heard in the Johannesburg-based English papers. Dutch papers from Pretoria tended to favour the government. (Of course they did – Kruger pushed significant advertising revenue their way!)

In July 1890 the owners of the English-language *Transvaal Observer* bought *Land en Volk* as part of a plan to advance the Progressive cause among Dutch readers. On 10 October Oom Paul Kruger received an unwanted birthday gift when eighteen-year-old Eugène Marais was appointed editor. Using the pseudonym 'Apteker' (pharmacist), Marais dispensed biting criticism of Kruger, the Volksraad and the concessionaires via his 'Swart Pilletjies' (Little Black Pills) column. On 7 July 1891, Marais and Jimmy Roos bought *Land en Volk* for £500,

Afrikanus Junior
aka Eugène Marais

with Esselen providing surety for the bank loan. Interestingly, Roos had been employed by the Cape Town *Argus* (clandestinely owned by Rhodes).

According to Herman van Niekerk, in the lead-up to the 1893 election Kruger passed a press law that 'curbed freedom of speech and editorial expression' and which was 'clearly aimed at Eugène Marais'. But Marais – who would later go on to practise as an advocate – spotted a loophole: the ruling did not apply to readers' letters. Suddenly, *Land en Volk* was awash with angry letters from someone called Afrikanus Junior. As Van Niekerk continues:

The typesetter at *Land en Volk* informed Eugène Marais that a government official [had] offered a considerable reward to him for revealing the identity of 'Afrikanus Junior'. It was clearly a witch-hunt by Paul Kruger. Eugène Marais set a trap for the government official and supplied him with a bogus name of a farmer in Waterberg. Eugène Marais subsequently wrote a juicy article in *Land en Volk* about the matter.[36]

To the Oom's great embarrassment, Marais donated the reward he received for revealing the author's identity to a local hospital.

Later, *Land en Volk* was bought by a consortium funded by the mining magnates Julius Wernher and Alfred Beit (the mining industry, as we shall see, has always had overly intimate ties to the South African press) for £2 500. After the Jameson Raid, to avoid a PR fiasco, the magnates handed the paper back to Marais for nothing. But he would not be a newspaperman for much longer...

In 1895 Marais suffered a personal tragedy when his beloved wife, Lettie, died in childbirth. A year later Kruger passed yet more draconian press legislation, which Marais dubbed the 'hou-jou-bek-wet' (hold-your-tongue-law). When his parents died within six weeks of each other, Marais decided it was time for a change. On 3 December 1896 he appointed James O'Brien editor of *Land en Volk* and sailed for England to study law.

Aged only twenty-one at the time of the campaign, and that rare breed of well-to-do urban ZAR burgher who spoke English at home (ironic considering he is one of the founding fathers of Afrikaans literature), Marais would never have dared address the electorate in person. But when lobbing sticks of dynamite from behind the parapets of his tabloid, nothing was off limits. As Sandra Swart explains in her memorably titled academic paper 'An Irritating Pebble in Kruger's Shoe',

> Under Marais's control, *Land en Volk* introduced a new kind of journalism, a break from the staid Anglo-Dutch journalistic tradition, and a shift towards the muckraking of the American yellow press and the radical English penny-press. *Land en Volk* became the vehicle for the polemics and diatribes of the young Turks of the Progressive faction. Matters of the day were discussed in regular columns, like 'Sonder Reserf' (Without holding back) and 'Hans se Brief' (Hans's letter) ... As a contemporary observed, he started making a name for himself as the *enfant terrible* of South African journalism.[37]

These excerpts from *Land en Volk* should give you a fairly good idea of the paper's vibe:

26 APRIL 1892 – PARODYING OOM PAUL

I'm for Concessions, Monopolies etc ... I'm for appointing two financial ministers (they have to be Hollanders), the Volksraad has to be satisfied with my will, and must not dare think. Or I'll threaten to resign.

15 OCTOBER 1892 – POSING TOUGH QUESTIONS

Why was Dr Leyds re-appointed? Why not a competent Afrikaner? Why is our country the only one in the world where a foreigner holds the reins? ... Why were we told that the Delagoa Bay Railway must be built by a Hollander company to free us from dependence on England, and now we find ourselves dangerously in debt to England?

2 FEBRUARY 1893 – UNASHAMED PLEADING

Citizens of the Transvaal! Don't sleep, vote for PIET JOUBERT, the hero of Amajuba, the man of honour, the beloved of his volk. Don't be fooled by clever talk.[38]

Botha's backing

One of the more telling yardsticks of the measure of support for Joubert is contained in a letter he received from Field Cornet Louis Botha, who would go on to become a revered Boer War general and the first president of the Union of South Africa.

My dear friend,

You will be very surprised to receive a letter from me; but with politics going the way they are at the moment I feel I must express my gratitude at having heard from my friends Mr Lucas J. Meyer and Esselen that you will stand in the coming Presidential elections.

Our country is certainly in need of a great change, and in you we have a man who cherishes the independence of our beloved country in his very heart, and who is a true friend of the Afrikaners. So just take this to show you that you have friends here also who will stand or fall with you. In my ward [Vryheid] the requisition to you to stand has been signed by every well-disposed Afrikaner, and they will support you to the end. I hope that the day will speedily come when we shall be able to say – away with Kruger's politics, concessions and Hollanders.[39]

The letter also lays bare the very real possibility of a military response should Joubert fail to win the election.

One named Pieter, one named Paul

After a campaign that featured what the pro-Kruger *Volkstem* described as unprecedented 'requisitions, counter-requisitions, manifestoes and anti-manifestoes', the burghers finally went to the polls in January 1893.[40] Although voting could continue until 20 February, by the end of January 'election results [began to come] in slowly over the hot Transvaal roads and not before early February was it clear that Kruger would beat Joubert with a very small majority and that Chief Justice Kotzé had received almost no support'.[41]

In a slo-mo version of the modern news cycle, newspapers published preliminary results that laid bare the deep regional divisions in the ZAR and fomented myriad rumours about irregularities in the electoral process. Kruger, it became clear, had mopped up in his western Transvaal home base, while Joubert had taken the lion's share in the northern and central Transvaal. But in every poll, by hook or by crook, Kruger maintained a slender lead. On 2 February *Land en Volk* gave Kruger a lead of 934 votes. By 18 February, two days before the polls closed, this lead had shrunk to around 650, according to the *Volkstem*.

The rules of the election stated that a full month had to pass after the polls closed for votes from distant districts to be counted and only after this date could the official scrutiny take place. While Joubert didn't go public with his misgivings, as early as 23 February he was writing to a friend to say,

> Well ... our President has come in again, by a small majority. I am glad that I did not obtain a majority in such a manner. I would ten times rather be in the minority than obtain a majority in such a manner.[42]

True to form, Esselen and Marais were much more vocal in making their grievances known. On 2 March *Land en Volk* was already threatening the possibility of a violent response if a recount was refused: 'If Paul Kruger's Government desires to maintain peace, it must see to it that an honest scrutiny takes place.'[43] Two weeks later they lodged an official request that four members of each election committee be allowed to observe the scrutiny – a request that was conveniently brushed aside. When the scrutiny began on 21 March, only Kruger himself and the mild-mannered Joubert were allowed to observe.

On 28 March, while the scrutiny was still ongoing, the Joubert Committee (i.e. Esselen) lodged an official complaint, which stated among other things

> [t]hat the ballot boxes had been opened and the votes counted by landdrosts and mining commissioners ... That innumerable unqualified people had been allowed to vote, including lunatics, children under 16, persons resident in other constituencies, persons whose names had been removed from the voting lists and persons who had not even been to the polls [and that] qualified voters had been refused permission to cast their votes.[44]

The scrutiny was concluded on 5 April and, notwithstanding another official complaint from Joubert, on 15 April Kruger was announced the official winner. While Oom Paul urged the populace to accept the result calmly, Joubert's election committee went into overdrive, calling a full congress of the party and, on 20 April, launching a more-stinging-than-usual rebuke in *Land en Volk*:

The party Committee has protested strongly to the Executive Council against any taking of oaths of office by members or officials, on the ground that the election was, for various reasons, illegal. Yet the senders of this protest have been treated with less courtesy than if they were Hottentots or dogs. Leyds did not even acknowledge it, and the President says he will put it before the Volksraad, and adds in his usual oily manner that he is ready to submit himself to their decision. Submit himself to the decision of a Volksraad packed with Kruger-men, such honest and upright people as Lombard and de Beer! The people demand a thorough and impartial scrutiny.[45]

Which brings us to the real challenge facing Joubert and his cronies: while Slim Piet had by all accounts put in a very strong performance in the presidential race, the members of his fledgling party had only won a handful of constituencies. As Gordon notes,

The outcome of elections for the First Raad gives no evidence of anything even remotely resembling a significant swing towards the Progressives. Of some seventeen constituencies in which First Raad elections were held, only six returned Progressive candidates ... Of these, only two ... were new choices.[46]

In perhaps the most shocking result of all, Ewald Esselen had lost in Potchefstroom. As Marais' biographer Leon Rousseau puts it,

An almost equally bitter pill to swallow was Ewald Esselen's defeat in Potchefstroom by only seven votes. Eugène knew what a thorn in the flesh Ewald had become to the Government; he was the only man who could unite the Opposition in the Volksraad. In this case he had no doubt there had been foul play. They could not yet prove it, but they were certain that Jan Kock, the electoral officer, had watched the voting (which was public) very thoroughly and exerted considerable pressure on voters to vote against Esselen. According to the stories, people who were known to be supporters of Esselen were disqualified on various pretexts, while the dead rose from their graves to support the Kruger candidate. And in the end Ewald had nevertheless been only seven votes short of victory. Seven![47]

On 4 May the strongly pro-Kruger Volksraad finally turned its attention to the legality of Kruger's election, with Leyds officially announcing the results (which had been known for some time). The following day Joubert and Esselen lodged their formal objection to the results and asked that the dispute be resolved by either a commission of inquiry comprising members chosen from outside the Raad or an arbitration overseen by the High Court. Kruger magnanimously announced that he quite liked the idea of a commission of inquiry, explaining that he had no desire to occupy a position that wasn't rightfully his. Lying through his teeth, he stated:

> I hope that the Committee will show no favour or bias towards myself, and that right and justice will sway them in their decisions. You will please institute a thorough and searching investigation upon each point in the matter ... I ask for a fair field and no favour.[48]

And with that he exited stage left and allowed his henchmen to see that (in)justice was done. 'After a very short debate', the Raad decided that the commission would be chosen from within the Raad and would comprise three Krugerites and three Jouberites. Soon after the commission got under way, however, one of the three Jouberites – a certain Schalk Burger – conveniently switched allegiances, ensuring that the result was a foregone conclusion. (Kruger rewarded Burger with the chairmanship of the Volksraad in 1895 and, a year later, elevation to the Executive Council.) The commission (like a fair number of other South African commissions) 'regarded speed as the essence of its task',[49] taking only three days to prepare its report on Joubert's complaints. While the report did address each of the fifteen complaints lodged by Joubert's committee individually, it did so off the back of little (or no) proper investigation and quickly concluded that only twenty-seven Kruger votes (and no Joubert votes) should be discarded.

The two remaining Jouberites on the commission, Lukas Meyer and Lodewyk de Jager, 'refused to accept the majority finding and insisted on submitting minority reports'.[50] As one opposition member put it in the subsequent debate, he found it hard to comprehend how such a complicated and important task 'could have been completed in a couple of hours'. *Land en Volk* pointed out that it was 'impossible for the Executive Council to examine the allegations with any thoroughness'.[51] Gordon concludes that 'a court of law would not have decided a dispute about the possession of a stray donkey – let alone the legality of the most crucial presidential election in the history of the Transvaal – in this cavalier fashion'.[52]

They were all, of course, farting against thunder, and on 10 May the Raad adopted the commission's report by eighteen votes to three before immediately passing another motion recognising Kruger as president. Three months of accusations and counter-accusations had done nothing to change what most burghers knew all along – that Oom Paul would not give up without a fight.

The table below shows how Kruger clung to his slender lead as the results were first counted and then scrutinised.

	Date	Kruger	Joubert	Kotzé
Partial results	2 Feb	5 741	4 807	45
First 'final' results	1 March	8 114	7 310	86
Results after scrutiny	15 April	7 881	7 009	81
Final results announced by commission	10 May	7 854	7 009	81

Now, more than a century later, there's no way of knowing who actually won the election. The fact is that even a full rerun of the election might not have come any closer to revealing the truth. This editorial from the *Volkstem* warrants quoting from at length:

> What guarantee is there that [another election] would be any better? We have already indicated that our electoral system is wholly unsatisfactory. In many places the registration of enfranchised burghers was defective or inaccurate; in others officials have shown themselves incompetent to carry out the provisions of the law; in yet other instances the law itself is so ambiguous that one could ride around it with cart and horses.
>
> In short the existing organization was not designed to cater for such a sharp election struggle as that which has just been thrust upon it by the Kruger and Joubert parties.
>
> Is there any point in forcing our creaking and sighing electoral machinery into action once again? ... That irregularities occurred is possible, when one takes into account the slapdash manner [*de slordige manier*] in which the matter was sometimes dealt with. But it is difficult to accept that only the Joubert party suffered. There is no one who swears that the Joubert people were invariably honest and legal and the Kruger people on the other hand shockingly dishonest and illegal.[53]

General Joubert's Election Committee aka the Progressive Party

Enough starch to stand stiffly?
On 12 May 1893, as Kruger put it,

> I was installed as State President for the third time. After being sworn in,
> I once more addressed the people, this time from the balcony of the new
> Government Buildings, while the public stood crowded in large numbers in
> the Church Square in front. I exhorted the burghers to remain unanimous,
> spoke a word of greeting to the women of the country and, lastly and particu-
> larly, admonished the children, with whom the future lay, to continue true to
> their mother tongue.[54]

Despite their losses, the Progressive faction was hopeful that the close-run election and the upswell in support for their cause would mean that, as the *Press*
put it, Kruger would no longer be 'supreme in the Raad and able to override all
opposition with impunity, with placidity and even with amusement'. A few lines
later, in a metaphor for the ages, the same article raised the obvious stumbling
block to this logic: 'Whether the opposition will succeed in putting enough
starch in General Joubert to make him stand stiffly to the programme issued by
his supporters remains to be seen.'[55]

Newspaper reports and Volksraad records show that in the period between
the election and the Jameson Raid in December 1895, the Progressives did gradually increase their influence in the twenty-four-man Volksraad, swelling from five
or six members in 1890 to ten or eleven at the end of 1895. This increase required
Kruger to proceed with more caution than he was used to. But the fact that at
least half of six 'floating votes' (party lines were not nearly as rigid back then)
would side with the president on any matter of consequence meant that he usually
got his way in the end. The Progressives did make some fairly meaningful strides
with regard to modernising railway policy, but they were only able to achieve
small modifications to the education policy and the dynamite concession (which
was effectively reissued to the same person, Edouard Lippert, despite his being
implicated in dodgy dealings). Kruger, however, refused to budge on the franchise
question.

Two events in 1894 suggested that the opposing factions might finally be finding some middle ground. Esselen, Kruger's harshest critic but also one of the ablest
minds in the ZAR, was appointed state attorney. And, outside the Raad, there
was an attempted '*toenadering*' (rapprochement) between the Volksvereeniging

(a committee of Progressive-leaning citizens) and the conservative Krugerite Burgermacht. The honeymoon would not last long, however. Esselen proved himself predictably incapable of being a yes-man. And the Volksvereeniging and the Burgermacht could not get any *nader* on the Uitlander issue.

Disappointments aside, there remained a strong feeling from both within and without the ZAR that change was imminent, as this discussion, which took place in the first few months of 1895 between the influential Cape newspaperman Francis Joseph Dormer (who owned both the *Cape Argus* and the *Star*) and Rhodes, attests:

DORMER: There is a strong Progressive party in the Raad and if we go the right way about the business, some man of liberal tendencies will become the President in the next elections. Then we shall get all that is necessary in the way of reforms.

RHODES: But I don't want your reforms, or rather your reformed Republic. The ideal system is that of a British colony... I also do not like the idea of British subjects becoming burghers.[56]

What if?

These are, of course, the two words that no historian should ever utter. But we hope that you will forgive us two paragraphs of fantasising. History shows that Rhodes – as was almost always the case – got his way. But it is still worth asking what might have happened if Dormer had got his. It seems fair to suggest that if Slim Piet had prevailed in the 1893 election, there's a possibility that both the Jameson Raid and, in turn, the Anglo-Boer War might have been avoided. Take these two events out of our history and who knows how South Africa might have turned out.

This is not to say that our country wouldn't have been subjected to some kind of racial segregation for the best part of the twentieth century, but a victory for Joubert might have helped us avoid grand apartheid. Then again, we might have ended up with something even worse.

Fun though this game may be, we have more pressing matters at hand. Like working out why on earth Rhodes, the man behind the criminally scandalous Jameson Raid, was even on the ballot in the 1898 Cape elections...

CHAPTER 4

RHODES:
PAVING THE CAPE
WITH BAD INTENTIONS
1898

'One lives in an atmosphere heavily charged with carbonic.' – *James Rose Innes*[1]

Voters at Barkly West electing for Rhodes

THE 1898 ELECTION WAS THE most fiercely contested, the most corrupt and the most libellous in the Cape's history. At the centre of these shenanigans was one man: Cecil John Rhodes, perhaps *the* most divisive politician ever to darken Cape Dutch doorways. As one politician put it, the Cape's 'body politic was virgin soil for the new infection' Rhodes subjected it to.[2] He was in many ways a nineteenth-century Donald Trump: egotistical, venal and loaded. And, as the philosopher Hannah Arendt expressed in her *Origins of Totalitarianism*, Rhodes and his activities in the Cape were instrumental in promoting 'mob rule' (what we call populism).

Much had changed in the Cape since 1854 – and very little for the good. Historian Stanley Trapido asserts that before the discovery of diamonds and gold, the Cape was developing an economy of merchants and trade. In this environment the inclination was towards inclusion: all cultures and communities were potential clients and partners. At the crucial moment of the discovery of diamonds in the Kimberley area, 'blacks and whites stood ready to cross a threshold together,' writes Antony Thomas, 'but this was not to be.'[3]

Rhodes in particular helped develop an anti-free-market and illiberal economic system that functioned in such a way that 'whenever rational labour and production policies came into conflict with race considerations, the latter won.'[4] As Olive Schreiner, a writer and fierce political opponent of Rhodes, wrote:

> the Retrogressive Party in this country regards the Native as only to be tolerated in consideration of the amount of manual labour which can be extracted from him; and desires to obtain the largest amount of labour at the cheapest rate possible; and rigidly resists all endeavours to put him on an equality with the white man in the eye of the law.[5]

Another factor creating racial tension in the Cape was that the British had merged two areas into the Colony, both of which had large black populations. The Ciskei had been incorporated in 1865, against the wishes of the Cape Parliament. And in 1885, after the ninth and last Frontier War, the Transkei was drawn into the Cape's borders. These areas, like the rest of the Cape, had no colour-bar restrictions – so long as a voter could fulfil Porter's '£25 franchise' requirement – and their incorporation would add six more representatives to the Cape Parliament. As Rodney Davenport puts it, with this new development, many conservative whites, both English- and Afrikaans-speaking, 'feared that unless they changed the electoral rules they would one day lose political control of the Cape legislature.[6]

Where's the Party at?

The Cape had not developed a party political system along British or American lines. However, by the 1880s an Afrikaner political movement called the Afrikaner Bond under the leadership of 'Onze Jan' Hendrik Hofmeyr had emerged. The Bond was avowedly anti-imperialist, its aim being to bring South Africa together in a federated state that was free from British influence. But although the Bond acted in some ways like a political party, it was 'retarded by two circumstances'.[7] One was that Hofmeyr did not like taking centre stage, preferring to work the smoke-filled backrooms. For this behaviour fellow parliamentarian John X. Merriman nicknamed him 'the Mole'. As Merriman wrote, 'the Mole is an industrious little animal … You never see him at work, but every now and then a little mound of earth, thrown up here or there, will testify to his activities.'[8] The other reason was that Hofmeyr feared that a monolithic Bond party would divide the Cape along racial lines and set the English against the Afrikaners.

The Bond nevertheless had a large, if not controlling, block of members in Parliament. The rest was made up of independent, largely English-speaking MPs who formed alliances according to their political beliefs. When conservative politician Sir Gordon Sprigg started his second term as prime minister in 1886, he was determined to apply the handbrake to racial inclusivity. In 1887, reacting to the British government's inclusion of the Transkei in the Colony, he pushed through the Registration Act, disallowing land held in communal tenure to be included in the property qualification. Sprigg is said to have drawn up the legislation when he received advice that a hut with some adjacent land might fulfil the £25 voting qualification. According to historian Robert Rotberg, Sprigg, with the backing of the Bond, wanted to 'cleanse and purify' the Cape voters' register. That is, they wanted to make sure that no MP could be voted in solely by the black electorate.

There were, however, those who stood against Sprigg – the movement generally referred to as 'the Cape Liberal tradition', the inheritors of Fairbairn's politics. James Rose Innes, John X. Merriman and J.W. Sauer all opposed Sprigg's Registration Bill on the grounds of 'truth', 'liberty' and 'justice'. Merriman would stand up in Parliament and declare that the bill was a 'miserable sham'. 'We have no right,' he went on to state, 'to take away the rights that have been conferred upon the Natives.'[9] Nevertheless, Sprigg's bill was passed with the help of the Bond and one young malignant member named Cecil John Rhodes.

The rise and rise of Cecil Rhodes

Until Rhodes became the member of Parliament for Barkly West in 1881, he had largely focused on developing his financial interests. When Sprigg's government began to suffer flagging fortunes in 1890, Rhodes saw his chance: in addition to being the wealthiest and most influential businessman in the Colony, he could truly control its politics.

Sitting pretty but standing
for the unpleasant

Sprigg, in a desperate attempt to retain popularity, had put forward a proposal to extend the railway network in the Cape. It was something he thought would resonate with rural voters. But he had not reckoned on the possibility of absolutely nobody liking it. The Bond and Rhodes pilloried him in and out of Parliament. Rhodes told a crowd in Kimberley that Sprigg's railway bill 'would place too great a burden upon the revenue of the Cape'[10] and, using the *Argus* newspaper, which he secretly owned, launched a full-scale media attack on Sprigg, who, having received it from all sides, resigned.

Rhodes and Hofmeyr had in fact been in secret alliance discussions since July 1889, and when Sprigg stepped down, the Bond offered Rhodes 'fair play'. Rhodes slipped effortlessly into the position of prime minister without a challenge. As Rotberg says, 'Rhodes could neither have taken nor have kept office without the Bond'.[11] He then made a deal with the Afrikaners that if they supported his expansionist dreams, he would support 'an appropriate Afrikaner order in the Cape'.[12] Importantly, both Rhodes and the Bond had dreams to unite South Africa. Rhodes had promised the Bond that this unity would come 'without forcing the British flag on the reluctant [Boer] republics'[13] and, in return for the Bond's support, he offered them the 'additional lubricant', as Mordechai Tamarkin puts it, of liberally distributing some 125 000 shares of his British South Africa Company (BSAC) to MP Bondsmen, including Hofmeyr.

Surprisingly, Rhodes brought many of the liberal voices of the Colony into his first cabinet, which became known as the 'Cabinet of all talents'.[14] Among these were the Eastern Cape–born Rose Innes, the towering moral presence of Merriman, and the great champion of black and women's rights, Sauer. But the three knew their engagement with Rhodes would not last. As Merriman wrote, '[I have] a good many things to gulp down. I therefore hardly like to predict a very long life for our craft... [and] I cannot say that I feel either proud or pleased'.[15] Also included in the cabinet was the Scottish-born Bondsman Sir James Sivewright, a man widely known to be a crook.

A Liberal line-up: Merriman, Sauer and Rose Innes

The carbonic air of Cecilian politics

True to Merriman's words, the three liberals quickly found their little craft in troubled waters. Rhodes twice supported the failed Masters and Servants Bill, known colloquially as 'the Strop Bill'. This legislation would have allowed black servants to be flogged by magistrates on evidence provided solely by their 'master'. As several commentators have observed, the bill would have returned servants to the status of something very close to a slave. It was defeated by thirty-five to twenty-three, however, largely because of Rose Innes, Merriman, Sauer and (interestingly) Hofmeyr's opposition to it.

But with the help of the Bond, Rhodes managed to push through the Franchise and Ballot Act and the Glen Grey Act, in 1892 and 1894 respectively. The first raised the £25 property franchise qualification to £75; the second was the first attempt at creating a Bantustan while at the same time enforcing migrant labour.

The Franchise and Ballot Act almost caused Rose Innes to resign from the cabinet. As he would write to Merriman, 'my inmost soul abhors the whole thing'. 'One lives in an atmosphere heavily charged with carbonic,' he continued; 'there are so many things to be considered apart from one's own honest opinions.'[16] Merriman too found himself compromising on the Franchise Bill, agreeing to support it on condition that a secret ballot clause be inserted, thus making all voting a private matter. Rhodes grudgingly agreed to the secret ballot, but he was unhappy with the compromise – 'I like to know how a person votes,' he whined.[17] But as he famously said, 'every man has his price' – and this price could be applied to the way every man voted.

The Franchise and Ballot Act was not the only attack on the non-racial franchise – there were many others throughout the Cape's history. As Davenport argues, the whole thing was compromised from its inception by miserable white administrators who did their best to remove legal black voters from the roll. One man who would do his best to counteract this was Rose Innes's friend, the newspaper editor John Tengo Jabavu.

Two good men

Jabavu was of Mfengu origins. Like many of his people, his family had settled in the Cape Colony largely as a result of the upheavals commonly referred to as the Mfecane. As Davenport and Saunders put it, the Mfengu who settled in the Eastern Cape 'found favour with the [British Colonial] authorities as soldiers fighting for the colonial interest, as peasants, farmers and townsmen holding European title, as successful scholars and religious converts, as hard-bargaining traders, and ... parliamentary voters'.[18]

A son of Christian converts, Jabavu was educated at a mission school and would go on to become a teacher, preacher, newspaper editor and political agent. He founded the newspaper *Imvo Zabantsundu* (African Opinion) and would use

John Tengo Jabavu and his son
Davidson Don Tengo

it not only as a means of giving a voice to black political opinion in the Colony, but also as a means to spread voter education. In *Imvo* he regularly discussed the advantages of registering to vote and informed readers of the qualifications required and the steps to be taken in order to be placed on the voters' roll.

Jabavu worked as a political canvasser in the 1884 Cape election for a young Rose Innes. Although they sometimes differed in opinion, the two men worked together in an attempt to protect the non-racial franchise in the Cape. As historian André Odendaal writes, it is beyond any doubt that Jabavu 'influenced Cape elections, being instrumental for example in the nomination and return of J.C. Molteno in the Tembuland constituency in 1894'.[19]

Cracks in the cabinet

What broke Rhodes's alliance with the liberals was a letter published in the *Cape Times* on 5 November 1892. It blew the whistle on a corrupt contract for refreshments along the railway line from Cape Town to the Free State that had been given to Mr James Logan, a friend of Rhodes's chum and cabinet minister James Sivewright.

The three liberals, Rose Innes, Merriman and Sauer, were incensed and pointedly raised the issue with Rhodes. But instead of receiving assurances that this corruption would be dealt with, Rhodes's paper, the *Argus*, went on the attack, referring to them as 'the three mutineers'. Rhodes then did a backroom deal with Sprigg and Hofmeyr and promptly resigned before calling for a new election. With the Bond and Sprigg on his side, Rhodes won easily, without the pesky liberals, and duly resumed his premiership in 1894.

But by the end of the following year, Rhodes would be in even hotter water.

Jameson's wretched raid

On the surface, the Jameson Raid might seem like a slightly innocuous joyride by Rhodes's best man and his group of merry bachelors, ending with them waking with a serious hangover in a ZAR prison. But for South African politics it would have cataclysmic repercussions that lasted nearly a century.

In short, the escapade was a monumental cock-up from beginning to end, not least due to Rhodes's miscalculations. As Arendt suggests, he was a megalomaniac very rarely touched by reason. Disregarding the fact that Britain's influence in the ZAR was complete anathema to his Bond supporters, Rhodes gained the empire's backing in his quest for the ZAR. (Despite his previous assurances to the Bond, he was entirely ambivalent about what flag would fly over the ZAR after the raid. Britain would support him, and that was all that mattered. 'Expansion is everything,' he claimed. 'I would annex the planets if I could.'[20])

In preparing for the raid, Rhodes attempted to collude with the Uitlanders of the Johannesburg Reform Committee in the ZAR. It was their job to rise in rebellion against Kruger, providing a reason for Rhodes to send in his own troops and take control of the republic. When the Reform Committee failed to do their bit (their gripes with Kruger were not as significant as Rhodes believed), Jameson took matters into his own hands and rode in to the ZAR with 500 men from Rhodes's private BSAC army.

Jameson's men were, for the most part, four sheets to the wind and, as a result, failed to cut all the communication lines to Pretoria – one drunken trooper apparently mistook a farmer's fence for a telegraph line and cut that instead. With Jameson's border incursion reported to Kruger in Pretoria via telegraph, a commando rode out to shadow Jameson's raiders. The commando struck at Doornkop, and Jameson, hopelessly outclassed and outmanoeuvred, was forced to surrender after seventeen of his men (many of whom were in their teens) were killed and fifty-five wounded. The Boers lost four men.

The Bond becomes unstuck and Rhodes becomes a jingo

The fallout of the raid was catastrophic. Realising that the Bond would no longer support him after his betrayal, Rhodes resigned as prime minister, and Gordon Sprigg once again took over the premiership. When the Cape parliamentary inquiry into the raid took place, the Bond-affiliated newspaper *Onze Courant* stated somewhat prophetically: 'Rhodes the Afrikaner has become an impossibility – thus now begins the career of Rhodes the jingo.'[21] Although some Bond members remained loyal to Rhodes, the tide had turned. As one Bond MP said of pro-Rhodes Bond members or 'wobblers', these men had been 'captured by the greatest enemy of South Africa'.[22]

The Jameson Raid created deep distrust between Afrikaners and English-speakers in the Cape. And at its congress in 1897, the Bond passed a resolution affirming never to grant Rhodes 'fair play' again. The Bond would go on to oppose Rhodes and his policies at every conceivable turn.

The regressive Progressives

It was now becoming apparent to many English-speakers that they needed a party of their own. A political organisation called the South African League was formed, and at its conference in Port Elizabeth in February 1897 it called on all MPs who were its members to form a parliamentary party. A resolution was adopted on 12 February that can be regarded as 'the birth of the Cape Progressive Party'.[23]

When Sprigg succeeded Rhodes as premier in 1896 he had been an independent, and he had included several Bondsmen in his cabinet, including the crooked James Sivewright. In fact, the Bond continued to support Sprigg until 1897, when a vote of no confidence was tabled against him by Merriman, backed by the other liberals, Rose Innes, Sauer and W.P. Schreiner. At that point, Bond members deserted Sprigg and voted against him. Nevertheless, his government survived because the Progressive Party rallied to his side, and in due course he became a Progressive. Sprigg was now a proxy for Rhodes – despite the fallout of the raid, the latter had remained the MP for Barkly West and was, in real terms, in control of the new Progressive Party.

Sprigg limped along in this state until trouble arose over getting the new Redistribution Bill through Parliament. The bill would add eighteen new members to the House of Assembly and as such met some serious headwinds from the Bond, as the constituencies would be made in cities and towns and would almost certainly be won by the Progressives. The bill was initially passed, but when W.P. Schreiner put forward another vote of no confidence in Sprigg's government, Sprigg was defeated after Rose Innes voted against the government. As a result, the Colony had to go to the polls.

Schisms and bonds

When Sprigg called for an election, it left several people in a dilemma. The English-speaking former Bond members Sivewright and Thomas Smartt had naturally followed Rhodes into the Progressive Party. But the liberals (or 'real' progressives) like Merriman, W.P. Schreiner, Rose Innes and Sauer were now technically partyless in an increasingly polarised political environment. After 1896 Schreiner was largely seen as the leader of the opposition in Parliament, but just what this meant was not initially clear. The Bond was certainly part of the opposition, but the best of the rest were a cobbled-together bunch of liberals whose views, certainly on race, were vastly distinct from those of Hofmeyr's men.

W.P. Schreiner goes to the pole

Nevertheless, some liberals and the Bond began to form an alliance. This alliance was named 'the South African Party' (SAP) by Schreiner, although Rhodes's supporters refused to use the name. According to historian Phyllis Lewsen, the

SAP 'had a curious identity for it functioned only in Parliament, with no distinctive branch structure'.[24] With the SAP came a new newspaper, started with the help of W.P.'s sister Olive. The *South African News* was edited by the anti-Rhodes journalist Albert Cartwright, a friend of the Schreiners and Rose Innes who had recently left the editorship of the *Diamond Fields Advertiser* after Rhodes's Argus group bought it out as part of his election strategy.

Despite all this, Rose Innes did not join the SAP. He was adamant that he would stick to his Progressive roots, and although running technically as an independent, he continued to support selected Progressive candidates. He had always distrusted the conservative strain within Bond politics and refused to see how an alliance with them could further a Progressive cause.

The liberals divided

What is perhaps baffling to the modern mind (given what was to follow with apartheid) is that Merriman, the Schreiners (W.P., Olive and her husband, Samuel Cronwright-Schreiner), Sauer and Henry Burton supported both non-whites and the Afrikaners. It was perhaps Jabavu who expressed the position best when he wrote to Rose Innes saying, '(Mr Merriman and Mr Sauer among them) think that the honest, simple Dutch farmer is more to be depended upon for the ends all of us hold in common.'[25]

What Rose Innes, in his particularly stubborn manner, refused to accept was that he was possibly the only 'real Progressive' left. When faced with whose side to take, Jabavu followed Merriman and Sauer. Jabavu had supported the Progressives, but with Merriman, Sauer and W.P. Schreiner now committed to the Bond, Jabavu wrote to Rose Innes:

> I think you would do your country good by going in with moderate men from both sides to carry out a Moderate as against a so-called Progressive policy. As you are aware, for myself I should much rather see you coming in as Prime Minister of the Moderate men, taking Schreiner, Sauer and Merriman from those who may be supposed to enjoy the confidence of the other side. From my standpoint, which is solely that of the Native Policy, such a ministry would be the ideal one. I may be wrong, but I feel like I can no more run away from looking at affairs by the light of Native policy than I can run away from my shadow.[26]

Rose Innes outright refused to join the Bond, believing firmly in the (Progressive) independent's role to judge issues on their merits and not by what party supported them. As he would write to Jabavu, 'for me to go over to the Bond is simply out of the question; I could not bring myself to do it'. He would go on to reprimand Jabavu, stating: 'I think it would have been better had you drawn a firmer line between yourself and the Bond'. For Rose Innes, to have joined the Bond would have meant political 'annihilation' for both himself and his political point of view. Being a Progressive had a particular meaning for him, a meaning that Rhodes was in the process of trampling.

Jabavu's support of the Bond came at another cost. In 1898 a new Eastern Cape newspaper, *Izwi Labantu*, emerged. The paper was set up to rival Jabavu's *Imvo* by people sympathetic to the Progressive Party. As Odendaal notes, some of the 'capital needed to start up the newspaper seems to have been provided by Rhodes'.[27] *Izwi*'s editorial line in the lead-up to the election was sternly pro-Progressive, and it set up a rivalry with Jabavu that would result in the black vote fracturing along the Bond vs. Progressive fault line.

Rhodes's resurrection

Rhodes, meanwhile, was pretending he had no real interest in being prime minister, even though most knew that Sprigg had been largely controlled by him. As one contemporary wag put it, Sprigg was running a 'warming pan government'. But on 9 March 1898, the *Cape Times* and its Rhodes-supporting editor published an interview with Rhodes in which he outlined his views with his brand of Trump-like egoism:

> Don't talk as if it was I who want your Cape politics. You want me. You can't do without me. You discuss; 'Ought Rhodes to do this' and 'Will Rhodes keep in the background' and so on – I am quite willing to keep out, but you have to take the feeling of the people; and the feeling of the people – you may think it egoism, but there are the facts – is that somebody is wanted to fight a certain thing for them, and there is nobody else able and willing to fight it.[28]

Three days later, at a mass meeting held at Good Hope Hall in Cape Town, he agreed to take over the leadership of the Progressive Party. As Merriman wrote in a letter to his mother some months later, Rhodes's followers intended on making 'him a sort of dictator, in which case – woe to the Transvaal and woe to the Natives'.[29]

THE
ABSENT PRESENCE

Sprigg warming the bench for Rhodes

The race to volte-face

One problem for the Progressives was that Rhodes could not now count on Bond support, and he would at the very least need to not bite his thumb at the non-white vote. Rhodes had never cut his punches when talking about the black vote; he had always been more comfortable playing to the English and Afrikaner racists in the Colony, as seen in his past statements: 'I am not going to the native vote for support', 'the native is to be treated as a child and denied the franchise' and '[is it right that] men in a state of pure barbarism should have the franchise and vote? The natives do not want it.' And of course, for the past two decades he had been central in passing racial legislation through Parliament.

But in the 1898 election this would all have to change. Bondsmen and Progressives now realised that without each other's support they would have to go cap in hand to coloured and black voters to get their parties over the line. Hofmeyr was first out the gate in an attempt to deny his past racist record. Sixteen days after Rhodes announced his leadership of the Progressive Party, Hofmeyr spoke at a meeting in Cape Town. In his speech, he pointed out that he had never voted for the infamous Strop Bill and claimed that he had 'never tried to deprive a single native of the vote' nor joined in Rhodes's 'insensate cry of "Equal rights for all white men south of the Zambezi"'.[30]

Rhodes, too, would change his tune. In a speech reported on by the *Eastern Province Herald*, he reiterated that he was fighting for '[e]qual rights for all white men south of the Zambezi' – a statement directed at the Uitlanders in the Transvaal, which stemmed from Rhodes's hope to one day rule over the Rand. As Rose Innes suggested, on the eve of the election Rhodes seemed to have momentarily lost his political bearings – in adopting his previous position of courting anti-Kruger, pro-British sentiment, Rhodes had apparently forgotten that without the Bond his political supremacy now relied in part on the coloured and black vote. When the newspaper containing his speech was sent to him by an association of coloured voters (possibly from around Barkly West) asking him if he had in fact said these words, he backtracked, sending back the newspaper with a note written in the margin:

My Motto is – Equal Rights for every civilised man south of the Zambezi. What is a civilised man? A man, whether white or black, who has sufficient education to write his name, has some property, or works. In fact, is not a loafer.[31]

This, Rose Innes pointed out, was simply a 'vote-catching device' and the 'crudity of the definition [of "civilised"] that Rhodes himself supplied' showed his total lack of respect for coloured and black voters.

Making the papers

The election was, as Eric Walker puts it, 'fought with a ferocity and expenditure of money unexampled in the sober annals of the Cape Colony'.[32] The gloves were off, and the fact that the likes of W.P. Schreiner, Sauer, Merriman, Rose Innes and many of the Bond members had once been in bed with Rhodes would mean that much of their 'pillow talk' would now be exposed in Rhodes's extensive media empire. Rhodes had not only put up the money for the Xhosa-language *Izwi*, but it was also a pretty open secret by then that he owned the Argus group, which, in the lead-up to the election, bought Kimberley's biggest newspaper, the *Diamond Fields Advertiser*, and several others. Rhodes would be generously quoted in these papers, calling the liberal–Bond alliance (i.e. the SAP) 'a little gang' 'terrorizing the country'.[33]

As Antony Thomas puts it, 'in the murk of lies and abuse, it was easy to lose sight of what this election was about. South African Party supporters feared that Rhodes, Milner and Chamberlain were hell-bent on pushing South Africa into a war and they were determined to prevent them.' As Merriman wrote in a letter to a British civil servant, 'war for you would be an incident of what you call "Empire", as it would mean absolute ruin, financially and socially, undertaken at the bidding of the subsidised press in order that those who are bursting with riches may grow richer'.[34] And Rhodes would not spare a penny to win the election that would bring on that war.

As Rotberg suggests, there is clear evidence that Rhodes began to pay and bribe people from the get-go, not only to not affiliate themselves with the Bond, but also to stand against Bondsmen in Bond strongholds. It would also be uncovered that Rhodes made payments amounting to £21 000 (R55 million today) to the MP Thomas Fuller (ex-editor of the *Argus*) 'to purchase favour and unexpected advantage'.[35] Merriman bemoaned this in a letter:

> Rhodes and his friends the capitalists are credited with having spent £50,000 on the elections, and I believe this to be within the mark. Our election fund (do not laugh) was £600!![36]

Rhodes had also 'taken steps to regulate the recruitment and discipline of his new battalions'. As Rose Innes wrote:

> No expense was spared. He imported from England an astute election agent – Owen Lewis by name – well versed in electioneering wiles and stratagems. The list of Progressive candidates was scrutinized, and those deemed unsatisfactory received no assistance, material or other, from the central committee. The test applied was loyalty to the Führer [i.e. Rhodes]. I was not behind the scene, but the matter was of common report. Nor was I sounded, for I had publicly declined to serve under the banner of Rhodes; fortunately mine was a safe seat, and I was returned without a contest.[37]

The same could not be said for the other liberals who had decided to throw in their lot with the Bond. Merriman, realising that he would not win his usual Namaqualand seat because of Rhodes's financial influence in the area, had opted for the Wodehouse seat in the Eastern Cape with its relatively large black voting contingent. There he would run against Thomas Smartt, the Irish-born ex-Bondsman who had recently allied himself with Rhodes's Progressives.

The minute Merriman announced his plans, Rhodes and his minions fired their opening broadside. In a coordinated attack on 3 August, Rhodes, Sivewright and Smartt all gave speeches revealing that Merriman had written encouragingly to a prominent member of the Johannesburg Reform Committee before the Jameson Raid. As Lewsen writes, 'the next day lurid reports appeared in the banner headlines in every Progressive newspaper in the Colony with enormous posters in the streets labelled "MERRIMAN UNMASKED".[38]

Rhodes's suggestion that Merriman had some empathy for the Reformers in the Transvaal would certainly not bring any Bond voter around to vote Progressive; the move was entirely an attempt to discredit rather than to change hearts and minds. As Merriman would write to his wife, he regretted the letter, but simply because he sympathised with some of the Reform movement did not mean that he had any sympathy for the raid. He hoped 'sensible people would see that'. 'Of course,' he went on, 'the enemy will do anything to blacken me, but they will fail ... My letter does not go much further than Hofmeyr's interview in the *Cape Times* of 26th December 1895.'[39] (In the interview, Hofmeyr had stated that the Uitlanders *did* have 'legitimate aspirations'.)

Rhodes and his electoral machinery also tried to tar Merriman with the brush

Walter Rubusana and the Cape Provincial Legislature

Walter Rubusana
dressed for success (and failure)

One of the most controversial aspects of the election was Walter Rubusana's decision to run for the Cape Provincial Council. He stood for the Tembuland district, where 49.5 per cent of the voters were black, yet all local newspapers were dead against him running. In a piece of absurd logic, one stated that if he won it would close the 'open door' that had so generously been offered to black politicians. *Imvo* only acknowledged, very late in the day, that he was running and stated that there was no reason to vote for him simply because he was black. Not only could Jabavu not manage to swallow his pride and back Rubusana, but such was the discord between them that he called on black voters to vote against his rival. Rubusana was nevertheless warmly supported by Abdurahman.

Rubusana made it clear in his campaign that he would work for all Tembuland's constituents, regardless of race. He ran against a Unionist candidate, T.G. Houghton-Grey, and an independent supporter of Botha, W.J. Clarke. Houghton-Grey attempted to make a deal with Clarke for only one white candidate to run against Rubusana, but Clarke refused.

When the ballots were finally counted, Rubusana was announced the winner with 766 votes, 25 more than Houghton-Grey, and he was duly elected as the first black member of the Cape Provincial Council. Interestingly, as historian Timothy Stapleton discovered, '[i]t appears that Rubusana gained slightly more white votes than black ones and that Houghton-Grey obtained more black votes than white votes'.[51]

Dawn of a divided Union

Union had been launched on a wave of political enthusiasm and false hope. But by the end of the election in September 1910, the wave had become a rip current.

The idea, sincerely believed by Botha, Smuts and Merriman, that *rooinek* and Boer would magically fuse together into one people was wishful thinking of the woolliest merino variety. Their distinctive cultures and recent history on the battlefields, and the Boers' experiences of scorched farmlands and concentration camps, could not simply be wished away.

Also, in Hertzog, Botha had in his own cabinet the very dynamite to blow open the divisions. As Jameson rightly predicted, Botha and Hertzog's proximity accentuated their differences to breaking point. Hertzog was expelled from the cabinet in 1912 with a relative hornet's nest in his Voortrekker's bonnet, and in 1914 he would form the National Party to oppose Botha's imperial complicity. When, in the same year, the Union Parliament took South Africa into World War I on the side of the Empire, many Boers took up arms against Botha's government in an act of open revolt. While Botha crushed the rebellion (at the cost of hundreds of lives), the wounds that it caused were left to fester.

Merriman's dream that white South Africans would naturally evolve towards liberalism turned out to be a fiction – more Charles Dickens than Charles Darwin. Not only did Merriman have zero evidence for his evolutionary theory, he'd also allowed the concept of segregation to be enshrined in the constitution so that he could push through union. Alas, legislative segregation would prove far easier to nurture than to eliminate.

And then there was the English-speaking Labour Party, which had set a worrying precedent with its explicitly racist constitution. As Thompson asks, '[W]hat if such a policy were to be adopted by one of the major parties?' What if, indeed.

But race was not the only issue. Class was another major factor in South Africa's early politics. And Creswell's Labour Party would soon find out just who it had got into bed with. In 1913 Smuts again used the army to suppress a miners' strike on the Rand. During the strike, he had his political ally Creswell arrested and thrown in jail for a month – an act that would have considerable repercussions ...

CHAPTER 6

PACT LUNCH: BOEREWORS AND MASH

1924

'The Prime Minister's footsteps drip with blood!' – **J.B.M. Hertzog**[1]

A 1924 SAP election poster shows a gallant
Smuts trying to wrest control of South Africa
from the two-headed monster of the Creswell–Hertzog Pact

F AST-FORWARD TO 1924, and Jan Smuts's SAP (which had hopped into bed with the Unionist Party and now spoke for most moderate whites) controlled Parliament. Hertzog's National Party had fast established itself as the official opposition.

Worryingly for Smuts, the twenty-four-seat majority the SAP had gained in the 1921 general election had been whittled down to only eight thanks to a succession of disappointing by-elections. But while the downward trend was by no means ideal, the next election was still two years distant and there was no apparent need for Smuts to panic. Most of the SAP's misfortunes in the by-elections could be attributed to an ongoing economic recession. But there was plenty of time for a recovery to kick in before he would have to call the next election. In fact, if he'd waited it out, he could have held the election when the recovery eventually began.

Smuts skrik Wakker(stroom)

Wakkerstroom, a small town in the eastern Transvaal, had always been a safe SAP seat. But the party's recent slide meant that a by-election there in 1924 assumed nationwide importance. Taking no chances, Smuts persuaded Alfred George Robertson to resign as administrator of the Transvaal to contest his home seat. Robertson spoke Afrikaans at home, had farmed in Wakkerstroom for three decades and was well liked in the area. In fact, writes Oswald Pirow in his hagiography of Hertzog, Robertson had

> only one vulnerable spot, viz., his [poor] record in the Anglo-Boer War. The Nationalists decided to hit him where he would feel it most and put up against him Mr A.S. Naude, an unknown farmer but a man who had been shot to pieces in 1900 and had lost the use of both legs. Every newspaper in the country took part in the campaign and the South African Party money flowed like water. But nothing could stop the crippled veteran; he won by a majority of over 200.[2]

These days they call it 'optics'. And the optics of losing Wakkerstroom by such a significant margin were bad. On Monday 7 April, two days after the result had been declared, Prime Minister Smuts blindsided Parliament by announcing a snap general election. Smuts explained to Parliament that the by-election loss had 'a very special significance … After Wakkerstroom the government is doubt-ful whether it still enjoys the confidence of the country.'[3]

As Pirow tells it, 'The South African Party was dumbfounded. Neither the caucus nor the cabinet had been consulted. The opposition cheered wildly; only General Hertzog remained calm. He had foreseen all of this.'[4] While Pirow was by no means an objective psychoanalyst, his evaluation of the two Boer generals' vastly different skills and personalities warrants further examination.

Like chalk and cheese

James Barry Munnik Hertzog was born near the Boland *dorp* of Wellington in 1866, the eighth of twelve children. His father, Albertus Hertzog, tried his hand at farming in Malmesbury before seeking his fortune on the diamond fields and finally establishing a successful butchery in the Free State town of Jagersfontein that would enable his son to pursue a university education.

Jan Christian Smuts came into the world four years after Hertzog, in the Swartland town of Riebeek West. A sickly kid who was fascinated by nature, he was considered by his father 'a queer boy without much intelligence' and he was only sent to school at the age of twelve because his elder, more promising brother had died of typhoid. But from the moment he set foot in a classroom, Smuts's incredible thirst for knowledge (not to mention his photographic memory and unflinching work ethic) would set him apart from his peers.[5]

What's in a name?

Curiously, the father of Afrikaner nationalism was named after a very British 'woman doctor' who lived at the Cape for ten years from 1816. The controversial Dr James Barry performed one of the first recorded Caesarean sections where both mother and child survived. And the least the patient, Mrs Munnik, could do was to name her son after the doctor who had saved her and her child's life. Almost half a century later, James Barry Munnik (the boy who survived the Caesarean) was chosen as Hertzog's godfather, and all three names were passed on to the future prime minister. In retrospect, it's kind of odd that the anti-British Hertzog bore the names of an English person who, by various accounts, literally got into bed with British governor Lord Charles Somerset. (You can read all about Dr Barry's exploits in our book *Rogues' Gallery*.)

Both Smuts and Hertzog had toyed with becoming *predikante* in their youth, and both ended up studying at Victoria College (the precursor to Stellenbosch University) at the same time, where they met their respective wives. But while Hertzog was 'a hard working conscientious student whose results were adequate if not distinguished',[6] Smuts's academic achievements were never short of excep-

'Adequate if not distinguished': J.B.M. (centre) with some of his Amsterdam law buddies

tional. On graduating from Victoria College, he was awarded a scholarship to Cambridge, where he studied law. Lord Todd, a former master of Christ's College, considered Smuts to be one of the three finest minds ever produced by the college. The other two? Charles Darwin and John Milton.

Hertzog studied law in Amsterdam, a choice that 'brought him into closer contact with his own Afrikaans-speaking people'.[7] Terry Eksteen notes that his time there 'probably laid the foundations of his own lengthy political reasoning which so exasperated friend and foe alike'.[8]

After qualifying as lawyers, both men ended up in politics: Hertzog in the Free State and Smuts as Kruger's right-hand man in the ZAR. D.W. Krüger makes an insightful observation about their contrasting *modi operandi*:

Like Smuts, Hertzog loved the law, but whereas Smuts was quick of mind and wit, [Hertzog] was laboriously painstaking. He liked to make fine distinctions which often had little practical application. Mentally he was not as agile as Smuts, but he was passionately and painfully logical.[9]

Both men excelled on the battlefield during the Anglo-Boer War. Smuts's incursion into the Cape Colony in 1901 has gone down in history as one of the most heroic episodes of a war in which tales of heroism were plentiful. And Hertzog was one of the *bittereinders* who advocated fighting the *rooinekke* to the last man. Only when the commandos were in rags and animal skins did he eventually come to his senses. In fact, he and Smuts were pivotal in hammering out the precise legal terms of the Treaty of Vereeniging in 1902. While this was by no means the last time the two Boer lawyers would work together, their contrasting views on Afrikaner nationalism meant they were more comfortable being ideological foes.

Smuts believed that South Africa could only prosper as part of an international commonwealth of nations. While remaining a proud and devout Afrikaner at home and in church, he felt that English was a more appropriate language in which to conduct politics and business. Hertzog, by contrast, believed that South Africa should become an independent republic where Boers and English-speakers would be treated equally. This meant that pupils should have the right to learn in Afrikaans and all government officials should be bilingual – a tall order when you consider that *die taal* was still in *kleuterskool* and many English-speakers could barely manage a *goeiemôre*.

When it came to the 1924 election, perhaps more important than the two politicians' opposing ideologies was the fact that, according to many critics, the concerns of South Africa were 'too small' for the internationalist Smuts. As Pirow put it, 'The country did not want to hear what Smuts thought of the French Ruhr occupation. It wanted to be told what the Government was going to do about the people's bread and butter. In fact, they did not merely want promises; they wanted action, and prompt action at that.'[10]

The little *taal* that could

While Afrikaans has been spoken on farms and in homes across South Africa for centuries, its emergence as a bona fide written language is a relatively recent phenomenon.

1875–99: On 14 August 1875, the Genootskap van Regte Afrikaners was formed in Paarl. The following year a newspaper, *Die Afrikaanse Patriot*, was produced, with Afrikaans grammars, dictionaries and religious materials following. The first *taalbeweging* (language movement) failed, largely because in the 1870s and '80s Afrikaans was still regarded as a *kombuistaal* (kitchen language) lacking literature and a culture of its own.

1902–25: This perception changed after the conclusion of the Anglo-Boer War, when the journalist Gustav Preller and poets including Eugène Marais (ironic,

The editorial board of *Ons Moedertaal* in 1914 – a magazine
that aimed to teach Afrikaners to read and write in
their own language and later merged with *Huisgenoot*

considering he spoke English at home), Jan F.E. Celliers and Totius demonstrated
the creative potential of Afrikaans. But at the same time, a significant group of
Cape Afrikaners led by 'Onze Jan' Hofmeyr argued that Dutch should be retained
as the language of the Afrikaner people.

1919–36: In 1919 the NG Kerk officially sanctioned the use of Afrikaans during
services, and in 1925, immediately after Hertzog came to power, Afrikaans was
officially recognised as a language in its own right (which meant that it could
finally be taught in schools). After a decade-long process, the first Afrikaans Bible
was published in 1933. The 1936 census showed that 56 per cent of whites spoke
Afrikaans at home; in the 7–21 age group, this figure jumped to 64.6 per cent.
The writing was very much on the wall.

Back to the future

Before we unpack the mud-slinging details of the campaign, we should look at
how things had changed since union.

Once the Boer rebellion had been crushed, South African troops under Botha and Smuts played an important role in delivering an Allied victory in German South-West Africa in World War I. When Botha died in 1919, a year after the conclusion of the war, Smuts was a shoo-in for prime minister. As Krüger notes, Botha's death 'cleared the way for a man of sterner mould and stronger character. It remained to be seen whether he would be able to deal with the new political and economic situation which had been developing during and since the war.'[11]

Spoiler alert: Smuts flunked it.

A general election in 1920 saw Smuts – who had excelled during WWI, first on the battlefield and then on Britain's Imperial War Cabinet – only just cling to power thanks to the support of the pro-British Unionists. But there was already an inkling that while the rest of the world couldn't get enough of the brilliant Boer general, many of his Afrikaner people felt betrayed by him. Hertzog's National Party, which had won an impressive twenty-seven (mostly rural) seats in its very first election in 1915, snapped up a further sixteen in its second. And they would not stop there – the Nats were on the rise!

Smuts should have seen it coming. His big mistake was to regard the quashing of the Boer rebellion as an end to the problem of Afrikaner nationalism, when really it was only the beginning. While he was away fighting on the side of the British, Afrikaner nationalists including Hertzog, Tielman Roos and D.F. Malan stayed home to fight a cultural war, railing against British influence on South Africa and working tirelessly to cement the status of Afrikaans as an official and literary language. As Krüger writes,

If Smuts was aware of the importance of the Afrikaans movement and its possible bearing on politics, he gave no sign of it. For Afrikanerdom its future as a people was at stake, but Smuts remained aloof, preoccupied by other thoughts and grand conceptions which left his audiences of farmers and small middlemen completely cold. He was out of touch with the national aspirations of his own people and it was to cost him dear.[12]

Malan and Hertzog: No guns, but still soldiers

Colonel Creswell contemplates
the 'native problem'

But, in the 1920s at least, Afrikaner nationalists simply didn't have the numbers required to win a general election. The extra push they needed would come from an unusual source: Colonel Creswell's South African Labour Party. After the 1920 election, these white brothers from different mothers tentatively began to collaborate on parliamentary issues.

While the Labour Party did in some ways draw inspiration from the working-class Bolsheviks who had overthrown the Russian government in 1917, you'll remember that they had the most racist manifesto in the 1910 election. As the slogan of the Communist Party of South Africa (closely linked to the Labour Party until 1923) proclaimed:

WORKERS OF THE WORLD FIGHT
AND UNITE FOR A WHITE SOUTH AFRICA

The Labour Party drew almost all its support from urban areas in the Transvaal, which, in 1920, produced 49.7 per cent of the world's gold and directly employed over 200 000 people.[13] On the mines a colour bar existed whereby only whites could do skilled jobs. As Krüger puts it, 'Natives were untrained and were expected to do only the simplest [i.e. most physically demanding] jobs ... They were able to exist on a very low scale.'[14]

The Labour Party was born out of the trade unions formed by British workers in the 1900s as protection against the dual spectre of profit-hungry Randlords hellbent on keeping them down and the 'pesky' 'native' labourers beneath them who had the audacity to suggest that blacks could do more than wield pickaxes and push wheelbarrows. By 1912 these trade unions had extracted from the government three promises that they would hold very dear:

1. That Africans could never earn as much as whites.
2. That whites should have a monopoly on skilled work.
3. That there must be a fixed ratio of skilled (white) to unskilled (black) labour.

For the mining magnates, the industrial colour bar was all very well while the price of gold was sky high, but after the gold-price bubble created during WWI burst, the Chamber of Mines appointed a commission to investigate how all mines might remain profitable. Against this backdrop, Labour gave a very impressive showing in the 1920 election: their seventeen-seat jump since 1915 saw them outdo even the Nationalists.

Hamstrung by the near parliamentary impasse that resulted from the 1920 election, Smuts made official the SAP alliance with the mine-owning Unionists and formally merged the two parties. In the 1921 snap election, he established what appeared to be a vice-like grip on the country, which would surely last until the next election in 1926 – and possibly beyond.

While the National Party maintained its support levels, a disappointing showing by Labour saw them lose ten seats in only a year. Richard Steyn attributes this to the fact that 'the threat of creeping "Bolshevism" with its associated brutalities had become much more apparent, and frightening'.[15] Creswell couldn't have dreamt he'd be holding the trump cards at the next election.

The Rand is revolting

Everything changed in late 1921 when the commission set up by the Chamber of Mines advocated removing the colour bar. The proposal was underpinned by simple economics: since WWI, white wages (which were much higher in the first place) had risen 60 per cent, compared with 9 per cent for blacks.[16] But the changes would mean that 2 000 white men would lose their jobs to blacks who were, as Krüger offensively puts it, 'sniffing round the perimeter of the stockade like a wild animal from the primeval forest'.[17]

All hell broke loose in the first days of January 1922, while negotiations between the Chamber of Mines and the unions about a proposed wage cut for white coal miners were still ongoing. After 800 white coal miners got fed up with talking and downed tools, the gold miners joined them in solidarity. Soon, 22 000 whites were on strike.

Smuts's government attempted to mediate, but the miners rejected the Chamber's offer of a revised employment ratio of 1 European to 10.5 blacks, demanding 'a ratio of 1 to 3.5 in conformity with the general population ratio' and across all industries.[18] The miners now added Smuts to their list of *personae non gratae*, having become convinced, as Krüger puts it, 'that Smuts was hand in glove with capitalism, represented by a Nationalist cartoon as Hoggenheimer, a big flashingly dressed man with a Jewish cast of face, smoking a fat cigar'.[19]

Drawing on their experiences in both the Anglo-Boer War (on both sides) and WWI, the strikers broke up into commandos organised along military lines. On 6 February, writes Jeremy Krikler, they sent a memorandum to NP and Labour politicians asking them to 'proclaim a South African Republic and immediately to form a government for this country'.[20]

The name of their proposed republic – SAR – was clearly chosen to tempt Tielman Roos, the Transvaal leader of Hertzog's NP, who had long dreamt of reasserting Afrikaner independence. But, according to Roos's biographer, he quickly realised that the workers 'desired a republic differing radically from that which he envisaged'.[21]

Roos made it clear to the strikers that the Nationalists would only support peaceful, constitutional progress towards a republic. Even in the Central Strikers' Committee there was disagreement on how to proceed. But the Council of Action, a fringe grouping led by Percy Fisher and Harry Spendiff (it has long been claimed that they were members of the Communist Party, but historian Tom Lodge has found no evidence of this), cut through the din. At a meeting on 7 February, Fisher said: '[T]he first man to return to work should be smashed until not a breath was left in his body.'[22] The following day Fisher, Spendiff and a few others were arrested on charges of inciting public violence.

Smuts tried to stay out of the dispute for as long as possible.[23] But as the strike wore on and the cost to the economy multiplied, the government eventually announced, on 11 February, that it would provide protection for men attempting to return to work. The strikers were incensed.

The first wave of violence was directed at white strike-breakers (scabs). In Krugersdorp, a taxi carrying a woman

The Fordsburg Women's Strike Commando

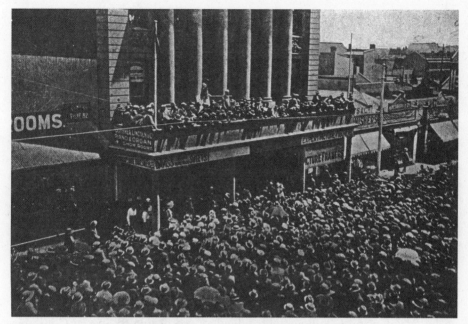

The general strike was declared at a mass meeting
outside the Trades Hall in Rissik Street on 6 March

to the mines to visit her scab husband 'was immediately surrounded by an
infuriated mob [and the driver] was violently assaulted and thrashed with sjam-
boks by a mixed gathering of women strikers'. At City Deep mine near central
Johannesburg, a women's commando came upon a man leaving work and
'knocked him down and beat and kicked him unmercifully'. But all this had
nothing on Benoni, where women attacked scabs 'with bicycle chains connected
to pickhandles, leaving them looking like a red pulp'.[24]

No sooner had Fisher and his cronies been released from custody on 22 February than they began to 'preach violent action', explaining to crowds of strikers
that 'all great political and social changes had only been achieved through militant
action'.[25]

The following day three strikers were shot and killed by police. Their
funeral attracted a procession that stretched for three kilometres. At this point
the majority of moderate strikers requested a meeting with the Chamber of
Mines. But the Chamber, clearly feeling that it had broken the will of the strikers, was having none of it. The Council of Action then announced a general
strike.

On 7 March railway employees were forcibly prevented from going to work. The next day a railway line near Driefontein was sabotaged and a train was shot at. This was also the first day in which violence was directed towards black workers.[26] On 9 March, after writing his last will and testament, Percy Fisher gave orders for the strikers to 'take' the Reef and the West Rand. The Rand Revolt had begun.

Beware the Ides of March[27]

Friday 10 March (aka Black Friday)

4.45 a.m. Striker commandos attack the Newlands Police Station, lobbing home-made bombs into the precinct and peppering the building with gunfire. One of the bombs kills four horses. The police surrender by 8 a.m.

6.30 a.m. Brakpan Strike Commando attacks a small armed garrison at the offices of the Brakpan mine, killing eight 'defenders'. According to Special Constable Joseph Stephens's testimony in court,

> There was a general slaughter ... A wounded man pathetically waved a handkerchief and begged for water, but one of the attackers turned round and said 'You bastard, it is too late to talk about water now. Take this', and got a bullet through his head ...[28]

7 a.m. The South African Air Force (SAAF) suffers its first-ever casualty when aerial observer Major W.W. Carey-Thomas, the sole passenger in a DH.9A aircraft, is shot by one of the Brakpan strikers.

9 a.m. Martial law is declared, and additional Active Citizen Force units and twenty-six burgher commandos are called up. Police arrest several delegates of the Council of Action, but Fisher and Spendiff evade capture. Meanwhile, a Benoni camp holding police reinforcements is 'raked with gunfire'.[29] The attack lasts an hour, until it is cut short by the arrival of an SAAF plane that sprays the attackers with machine-gun fire.

2 p.m. A train carrying 200 troops from the Transvaal Scottish regiment is forced to stop at the Dunswart Crossing as the line has been sabotaged. The Benoni strikers' commando launches an attack on the soldiers, killing twelve and wounding thirty.

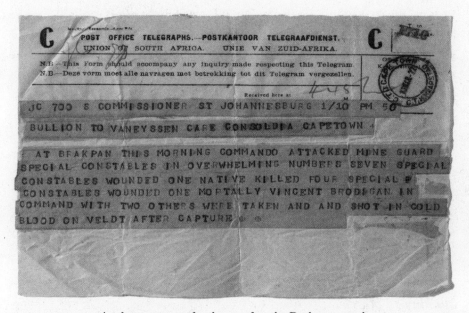

A telegram sent a few hours after the Brakpan attack

6 p.m. Police at the Fordsburg Charge Office, who have been under assault all day, eventually run out of ammunition and are forced to flee to the nearby barracks. A shopkeeper who helps to conceal the fleeing policemen is captured by the strikers and shot dead.

Saturday 11 March

10 a.m. Benoni becomes one of the first places in the world to be subjected to aerial bombing. The SAAF drops four bombs, accidentally hitting a café and the courthouse. Over the course of the revolt, SAAF bombs claim a dozen civilian lives.

1.30 p.m. One hundred and fifty soldiers of the Imperial Light Horse who have gathered on a field (which will become Ellis Park rugby ground in 1928) come under attack from commandos hidden in bushes at the edge of the field. Eight men are killed and fifteen wounded.[30]

3 p.m. The Langlaagte Police Station is attacked by a small group of strikers who arrive on motorbikes with sidecars. Within minutes one constable has been killed and the police lift a white towel in surrender. The strikers capture twenty policemen and, more importantly, fifty firearms and a veritable bounty of ammo.

10 p.m. Fresh off the train from Cape Town, Smuts heads straight for the action in a car chauffeured by 'a brilliant racing driver', accompanied by SAP secretary Louis Esselen (nephew of Ewald).[31] Smuts's son Jannie picks up the tale:

> Hodgson drove furiously. They had rifles with them in the car. Louis Esselen returned the fire for all he was worth. In his excitement he said to my father, 'Shoot, Oom Jannie, shoot!' But my father just sat impassively. Later on, a striker's bullet punctured the back tyre and ... they pulled up to change the wheel. Then my father said to Esselen: 'You have kept on telling me to shoot, now how many bullets have you left?' Oom Louis replied that he had used his up. 'A fine fix we might now be in,' my father retorted, 'if I had also used up all my ammunition.'[32]

Tuesday 14 March

6.30 a.m. A plane drops pamphlets over Fordsburg, calling upon 'all women, children, law-abiding citizens and natives' to evacuate the area.[33]

11 a.m. Just in time for mid-morning tea, the shelling commences. Over the next hour 140 shrapnel shells rain down on Fordsburg, while ground troops close in on the area from all sides. A Whippet tank is deployed, but it breaks down in the Fordsburg subway and one of the men onboard is killed. According to the *Cape Times*, 'practically the whole of Johannesburg was watching this terrible drama in clear, beautiful sunshine. On the tops of buildings, houses, water tanks – everywhere – there were crowds of spectators.'[34]

12.30 p.m. The Durban Light Infantry and Transvaal Scottish regiment come under heavy fire in Main Road (today's Albertina Sisulu Road), losing two men. They conceal their Vickers machine gun behind the frosted windows of a bottle store and open fire on passing strikers at point-blank range. While combing the Market Square building for stragglers, they come across the bodies of Fisher and Spendiff. A bloodstained note reveals that they have committed suicide: 'I died for what I believed to be right, the cause.'[35]

At midnight on 17 March, the strike committee officially called off the strike. At least 214 people had died, including forty-three members of the army, twenty-nine policemen and eighty-one civilians.[36] But there was still hope among the strikers that the mine owners would now take their demands seriously. They were wrong.

The bosses chose to make an example out of the men. More than 850 strikers were criminally charged, including forty-six with murder. In the end sixteen were sentenced to death, but following a public outcry only the first four were hanged. Before the dust had even settled, strikers anxiously reported for work, hoping to find that their jobs had been held open for them. Many were turned away because of their activities during the revolt.

Most damaging was the long-term impact. 'After the strike,' write J.P. Brits and Burridge Spies, 'the wages of semi-skilled white workers were decreased and mine owners were free to allocate underground work as they saw fit. This meant that semi-skilled whites were replaced at an accelerated pace by cheaper black labourers.'[37] The whole episode would also prove disastrous for Smuts. Three months after the revolt, Hertzog and Creswell had their first meeting about a possible political coalition.

When in doubt, drop some bombs

For someone so committed to the rule of law, Smuts was rather keen on blowing poorer and/or darker people to pieces. The Rand Revolt marked the third time in less than a year that he had opted for a military solution to a political problem.

Exhibit A: The Bulhoek massacre

On the morning of 24 May 1921, over 600 white policeman and soldiers opened fire on prophet Enoch Mgijima and some 3 000 of his followers (known as Israelites) who had been awaiting the end of the world at Ntabelanga near Queenstown in the Eastern Cape. The Israelites were accused of illegally occupying government land and not paying taxes.

The massacre was the culmination of two years of negotiation between Mgijima and the authorities. Smuts's failure to view 'natives' as equals, or to entertain their claims to the land as legitimate, dogged every step of the process. (At the Rhodes Memorial Lectures at Oxford in 1929, Smuts would declare that '[t]he negro and negroid Bantu form a distinct human type. It has largely remained a child type, with a child psychology and outlook.'[38])

Enoch Mgijima: Religious
zealot or political activist?

The police and the Israelites had almost
come to blows in December 1920, and the
Israelites had demanded that Smuts come to
Ntabelanga to discuss the issue in person.
A month later, the prime minister had spoken
to white voters at nearby Tarkastad but,
concerned about being seen to negotiate
with 'fanatics', he had stayed away from
Ntabelanga.

General consensus among whites and
some blacks, including Tengo Jabavu, was that
the Israelites' intransigence made what was to
come essentially unavoidable. Tembeka
Ngcukaitobi disagrees: 'This was not an
inevitable tragedy. If Smuts had talked to
them, it could all have turned out differently.'[39]

During last-ditch negotiations on the
morning of the massacre, police commander
Colonel Truter claimed that he did not want to make war. But as Robert Edgar,
who has been researching the massacre since the 1970s, points out, his arsenal of
modern weapons told a different story:

> The outcome of the battle was a foregone conclusion. The police arrived with
> rifles, machine guns, and cannon, while the Israelites carried only
> knobkerries, swords and spears. After a twenty-minute skirmish nearly two
> hundred Israelites lay dead and many more were wounded.[40]

Most white South Africans saw the massacre as unfortunate but necessary. As
one *Cape Times* reader put it, 'If you taught these people that those miracles of
the Bible had really happened in the past, what was to prevent their believing
that they were to happen again?'

Abantu-Batho, the mouthpiece of the South African Native National Congress
(SANNC, later renamed the ANC), asked whether the government would have
'treated a white religious group in the same callous fashion'. As *Abantu-Batho*
saw it, the government was just as fanatical as the Israelites. How and why, it
asked, 'did the Israelite defiance of the government escalate from being a simple
case of trespassing to become a major threat to the state?'[41]

Exhibit B: The Bondelswarts Rebellion

The Bondelswarts Rebellion took place in the arid scrubland surrounding the Fish River Canyon in mid-1922. After WWI, South Africa had been granted a League of Nations mandate over the former German colony of South-West Africa, and Smuts hoped that it would be the first step towards its eventual incorporation into South Africa. But no sooner had the mandate been granted than the new administrator, Gysbert Reitz Hofmeyr, decided to drastically increase the dog tax in the territory.

Under German rule, writes Gavin Lewis, a tax of thirty marks for the first dog and ten marks per additional dog had been levied, but this only applied to urban areas. (Whites were allowed one tax-free dog to serve as a watchdog.) After touring the country and being shocked by the 'vast numbers of dogs' used by blacks to 'hunt game instead of earning a living by ... honest labour' (i.e. working on farms owned by whites), Hofmeyr imposed a sixfold increase to the dog tax that would now apply to both rural and urban areas.[42]

The Bondelswarts (a subset of the Nama people) were 'unusual in their sporting instincts and love of hunting'[43] and did not take kindly to the new law, nor to the new administration's even stricter implementation of an existing ban on them owning firearms. Their barter economy also meant that coming up with cash was tricky. Mindful of the fact that the Bondelswarts had caused the Germans no end of trouble with their first rebellion (1904–6), Hofmeyr took their objections seriously, even going so far as to suggest that the Bondelswarts might inspire a 'general rising' that would spread across SWA.[44]

Morenga, chief of the Bondelswarts,
and officers during the first Bondelswarts rebellion in 1905

When Abraham Morris, one of the heroes of the first Bondelswarts rebellion, took it upon himself to return to his people from involuntary exile in South Africa (with a rifle, *nogal*), Hofmeyr was not amused. While there were some attempts at negotiation, it didn't take him long to turn to a military solution. At first he hoped to be able to quell the uprising without South African aid, but realising how scant his reserves were, he 'reluctantly' telegrammed Pretoria. On 26 May 1922, two aeroplanes, two mountain guns and four Vickers machine guns were delivered.

The Bondelswarts had four times as many men as they had rifles, not to mention a severe shortage of ammunition. Their only hope lay in capturing arms from vanquished government soldiers. Unfortunately, things didn't go as they had hoped, and the larger and far-better-armed government forces soon brought them to heel. The moral low point of the campaign was the early morning aerial bombing of a Bondelswarts settlement that had been abandoned overnight by all men of fighting age, as Hofmeyr was well aware. One woman and two children were killed in this episode and a further twelve were wounded.

Over the course of the rebellion, 110 Bondelswarts men were killed, 53 were wounded and all of their livestock was confiscated. After the conflict, those Bondelswarts who had not participated in the rebellion were given back half their livestock. Smuts believed that 'to restore all their captured property would only serve to make them think they can go into rebellion'.[45]

The impact on the Bondelswarts was catastrophic. But the rebellion would also have a long-lasting impact on the reputation of the South African government, which had abused the 'sacred trust' placed in it by the League of Nations to protect indigenous interests in SWA. The legacy of the rebellion went a long way to ensuring that SWA was never incorporated into South Africa.

'The Prime Minister's footsteps drip with blood!'

When Smuts proposed a motion that all government forces be granted indemnity for their actions during the Rand Revolt (while at the same time arguing that the strikers must feel the full might of the law), Hertzog sniffed blood – literally. As Smuts's son writes,

He paraded my father's long sequence of bloody events from the 1913 strike to the present one, ending on a high shrieking note: 'The Prime Minister's footsteps drip with blood! His footsteps go down in history in that manner!'[46]

In ten years, Hertzog pointed out, Smuts had declared martial law three times, and on each occasion he had sought to indemnify the government. But Hertzog could not be too outspoken in his criticism of the Bulhoek and Bondelswarts affairs, notes W.K. Hancock: 'It must have irked [the Nats] not to take up this new stick for beating Smuts with, but they could hardly run the risk of branding themselves in the platteland constituencies as the champions of the Hottentots.' Luckily, 'they had friends in the Labour Party ready and eager to flail Smuts',[47] as this memorable exchange between an unnamed Labour MP and the prime minister attests:

> SMUTS: Tonight the whole fire seems to have been concentrated on me. It leaves me cold.
> A LABOUR MEMBER: Murder always does.
> SMUTS: Then take Bulhoek. I am posted in Moscow as the Butcher of Bulhoek. That is my reputation in Russia.
> A LABOUR MEMBER: Yes, and not only in Russia.[48]

The final straw came in November, when Smuts insisted that the first four strikers of the Rand Revolt who'd been sentenced to death should indeed be executed. Creswell and Hertzog, who had deliberately stayed out of the revolt, seized the opportunity to team up against Smuts. The 'ticklish obstacles' posed by 'the Republican objective of the Nationalists and the Socialist ideal of the Labourites'[49] were glossed over with an agreement known as 'the Pact', whereby Labour and the NP agreed to avoid 'three-cornered contests'[50] by only putting up their strongest candidate in each constituency and thus making it doubly difficult for the SAP to claim every seat.

As so often happens in politics, the Pact also saw each party cede a fairly hefty swathe of ideological ground. As Pirow tells it,

> neither side fully understood what the other was reserving, but they were too busy worrying about hating Smuts to worry about such trifles ... For example, Colonel Creswell once addressed a meeting on the Platteland on Socialism and Trades Unionism. He spoke in English and less than half the audience could follow him. But with the perfect courtesy which is the heritage of the Boers they looked as appreciative and friendly as possible. At the conclusion of the speech Mr Louis Karofsky, a Labour extremist but a great personal

friend of Tielman Roos, rose to give a short summary of what had been said. He stated as follows: 'The leader of the Labour Party has just explained that his policy is to put the n****r in his place and repatriate all Asiatics.' There was wild cheering and Colonel Creswell ... was carried shoulder high to his car.[51]

Aware that he was up against it, Smuts attempted to increase his voter base by bringing Southern Rhodesia (which was still controlled by the BSAC) into the Union, generously offering to pay the Company almost £7 million for the privilege. But in a referendum held on 22 October 1922, the voters, who were mostly white and numbered a mere 14 000, opted for responsible government (i.e. a pathway to eventual independence) by a margin of 59.4 per cent to 40.6 per cent.[52] Ironically, the only community that voted in the majority for union was Rhodesia's Afrikaners – everyone else had been scared off by Hertzog's electoral gains down South, and in particular Afrikaner nationalists' agitation for a republic. As Walker notes, 'many Rhodesians feared centralised Pretoria rule and the republicanism and bilingualism of the Union. They prided themselves on being a British community in spite of the Jews, Greeks and Moslems in the towns and the Afrikaners, perhaps one-eighth of the total European population, who lived in groups in the countryside.'[53]

Southern Rhodesian women, who had gained the vote in 1919, eleven years earlier than South Africa, were especially vehement in their rejection of union. As Donal Lowry writes:

In 1923, in a speech to the South African House of Assembly in support of a bill to grant white women the vote, Smuts argued that women were more politically cautious than men, as had been demonstrated in the referendum of 1922 in which their vote had been 'the decisive factor'. An estimated 75% of Rhodesian women voted for responsible government, including some whose husbands had voted for Union.[54]

The 1923 Native Urban Areas Act, which was passed by Smuts's government based on the recommendations of SAP stalwart Colonel Charles Stallard (a man who later decried Hertzog for being 'too liberal'[55]), deemed all urban areas in the country to be 'white' and required all blacks in cities and towns to carry 'passes'. Urban blacks could only live in racially segregated areas.

In Stallard's view, it was especially important to impose passes on 'skilled and educated natives' because to do otherwise would be 'to expose the white population to the most deadly competition which the black race is capable of offering, and to ensure the ultimate subordination of the most hopeless portion of the white race to the most competent portion of the black race.'[56]

Later that year, the Imperial Conference enabled Smuts once again to bask in the adulation of an international audience. But when he returned to South Africa, he was brought swiftly down to earth by the disastrous by-election at Wakkerstroom.

'Die Volk Moet Kies'

Using the slogan 'Die Volk Moet Kies', Smuts and the SAP painted the 1924 election as a choice between the relative calm of a Smuts-led administration and the chaos that would surely result from being led by a two-headed ~~monster~~ government of racists and communists. Hertzog and Creswell were, of course, quick to point out that far from being calm or orderly, the Smuts administration had unleashed the full might of the military on Benoni, Brakpan, Bulhoek and the Bondelswarts.

But even more important than this was the Pact's success in getting the white working class (both English- and Afrikaans-speaking) to vote for them. Hertzog and Creswell decried the SAP's ties to big financial institutions, depicting Smuts as a 'puppet who moved his arms and legs when Hoggenheimer pulled the strings',[57] and the Pact's slogan, 'Civilised Labour', asked voters to make a simple choice between 'the People and the Mine Magnates'. Of course, by 'People' they meant white people. As historian Thula Simpson notes, at the Nats' manifesto launch on 3 May 1924, Hertzog declared he would seek a 'solution of the native question' that would protect '"civilised labour" in the white man's territory, and develop Africans in their own areas'.[58]

Die Volk moet kies.

„Ik laat met vertrouwe die beslissing aan U."

Gepubliseer deur die Hoofkantoor van die S.A. Party.
Gedruk deur Wallachs' Beperk.

'I confidently place the issue before you' – not the most rousing of battle cries

The Puppet of the Goldbug.

PULL THE STRING AND "JANNIE" MOVES!

Opposition cartoonists reckoned
Smuts moved when the Goldbug
(aka Hoggenheimer) pulled the strings

The Pact made much of the fact that the three-year-long economic recession had left a reported 50 per cent of white school-leavers unable to find employment. And with their colour bar policy, they virtually guaranteed these people jobs. No matter that every new white job meant the loss of a black job.

For the Pact, the 1923 Native Urban Areas Act didn't go nearly far enough: they reckoned, stricter segregation and harsher discrimination were required to ensure that South Africa remained what Hertzog called a 'witmansland' (white man's country). Natives must, he said, be banned from semi-skilled or skilled work. Tielman Roos, his fiery adjutant in the Transvaal, told voters that 'the native is not an asset to the white man in this country; he is a curse'.[59]

The Labour half of the Pact urged white workers to vote against Smuts because 'it is the tradition of the people of every British Dominion to insist that their country shall be the home of an ever-increasing civilised and contented people ... South Africa shall be no exception and shall not be permitted to degenerate into a big, cheap-labour compound, in which the people will find it harder to earn a civilised livelihood'.[60]

But the real genius of the 'Civilised Labour' slogan (as opposed to 'White Labour') was that it allowed them to pick up votes from coloured people who comprised a not-to-be-scoffed-at 11.6 per cent of voters in the Cape. In a speech Hertzog gave shortly after the election, he reiterated his pitch:

Economically, industrially and politically the Cape Coloured must be accepted within our ranks. Socially it is their wish just as much as ours that they will be on their own and will seek no association with the white man.[61]

In other words, Hertzog wanted very much for coloured people to vote for him, but he would never have dreamt of inviting them round for a *tjop en dop*.

The Pact and the black vote

Against this backdrop (and especially given what was to follow), it should come as something of a surprise that the Pact bothered to try to appeal to the black vote in the Cape. But they took a shot, employing the age-old political strategy of lying through their teeth.

Deep down, both heads of the Pact saw 'natives' as 'a curse' who must be aggressively segregated and discriminated against. But they sang from a very different *loflied* when campaigning among black voters in the Cape. At a meeting of black voters in Queenstown, D.F. Malan, the Cape leader of the NP and the man who would introduce apartheid in 1948, somehow managed to keep a straight face as he declared:

> No race has shown a greater love for South Africa than the native and in that respect he is certainly an example of true patriotism. He should therefore take his place alongside the nationalist in the same area.[62]

You may remember Rhodes giving a similar performance in the lead-up to 1898...

Meanwhile, the All-African Convention (AAC), which took place in King William's Town on 15 and 16 May 1924, brought together representatives of the ANC, the Industrial and Commercial Workers' Union of Africa (ICU, the first major black trade union in southern Africa), Dr Abdurahman's APO, Rubusana's Bantu Union, the Cape Native Voters' Association, the South African Indian Congress, and several others. It was hoped that the AAC would pass a resolution instructing African voters which party to vote for. So-called 'conservatives' including D.D.T. Jabavu and Rubusana were steadfast in their backing of Smuts's SAP, but others saw his inaction on the 'native question' (and his poor human rights record) as problematic. 'No policy, no vote' was their mantra. In the end the AAC declined to put its head on a block and urged voters to choose on a candidate-by-candidate basis.

The ANC's annual conference, which was held in Bloemfontein a couple of weeks later, reached an even more damaging conclusion. A motion was put forward by Clements Kadalie, the flamboyant Malawian-born leader of the ICU, stating that 'a change of government was necessary and would be in the best interests of South Africa'. In his autobiography Kadalie notes:

> In speaking to the motion, I reminded the conference about the sins of the government in power. I mentioned forcibly the shootings at Port Elizabeth in 1920, the Bulhoek massacre, the calling of troops to the Cape Town dock strike in 1919, and many other acts too numerous to mention here. When the vote was taken and declared by the 'Speaker', the [motion] was carried by a large majority.[63]

In simple terms, the ANC was prepared to back Hertzog.

While he was in Bloemfontein, Kadalie took the time to meet Hertzog at his office in Maitland Street. 'The General was interested to see me,' Kadalie recalls. 'He was also quick to appreciate the resolution adopted by the ANC conference.' So appreciative, in fact, that he offered to print thousands of copies of the resolution on the 'Nationalist printing press' gratis. To further underline the depths of his 'appreciation', the wily general offered to foot the bill for the printing and distribution of 10 000 copies of the general election issue of the ICU's mouthpiece, the *Workers' Herald*. (Hertzog's free print job ultimately did not reach the majority of black voters – the ANC didn't have many members back then, and Kadalie's support base was concentrated in Cape Town, where there were few black voters.)

Less than a week before the election, *Umteteli wa Bantu*, which was funded by the Smuts-friendly Chamber of Mines, published a passionate leading article titled 'Dolts in Council', which concluded:

> If the Native voters permitted themselves to be influenced by the drivel broadcast by Congress they would deserve all that the Pact promises them; and to those who may be disposed to follow the doltish advice to 'vote solidly for a change of Government' we would repeat Dr. Rubusana's warning that the Native who casts his vote for a Pact candidate may never have another vote to cast.[64]

The day after the election, the same paper argued that '[t]he ICU and the African National Congress might safely be scrapped because there is no evidence that they serve any useful purpose.'[65]

'Which way the cat jumps'

Despite Smuts's problems, in the weeks leading up to the election the English press still appeared fairly sure he would win. Five days before voting day, *The Times*'s Cape correspondent wrote that 'unless there is an extraordinarily deep and pervasive feeling of hostility to General Smuts and his colleagues ... a Smuts victory is certain ... he must win by five and his probable majority is from 10 to 15'.[66] Just one day later, the same correspondent dialled it back: 'the result in many of the Rand constituencies is on a hair balance and a breath at the last minute may turn the majority. There has been much less rowdyism at the final South African Party meetings.'[67] But he stuck with his prediction of an SAP victory. His Johannesburg counterpart, on the other hand, declined to stick his neck out. Reminding readers of the Rand Revolt, he wrote:

> Undoubtedly the Rand workers are solid for the Pact. The feeling among miners and others against General Smuts and the Government is increasingly bitter. They are still smarting from their defeat in 1922 and thirsting for revenge ... It is significant that the mining engine-drivers have not carried out their intention, declared weeks ago, to apply for a Conciliation Board to settle the wages dispute. Evidently they and other mine workers are waiting to see which way the cat jumps tomorrow.[68]

Smuts, who was clearly exhausted, was not nearly as confident as he had been when calling the election. In a telegram to friends in England, he wrote:

> I have once more gone and done it and another General Election is pending. The trouble with us is that the business lasts 2 months instead of a week as with you. And by the time that end is reached everybody is half or quite dead. I hope I shall survive in more than one sense. But you will know that a little spell of political rest will not be unwelcome to me. The indications are that I shall get it.[69]

As it turned out, the result was not even close. Despite the fact that more people voted for Smuts than for Hertzog and Creswell combined, the Pact won a twenty-seven-seat majority over the SAP, and Smuts lost his seat in Pretoria West to a Labour candidate. The NP mopped up in the platteland, while Labour put in a strong showing on the Rand. The SAP 'won more than half its seats in the Cape

Province, which had an abnormally high proportion of voters per constituency,' writes Hancock. 'Moreover, most of its victories in all four provinces were in urban constituencies which were similarly "loaded" in comparison with country constituencies.'[70] The 30 per cent wiggle room on constituency size, which Smuts had devised in the lead-up to union, had come back to bite him where it hurt most.

For all its superficiality, Hertzog's ploy to nab the coloured vote seems to have worked. The 1924 election results saw 'a strong swing to the NP in several Cape constituencies where there were concentrations of coloured voters.'[71] The Pact's attempts to corner the black vote don't seem to have been nearly as successful, however. Sylvia Neame notes that 'it is more or less certain that the overwhelming majority of African voters in the eastern Cape [which accounted for around 70 per cent of the Cape's 14 000 African voters] voted for the SAP'.[72] As the Cape Town–based trade unionist I.B. Nyombolo noted in a letter to the *Cape Times*, 'While the native is not easily bluffed, the coloured man seems to be the victim of the propaganda of the Pact.'[73]

Which all added up to a bloody nose for the SAP.

Party	Votes	%	Seats	+/−
South African Party (Smuts)	148 769	47.04	53	−24
National Party (Hertzog)	111 483	35.25	63	+19
Labour Party (Creswell)	45 380	14.35	18	+8
Independents	10 610	3.36	1	0
Total	316 242	100.00	135	

'Not a single white person should be allowed to go under'

There were many reasons for Hertzog's victory: the economic recession, the Rand Revolt, the coloured vote and Smuts's apparent inability to read the electorate. But these all paled in comparison to the rise in Afrikaner nationalism, which had carried the Pact to victory. As Brits and Spies write, the SAP's defeat can

be seen as the culmination of a process which started as early as 1912 ... From the time of Hertzog's exclusion from the Botha cabinet in 1912, the SAP began to lose Afrikaans-speaking followers. Gradually the NP grew stronger, gaining more Afrikaner support in each election. In 1920 the SAP absorbed the Unionist Party, which meant that the English-speaking group was no longer as divided as before, but the price Smuts paid was a further loss of Afrikaner support, particularly in the rural areas.[74]

The Pact may have had to rely on a scurrilous marriage of convenience to get there, but for the first time in the Union of South Africa's history, the Nationalists controlled the government. One need look no further than a speech given to Parliament on 12 August 1924 by newly elected Nationalist MP Dr A.J. Stals to see where the party would take the country:

In this country, there is a small number of whites against the natives, a few civilised people against uncivilised hordes, and for that reason it is so important that not a single white person should be allowed to go under ... There is no greater problem than this, because the existence of the European civilisation in this country hinges on it.[75]

Life for black South Africans was about to get much tougher.

EERSTE NAT. KABINET 1924

A cabinet jam-Pact with racists, English and Afrikaans

What would Jannie do?

The 1924 loss gave Smuts the 'little spell of political rest' he had hoped for. And according to Richard Steyn, 'the years from 1924 to 1933 were some of the most fulfilling and productive of Smuts's life. Freed from the burdens of high office, he found time to read, to think and to write'. In 1926 he published *Holism and Evolution*, a philosophical tome he'd been working on for years, which sought, in Steyn's words, 'to link the physical to the metaphysical and make sense of the vast complexity of the world around us'. Smuts was more modest about his opus: 'I have simply tried to hammer out some rule of thought to carry my action along'.[76]

Albert Einstein, who considered Smuts to be one of only a dozen people who actually understood his theory of relativity, was full of praise for the book. But Roy Campbell, the poet who was as famous for the quality of his verse as for the vehemence of his pro-black sentiments, was less convinced:

> The love of Nature burning in his heart,
> Our new Saint Francis offers us his book.
> The Saint who fed the birds at Bondelswaart
> And fattened up the vultures at Bull Hoek.

Hancock argues that the poem, while 'brilliant satire', was 'a travesty of the truth', as Smuts was by no means a 'butcher'; he had tried hard to avoid both massacres, especially in the case of the Bondelswarts, where he had urged Gysbert Hofmeyr 'to use every effort towards a reasonable settlement'.[77] Perhaps, but it seems clear that as soon as what Smuts considered to be 'native insubordination' crossed a certain line, he could see only one solution. In *Farewell the Trumpets*, Jan Morris suggests that Smuts, despite being educated at Cambridge, estranged from the NG Kerk and 'detested by Afrikaner republicans', was just too much a 'Boer of the Volk' to back down in the face of black opposition:

> Fundamental to Boerness was the question of race, and behind every episode of
> Boer history ... lay the inescapable truth that the white man was outnumbered
> in South Africa by the black. The profoundest Boer intention was to maintain
> the sovereignty of the white race.[78]

CHAPTER 7

SWART GEVAAR
AND THE
CONFUSION OF FUSION
1929 and 1933

'Hertzog and Smuts had removed the war paint and buried the axe.'
– D.W. Krüger[1]

Barry and Jan: Let the bromance begin

THE TWISTING PLOTLINE OF SOUTH AFRICAN politics in the late twenties and early thirties is not dissimilar to that of a nineties romcom: after nine years of feuding, Hertzog (played by Adam Sandler) promptly hops into bed with Smuts (played by Drew Barrymore) and all the underlying cracks in their relationship are magically plastered over. The movie even has a name: *Fusion* (not to be confused with its prequel, *The Pact*).

On 28 February 1933, Hertzog announced to 'general bemusement' that he and Smuts planned to form a coalition government based on seven principles:

1. The administration was to be based on national principles in harmony with the independent status of the Union.
2. The Union of South Africa was to be symbolised by the national flag.
3. Equal language rights for Afrikaans- and English-speakers would be ensured.
4. Efforts would be made to maintain a rural population.
5. The government would continue to apply the 'white labour' policy.
6. The 'native question' would be solved in such a way as to safeguard white civilisation, while natives would not be deprived of the right to develop. The political developments of white and black people would be separate.
7. A sound national economy would be maintained.[2]

STATEMENT

by General Hertzog and General Smuts

in regard to Co-operation.

———

With a view to ensuring racial peace and co-operation, and having regard to the national emergency which has arisen as a consequence of the world depression, the two leaders of the Nationalist and South African Parties respectively have decided to co-operate in forming a Government, which will make it possible to work together on a basis of more or less equal participation and upon agreed principles, so that, while the identity of their respective parties is retained, there may be cordial co-operation between the members of the Government along agreed lines of national policy.

The signed marriage certificate

During the negotiations, provision no. 6 had threatened to derail the coalition. But when they again agreed to delay answering the native question, the Fusion train could chunter on again. As D.W. Krüger puts it, 'The incredible had happened in South African politics. Implacable enemies had been reconciled within a few weeks and what a few had feared and most had hoped, had come to pass. Hertzog and Smuts had removed the war paint and buried the axe.'[3]

The problem with Hertzog and Smuts's real-life romcom was that after the great coming together that resulted in what was called the Fusion government in 1934, they couldn't just sit back and watch the credits roll. Instead, they had to get on with the hard work of making their arranged marriage work. But let's return to a time when our two protagonists still detested each other ...

After the shock victory of the Nat–Labour pact in 1924, Prime Minister Hertzog had a lot on his plate, not least answering the native question, safeguarding white labour, advancing the cause of the Afrikaans language and Afrikaners in general, and securing the constitutional independence of the Union. Neither Smuts nor the press gave Hertzog's cabinet of newbies (which Smuts called an 'unholy alliance') much chance of holding a government together, let alone actually getting stuff done. The SAP expected that they would be fighting a new election relatively soon.

Smuts was surely kicking himself when he noted: 'Great rains in the interior, a general lifting of the depression and great platinum discoveries in the Transvaal gave them all the luck possible.'[4] Wakkerstroom, he must have realised, need not have been his Waterloo.

The Pact takes the native question by the horns

Hertzog and Creswell used their luck wisely, taking swift and definitive strides to advance their separate but overlapping causes. When it came to the native question, where, as Richard Steyn puts it, Smuts chose to 'kick the can down the road', Hertzog was determined to tackle it head-on. The nature of his solutions would leave much to be desired, however.

In 1926 Hertzog put no fewer than four separate 'Native Bills' (aka the Hertzog Bills) in front of Parliament, in which he

1. Asked to extend the voting rights of coloured people across the Union (before you get the wrong impression here, bear in mind that most coloureds lived in the Cape and that Hertzog had won much of the coloured vote in 1924).
2. Proposed removing 'Cape Natives' from the common voters' roll and

allowing them instead to vote 'through their Chiefs, Headmen and Councils' for *white* native representatives in Parliament.

3. Tabled the establishment of a toothless Native Council, which would constitute only blacks and be restricted to 'ordinances dealing with Natives only'.

4. Expressed his intention to release further land for sole ownership and occupation by natives. (It is important to remember that the Natives Land Act of 1913 – a piece of legislation originally conceived by Hertzog – assigned a mere 7 per cent of South Africa's arable land to more than 80 per cent of its population.)

As agreed before union, any law that dealt with the native franchise needed to pass by a two-thirds majority. And because the Cape franchise was tied to land-ownership, the same requirement applied to the fourth bill, which concerned land.[5] This meant that Hertzog would require significant SAP support to get his bills through Parliament. In the end, while some of the more conservative members of the SAP muttered their approval of the bills in private, the opposition voted along party lines and all four of Hertzog's bills were defeated. But Hertzog was prepared to play the long game...

'A European problem of weakness, greed and robbery'

At the ANC's national conference in 1926, Reverend Pitso from Winburg stood up and asked the congress to 'place on record "its sincere and hearty appreciation"

of Hertzog's courage in dealing with the "vexed question known as the native problem" in a practical and sympathetic manner'. Despite some mumblings of discontent, the motion was initially seconded by none other than ANC president-general Z.R. Mahabane, who thanked Hertzog for stating his intentions like 'a snake that has come out of the grass'.[6]

The mood changed when Clements Kadalie, who had backed the Pact in the run-up to the 1924 election, came out in rampant opposition to Hertzog's Native Bills. Kadalie, who felt that he had been betrayed by Hertzog, argued that while Smuts and Botha may have been guilty of extreme

Clements Kadalie:
Betrayed by Hertzog

fence-sitting, Hertzog was worse, as he made no bones about his desire to obliterate the native franchise. As Tembeka Ngcukaitobi tells it:

> The prime minister and the white people had to be told that their proposals were rejected. Kadalie wanted it placed on record that Africans would not allow white people to relegate them to a position of inferiority in the land of their birth. He declared that there was no such thing as a 'native problem' – instead, there was a European problem of weakness, greed and robbery. White people had robbed the aboriginal races of South Africa of their inheritance, and for this, Kadalie concluded, they could not be thanked or congratulated.[7]

A cartoon by J.S. Scott, a friend of the ICU and one of South Africa's first black artists, showing just how the 'natives' felt about their bills

After giving Kadalie a cacophonous ovation, the ANC unanimously voted to reject the bills. A few months later, Dr Abdurahman convened a large Non-European Conference in Kimberley. There, attendees including D.D.T. Jabavu (son of Tengo), Sol Plaatje and Walter Rubusana came out against the gradual erosion of coloured, Indian and black rights. Jabavu 'rejected the government attempt to portray South Africa as a land of different races and nations. With remarkable prescience he warned, "A nation within a nation is an impossibility."'[8]

While Hertzog's four bills were again defeated in 1927 (because of the two-thirds stipulation), he did come away from that parliamentary session with a few more whiskers in his moustache. The Immorality Act (1927), which only needed a simple majority in Parliament for it to pass, made sex between blacks and whites illegal:[*]

Any European male who has illicit carnal intercourse with a native female, and any native male who has illicit carnal intercourse with a European female, in circumstances which do not amount to rape, an attempt to commit rape, [or] indecent assault ... shall be guilty of an offence and liable on conviction to imprisonment for a period not exceeding five years.[9]

The Native Administration Act (1927), meanwhile, gave the governor-general 'wide discretionary powers over every native in the Transvaal, Natal and the Free State'.[10] (In practice these powers were given to Hertzog, as the governor-general was a largely ceremonial figurehead.) The Act effectively gave Hertzog the power to remove any native group or individual 'from any place to any other place within the country on any conditions he may determine expedient in the public interest'.[11]

Ngcukaitobi has shown how the black lawyer Richard Msimang challenged the implementation of these wide-ranging powers in the courts. One case involved the 'politically undesirable' Munjedzi Mpafuri, who had been ordered to relocate from Louis Trichardt to Barberton for refusing to 'serve as a government stooge'. In arguing that the wording of the governor-general's order was overly vague,

---

[*] The other Immorality Act, which banned all interracial sex, was passed in 1950. This was expanded in 1957 to include other sex offences.

Msimang found some judicial relief. Judge Tindall noted that the powers given to the governor-general were 'certainly drastic' and described the order as one which may be 'despotically issued'. Tindall went on to explain that 'bearing in mind the extraordinary powers granted by the Act to the governor-general, there was no need to read the order with any level of generosity to the governor-general'.[12] If the governor-general wanted to enjoy his despotic powers, the judge insisted, he would have to make sure his i's were dotted and his t's crossed. Sadly, such victories were few and far between.

At the insistence of Tielman Roos, the Act also contained what became known as the 'hostility clause', which imposed jail terms on 'any person who utters any words or does any other act or thing whatever with intent to promote any feeling of hostility between Natives and Europeans'.[13] This made it much easier for the government to clamp down on black (or white) activists, agitators and trade unionists.

While the official construction on the apartheid edifice only began in 1948, Hertzog's first government provided its foundations and some preliminary drawings for its architecture.

'An ugly flag unworthy of South Africa'

Despite their pact, the Labour–Nationalist dalliance was not always lovey-dovey. While Creswell was A-OK with Hertzog's racist policies, he was a little touchier when it came to the topic of South Africa's independence from dear old Blighty. And as it happened, the belligerent *Vrystater* Hertzog would be faced with an early test of his political marriage vows. In May 1925 it fell to J.B.M. to play the perfect host to the Prince of Wales, who Smuts had invited to South Africa just before losing the 1924 election. As Smuts would write with a mixture of schadenfreude and genuine optimism,

> Perhaps it is as well that the visit came after a change of Government in this country. Instead of the Nationalists now standing aloof and pointing to us as jingoes and snobs, they have to do the job themselves with our approval and the national unanimity of South Africa is far greater than it would otherwise have been.[14]

Smuts would get his wish. The prince's three-month tour, during which he wooed Boer commandos and avowed nationalists across the length and breadth of the platteland, was hailed in the English press as a triumph of what today would be known as 'soft power'. As Dorothea Fairbridge wrote in a letter to *The Times*,

> the Prince's visit has been a triumph of courtesy, of kindliness, of chivalry and tact. It has done more to consolidate the two white races in South Africa – who of all peoples on earth, need consolidation in the face of an over-whelming native population – than years of mere diplomacy could have achieved.[15]

But of course an avowed Unionist writing to *The Times* of London would say this! The truth is more complex. According to historian Hilary Sapire, 'Afrikaner engagement with the royal visit of 1925 was layered and ambiguous. Deference, curiosity, and admiration mingled with lingering war resentment, satire, defiance, and expressions of courtesy that often masked distaste.'[16]

Afrikaner nationalism had not simply been washed away by one royal visit. The following year it reared its head when none other than D.F. Malan, the portly, bespectacled *dominee* who was minister of the interior, introduced the Nationality and Flag Bill in Parliament. It proposed that a new national flag should replace the Union Jack as an 'outward expression and symbol of the Union's independence'.[17] Malan's proposal, writes H.C. Armstrong,

> roused all the hostility, which had begun to disappear, between the English and the Dutch. It became the topic of conversation in every village and dorp, and the burning argument in every hotel and bar and farm. It grew quickly into a quarrel, which boiled up angrily. Englishmen and Dutchmen insulted each other openly, swore they would shoot each other rather than give way.[18]

It is telling that the Flag Bill was seen at the time as a far bigger deal than the four Native Bills tabled in the same year. Smuts, the Boer War hero, took up the fight for the Union Jack. At a meeting in Bloemhof in the Transvaal, 'Hertzog's supporters raided the hall where Smuts was due to speak, broke the furniture, chased out the police, tore up the Union Jack which was on the platform, and swore that they would kill Smuts if he persisted.'[19]

Eventually a compromise was reached whereby a hodgepodge national flag comprised of 'the old orange, white and blue banner of the House of Orange, with the two Republican flags and the Union Jack imposed upon its white field'[20] (i.e. the old South African flag that still makes the odd appearance at Loftus Versfeld) would fly alongside the Union Jack. The compromise left no one happy. As Armstrong describes it, the new national flag was 'an ugly flag unworthy of South Africa'.[21] And the Nats moaned about having to put up with two Union Jacks instead of one!

Talking the *taal*

While the flag issue dominated the headlines, Hertzog's Afrikanerisation of the civil service was probably more important. In 1925, after a commission had found that Afrikaans had developed sufficiently to be considered a language, a law was passed stating that wherever the word 'Dutch' appeared in the Constitution, 'Afrikaans' should be included too. And so Malan set about enforcing his policy of compulsory bilingualism.

Back then, there was a huge segment of English-speaking South Africa who couldn't string so much as a *ja-nee* together. Among the 13 000 civil servants in 1925, there were 3 792 who could speak only English, compared with twelve who could only converse in Afrikaans! By 1931, Malan had seen to it that Afrikaners made up 36 per cent of the civil service, albeit mainly in lower-paid positions. The growth of the Broederbond, which had been founded in 1918, and the establishment of other cultural and charitable organisations like the Federasie van Afrikaanse Kultuurvereniginge, the Reddingsdaadbond and the Afrikaanse Handelsinstituut would combine to foment a socioeconomic realignment that leaves B-BBEE in the shade (more about that later).

In the middle of the flag controversy, Hertzog sailed to London to attend the Imperial Conference of 1926, intent on getting some kind of formal recognition of South Africa's relative independence from Britain. But his pact with Creswell meant that he couldn't gun for a republic – much to the chagrin of arch-nationalists like D.F. Malan and Tielman Roos.

In one of the more deliciously ironic episodes in our history, Hertzog relied on a memorandum prepared by none other than Jan Smuts (who had tried and failed to get a very similar resolution passed at the 1921 Imperial Conference) to argue his case with the king. 'Both in its broad outline and its specific details, the

Smuts memorandum anticipated almost every demand which Hertzog was proposing to make,' writes Hancock.

> Smuts had saved Hertzog an immense amount of work and had presented him with a superb tactical opening, but had also created some embarrassment for him. In his ... discussions with the Commonwealth Prime Ministers, Hertzog emphasised the wide area of his agreement with Smuts; but he also knew that the republicans in his party would not thank him if the sovereign status which he offered them bore Smuts's trademark. Consequently, he had to persuade [the other Commonwealth prime ministers], and if possible to persuade himself, that he and Smuts were at odds on some issue of fundamental principle.[22]

Without any justification, Hertzog claimed in Parliament that Smuts had wanted Britain to rule over South Africa like 'an authority holding everybody by the throat, something like a super-authority and a super-state'.[23] No matter that the piece of paper he proudly brought back with him to Pretoria may as well have been written by Smuts. The Balfour Declaration of 1926 (not to be confused with the 1917 Balfour Declaration, which paved the way for the establishment of the Jewish state of Israel – itself a colonial, settler state) made it clear that the dominions (Australia, Canada, the Irish Free State, Newfoundland, New Zealand and South Africa) were

> autonomous Communities within the British Empire, equal in status, in no way subordinate one to another in any aspect of their domestic or external affairs, though united by a common allegiance to the Crown, and freely associated as members of the British Commonwealth of Nations.[24]

Hertzog had 'failed to get his favourite word "independence" written into the Declaration' because the Canadian prime minister, William Mackenzie King, had argued that including the word would 'get him hanged when he got back to Canada'.[25] Nevertheless, Hertzog declared himself 'absolutely content' on his return. Smuts, too, claimed to be 'satisfied', and even Malan and Roos expressed their support for the Declaration. Only time would tell if they meant it.

All the King's men: Hertzog (standing, second from right)
pays homage at the Imperial Conference of 1926

Swart gevaar: Know your enemy

The 1929 election is significant due to the role racial issues played in the Nationalist campaign – and the incredible success this approach brought them. The
concept of *swart gevaar* (black peril) had been championed by Tielman Roos
since at least 1924. But in 1929 fear of 'black inundation' played such a pivotal
role in the political messaging of Hertzog, Roos and Malan that the election
became known as the 'Black Peril Election'.

For all its repulsiveness, it was a highly effective piece of electioneering. As
Govan Mbeki concedes in his essay 'Rise and Growth of Afrikaner Capital',
swart gevaar 'skilfully' united English- and Afrikaans-speaking whites: 'Thus a
common fear and common hatred were generated against a common enemy –
the African ... [giving] the Nationalist Afrikaner a free hand to carry on with his
allotted mission to put *die k***** in sy plek*.'[26] Hancock writes:

The colour issue was dominant. The Nationalists staked their fortunes on a gigantic campaign to convince the constituencies that white civilization was in danger. It was in danger, they said, because Smuts stood for *niksdoen*, for 'letting the situation develop', which meant letting white civilization drift onto the rocks. Worse than that the country was in danger because Smuts stood for *gelykstelling*, the equality of black and white.[27]

'Alien natives'! The Pact and immigration

Migration was a hot topic the world over in the period between the two world wars. Even by global standards, South Africa was a pioneer of immigration controls, which had first been implemented against Indian immigrants in Natal during the late 1890s. In the 1900s curbs were placed on Chinese and central African workers coming to the Transvaal mines. And in the early 1920s, Smuts tried to introduce partial restrictions on the employment of Mozambican workers on the gold fields.

When the Pact alliance came to power, they took these wishy-washy attempts at safeguarding white labour several steps further. After anti-immigrant riots in Johannesburg and Lichtenburg at the end of 1927, the Native Affairs Department established a scheme of self-funded repatriations and labour bureaus, directing 'foreign labour' to farms. In February 1929 it was reiterated that 'in its care of national interests the Government is not prepared to allow the ceaseless infiltration and permanent settlement of alien natives'.[28] Many in the ANC, including Henry Selby Msimang, Thomas Mapikela and Eddie Khaile, supported these moves.

A period of mass deportations followed amid the onset of the Depression. Thousands of central Africans in urban areas were forcibly repatriated. And, after hitting a peak of just under 91 000 in 1928, the number of Mozambican mineworkers almost halved to 48 000 in 1933. The number of black South African mineworkers, meanwhile, increased exponentially.[29]

While addressing voters in Ermelo, Smuts made a massive *oepsie* when he talked of his dream of a 'confederation of African states ... a great African Dominion stretching unbroken throughout Africa'. While Smuts later denied he had used the term 'African Dominion', the Nats didn't need a second invitation to pile on to Slim Jannie. They disseminated their 'Black Manifesto', which implored voters to '*Stem vir 'n witmansland*' (vote for a white South Africa) and tarred Smuts as

the man who puts himself forward as the apostle of a black K****r state ...
extending from the Cape to Egypt ... And already foretells the day when even
the name of South Africa will vanish in smoke upon the altar of the K****r
state he so ardently desires.[30]

'Day after day from January to June', the pro-Nationalist newspapers owned by
Nasionale Pers (most notably *Die Burger*, which had been founded by D.F. Malan
in 1915) claimed that if Smuts got his way, 'White South Africa would be drowned
in the Black North'.[31] The newspapers' cartoonists took to their task with glee.
One cartoon depicted South Africa as a tiny white spot on the tail of a black dog,
while another showed a Griqua soldier with a white bride on his arm. Arguably
the most effective of the bunch was a simple cartoon published in *Die Burger*
a week before the election showing a white farmer staring forlornly at an SAP
election poster that read: 'Stem vir die Swart Afrika Party'.

Die Burger's take on the SAP

Labour's love lost

Another notable feature of the '29 election was the dismal showing of Creswell's Labour Party, which only managed eight seats – including three members who routinely and openly voted against their own party in the subsequent Parliament. The 'hostility clause' of 1927, which allowed government to throw black activists in jail on the slightest misdemeanour, had forced Labour into a crisis. While Creswell and the party's other proponents of the colour bar thought discrimination a damn fine caper, the socialist-leaning 'true Labour' faction dismissed it as unashamed racism, and a dramatic internal schism developed.

First, Bill Andrews (an ex-Labour MP who subsequently served as the first secretary of the Communist Party of South Africa) brought a dozen black trade unions together under the umbrella of the Non-European Trade Union Federation. In an open act of provocation, the 'true Labour' cabinet minister Walter Madeley made a point of receiving a deputation from Andrews and the militant ICU against Hertzog's wishes, causing a cabinet crisis. Hertzog predictably sided with Creswell in giving Madeley the boot. In retaliation, the National Labour Council – which, much like the ANC's National Executive Committee, had a lot of behind-the-scenes heft in the Labour Party – expelled Creswell and eight other Labour MPs.

When Hertzog replaced Madeley in the cabinet with a Creswellite (i.e. a racist), the die was cast. Although Labour was listed as one party on the ballot papers, the ideology of its candidates ranged from red-blooded commie to racist right-winger.

Communists and the Congress

After Hertzog's win in 1924, the CPSA and the ANC engaged in the first flirtations of a long and at times fractious affair. By 1926, 1600 of the CPSA's 1750 members were black (remember that during the Rand Revolt it had sided with strikers fighting to preserve the colour bar) and in 1929 it officially demanded black majority rule when it adopted the call for a proletarian Native Republic. Robert Edgar points out that the number of *committed* party members was much lower than 1750, however, as the early CPSA 'was like a revolving door with new members coming and going and not really understanding what the Party stood for ... The Native Republic thesis created enormous splits in the Party and contributed to the Party virtually disappearing in the 1930s.'[32]

Be that as it may, in 1932 the CPSA nominated a black man for Parliament. As the party's newspaper, *Umsebenzi*, reported at the time,

> The Communist Party has decided to put forward Comrade J B Marks, a Native
> worker, as a candidate in the Germiston by-election. The laws of the white
> imperialist ruling minority deny a Native the right to stand for Parliament in
> this country ...
>
> Why then does the Communist Party contest this election? The Communist
> Party, the only political party of the working class and the leader of the toiling
> masses, tells the workers, white and black, that Parliament does not and cannot
> solve the burning questions affecting the interests of the toilers. The CP mobilises
> the masses to fight for their demands, not in the house of the slave owners'
> representatives, but outside in the mines, factories, farms, locations, streets, etc.[33]
>
> In the mid-1930s, the ANC, which was in danger of becoming defunct, temporarily
> turned its back on communism. But the romantic spark between the parties would
> not be snuffed out that easily, and in the 1950s their alliance would become the
> major multiracial political force in the country.

One step forward and two steps back:
Coloured and women voters

You will recall that the Pact victory of 1924 had been achieved partly thanks to
the coloured vote. Once in government, the Pact tried to consolidate its coloured
support by increasing spending on coloured education, introducing a coloured
pension and doubling down on their 'civilised labour' policy, which supposedly
put coloureds on the same plane as whites.

But actions speak louder than words. During Hertzog's first government, whites
were always preferred over coloureds when applying for jobs in the public sector;
salaries for white civil servants were, by definition, higher than coloured salaries;
and the coloured pension was capped at 70 per cent of the amount received by
whites. Surprise, surprise, in 1929 the Nats didn't get nearly as many coloured people
to vote for them. Luckily for them, an improved showing among Afrikaner voters
thanks to the highly successful *swart gevaar* messaging meant that they could stop
worrying about the coloured vote and focus instead on doubling the white vote.[34]

Only in South Africa could allowing women to vote actually take democracy backwards. But that is exactly what Hertzog managed with the Women's
Enfranchisement Act of 1930. By granting a Union-wide unqualified franchise to
white women over the age of twenty-one, Hertzog reduced 'the coloured vote

from 12.3% of the electorate to 6.7%' overnight.[35] The even smaller black vote was also effectively halved by the Act.

As Mohamed Adhikari explains,

[The Act] represented an about-face on the part of... Hertzog. Throughout the latter part of the 1920s he had tried to entice coloured voters into supporting the National Party with the prospect of a 'New Deal' that would give them economic and political, but not social equality with whites. This act was but the latest development in a decades-long trend of the erosion of coloured civil rights.[36]

Baking bad: Coloured women vote with their ovens

When Hertzog promised to give coloured women the vote, some Cape Malay women created a tartlet in his honour: a delicately spiced biscuit cup filled with apricot jam and desiccated coconut called the *hertzoggie*. After the disappointment of the Women's Enfranchisement Act of 1930, the women once again took to their ovens, creating a sarcastic new version of the tartlet with brown and pink icing, calling it the *tweegevrietjie* – the 'two-faced cake'.

Hertzoggies and *tweegevrietjies* at the legendary Wembley Bakery in Athlone

At a meeting held in Cape Town City Hall on 27 April 1931, Dr Abdurahman and his daughter Zainunnisa ('Cissie') Gool both gave withering assessments of the Act. 'One of the most recent actions of this Nationalist Parliament,' stated Dr Abdurahman,

> is to say by virtue of the Women's Suffrage Act, that the Virgin Mary, an Asiatic, may not have a vote. That is a doubly blasphemous thing to do ... the Rev. D F Malan ... has forced through Parliament an Act which lays down that the Mother of Christ shall not have a seat in Parliament.[37]

The *jool* of District Six

The 27 April meeting launched the political career of Cissie Gool, whose impassioned oratory reportedly sent the crowd into raptures. Only a few snippets have survived: 'In the face of so much oppression it is hard to keep one's temper,' she said, before concluding with a flourish: 'A civilised people is being ruled by an ignorant oligarchy.'[38] At the end of the meeting, Gool led a march to Parliament and demanded in vain to speak to Hertzog. 'Swaying the masses with her eloquence and charm and then taking direct action would remain a favourite tactic throughout her political career,' notes Gairoonisa Paleker, who explains that '[w]hile Dr Abdurahman and his generation believed in politics of accommodation and petition, the younger generation, including his daughter, espoused a more radical approach to the issues at the forefront of Cape politics.'[39]

Her entry into politics was perhaps an inevitability: apart from her father's political achievements, her Scottish grandfather, John Cummings James, 'is credited with having secured free and compulsory education for Scottish children', and her mother, Helen 'Nellie' James, continued her father's fight when she arrived in Cape Town. And young Cissie wasn't only exposed to her parents' political views; their home on Mount Street ('the most prestigious mansion in the whole of District Six') was a thoroughfare for the liberal thinkers of the day, and she must surely have been inspired by the fireside chat of Mahatma Gandhi, Sol Plaatje, W.P. and Olive Schreiner, and John X. Merriman, among many others.

Cissie Gool was a trailblazer in every way. As Patricia van der Spuy notes in her PhD thesis, she was the 'first Black woman to be awarded a Master's degree at the University of Cape Town'; the 'first Black woman to be called to the Cape bar'; the 'first black South African woman to preside over a national political

BC506 A5.5

MUNICIPAL ELECTION

WARD 7   5th SEPT., 1938

VOTE FOR

"The People's Own Candidate"   "The People's Own Candidate"

Mrs. Z. GOOL
M.A.
(PRESIDENT OF THE NATIONAL LIBERATION LEAGUE OF S.A.)

Who stands for

1   DECENT HOUSING AND SANITATION
2   ADDITIONAL REFUSE REMOVAL SERVICES
3   MORE CRECHES AND CLINICS FOR THE POOR
4   OPEN SPACES FOR CHILDREN
5   THE ABOLITION OF SLUMS AND THE REFORM PARTY
6   EQUAL OPPORTUNITY FOR THE EMPLOYMENT OF COLOURED PEOPLE IN THE COUNCIL
7   HIGHER WAGES FOR MUNICIPAL EMPLOYEES
8   RECREATION GROUNDS AND A SWIMMING BATH FOR WARDS 6 & 7
9   **NO RESIDENTIAL SEGREGATION**
10   THE IMMEDIATE CONSTRUCTION OF A PUBLIC HALL FOR WARDS 6 & 7

STEWART, CAPE TOWN

Apart from a brief expulsion in 1952, Cissie Gool represented District 6
on the Cape Town City Council from 1938 until her death in 1963

organization'; and the first and 'only black woman to be elected to the Cape Town City Council before 1994'.[40]

But it was not only in her public life that Gool ruffled feathers. In 1919 she married Abdul Hamid 'AH' Gool, who came from a prominent and politically active Cape Indian family and, like Cissie's father, had studied medicine in the UK. They had three children but separated in 1936. Cape Town was atwitter when, without allowing the paint of their failed marriage even a minute or two to dry, Cissie rented a house in Vredehoek and moved in with a young Jewish lawyer named Sam Kahn.

Despite this snub, AH and Cissie remained good friends until her death in 1963. He was always first in line to hear her speak at political rallies and, after her imprisonment in the wake of the Sharpeville massacre in 1960, he was one of her frequent visitors. His extended family (with the exception of his radical younger brother Goolam) were not such big fans and she had other vocal critics. Either way, 'her wit and sharp tongue are what people remember best'.[41]

Small silver linings

The passing of the Women's Enfranchisement Act wasn't entirely a bad thing. It did, after all, mark a massive step forward for the 469 000 white women who were added to the voters' roll. The ease with which it sailed through the House (seventy-three votes to thirty-four) and the Senate (thirty votes to six) showed that unabashed chauvinism was on the decline. (Racism, of course, was an entirely different beast.)

Among the six naysayers in the Senate was a Dr T.C. Visser, who claimed that 'it was a scientific fact that the development of a woman's brain stopped at a stage beyond which a man's brain went on'. Senator Van der Walt, meanwhile, argued (somewhat confusingly given the fact that the Act effectively halved the black and coloured vote) that

> [t]he South African man, well known for his courtesy to the weaker sex, was accustomed to hard hitting in his politics. [The Act was] merely aping Europe, while the conditions in South Africa were vastly different. Our problem was not so much one of economics as of racial survival, and this demanded that the political role should be confined to men.

Senator C.J. Langenhoven (of 'Die Stem' fame) declared, before grudgingly voting in favour, that he viewed the Act as 'a movement away from the home ... What did the woman who occupied a professional position accomplish? She kept a man out of a position, she shirked the responsibility of marriage and prevented a man from marrying because he did not earn the income which would make it possible for him to marry'.[42]

Fortunately, these men were in the minority. The *Cape Times* of 15 May 1930 called Dr Visser a 'shallow thinker' whose claims were 'grossly unscientific'.[43] Senator S.P.C.R. van Niekerk dismissed Senator Van der Walt's claims as 'nonsensical talk'. And Senator R.A. Kerr claimed that twenty-one-year-old women were 'infinitely better balanced' than men of the same age.[44]

Two days later, in a show of strength, female students and staff at the Paarl Training College refused to serve tea to their male counterparts at break time. Instead, writes Vic Alhadeff, 'they paraded around the college campus with banners bearing the words: "Who is to be the first woman in Parliament? Come along girls!" Marching in the opposite direction was a small but distinguished army of anti-suffragists brandishing the slogan: "Men every time."'[45]

Bertha's Bill

Bertha Solomon (née Schwartz) and her family moved to South Africa from Russia when she was four years old. After completing a master's in classics at UCT, she

got married, moved to Joburg and had two kids. Declaring herself 'bored', at the age of thirty-four she took advantage of a change in the law to become, in 1926, one of the first women in South Africa to qualify as an advocate. She soon found herself working on cases that hammered home to her 'the evil of marriage in community of property'. Most of her clients were women, including a teacher 'who had married unwisely' and then moved out. When the client's hubby wrote to the Department of Education 'demanding that he should be paid his wife's salary, [under the laws of the time] the Department was obliged to comply'.[46]

More Bertha control

While her main aim was overhauling the domestic rights of women, Solomon realised that no real change could be effected until women were given the vote. So, she threw her weight behind the women's suffrage campaign and was soon elected their chairperson. Despite 'stiff opposition' from the Dutch Reformed Church, which reckoned that women voting was 'in direct conflict with the word of God', she managed to get the Act through Parliament.[47]

In 1933 she ran for (and won) a seat on the Transvaal Provincial Council, and five years later she was elected the MP for Jeppe. But this was only the first battle won. Despite the challenges of working in a male-dominated environment (Smuts once quipped 'What this house needs is more Bertha control!'), Solomon almost brought her women's rights bill before Parliament in 1939. But the outbreak of World War II kiboshed it. Five years later she finally managed to get a similar bill through the lower house, but it was rejected by the Senate.

Solomon then persuaded Prime Minister Smuts to set up a judicial commission to investigate the position of women in South Africa. 'The findings were horrifying,' writes Jordan Moshe. 'Even the commission's chairman, who had initially been opposed to such a bill, changed his view.' Unfortunately, '[b]y the time the commission presented its findings, the conservative National Party had come to power, and it was more interested in legislating apartheid than antagonising the church.'[48]

Eventually, twenty-seven years after taking up the fight, the Matrimonial Affairs Act of 1953 was passed. The opening lines of the Act, which was nicknamed 'Bertha's Bill' by Prime Minister D.F. Malan, stated emphatically that 'No husband shall be entitled, without his wife's written consent, to alienate, mortgage, burden with a servitude or confer any real right in ... any immovable property which is the separate property of the wife; or any immovable property held in community.'[49]

The ensuing clauses went on to enact sweeping changes to the law relating to orders for maintenance, the guardianship and custody of minors, and divorce.

Giving the finger to the gold standard

In hindsight, the 1929 election was decided as much by the prevailing economic conditions of the country as it was by party policy. In the same way that voters who were feeling the economic pinch in 1924 had rejected Smuts, now Hertzog took the credit for the slightly more prosperous state of the nation. How different things might have been if the Great Depression, which kicked off in October 1929, had come a few months earlier.

Armblankes (poor whites) had been around in South Africa since at least the conclusion of the Anglo-Boer War, when destitute Afrikaners returned to their razed farms. Fixing the problem – mainly by ensuring that every white kid went to school – had been a focus of every government since union. But the Depression, coupled with an almost biblical plague of locusts and a prolonged drought that lasted into the 1930s, ratcheted up the problem by several notches.

The famous Carnegie Commission of Investigation (funded by a US 'philanthropical' organisation concerned 'that if the Bantu were given full economic opportunity, the more competent among them would soon outstrip the less competent whites'[50]) found that there were 300 000 poor whites in South Africa. In 1934, Hendrik Verwoerd (then a professor of sociology and social work at Stellenbosch University with a particularly soft spot for poor whites) reasoned that 250 000 of these were Afrikaners – a quarter of the entire Afrikaner population.[51]

In the first few years of the 1930s, fifteen million sheep died of starvation and the price of maize halved. For reasons known only to them, Hertzog and his finance minister Nicolaas 'Klasie' Havenga clung to the gold standard (back in the day, most major currencies were pegged to the gold price) while most other nations, Britain included, abandoned it. This artificially overvalued the South African currency and pushed many farmers into debt. There was, writes Hermann Giliomee, 'a real danger that a number of the commercial banks might close'.[52] As Armstrong memorably puts it, even 'the dullest clerk in a counting-house could see that the country was going bankrupt, but Havenga still held steadily on'.[53]

Smuts, just back from yet another triumphant tour of England and the US, went on the attack, accusing Hertzog of the three-course dinner of bribery, nepotism and incompetence. He promised to take South Africa off the gold standard immediately if he was returned to power. While Smuts's status as a senior statesman meant that he was taken seriously, it was Tielman Roos's intervention that ensured the gold issue was on the lips of voters from Newlands to Nelspruit.

Roos, who had become a judge in the Supreme Court of Appeal after being overlooked for the position of justice minister by a mistrustful Hertzog after the 1929 election, came out guns blazing. As Armstrong puts it, when Hertzog reprimanded him for compromising his office by engaging in politics, he promptly

> stripped off his robes as a judge, and, disregarding the protests of his doctor [he was plagued by ill health], dashed into politics, shouting that he had come to save South Africa, and that South Africa must at once, under his guidance, without a minute's hesitation or delay, come off gold.[54]

In November 1932, Roos approached Smuts about the prospect of a coalition, telling him that he had already secured the backing of twenty-four Nationalist MPs. While some in the SAP were tempted by the offer, Smuts knew better. Not only did Roos reside in the dingier and more racist corners of the Afrikaner nationalist cathedral, he also had a long and proud track record of back-stabbing. As Armstrong notes, Smuts 'was not going to be tied up with this mercurial, haphazard, unreliable fellow, especially as Tielman Roos wanted everything, to be Prime Minister, and to nominate half the Cabinet; and he could not show any proofs that he could carry out his boasts'.[55]

Tielman Roos: A caricature of himself

In the week before Christmas 1932, as capitalists started to take their money out of South Africa, it seemed as if Roos might be able to go it alone. But everything changed on 27 December when Havenga, at Hertzog's insistence, finally took the country off the gold standard. The effect was immediate: money poured into the economy, the gold price soared and the mining houses laughed all the way to the mint.

But this newfound prosperity did not spell the end of Hertzog's problems. He had, writes Krüger, 'always stated that the Government would stand or fall with the gold standard. People asked: now that it was gone, why did he not resign?'[56] What's more, he'd lost a few seats in by-elections in 1932 and his party had been so rocked by the crisis that the old fault lines had re-emerged and he no longer knew who to trust.

Smuts, meanwhile, made a point of reminding the country that Hertzog and Havenga had only done what he'd been advocating all along. Smuts knew he could count on the support of his traditional voter base of English-speakers, entrepreneurs and most city dwellers, and he felt that he even had a shot with Hertzog's *volk*, who were still struggling to put food on the table. Leaving the gold standard had, after all, done nothing to alleviate the once-in-a-generation drought, which was at its very worst in the summer of 1932/3. (The drought broke a year later.)

And then there were two

To return to the Hollywood romcom analogy from the beginning of this chapter, the only thing that was certain as the flick neared its end was that the alternative love interest, Tielman Roos, was done for. As one of Smuts's biographers, F.S. Crafford, put it,

[Roos] had thrown the generals into each other's arms and in doing so, had brought disaster on himself. Had the Hertzog government been able to remain on gold, Roos might have secured Smuts' cooperation on his own terms. But Finance Minister Havenga's all-too-prompt acceptance of sterling upset his applecart. No sooner was the gold issue a thing of the past than Roos discovered that his magnetism had died with it.[57]

While Hertzog was clearly standing on shaky ground, Smuts was not super confident either. (The 1924 defeat must have been weighing heavily on his mind.) When Parliament reconvened in January 1933, everyone was talking about the prospect of cooperation between the two main parties. Hertzog and Smuts made a point of being nice to one another. Smuts even publicly proposed the formation of a national government. According to Steyn, 'Hertzog laughed openly when conciliation was suggested, but behind the scenes his lieutenants were already sounding out SAP MPs.'[58]

First, Hertzog put the idea to his own party. He argued that now the language and constitutional issues had been clarified, not much separated the two parties. Besides, the Nats couldn't bank on winning the election on their own. In Krüger's words, 'If the opposition came to power with the help of federalist Natal, the reward for that support might well be the introduction of federalism to such an extent that the Afrikaans language would disappear from that province.'[59] Most members of the National Party – with the very notable exception of D.F. Malan – agreed that this was too big a risk to take.

On 16 February 1933, Smuts provided Hertzog with a typed proposal, which they discussed in person the following morning. The major sticking point was Smuts's keenness to exclude any mention of proposed native legislation from the agreement. And so the discussions dragged on. (Pirow describes Smuts as 'the arch procrastinator.'[60]) Eventually, on Tuesday 21 February, Smuts climbed down from his pedestal.

A week later Hertzog announced that 'he and his former opponent had agreed to form a coalition government based upon the seven-point programme of principles' described at the beginning of this chapter.[61] The document's conclusion stated that a general election would take place immediately.

The election itself: 'Heedless of the claims of housework'

As the *Cape Times* stated in its election-day issue: 'For the first time in Union history, the issue is not between the parties, but simply: coalition.'[62] (It would not be the last South African election to be a foregone conclusion!) A staggering 78 of the 150 seats were returned unopposed and, despite the addition of almost half a million white women to the roll, the overall turnout was lower than the 1929 election. This is not to say that the election day was not reported on with interest. One theme stood out in all the papers. This snippet from the *Cape Argus* is representative:

> The outstanding feature of today's general election, is the flocking of women
> to the poll in their thousands… the keenness which they everywhere display
> is remarkable. Heedless of the claims of housework or small children they are
> finding their way to the polling booths.[63]

Gwendoline Ellen von Wiese becomes the first woman in South Africa to register to vote

The same paper also noted, with more than a hint of chauvinist bias, the 'curious ways in which voting papers were spoiled':

WITHOUT MAKING A CROSS

A great many voters, presumably women, evidently thought that by getting their number on the voters' roll outside the polling station and indicating their wishes they had no further responsibility. They simply folded their voting papers and put them in the ballot box without making a cross.[64]

Close analysis of election results shows that there was actually a lower percentage of spoilt ballots in 1933 than there had been in the previous election, so perhaps the culprits were – whisper it – men!

There is much less doubt about the piss-poor showing of the Labour Party, which with two measly seats had fallen a long way since the triumph of 1924. Tielman Roos's Central Party could also only muster two seats. Roos's own contest in Rustenburg with Pieter Grobler, the minister of native affairs, was arguably the most keenly watched of all. As *The Times* of London reported,

Close as it is to Johannesburg, Rustenburg has never lost its character of an old-time town dominated by a statue of Kruger, and men and women who came in from the farms to vote wore the old-fashioned clothes of their forefathers and found parallels for the present struggle in heroes and profits of the Old Testament. Mr Roos and his supporters had, however, nearly 200 motor-cars plying in the district... Women are sitting at Mr Roos's election table wearing his blue, white and gold colours while their husbands drive Mr. Grobler's supporters to the polls. Good humour prevails nevertheless.[65]

Once all the ballots for Rustenburg had been counted, Roos was found to have been defeated by 2466 votes to 1922. In 1935, shortly after advising his few remaining supporters to switch to the United Party (the name of the party Smuts and Hertzog would form in 1934), he died, impoverished and broken, aged only fifty-six. 'A fund raised on behalf of his widow and children raised £6,000,' writes Crafford. Included in this amount was a £250 contribution from one of the mining houses 'which Roos's intervention had saved from utter ruin and furnished with unbelievable prosperity in the shape of profits amounting to millions of pounds'.[66]

The table below details the damage:

Party	1929 aka *Swart Gevaar*				1933 aka Fusion[67]			
	Votes	%	Seats	+/-	Votes	%	Seats	+/-
National Party	141579	41.17	78	+15	101159	31.61	75	-3
South African Party	159896	46.50	61	+8	71486	22.34	61	0
Central Party (Roos)					27441	8.58	2	New
Labour Party	33919	9.86	8	-10	20276	6.34	2	-6
Natal Home Rule Party					12328	3.84	0	New
Independents	8503	2.47	1	0	87321	27.29	10	+9
Total	343897	100.00	148	+13	320011	100.00	150	+2

Malan and the Mevrou

One other prominent coalition member who was forced to contest his seat was D.F. Malan, who had never before come up against much opposition in conservative Calvinia. The Women's Enfranchisement Act presented Dr W.P. Steenkamp with a chance to upset Malan's apple cart, however. A Dutch Reformed dominee turned medical doctor who had written a book in support of the theory of evolution, Steenkamp 'regarded it as his highest calling to be a thorn in Malan's side'.[68]

Mevrou Steenkamp

The Steenkamp family went about this in an unusual manner. The good doctor's wife, Mrs A.C. Steenkamp, ran against Malan in Calvinia, while Dr Steenkamp contested the neighbouring Namaqualand constituency. Although both Steenkamps ran ostensibly as independents, they campaigned unashamedly for the SAP vote – in flagrant disregard of the coalition agreement between Smuts and Hertzog. Dr Steenkamp would win his Namaqualand seat with ease, while his wife gave Malan a run for his money. Sensing a potential calamity, Smuts swallowed his pride and flew to Calvinia to campaign on Malan's behalf. In the end Malan won the seat by a relatively comfortable 621 votes.

Where to now?

The overarching sentiment in the wake of the 1933 election was one of hope – hope that the union achieved on paper in 1910 would finally become a reality. Smuts released a statement praising 'the spirit of good will and friendliness among the people', proclaiming the laying of a 'firm foundation on which to build hopes for the future' and calling out 'those who entertained doubts'.[69] The *Manchester Guardian* also waxed lyrical, describing the outcome as 'one of the strongest governments in modern times' and an 'expression of popular revulsion from years of party bickering'.[70] Writing in 1937, Smuts's biographer Armstrong was even more emphatic: 'No opposition worth the name remained. There were no Dutch and English parties. They were united.'[71]

Unfortunately, they had all been beguiled by the romcom's promise: Smuts and Hertzog should have ridden off hand in hand into the Namaqualand sunset. But both they and their audience had failed to notice the sinister figure of D.F. Malan loitering, only half obscured, behind a halfmens.

No sooner had the election dust settled than the real negotiations began. Albert 'Ysterman' Geyer and his influential paper *Die Burger* came out all guns blazing against the idea of Fusion. The Ironman argued that all the gains made in the long-fought struggle for Afrikaans and 'civilised labour' and against the big money of the mining houses would be endangered by hopping into bed with Smuts the Anglophile strike-breaker.

Malan took some convincing – one of the architects of apartheid, Paul Sauer, famously said that 'we had to drag [him] out by the seat of his pants'.[72] Given Malan's physique this must have been quite a challenge, but once they'd managed, it set off 'a struggle without precedent' in the National Party.[73] As Charles Bloomberg points out, the clandestine Broederbond organisation also played an important role 'stiffening the morale' of Malan on this issue.[74] Try as he might, there was no way Hertzog could keep both Smuts and Malan happy in the same government.

When the NP met in the winter of 1934 to officially endorse the fusion of the NP and SAP into the new United Party, Malan was having none of it. The UP was, he said, a bulwark of 'imperialism and capitalism'. Fourteen Cape members of Parliament (including Sauer), four *Vrystaters* and one *Vaalie* broke away from the party to form the Gesuiwerde (Purified) Nasionale Party.[75] Though maligned and ridiculed by all quarters, the Gesuiwerdes would have the last laugh.

As an aside, there was also some English opposition to Fusion. When the idea was first proposed, Alan Paton (who would go on to form the Liberal Party) memorably remarked that English-speakers were 'more inclined to believe in cooperation than we are in "*samewerking*" [cooperation]. I believe we are more inclined to co-operate in English.'[76] And the SAP also suffered a small – but ultimately irrelevant – schism of its own when a handful of ultra-jingoes under the leadership of Colonel Stallard (the stiff-upper-lip racist behind the Native Urban Areas Act of 1923) broke away to form the Dominion Party.

Leaving a Sauer taste

With the famous liberal J.W. Sauer for a dad and Olive Schreiner (from whom he acquired his second name) as an aunt, Paul Oliver Sauer might have gone on to

Sauer hour

become a leading liberal figure. Things started well enough. During his schooling at SACS, a bastion of Anglo-Saxon education, he served as both head boy and captain of the First XV. But he soon lost his way at university, where he became a vocal proponent of right-wing republicanism.

By his mid-thirties he was, as we have just seen, an even stauncher nationalist than D.F. Malan. A chastening election loss in Stellenbosch in 1924 had set him against the coloured vote for life, and in 1947 a commission chaired by him provided the blueprint for what he termed 'total apartheid'. While he did later soften his stance in the wake of Sharpeville in 1960, arguing for 'conciliation' with blacks and the abolition of pass laws, he didn't kick up much of a fuss when he was ignored.

It is one of the stranger quirks of our history that the first South African wine ever to receive 100 points from an international critic bears his name. The Kanonkop Paul Sauer, which retails for around R700, is 'named after the legendary former owner of Kanonkop who was a statesman and wine-lover as well as being the grandfather of Kanonkop's current proprietors Johann and Paul Krige'.[77] One wonders why they didn't name it after one of their more palatable ancestors. Perhaps they were going for layered complexity?

PART THREE
APARTHEID

In 1948, after almost three centuries of practice, the South African government finally perfected the art of racial discrimination and segregation. In the decades that followed, white voters would back the fine-tuning of apartheid legislation to truly cruel ends.

CHAPTER 8

ELECTING FOR APARTHEID
1948

'The Magic word "Apartheid" suddenly flamed into the headlines as the main election slogan.' – **D.W. Krüger**[1]

Malan and wife: Ons premier racist

O N 28 MAY 1948, SOUTH AFRICA woke up to the shocking news that D.F. Malan, leader of the Herenigde Nasionale Party, had slunk into office. He had won a nanoscopic majority in the House of Assembly, and Smuts, who had (again) invited the British royal family to South Africa in 1947 and become deeply unpopular among nationalist Afrikaners, had been toppled. All the king's supporters and all the white men would never put the United Party back in power again.

A multitude of issues had been stacking up against Slim Jannie Smuts. Not only had his United Party lost the election, but he had been spat out by the electorate, losing his Standerton seat to a little-known member of the Broederbond. Smuts had come out the day before the election to state that the nation faced a choice between 'a fight for decency and justice and fair living conditions for all' and the 'crazy concept' of apartheid. 'Keep steady, vote right. Do not be confused,' he declared.[2]

But the country was confused, and Smuts was very much at the centre of this confusion. 'Justice for all' was certainly not where his Fusion government with Hertzog had sailed the ship.

'Any white moron': What Fusion segregated

A lot had happened in the preceding two decades. In 1929 James Rose Innes and Henry Burton, who had both left politics, formed the Non-Racial Franchise Association in an attempt to slow Hertzog's pursuit to remove black voters from the Cape voters' roll. As Rose Innes stated at the time:

> In the Transvaal and Free State any white moron can vote, but no coloured or black man, however wealthy and civilised he may be. A white minority with manhood suffrage rule a black majority with no suffrage at all. That is the very negation of democracy.[3]

But in many ways the notion of an inclusive non-racial democracy boat had already sunk – Hertzog had been driving stakes into its hull from the very beginning of union. Some black and white liberal activists felt that after Fusion their only hope was to secure a set of concessions from Hertzog. The fight for a non-racial democracy was over. The first president of the ANC, John Dube, was one of those who took this line. But as Rose Innes warned, it was vitally important to 'stand upon the principle of no colour differentiation'. Taking away the black

Cape franchise, no matter what other form of representation was on offer, would be reducing blacks in the Cape and the rest of South Africa to the status of second-class citizens forever.

In response to Hertzog's actions, D.D.T. Jabavu (now a professor at Fort Hare) and Pixley Seme (the president-general of the ANC) organised the All-African Convention in Bloemfontein in December 1935. Around 400 black leaders from an array of organisations and ethnicities gathered to coordinate resistance to Hertzog's 'Native bills'. The AAC found that

> the policy of political segregation of the White and Black races embodied in the Representation of Natives in the Senate Bill is not calculated to promote harmony and peace between the two races, for the logical outcome of its operation will be the creation of two nations in South Africa, whose interests and aspirations must inevitably clash in the end and thus cause unnecessary bitterness and political strife.[4]

During the debates on the decision to remove blacks from the Cape franchise, Burton cautioned against changing the Constitution via a two-thirds majority. However, Hertzog, Smuts and the now-United Party were deaf to Burton's advice and proceeded in a joint sitting to pass the Representation of Natives Act 1936 by 169 votes to 11 – easily making the two-thirds requirement. A tiny smattering of white liberals raised objections, among them J.H. Hofmeyr (nephew of 'Onze Jan'):

> If we were starting with a clean sheet it would certainly be possible to devise a system of separate representation in separate assemblies which would be fair and just ... but we are not starting with a clean sheet. We are starting with the existence of a vested right which has been in existence ... for more than 80 years, and once the franchise rights have been given and exercised by a section of the community, then no nation ... should take away those rights without adequate justification.[5]

Black people in the Cape were taken off the voters' roll, their rights reduced to being allowed to vote for three white politicians who would represent them in the lower house, while four senators would represent their interests in the upper. A Native Representative Council (NRC) was created to help 'advise' the government on 'native issues'.

Defusing and refusing

When Britain declared war on Germany on 3 September 1939 in response to Hitler's invasion of Poland, the South African Parliament had an important and potentially government-breaking decision to make. The United Party would have to decide on the question about which they were most divided: to join the Empire in its battle against the Nazis or express South Africa's ultimate independence and remain neutral?

Hertzog, mistakenly believing that he could command the majority in Parliament, put a motion before the Assembly to reaffirm South Africa's neutrality. However, Smuts, in an act of 'ultimate betrayal', put forward an amendment favouring cutting ties with Germany. With Labour and the Dominion Party behind him, Smuts surprisingly won the vote by eighty votes to sixty-seven. Fusion was done for, Hertzog resigned, and Smuts then managed to form a pro-war government with some vestiges of the UP and the smaller, largely English-speaking parties.

This was, as D.W. Krüger states, 'the beginning not merely of a military struggle against an external enemy but also a political struggle at home. That struggle was not only one between Smuts and the opponents of the war policy but also a struggle of the opposition groups amongst themselves.'[6] It now seemed as if Afrikaner nationalism could at last fuse more naturally on one issue – a purer form of anti-Englishness.

Volking off

On 27 January 1940, the 'Purified' National Party and what was known as the 'Hertzog group' signed a conciliation agreement reuniting into what would be called the Herenigde Nasionale Party (HNP), or simply the Volksparty. But the moment of united ecstasy was short-lived. At the Volksparty's first congress in Bloemfontein, two statements were presented: one from the party's Broederbond-controlled Federal Council and one prepared by Hertzog himself. Despite what had happened in Parliament, Hertzog warned the congress: 'Germany is fighting her own battles. I am not one of those persons who say: "Let the Germans come to South Africa and all will be well." A jingo is always an intolerable person, whether he's English, German or Afrikaans.'[7]

The Federal Council's statement was radically republican and riddled with what Hertzog might have termed Afrikaner jingoisms. It made no reference to the political rights of English-speakers and stated that 'Die Stem' would be South Africa's only national anthem. Hertzog stormed out and was followed by Havenga and 100 of his supporters. Hertzog then offered his resignation. C.R. 'Blackie' Swart, who stepped into the void left by Hertzog, expressed regret that Hertzog had left simply because of 'the rights of the English-speaking people'.[8]

As Charles Bloomberg explains, this 'marked the end of Hertzog's political career and opened the way for Dr Malan, supported by the Broederbond machine, to take command of Nationalist Afrikanerdom'.[9] Hertzog retired to his farm, while several of his supporters formed the Afrikaner Party (AP), which would back neither Smuts nor the new HNP.

Hertzog's end

Hertzog would make one more public utterance before his death in 1942. In October 1941, alone, isolated and clearly still smarting from his recent political defeats, he suddenly issued a statement to the press. In it he offered a strange backpedal from what he had said in Bloemfontein, announcing that liberalism and multiparty democracy were anti-Afrikaans. National Socialism, he now declared, better reflected the traditions of the Afrikaner *volk*, and South Africa was ripe for a dictatorship:

> National socialism ... is a plant which owes its origin to certain circumstances and certain requirements and needs in state life; and where all the necessary circumstances, requirements, and needs exist, it will be valid – whether it is in Germany or in South Africa, does not matter ... The question of granting special powers to the governing person, or persons, by who the appropriate form of national socialism will have to be introduced or applied and administered as a governing measure; namely the so-called dictatorship.[10]

The gathering of Nazi sentiment was by no means unique to Hertzog. National Socialist organisations were everywhere, including within the HNP. That old Hitler admirer, Oswald Pirow, set up a pressure group within the parliamentary caucus of the HNP that called itself the 'Nuwe Orde' (New Order). Pirow preached the end of 'liberal-capitalist-democracy' in South Africa, stating, as historian Newell Stultz relates, that what would follow would be 'a Christian, white, National-Socialist republic, separated from the British Crown and founded on the principles of state authority and national discipline'.[11]

This brand of Christian National Socialism was also being championed by a new 'cultural organisation' with close links to the Broederbond – the Ossewa-brandwag (OB). In 1941 Dr J.H. 'Hans' van Rensburg, Pirow's old secretary of justice, was made commandant-general of the movement. A Germanophile, soldier and lawyer, he had met Hitler in the 1930s and was seemingly taken in by the Führer's *delightful* personality. Bloomberg states that Van Rensburg 'was greeted in some quarters as the new saviour of Afrikanerdom, his advent being reputedly foretold by the famous Afrikaner mystic and seer, N.P.J.J. "Siener" van Rensburg (no relation) who, only just before, had predicted that a man in a brown suit would suddenly emerge and lead his volk to its final salvation'.[12]

Van Rensburg saluting Nazi-style at a 'cultural concert' in Brakpan

Van Rensburg soon became *tjommies* with Dr Nico Diederichs and Dr Piet Meyer, who invited him onto the secretive Broederbond's executive council in an advisory capacity. The OB itself was filled with people who would become household names in the coming decades: B.J. 'John' Vorster, Hendrik van den Bergh, P.W. Botha, Paul Sauer and Anton Rupert. Rupert was then the young fire-brand editor of the Afrikaans-Nasionale Studentebond's newspaper, *Wapenskou*, which was 'a major OB mouthpiece'.[13]

OB quiet!

The Ossewabrandwag also developed a military wing known as the Stormjaers, led by Steve Hofmeyr (the grandfather of the right-wing singer-songwriter of the same name), a Rhodes Scholar and cousin of deputy prime minister J.H. Hofmeyr. In the early 1940s, Steve organised a campaign of terror across the country. Electricity pylons were blown up, attempts were made to destroy the power station at Delmas, and the black newspaper *Bantu World*'s office was bombed, as was the post office in Benoni, killing an innocent bystander. The Stormjaers were also seemingly behind the attempt to assassinate Steve's cousin J.H. Hofmeyr, Smuts's trusted liberal deputy – a bomb was planted outside his bedroom window, but it failed to detonate.

In December 1941 the Stormjaers' 'General' D.K. Theron and a man known as 'Doors' Erasmus attempted to blow up a train carrying troops destined for North Africa. As head of military intelligence Ernst Malherbe related:

> They went under a bridge and they had their dynamite there to blow up the bridge just before the train came. But – and I wouldn't say unfortunately – they blew themselves up. Had they succeeded they would not have blown up the troop train but the train of the families who were going to Durban to say goodbye.[14]

Stormjaers led by brothers Jan and Jacob Wilkens, who were also members of Parliament, once broke up a UP braai and severely beat Harry Lawrence, the minister of the interior and head of the country's internal security. They also regularly engaged in beating up servicemen and Jews. In 1940 at least seventy-nine cases of assault on soldiers were reported in the Transvaal alone.

In January 1941 a two-day-long running battle between Stormjaers and troops who had joined up to fight the Nazis took place in the streets of Joburg after an OB 'cultural concert' at City Hall. As the commission of inquiry into the unrest found, many of the 'civilians' (i.e. OB supporters) who attended the 'concert' came armed with clubs and knives. The commission also found that the police were often sympathetic to the OB. (Many policemen were, in fact, clandestine members of the organisation.) During the running battles, the police staged a baton charge against the soldiers who had gathered outside City Hall. The charge, it was found, had not been ordered by a senior officer and many 'civilians' had joined in to 'help' the police.

The OB's 'cultural weapons' used in the Joburg riots

The commission also uncovered that the police had repeatedly beaten soldiers who were either moving away from the area or had been knocked to the ground. In one incident a corporal was attacked – witnesses claimed without provocation – by the police. He later died of his injuries in hospital. During the two days of unrest, about 200 soldiers were admitted to hospital with stab wounds and other injuries. 'Civilian' (i.e. OB) injuries were far less numerous or severe.

After the commission into the violence in Joburg, Smuts acted to prevent what seemed like the very real possibility of a *coup d'état*. He first dismissed 400 policemen for pro-OB sympathies, and on 1 March he issued a decree stating that any civil servant belonging to the OB would be prosecuted.

At a time when the Allies were sustaining heavy losses and all bets were on a Nazi victory, the troops in South Africa took revenge. In one incident they chased an OB 'civilian' up a lamp post. The man, who had somehow lost his trousers during an earlier 'discussion', was then forced, while clinging to the top of the post, to sing 'God Save the King'.

Soldiers in Cape Town also set upon two Stellenbosch students for not observing the two-minute silence after the noon gun in recognition of the troops fighting in North Africa. When the news of this reached Stellenbosch, it sparked off a group of 'furious students, full of beer'. White Stellenbosch students armed with bricks, bottles and whips rampaged through a nearby coloured district, whipping children, beating up anybody they could find, and destroying property and vehicles.[15]

The end of the beginning

This all occurred when Hitler was thought to be winning the war. Things in South Africa began to change when the tide turned, but before that, as Patrick Furlong explains,

> The entire nationalist movement, despite its many different shades, had been caught up in a wave of extremist and revolutionary hysteria that left no component part unscathed. Almost everyone in the National Party, from outspoken younger radicals like ... Hendrik Verwoerd to ... Malan himself, had been affected to some degree by this baptism in the fires of war. For Hitler had, at least for a time, made so much seem possible.[16]

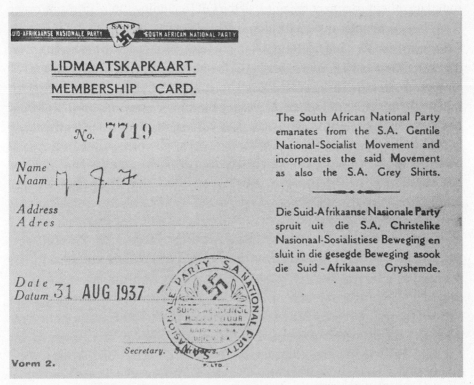

The National Party pinning the swastika to its cards in 1937

199

And despite the HNP and Malan's later climb down, they had all flirted with the idea of violent overthrow and dictatorship. In a meeting between the OB and the HNP facilitated by the Broederbond at Cradock in October 1940, Malan stated: 'Our greatest aim is now a Republic and we shall try to obtain it as a result of the war.'[17]

The 'Khaki Election' of 1943

The turnaround of Hitler's fortunes on the battlefield coincided with the 1943 election in South Africa, which would be a one-issue affair, that issue being the war. By election day on 7 July, Hitler's armies had been forced out of North Africa (with the help of South African troops) and halted in Russia.

Malan had already begun to realise that working with the OB was damaging to the HNP's image. He had denounced the Stormjaers in late 1941, disclosing that they were planning an armed rebellion. Smuts had acted quickly, arresting fifty-two Stormjaer officers and charging them with treason. He also began to round up other prominent members of the OB (including future prime minister B.J. Vorster) and interned them without trial at Koffiefontein.

Whatever Malan and his Broeders might have secretly desired, with Hitler on the back foot they were now wedded to change via the ballot. By 1942 the HNP had banned its office-bearers from being members of the OB. The Broederbond, too, was beginning to see that marching around with armbands and dark shirts was far less effective than clandestinely ensuring that the government bureaucracy was filled with its members.

But in 1943 these lessons were only beginning to be learnt, and with the HNP still in a state of disarray, Smuts, the UP and its pro-war allies in Labour and the Dominion Party had a relative cakewalk.[18]

Party	Votes	%	Seats	Change
United Party	435 297	49.68	89	-22
Herenigde Nasionale Party	321 601	36.70	43	New
Labour Party	38 206	4.36	9	+6
Dominion Party	29 023	3.31	7	-1
Afrikaner Party	15 601	1.78	0	New
Independents	30 185	3.44	2	+2
Native Representative Members			3	

The men in khaki go to the polls in North Africa in 1943 while Malherbe's information officers explain who the parties and leaders are

Word Wakkerstroom

Smuts now had a parliamentary working majority of sixty seats. But this was ignoring certain facts about the election. For one, thousands of Afrikaners abstained from voting and there was a very low turnout in many of the seats the UP won. With a higher turnout, Malan's HNP could well have come within reach of winning in at least forty-seven of these seats. Another factor was that the UP had won certain seats largely because of the presence of the Afrikaner Party (led by Hertzog's old ally Havenga). The opposition was divided.

If Malan could in some manner reconcile with certain elements of the OB and Nuwe Orde and arrange a deal with the AP, it would lead him into a much stronger position. This was proved in a by-election in 1944 after the death of the MP for Wakkerstroom, Colonel Collins, the minister of agriculture. Considering what had happened in 1924, the word 'Wakkerstroom' should have sent shivers of panic through Smuts's nervous system.

The HNP had put forward J.G.W. van Niekerk, known to his supporters as Jan Mielies, to run against the conservative UP member Bailey Bekker and an independent by the name of Len Hall who had some limited fame as a local wrestler. Van Rensburg instructed OB members to vote for Hall, but sadly he discovered that discipline in the organisation was distinctly defective. And besides, by 1944 the OB was a spent force. Not only had Smuts and Malan damaged its reputation, but with Hitler's defeat looming, the OB had become an unattractive prospect. In a constituency of around 6 000 voters, Hall received only ten votes and had to forfeit his deposit.

Jan Mielies stormed to victory by an impressive 221 votes, a swing of nearly 700 in one year. In order to win the seat, not only did Mr Mielies manage to persuade the OB members to ignore the will of its *Volksleier*, but he also came to an understanding with other groups like the Greyshirts, the Nuwe Orde and the AP. As Krüger explains, 'it was an ominous sign of what the National Party was capable of'.[19] Smuts was once again in trouble, but he did not seem to twig. As David Welsh puts it, 'Smuts's preoccupation with the war and its aftermath meant that little was done to galvanise the UP into an effective fighting force. Complacency bred sclerosis.'[20]

The band of Broeders

And of course, lurking in the South African political penumbra from the 1930s onwards was the clandestine organisation known as the Broederbond. As René de Villiers says, their day-to-day activities could never be determined with any accuracy, but their influence was 'always considerable and sometimes decisive'.[21] Although it can't be said that the Broederbond controlled Malan's party as it would Verwoerd's, their religious, economic and cultural networks made them hugely influential.

The Broederbond had been formed in 1918 after violence erupted between Englishmen and Afrikaners at a speech given by D.F. Malan at Selborne Hall in Johannesburg. According to one member of the Broederbond, somebody at the speech had pulled down the Union Jack at the back of the hall and torn it to shreds. On hearing about this, Englishmen in the area gathered outside the hall spoiling for a fight. The audience then 'did the manly thing' and went outside. A full-scale brawl broke out, and a car belonging to a member of the National Party was set on fire.[22]

The Broederbond had started out as a small cell intent on furthering Afrikaner ends in the face of English arrogance, violence and oppression. By the 1930s they had grown into a formidable presence in Afrikaner life, and they were decisive in persuading Malan not to join Hertzog in Fusion. By the 1940s they were controlled by a close-knit group of men including Drs Diederichs, Meyer and Verwoerd. The Broederbond's tentacles touched a breathtaking number of religious, social, cultural, youth and economic organisations that took control of and monitored a huge swathe of Afrikaans cultural life.

The breaking of the Broeders

Smuts had always been very wary of the Broeders, and during the war he secretly established a special division of military intelligence to investigate their activities. These investigations were headed by Dr Ernst Malherbe and his Department of Military Intelligence (DMI). Through ingenious clandestine methods, Malherbe gathered evidence against the Broeders, and in March 1944 he issued an extensive report. The report analysed the Broederbond's aims, internal structure and economic operations, as well as its infiltration into the civil service and the police. Its essential takeaway was this:

> If the Afrikaner-Broederbond is not similarly exposed [like the OB] and its strangle-hold eradicated root and branch – in particular its insidious hold on education – it WILL, AT ITS PRESENT RATE OF GROWTH, WITHIN A FEW YEARS DESTROY SOUTH AFRICA. Thus did the Nazi system, also starting with a small but powerful underground group, gain ultimate control ... Germany's nemesis was disguised in the form of a humble and poorly educated housepainter [i.e. Hitler]. South Africa's equivalent is a university professor [i.e. Diederichs, Meyer and Verwoerd]![23]

At the UP congress in early December 1944, Smuts began his public attack on the Broederbond, saying that it was 'undemocratic, crypto-Fascist, deceitful and a plague on society'.[24] Then, on the 15th, he issued a statement under the authority of the War Measures Act, banning the Broederbond as a political body and giving public servants

The battle of the moustaches: Piet Meyer's attempt to copy his beloved Führer fourteen days to resign their membership. Failure to do so would lead to prosecution.

Thousands of members duly resigned from the Broederbond, though others refused and resigned from their jobs instead. But as Bloomberg points out, 'although the ban disrupted and temporarily incapacitated the Broederbond, bringing its work in the administration to a standstill, in the long run it was a relatively minor interruption to the organisation's growth. Unlike members of the OB, no brethren were interned.'[25]

Brotherly hate

The Broederbond soon began to reconstruct itself while continuing to develop and spread its poisonous ideology of racist segregation and white Afrikaner supremacy. The most effective weapon against the Broeders was perhaps Malherbe's DMI. Malherbe, an educationalist by profession, not only investigated far-right activities during the war but also set up a highly effective education unit within the army. Over 300 information officers within the ranks gave lectures to the troops on subjects ranging from current affairs to economics and history. These officers were trained, as Malherbe put it, to protect the soldiers in their unit from other forms of attack:

> My men would find a soldier not eating and thoroughly miserable and they would press him to find out what was the matter and finally he would confess. Later we found out that the Broederbond was behind it, but it was mostly Nationalists and the Ossewabrandwag that did it. They'd send an anonymous letter to a man saying that his wife was unfaithful; they would even go so far as to write to a man and tell him that his child had died. There was enough authenticity attached to it that the man believed it and became utterly miserable. They deliberately poisoned the men's minds. So I got my men to intercept the letters, and that is how we started censorship.[26]

Malherbe's information officers seem to have had a decided effect on the troops and their political outlook. In a survey done at the end of the war, Malherbe discovered that the vast majority of the troops favoured a slow movement towards a non-racial solution to South Africa's politics. But at the end of the war Smuts closed down the DMI.

Time to upgrade the toy telephone

Black politics had also changed during the Second World War. Thousands of black, coloured and Indian civilians joined the army, and their experiences abroad shifted their expectations of what South Africa could be. As one of the intellectual giants of the ANC, Z.K. Matthews, wrote,

> All of them came back with wonderful stories about the countries they had
> visited: comparisons were drawn with their own country which was lagging
> behind. They had rubbed shoulders with men of different racial and cultural
> backgrounds who treated them as soldiers fighting the same enemy ... in the
> comradeship of war they had learned that colour was only skin deep and that
> 'A man's a man for all that!' ... now that they had served their country loyally
> they expected that they would not be forgotten.[27]

Soldiers without guns

Job Maseko, who did a
good job for South Africa

The Smuts government had approved the formation of a Non-European Army Service that allowed black, coloured and Indian soldiers to enlist, but strictly in non-combatant roles. Despite not being allowed to fight, many of these men received medals for their bravery.

Stretcher-bearer Lucas Majozi received the Distinguished Conduct Medal for his part in the Battle of El Alamein, where he continued to work under fire despite being wounded in the hip and neck. Job Maseko was captured at Tobruk when Hendrik Klopper surrendered the South African 2nd Infantry Division. As a POW, Maseko was forced to work loading ships. Having been a miner trained in explosives in South Africa, he devised an improvised bomb and placed it among oil drums on a cargo ship. The ship was destroyed in a massive explosion. Maseko felt impelled to do this 'because of our ill-treatment by the enemy ... and because I felt it a duty in this way to assist my own people'. Maseko then managed to escape and walked across the Sahara for three weeks, eventually finding his way back to Allied lines. He was awarded the Military Medal, although he was initially recommended for the Victoria Cross. According to the official war artist Neville Lewis, the reason Maseko did not receive it was that 'he was only an African'.[28] Maseko lived the rest of his life in poverty in South Africa and was killed when he was hit by a train on 7 March 1952.

After 1936 the ANC initially took the decision to engage with the Native Representative Council, which one of its members called 'the toy telephone'. The council consisted of white members of the Native Affairs Department, four Africans nominated by the governor-general and twelve elected African members. It was, however, strictly an advisory body with no legislative powers. As Z.K. Matthews, who was elected to the position of deputy chairman during the war, would say,

[The NRC] developed into a mere talking shop in which members debated various motions at great length, passed them more or less unanimously, and sent them on to various government departments for consideration, only to find that little or no attention was paid to their advice. This led to a sense of frustration and bitterness among the members and to an increasing loss of confidence in the Council among the African people.[29]

The ANC was slowly beginning to awaken to the truth of the matter: without an effective resistance strategy, they would always be handed toy telephones and toy political rights. With this realisation came several men who began to massage the organisation's failing heart. Two communists, Moses Kotane and the aptly named J.B. Marks, would take leadership roles on the ANC National Executive Committee, and Dr A.B. Xuma was elected as the organisation's president-general in 1940. A medical doctor who had trained in both the USA and the UK, Xuma not only helped the nearly bankrupt organisation with funds from his own pocket, but he also established grassroots membership. And he soon began to ramp up the rhetoric. Profits at the mines, he pointed out, had trebled between 1933 and 1939, while black mineworkers' wages had remained almost the same.

In 1941 the ANC made its 'first tentative plunge into the deeper waters of labour organization' with the formation of the African Mine Workers' Union (AMWU).[30] Marks, who had been trained at a Communist Party school in the USSR, where he had narrowly avoided being a victim of one of Stalin's purges, was elected president. He was a man of great energy, brashness and eloquence, and he attracted large numbers of mineworkers to AMWU. This extract from a police report of a speech he made to mineworkers during the war gives a feel for his political personality:

> the natives were to respect their Compound Managers, but should not be afraid of them. As African people they wanted their rights. They wanted decent wages, food and good accommodation. Some Compound Managers had an oppressive policy. Each time he met a bully Compound Manager he felt like taking his jacket off or kick[ing] him in the backside. The Government believed in cheap native labour. The natives had been robbed of their land and forced to come to the mines. The conditions on the mines were most unattractive and for this the management were responsible. When the Natives stood together they shall get what they want.[31]

As a result of the ANC pressing for a minimum weekly wage of £2, strikes began to break out during the war, not only among mineworkers but also among municipal, railway and dock workers. Smuts, who we have seen was not the greatest fan of strike action, passed the War Measures Act of 1942, which banned strikes and made African strike action punishable by a fine or three years' imprisonment.

Marks(ist) uprising

AMWU would flex its muscle after the war. A meeting was called on Sunday 4 August 1946 at Market Square in Newtown. Police reports claimed that around 1000 miners pitched up to listen to Marks explain that AMWU had asked Smuts for the War Measures Act to be lifted and the Chamber of Mines to raise the minimum wage, but that they had got nowhere. The gathering resolved to go on strike on 12 August. As Marks later stated at his trial:

> I explained to them what a strike would involve, sacrifices would have to be made, to refrain from falling for any provocation, to be non-violent. To do nothing else on the day of the strike but to remain in their rooms. That's what

I put to them. And many other things naturally, as a leader would put to people who are going into battle ... They were ready, they were ripe for it.[32]

On 12 August around 70 000 to 100 000 miners across the Rand downed tools and retired to their compounds. A journalist from the *Rand Daily Mail* reported that he

> found the strikers treating the occasion as a Sunday, except that a few were making purchases at the concession stores. They sat or lay about in blanketed groups, sunning themselves behind compound walls out of the wind. Others strolled along veld paths smoking and talking. At one mine, weekend musical programmes were being given through loudspeakers. Many of the giant sheave wheels which crown the headgears were still. The only signs of abnormal conditions were the frequent lorry-loads of armed police arriving.[33]

Smuts, in his usual manner, dismissed the strike as simply a bunch of agitators against whom 'appropriate action' would be taken. He declared himself 'not unduly concerned' and sent in 1600 armed police to seal off the compounds.

The following day police stormed a meeting between leaders of AMWU and the Council of Non-European Trade Unions, which had agreed to join the strike. Marks was arrested and his offices were raided. Several others were also arrested, including Bill Andrews, Moses Kotane and Betty Sachs, a member of the Communist Party and a Cape Town city councillor (along with Cissie Gool).

On the same day, six strikers were shot dead by police at the Sub-Nigel mine and another six lost their lives in a panicked stampede that followed the shooting. When miners staged an underground 'sitdown strike' the next day, they were baton-charged by police and driven up 'stope by stope, level by level' to the surface, where they were beaten back into the compounds.

Another group of miners staged a march to Johannesburg and were 'dispersed' by the police. As O'Meara puts it: 'Much was made of this march, the Press claiming a profusion of "weapons" indicated an intention to "attack" the city. Yet at the subsequent sedition trial the prosecution could establish no motive other than the desire to recover passes lodged with the Commissioner.'[34]

In total twelve miners were killed and around 1200 injured. Marks and the others were put on trial under the Riotous Assemblies Act and the Native Labour Regulation Act. They were given suspended sentences of nine months.

The toy telephone makes a call

As Z.K. Matthews reports in his autobiography, in the week of the 1946 strike, relations between the government and the NRC 'reached breaking point'. As a result of
the strike, the NRC adjourned to protest the government's 'breach of faith' and
passed, by a large majority, a resolution put to it by the ANC's National Executive:

The ANC
➢ Calls upon all counsellors to attend the meeting convened for
 20 November,
➢ Declares the Native Representation Act of 1936 to be a fraud and
 a means to perpetuate the policy of segregation, oppression and
 humiliation.
➢ Calls upon the African people as a whole to boycott all elections
 under the Act and to struggle for full citizenship.[35]

The NRC was pleasantly surprised when acting prime minister J.H. Hofmeyr, who
had voted against Hertzog's Native Acts in 1936, pitched up to the 20 November
meeting with a prepared statement. But whatever hope they had soon faded.
Hofmeyr put it relatively bluntly that it would not 'be practicable to accede'
to the NRC's request to end the Union's racist laws. This reforming of policy,
Hofmeyr claimed, was neither in white people's nor black people's interests.

Matthews replied directly to Hofmeyr, saying this was

merely an apologia for the status quo, apparently oblivious of the progressive forces at
work not only in the world in general but even
in South Africa itself. The Statement makes
no attempt to deal with some of the burning
questions of the day such as the Pass Laws,
the colour bar in industry, the political rights
of Non-Europeans... In his statement the acting Prime Minister virtually denies that the
native policy of the union is in need of revision
and proceeds to justify the policy of segregation and discrimination on the grounds of its
supposedly protective character.[36]

Z.K. Matthews:
Not simply an academic

He went on to tell Hofmeyr that the NRC was now resolved to ask government to reconsider its position. But they knew the answer. Everybody could now acknowledge the toy telephone in the room. The NRC was effectively over.

The Indian winter of discontent

Smuts and the UP were simply not prepared to offer black people in South Africa further representation. Hofmeyr had already received an early warning shot of just how unpopular even the slightest move by government to acknowledge 'non-European' rights would be.

In 1946 Smuts introduced the Asiatic Land Tenure and Indian Representation bills. The first prohibited Indians from buying land beyond designated areas or without government consent. The second confirmed that Indians in Natal and the Transvaal would not be admitted onto the common voters' roll. Like Hertzog's 'Native Bills', it would permit Indians to elect three white MPs to Parliament and one to the Senate.

Although hardly an act of liberal social reform, the bills were rejected by Malan's HNP and the English-speaking whites of the racist Dominion Party for being too soft. The bills were equally unpopular in the Indian community as they restricted property rights and relegated their franchise aspirations to the bin. After the Act was passed, a day of *hartal* (mourning) was called. A passive resistance campaign would follow.

Two-colour commies

The elections of 1948 were now fast being set up for a repeat of the 1929 'Black Peril' election, except this time Malan's HNP added a 'red menace' too. As they would frame it, the commies were coming to reside under South Africa's carpets with all the other goggas. Ironically, in the 1920s when Malan had attempted to attract white urban Afrikaner workers, he had said that 'Communism in Russia stands for the same things as Nationalism in South Africa'.[37] But since those days, the CPSA had done a full 180, advocating the abolition of the colour bar and the enfranchisement of non-Europeans.

In early 1948 the HNP published a pamphlet titled 'The Communist Danger'. It stated that communists were atheists and believed in miscegenation and were therefore a threat to 'white civilisation and Christianity'. The pamphlet also stated that Smuts and Stalin were 'comrades' (the 'proof' being that the USSR had fought with South Africa against the Nazis). In Parliament in 1947, Malan went on to reveal that minister Harry Lawrence was a patron of an organisation called Friends of the Soviet Union and that ex-mayor of Johannesburg and chairman of the Labour Party Jessie McPherson was a 'well-known communist'. (As an aside, McPherson was the only woman to have been elected mayor of Joburg until 2021.)

The problem with Smuts

Simple bread-and-butter issues were also relevant in the upcoming election. As Saul Dubow reflects, despite the often-noted intelligence of both Smuts and Hofmeyr, the rest of the Smuts government was widely known for its hopeless incompetence. To give one example, in 1947 it was announced in Parliament that 36 000 houses were needed for Europeans, while non-whites required 120 000. The National Housing and Planning Commission was given sixteen months to build 6 000 houses, but by the end of this period they conceded that fewer than half had been completed.[38]

They also admitted that only around 20 000 sub-economic houses had been built for non-whites. As Newell Stultz puts it, Smuts's government also became known for adding 'obnoxious official regulations and controls'.[39] On this were lumped the post-war food shortages and a significant rise in the cost of living.

All the cards were stacking up against Smuts. Even internationally, despite his role in forming the United Nations, he was pilloried for his racist policies and his desperate and illegal attempt to hold on to South-West Africa. Painted locally as both a communist and a capitalist-imperialist, Smuts was run-

J.H. 'Gogga' Hofmeyr

ning out of road. And it's difficult to see just how he could turn the car around. Realising the fix that Smuts was now in, Ernest Malherbe argued that he should court Havenga's Afrikaner Party. But Smuts turned up his nose at this, sniffily stating that they were 'a lot of fascists'. This was of course true, but they were also natural enemies of the Broederbond.

Klasie Havenga looking classy

Malan was quicker to realise what was at stake and proved the more flexible, hooking up with Havenga to form an electoral pact. When Hofmeyr announced in Parliament on 24 March that the election would take place on 26 May, Malan agreed to support the AP candidates in eleven constituencies. Havenga in turn agreed to uphold and promote the policy of something Malan termed 'apartheid'.

Interestingly, Malan also had issues with the AP's ties to the Ossewabrandwag. When OB general B.J. Vorster was put forward as the AP's candidate for Brakpan, Malan vetoed the decision. When John Vorster stood down from the AP and ran as an independent, the AP did not select a candidate to run against him. Vorster lost the seat by only two votes, to the UP's A.E. Trollip. (Trollip would later serve in Vorster's first cabinet.)

Campaign Apartheid

There was no doubt that Malan's HNP had its house in order – by-elections had proven this. And in January 1947, the UP suffered a shocking blow. In a by-election, the party's Sir De Villiers Graaff – godson of Louis Botha, decorated soldier and first-class cricketer – was hit for a six in the Hottentots-Holland constituency by the unheard-of HNP candidate Hendrik van Aardt. Many people put the loss down to a speech Hofmeyr made at a meeting the night before the election, where he had been asked by a Nationalist supporter about what direction he saw the franchise going. It was late in the evening, and Hofmeyr made the fatal error of speaking his mind: 'Natives will eventually be represented in parliament by Natives and Indians by Indians.'[40] Nationalists later heckled Hofmeyr, saying that since he was the reason for Van Aardt's victory, he and not HNP leader Malan should welcome Van Aardt into Parliament.

As opposed to the clown car that UP politics had become, Malan and the Nats had a one-word plan: apartheid. As Krüger puts it, 'the Magic word "Apartheid" suddenly flamed into the headlines as the main election slogan'.[41] It was a new word in a relatively new language, explains Dubow, and Malan 'deployed it for the first time in the South African Parliament' in 1944.[42] Martha Evans points out that as 'a former editor of the Afrikaner nationalist newspaper *Die Burger*, Malan had a talent for encapsulating ideals and coining catchphrases and slogans'.[43] To the voter, 'apartheid' was clear: it was not the stumbling, bumbling, piecemeal, patchwork approach that had characterised Botha, Smuts and even Hertzog's segregation policies – it was total onslaught.

Some suggested at the time that the word was simply old wine in a new bottle. But this old wine had developed a kick like a mule and it produced an ideology as basic as brandy and Coke. Apartheid, Malan argued, meant the following:

> Outlawing of marriages between whites and non-whites; abolition of the Natives Representative Council and African representation in the House of Assembly and the Cape Provincial Council; recognition of Native reserves as the true African 'homelands' and strict control of African influx to the city; segregation of whites and non-whites to the maximum extent possible wherever the two groups necessarily come together; protection of the European workers from the competition of Africans; and disallowance of African trade unions.[44]

Coloureds would be removed from the common voters' roll but would be handed their own toy telephone (i.e. a representative council). They would also be offered some protection from black labour. Startlingly, all Indians resident in South Africa would be 'repatriated' to India and Indian immigration would be halted.

Nat vs. UTD

Malan's HNP campaign was pretty simple: nothing could be easier to understand than their manifesto based on the 'apartheid principle'. On the other hand, the UP's 'weary, stale, flat and unprofitable' manifesto was far more a dog's breakfast than the dog's bollocks.[45] It stated that it stood for 'the maintenance of white civilisation in the way of life known as Western democracy with unswerving opposition to fascism, Nazism, communism and all the other forms of undemocratic government',[46] and its object was to 'achieve national unity'. It wanted the enlargement of the existing NRC and the recognition of the coloured people as an 'appendage' of the European community. Smuts would go on to publish a propaganda pamphlet titled *Election News* in which he stated:

> The United Party differs from the Nationalist Party in that it does not arrogate to itself the power or the knowledge to lay down the policy for all time. It will do its best to lay a firm foundation for the future … but cannot entail the future. Generations to come will decide their own policy, and it would be folly for us today to impede what will be their great experience and riper judgement.

As Welsh notes, 'this was not a stirring call to the blood'.[47]

Smuts had accepted the report of the Fagan Commission's findings, which declared '[t]he idea of total segregation … utterly impracticable'. But the HNP spat this out like *pruimtabak* and instead created their own commission. Headed by Paul Sauer and backed by little social science or statistical data, its report came up with far more dramatic solutions and more easily digestible soundbites. Sauer recommended 'total separation', 'elimination of miscegenation', and the creation of both black and white separate tribal 'volk-communities'. What Sauer created with three other politicians and one cleric was *melktert* in the apartheid sky. But as Welsh suggests, it would become the blueprint for both petit and grand apartheid.

In the lead-up to the election, Smuts and the UP attacked the HNP's war record. In return, the HNP opened a broadside of liquid manure on almost every issue, both real and imaginary. Smuts was a communist, a capitalist, a liberal democrat, a supporter of the black franchise, a traitor, a jingo and a handmaiden of the British Empire. However ludicrous and factually inaccurate the depictions, the shit stuck. Malan, a dour, unsmiling man, campaigned like his political life depended on it. In Paarl on 29 March, two months before the election, he hit his straps with 'a terrifying outline of a policy of social engineering',[48] stating:

> We can act in only one of two directions. Either we must follow the course of equality, which must eventually mean national suicide for the White race, or we must take the course of apartheid through which the character and the future of every race will be protected and safeguarded with full opportunities for development and self-maintenance in their own ideas, without the interests of one clashing with the interests of the other, and without one regarding

the development of the other as undermining or a threat to himself. The party therefore undertakes to protect the White race properly and effectively against any policy, doctrine or attack which might undermine or threaten its continued existence.[49]

The gogga in the ointment

And then there was the man characterised as a 'gogga': J.H. Hofmeyr. And 'Gogga' had that worst of all things: liberal views. Despite his *bloubloed* Afrikaner heritage, he was singled out for a torrent of foul language and was often openly referred to as 'the arch-K*****boetie of the UP'.[50] On 20 April Malan stated in Paarl that 'a vote for Smuts was a vote for Hofmeyr'.

Hofmeyr was then 'caught out' in Parliament suggesting that white supremacy could not last. This, coupled with his comments in Hottentots-Holland in 1947 and other liberal parliamentary slips of the tongue, was enough for the HNP. If Smuts could be a communist, then Hofmeyr could certainly be painted as a 'gogga' 'K*****boetie'. And as Davenport points out, the Nationalist press was far better at spreading its poisonous and skewed message than the liberal newspapers ever were.

Still, the naive liberal press were generally quietly optimistic that Smuts would pull off another victory. A correspondent for the London *Times* was a tinge more realistic. On the day of the election, he wrote: 'There are strong hopes for General Smuts, but lessons of unexpected results elsewhere have been well learned.'[51]

The ghost of 1910

Hopes for a Smuts victory lasted one more day as the results dribbled in from the platteland. On the morning of the 28th all was clear: Malan and his party had won, increasing their seats from forty-eight to seventy. Havenga's AP also won nine seats, giving the HNP–AP coalition a majority of five over the UP–LP coalition. Smuts's defeat at his seat in Standerton by the almost-unheard-of W.C. du Plessis by 3750 votes to 3535 was humiliating. Du Plessis, it turned out, was a civil servant who had been dismissed by Smuts's government in 1945 for refusing to resign from the Broederbond. As Smuts lamented, 'to think I have been defeated by the Broederbond'.[52] According to the *Rand Daily*

Smuts painted in 1953 after his death
(both real and political)

Mail, sixty-three of the ninety-two HNP candidates who ran for Parliament were known Broeders. C.M. Abbott, who had won by the largest majority in South African electoral history, offered Smuts his seat in Sea Point, but Smuts declined the offer.

As Stultz writes, 'Smuts's political humiliation was complete, but Malan's victory was far from overwhelming.'[53] In fact, the UP won the popular vote by over 120 000 votes. This was the legacy of the 1910 delimitation agreement that Smuts and others had so foolishly concocted. As Roger Southall puts it:

The imbalanced result was an outcome of two principal factors. The first was the practice of the Delimitation Commission ... This meant that fewer votes were needed to win seats in rural areas (where, on the whole, Afrikaners predominated) than in urban ones, a factor which favoured the NP. Second, the high rate of migration of whites from rural to urban areas during the 1930s and 1940s was largely a migration of Afrikaners, thus swelling the NP-leaning vote in a significant number of urban constituencies.[54]

As Kenneth Heard calculated, to win one seat the UP had to attract on average 9 124 voters while the HNP needed only 5 683. When the scores were tallied up the results were as follows:

Party[55]	Votes	%	Seats	+/–
United Party	524 230	49.18	65	−24
Herenigde Nasionale Party	401 834	37.70	70	+27
Afrikaner Party	41 885	3.93	9	+9
Labour Party	27 360	2.57	6	−3
Independents	70 662	6.63	0	−2
Native Representative Members		.	3	0
Total	1 065 971	100.00	153	

Hard to believe these were the winners: Strijdom, Malan and Sauer

Although it might be a fool's game to imagine just what might have happened if the black franchise had been retained in the Cape and the franchise had been extended to coloured women, it is worth noting that the UP lost heavily in many rural areas in the Cape. Uitenhage and Vryburg, both places where the black vote had once been meaningful and could sway outcomes, fell to the HNP. And across the western Cape, the UP was devastated in areas where the weight of the coloured vote had been halved. In the Kimberley district seat, an area that in times past had been decided by the black and coloured vote, the HNP won by a mere fifty-seven votes: 4153 to 4096.

Welsh points out that only one-third of coloured males who were eligible to vote in the Cape had registered. This was partly because it was not compulsory for coloureds to register, while it was for whites. Another ironic factor was that the Indian community boycotted the limited representation Smuts had offered them. This would have given an anti-HNP coalition another three seats in the House of Assembly. What's more, if Smuts had bothered to answer the toy telephone that was the NRC and given them the extra ten seats they had asked for in

1943, the UP may well have had enough seats in Parliament to avert the disaster that befell them and South Africa.

But, to be fair, who knows what the white sentiment may have been if these things had come to pass. Smuts may well have suffered a worse defeat with a white populace furious at his concessions. It is simply not possible to say.

Smuts had made his bed and would now go to sleep in it. Malan and his Broederbond friends with their slogan of 'apartheid' had won the day, and it would slowly also win the hearts and minds of a white majority. On 1 June 1948, Malan gave his first speech as victor: 'In the past we felt like strangers in our own country, but today South Africa belongs to us once more ... May God grant that it always remains our own.'[56]

CHAPTER 9

THE REPUBLIC
OF VERWOERD
1960 and 1966

*'The English-speaking vote is, in ever increasing strength,
and more and more openly, aligning itself with the Government policies.'*
– H.F. Verwoerd[1]

Murderer and murdered

'MR VERWOERD COULD NOT LOSE this election if he tries' was the
Sunday Tribune's pronouncement in the lead-up to the 1966 election. If
mainstream white politics had ever flirted with liberal ideas in South Africa, that
time had passed. The James Rose Inneses, Henry Burtons, John X. Merrimans
and J.H. Hofmeyrs had been replaced by one diminutive woman from Houghton
in Johannesburg, and that was it. The 1966 election would in real terms turn out
to be a battle between the National Party (the H was dropped from the HNP after
it officially merged with the Afrikaner Party in 1951) and a progressively reactionary United Party to see who could be the most racist. And they gave each other
some pretty stiff competition.

Flying on a right-wing and a prayer

Between 1948 and 1960 a lot of dirty water had passed under the South African
bridge. As William Beinart puts it, Malan and his HNP built their policy of
apartheid 'on the foundations of the segregationist legacy laid by Rhodes and
Milner, Kruger and Shepstone, Hertzog and Smuts'.[2] But the Nats were in many
ways playing in a different league.

Malan and the HNP had passed a truly staggering amount of racial legisla-
tion in a very short period: the Mixed Marriages Act (1949), the Immorality Act
(1950), the Population Registration Act (1950), the Group Areas Act (1950), the
Suppression of Communism Act (1950) and the Prevention of Illegal Squatting
Act (1951). Another nail in the coffin was when Malan's HNP, disregarding the
Constitution, which demanded a two-thirds majority of a joint sitting of Parliament and the Senate, passed the Separate Representation of Voters Act (1951).
This law attempted to remove, with a simple parliamentary majority, coloured
voters from the common voters' role. But when four coloured men took the Act
to the Appeal Court, the liberal judges Albert Centlivres and Oliver Schreiner
(son of W.P. and nephew of Olive) judged the Act to be unconstitutional.

For the apartheid government, the gloves were now off. With the passing of
the Appellate Division Quorum Act (1955), they increased the size of the Appeal
Court as well as the number of judges who would sit on constitutional cases. As
Judge Dennis Davis and Michelle le Roux write, 'the government now moved
decisively to pack the court with judges made in its own political image'.[3] Five
judges who were politically compliant with the apartheid regime were accordingly appointed to the court.

But the Nats still needed to deal with the issue of attaining a two-thirds majority. And the Senate Act (1955) did just this, increasing the size of the Senate while ensuring that the NP would be able to elect a majority of the senators. After the bill was enacted, the Senate was dissolved and an electoral college vote was held. As Ian Loveland writes, 'as might have been expected, the result of the election was that the new senate contained an overwhelming majority of Nationalist members'.[4]

The NP miraculously increased their control of the Senate from 25 per cent to 87 per cent, and with this attained a two-thirds majority in a joint sitting of both houses. It was a shocking misrepresentation of their actual support: in the 1953 general election, the NP had only just scraped the popular vote, winning 49 per cent to the United Party's 48 per cent.

There was very little that could be done when the Senate Act was taken to the now packed-and-captured Appeal Court. Even liberal Chief Justice Centlivres capitulated, siding almost inexplicably with the government appointees. Only Oliver Schreiner refused to go along with the NP's political manipulations, writing a dissenting judgment.

Emboldened by their victories, the NP's white supremacy swept through the country like a virus. Alarmed and desperate, a large movement of ex-servicemen who had fought in North Africa and Italy formed an organisation called the Torch Commando, under the leadership of the pilot and war hero Adolph 'Sailor' Malan. In 1951 the Torch Commando staged various marches in Cape Town and Johannesburg to protest the direction D.F. Malan was taking South Africa in. But when the United Party, which they backed, lost the election in 1953, and after one of their marches turned violent, the Torch Commando collapsed – and with it organised popular white opposition to apartheid.

To add another blow beneath the belt, Malan, in an act of total disregard for the black people of South Africa, appointed H.F. Verwoerd as the minister of native affairs. Verwoerd in turn packed his department with Broederbonders. With these zealots in control, they managed to pass a raft of legislation, including the Native Laws Amendment Act (1952), which required all blacks to carry 'reference books'. A year later the Bantu Education Act was pushed through, which cancelled all funding to mission schools.

As Beinart writes, 'Education at the 5000 or so mission schools had produced, in the Nationalist eyes, an academic training with too much emphasis on

English and dangerous liberal ideas. It was seen as the foundation of an African elite that claimed recognition in a common society.'[5] Or, as the liberal senator Edgar Brookes put it, 'All these happy things have passed. Butchered to make an ideologist's holiday, the old missionary schools and colleges have, with a very few exceptions, gone.'[6]

Under Verwoerd's new system, all black children would be taught in their native language until the age of thirteen. Once suitably divided from each other and denied proficiency in a lingua franca, they would be allowed to learn 'technical subjects' from a government-controlled syllabus in English or Afrikaans (if they hadn't been forced by circumstance to leave school by then).

The resistance to passivity

Targeting the mission schools made political sense. They had, after all, educated many of the people who were and would be the most critical of and troublesome to apartheid: Dube, Plaatje, Seme, the Msimang brothers, A.B. Xuma, Z.K. Matthews, Albert Luthuli, Anton Lembede, Nelson Mandela, Oliver Tambo, Robert Sobukwe and Steve Biko were all educated at mission schools in the Cape and Natal.

Without the missionaries, the ANC would never have taken the form it did. But it is also fair to say that it was in many ways their missionary education that held the ANC back. The missions preached the word of non-violence and were generally against forms of protest that might destabilise the country. As president-general of the ANC, Dr Xuma had managed to pull the organisation out from the morass it had found itself in in the late 1930s. But he still had the traditionally cautious approach of many of his predecessors. Xuma, however, developed ties with the white communists of the CPSA and encouraged a young group of activists including Mandela, Sisulu and Tambo to develop new ANC policies. In doing this, Xuma ushered in his own demise. Although these young men admired Xuma, they all realised that the elitist non-confrontational approach the ANC had adopted had to change.

Xuma was voted out in 1949, at the same time as the Congress's Youth League was pushing for what they called a 'Programme of Action' that would include mass protests, boycotts and passive resistance. Mandela was initially sceptical of joining forces with radical whites, Indians and communists. But with Sisulu's influence, he slowly came around to the idea of multiracial collaboration. Against a backdrop of growing racial legislation, the ANC and the South African Indian Congress embarked on a defiance campaign.

The campaign was launched on 26 June 1952. Mandela, J.B. Marks, Yusuf Dadoo, Ismail Cachalia and Sisulu spearheaded the protests, marching into white areas, in the spirit of Gandhi's *satyagraha*, without their 'reference books' (which had become known as passes). By the end of the campaign, around 8 500 people had been arrested for breaking apartheid regulations. In the latter months, riots broke out in various cities, leading to the deaths of around forty people. As a result, the protests slowly lost momentum. Albert Luthuli, now the president-general of the ANC, denied that any violence had been instigated by the Congress Alliance, arguing that it was not in their interests to do so. Why, he argued, would they incite white violence against themselves? They were unarmed, unlike the whites, and provoking a violent response would allow the apartheid government to suppress them by force. Provoking violence, Luthuli maintained, would only allow Malan's government to gain an iron grip over the country.

Chartering the flight to freedom

In 1955 the Congress of the People, organised by Matthews, gathered together the African National Congress and its partners, the Indian Congress, the Coloured People's Organisation and the white Congress of Democrats, at Kliptown in Soweto. There they adopted the Freedom Charter, agreeing that

> We, the People of South Africa, declare for all our country and the world to know: that South Africa belongs to all who live in it, black and white, and that no government can justly claim authority unless it is based on the will of all the people; that our people have been robbed of their birthright to land, liberty and peace by a form of government founded on injustice and inequality; that our country will never be prosperous or free until all our people live in brotherhood, enjoying equal rights and opportunities; that only a democratic state, based on the will of all the people, can secure to all their birthright without distinction of colour, race, sex or belief...

The Charter endorsed a non-racial democracy, equal opportunities for all and the redistribution of wealth. On the last day of the congress, a contingent of police arrived with Sten guns to break up the meeting.

On 5 December 1956, 156 members associated with the Freedom Charter were arrested in dawn raids and imprisoned in the Johannesburg Fort on charges of high treason under the Suppression of Communism Act. Those held included the ANC's Luthuli, Mandela, Sisulu and Lilian Ngoyi, the Indian Congress's Dadoo and Ahmed Kathrada, and members of the (communist) Congress of Democrats Joe Slovo, Helen Joseph, Ruth First and Rusty Bernstein. What followed, as Rodney Davenport puts it, 'was one of the longest and largest trials in the history of mankind'.[7]

As Saul Dubow writes, the accused were 'a racially mixed and ideologically diverse convocation'.[8] And it was this diversity that several in the ANC began to question. There had always been a division within the Youth League with regards to consorting with white communists and Indians; the 'Africanists' in the league often spoke of this element as 'foreign' and their ideologies as 'un-African'. During the time of the seemingly interminable Treason Trial, a group under the leadership of Robert Sobukwe broke away from the ANC to form the Pan Africanist Congress (PAC). Their politics would be more closely linked to the anti-colonial movements sweeping through Africa, such as Kwame Nkrumah's in Ghana.

After this breakaway, the ANC believed that they now had to act on a national level in a show of strength that would nullify the growing support for the PAC. At a meeting in Durban in 1959, the ANC decided to hold a nationwide protest of the pass laws on 31 March the following year. However, the PAC pre-empted this and organised their own demonstrations for 21 March. Across the country, PAC-supporting demonstrators arrived at police stations without their passbooks and offered themselves up for arrest.

As Albert Luthuli stood in the witness box during the Treason Trial explaining the ANC's commitment to non-violence, news began to filter through that a massacre had taken place at Sharpeville. Sixty-nine demonstrators had been killed and 186 injured when police opened fire on what was a noisy, but not hostile, crowd. Many of the dead and injured had been shot in the back while fleeing the scene. On the same day, at a PAC demonstration in Langa, Cape Town, police charged a crowd of around 10 000 people, killing three and injuring forty-seven.

A clause for Sobukwe

Sobukwe before being subordinated by his clause

On the morning of the Sharpeville massacre, Robert Sobukwe had led a march to Orlando police station. There he entered the charge office and offered himself up to Captain J.J. de Wet Steyn, stating that he did not have his passbook with him. Captain Steyn initially told him to leave the station and stop wasting his time. But when Sobukwe stayed outside the station with the other protestors, he was arrested for 'incitement'. At the time the massacre occurred, Sobukwe had been locked in a cell for several hours.

Sobukwe was sentenced to three years in jail. After finishing this stint, mainly at Pretoria Central Prison, he was detained under an amendment to the Suppression of Communism Act that would become known as 'the Sobukwe Clause'. He was then transported to Robben Island, where he was imprisoned in isolation in a small warder's cottage for an unprecedented six years without trial.

In the days after Sharpeville, Verwoerd declared a state of emergency – during which over 11 500 people of all races were arrested – and, after the passing of the Unlawful Organisations Act on 8 April, the ANC and PAC were banned. What was more, the security branch of the police was strengthened and Ossewabrandwag old boy B.J. Vorster was appointed minister of justice.

Pratt and Paul

On 9 April 1960 Verwoerd made his first appearance since declaring the state of emergency after Sharpeville. At the Rand Show in Johannesburg, he wandered around the exhibitions and gave a speech about South Africa's willingness to cooperate with the rest of the world (just how long they would want to cooperate with him was another question). After Verwoerd sat down at the podium, a wealthy trout farmer by the name of David Pratt strolled up, pulled out a

.22 revolver and shot him twice in the head. Verwoerd was rushed to hospital in a critical condition but managed to survive, largely due to the gun's low calibre.

Pratt was arrested but would not stand trial because authorities classified him 'insane'. He is believed to have committed suicide a year later, although some people question

Verwoerd shot in the head but not dead

whether this was in fact the case. What does seem certain is that Pratt attempted to assassinate Verwoerd because he believed that apartheid was evil.

While Verwoerd was in hospital, Paul Sauer acted as prime minister and called for major policy changes. As he stated, 'the old book of South African history was now closed'. But when Verwoerd emerged from hospital, he snatched back the government from Sauer with an iron grip. Senior cabinet ministers lived in fear of Verwoerd and did little to stop the almost complete domination he had over them.

Verwoerd's Republic

After being released from hospital, Verwoerd was eager to put his long-desired apartheid and republican plans into overdrive, contrary to the wishes of many of his colleagues. He had long dreamt of making South Africa into an ideal Boer republic, along the lines of Kruger's ZAR. In fact, as far back as 1941, Verwoerd had drawn up a draft republican constitution with several other right-wing academics, which was published in his newspaper, *Die Transvaler*, in January the following year. The Boer republics were at the centre of this constitution – Verwoerd and his *tjommies* even intended to replace the South African tricolour flag with the ZAR's Vierkleur. As Verwoerd's biographer Henry Kenney states, he would later try to distance himself from this early draft, but 'there can be no doubt the final document represented his own thinking at the time'.[9]

The draft certainly makes for interesting reading:

The public tone of life of the Republic is Christian-National ... The propaga-tion of any State policy and the existence of any political organisation which is in strife with the fulfilling of this Christian National vocation of the life of the people is forbidden ...

[The prime minister is to be appointed by the state president] and the State President is further directly and only responsible to God and over against the people for his deeds in fulfilment of his duties ... he is altogether independent of any vote in Parliament ... The State President decides on all laws, which can only become valid by his personal signature ...

Afrikaans, as the language of the original white inhabitants of the country, will be the first official language, English will be regarded as a second or sup-plementary official language which will be treated on an equal footing and will enjoy equal rights, freedom, and privileges with the first official language, everywhere and whenever such treatment is judged by the State authority to be in the best interests of the State and its inhabitants ...

Individual citizens as well as the organs of public opinion, such as the existence of parties, the radio, the Press, and the cinema, whilst their rightful freedom of expression, including criticism of government policy, will be pro-tected, shall not be allowed, by their actions to undermine the public order or good morale of the Republic internally or externally ...[10]

As Brian Bunting puts it, a great deal of apartheid legislation was foreshadowed in the draft constitution, such as 'the Immorality and Mixed Marriages Acts, the establishment of Bantustans and the Coloured and Indian Councils, job reservation, decimal coinage, Press control and censorship, the Suppression of Communism Act, bannings, Group Areas, control of trade unions'.[11]

It took Verwoerd only four months after coming to power in September 1958 (following J.G. Strijdom's death) to make it clear that he had every intention of organising a referendum on the republican issue. Interestingly, Strijdom had believed that a vote of 50 per cent plus one was not enough to drag South Africa into a republic, deeming that such a decision could only be based on 'a broad basis of the people's will'.[12] Verwoerd tossed this idea to the wind: he was more than willing to accept a simple majority.

On 20 January 1960 Verwoerd announced in Parliament that he intended to hold a whites-only referendum on the issue. Coloured people had of course been removed from the common voters' roll, and Verwoerd argued they had no real historical interest in the republican debate. This was nonsense on stilts, but Verwoerd ploughed on, arguing that black voters would soon have their own representation and independence with the formation of the Bantustans; that is to say, they too had no skin in the game.

Some more oxygen was added to Verwoerd's republican aspirations when, on 3 February 1960, British prime minister Harold Macmillan delivered his 'Wind of Change' speech in South African Parliament. Macmillan declared:

> The wind of change is blowing through this continent and, whether we like it or not, this growth of national consciousness is a political fact. We must all accept it as a fact, and our national policies must take account of it.
>
> In this context we think first of Asia and then of Africa. As I have said, the growth of national consciousness in Africa is a political fact, and we must accept it as such. That means, I would judge, that we must come to terms with it. I sincerely believe that if we cannot do so we may imperil the precarious balance between the East and West on which the peace of the world depends.
>
> As I see it, the great issue in this second half of the twentieth century is whether the uncommitted peoples of Asia and Africa will swing to the East or to the West. Will they be drawn into the Communist camp? Or will the great experiments of self-government that are now being made in Asia and Africa, especially within the Commonwealth, prove so successful, and by their example so compelling, that the balance will come down in favour of freedom and order and justice?
>
> The struggle is joined, and it is a struggle for the minds of men. What is now on trial is much more than our military strength or our diplomatic and administrative skill. It is our way of life. The uncommitted nations want to

see before they choose. What can we show them to help them choose right? Each of the independent members of the Commonwealth must answer that question for itself. It is a basic principle of our modern Commonwealth that we respect each other's sovereignty in matters of internal policy. At the same time we must recognise that in this shrinking world in which we live today the internal policies of one nation may have effects outside it.[13]

Verwoerd is said to have been infuriated by the speech, which acknowledged the inevitability of African independence and faced up to the fact that white rule across the continent was over. But he was perhaps also in some sense motivated by it. If the wind of change that was sweeping through Africa was one inspired by nationalism and independence then, by God, why should that not be true of the Afrikaner nation?

On 11 March the Referendum Bill was introduced in the House of Assembly. All opposition parties, as well as the native and coloured representatives, opposed it on the grounds that the referendum would be confined to white voters. The United Party under De Villiers Graaff suggested that coloured voters should participate, while the Progressive Party members and Margaret Ballinger (a native representative and member of the Liberal Party) demanded that black and Indian voters also 'be given the opportunity of expressing their point of view'.[14]

Two liberal white women

In 1959 eleven men and one woman broke away from the United Party to form the Progressive Party. The woman was of course none other than the indefatigable Helen Suzman. What initiated the split in the United Party was the issue of the Bantustans. In a highly contentious debate, it became clear to the party's more liberal members that their leaders were trying 'to outbid the Nationalists in racism by rejecting the purchase of more land for Africans'.[15] At the United Party's congress in August 1959, the conservatives, who outnumbered the liberals, took to shouting down and booing the likes of Colin Eglin and Suzman whenever they rose to speak. The call of 'k*****boetie' was often raised and Suzman was verbally abused and laughed at. As the congress became more acrimonious, Suzman stormed out of the hall, stating to a *Rand Daily Mail* reporter: 'That's it, I am out.'[16]

With the financial backing of Harry Oppenheimer, Suzman, Eglin, Zach de Beer and nine others formed the Progressive Party. The new party's twelve MPs

Helen of Houghton

had all been voted in as United Party members, and all but Suzman would lose their seats in the 1961 election, leaving her the lone voice sounding against apartheid from within the parliamentary chamber until 1974.

In many ways Suzman took this mantle from Margaret Ballinger, who had been elected as native representative to Parliament in 1937. Ballinger had begun her working life teaching history at Rhodes University and Wits. In 1935 her academic career came to an end when Wits terminated her services due to her 'radical' liberalism. In 1937 the ANC nominated her to contest the Eastern Cape seat that would elect one of three white native representatives to Parliament. The ANC's secretary-general, J.A. Calata, went to Joburg specifically to convince her to stand. As some of the black voters who voted for her were quoted as saying, 'Queen Victoria gave us the vote – Men took it away – perhaps a woman will restore it to us.'[17]

In her early years in Parliament, Ballinger attempted to use reason to persuade her fellow MPs that change was necessary. In her maiden speech she called for a more equitable wage for black, coloured and Indian workers, stating this was not simply a moral question but also a practical one. She argued for 'the raising of the non-European wage level as the only guarantee that there will be a steady rise in the European wage level'. And in 1944 she stood up to contend that 'European prestige could not be maintained by falling back continually on the bludgeon.'[18]

When Malan's government took power, Ballinger changed tack, describing apartheid as 'a lunatic policy expressed in lunatic legislation'.[19] She would go on to be elected leader of the Liberal Party, which was formed after the failure of the United Party to defeat the Nats in the 1953 election. The Liberal Party attempted to form the first truly non-racial political movement in South Africa (the Congress Alliance was at the time racially divided into the ANC, the Indian Congress and the (white) Congress of Democrats).

Like Suzman and the Progressive Party, Ballinger and the Liberals believed

in and argued for the Cape liberal qualified black franchise based on property and education. But in 1960 the Liberal Party changed its position, calling for 'the right of franchise on the common roll to all adult persons'.[20] Despite this, Ballinger remained in the party, unlike some of the other members who jumped ship to the all-white Progressives. That year, Verwoerd's government abolished the 1936 Representation of Natives Act, effectively ending Ballinger's career in Parliament. This silenced one of the few voices standing against racism in an all-white Parliament.

Ballinger the white black representative

Ja-nee

Verwoerd knew that with the referendum he was in for the political fight of his life. The Nats had a tenuous relationship with the popular vote, having only ever won a majority in the 1958 election. On 21 March Verwoerd announced to Parliament that if they did indeed lose the referendum, the decision would in any case 'be taken by the majority in the Parliament elected for that purpose'.[21] Verwoerd knew that it would be so tight that he would almost certainly lose if he proposed anything as radical as the 1941 draft constitution. He would have to curry favour in some manner with not only the English, but also those Afrikaners who believed in the now well-established white 'democracy'.

With this in mind, Verwoerd proposed that in the republic the British monarch would be replaced as head of state by a president, but that the president would not be the head of the government. That is, the established white democracy under an elected prime minister would be maintained. More importantly, Verwoerd would make a considerable effort to woo what English-speakers he could. He reassured them that the status of English as an official language would be upheld and that he would attempt to keep South Africa within the Commonwealth.

Of course, it would not be a South African election if fear and race were not thrown into the mix. The wind of independence blowing in Africa had brought

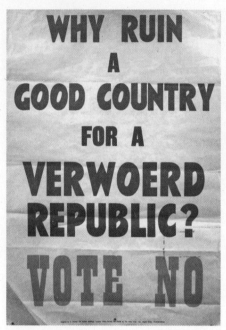

A poster for the campaign against Verwoerd's republic

with it concomitant violence and instability. The chaos and murder that had ensued when Belgium withdrew from Congo was the perfect straw man to animate before the eyes of the *swart gevaar* conspiracy theorists. The popular slogan for the republican campaign became 'Ons republiek nou, om Suid-Afrika blank te hou' (Our republic now, to keep South Africa white).

Even the opposition engaged in race-baiting. Anti-republicans spread the fear that Verwoerd and his segregationist Bantustan policies would ultimately lead to the creation of 'Congostans' in South Africa. As the *Rand Daily Mail* would put it in the lead-up to the vote: 'The whole republican referendum is reduced to the simple question of whether you want your daughter to marry an African, or, more to the point, be ravished by a Congolese soldier.'[22]

On 5 October 1960, the yes/no question 'Are you in favour of a Republic for the Union?' was finally put to white voters in South Africa and South-West Africa. Seemingly, SWA had been added to help ensure a Verwoerd victory. What is also said to have helped the 'yes' vote was the recent lowering of the voting age from twenty-one to eighteen. On the eve of the election, Verwoerd declared that even if he had a majority of one person, the Union would become a republic.

An unprecedented 90 per cent of registered white voters turned up at the polls in what was perhaps the first true gauge of exactly what proportion of the white population in South Africa supported the Nats and their policies. And although the initial (mostly urban) count favoured the 'no' vote, as the ballot boxes rattled in from the platteland, the defeat of the coalition of the United, Progressive and Liberal Parties was confirmed, with 52.14 per cent voting 'yes'. The Cape, Orange Free State and Transvaal provinces and the protectorate of SWA all had a majority 'yes' vote. Only the largely English-speaking province of Natal voted a resounding 'no'.

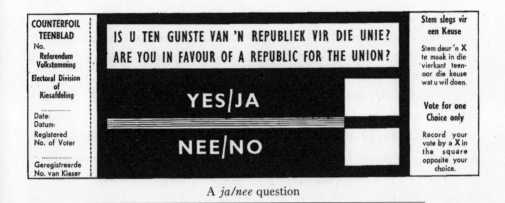

A *ja/nee* question

The final tally (which excluded 7 436 spoilt ballots) revealed the following:[23]

Province	For a republic	Against a republic
Cape	271 418	269 784
Transvaal	406 632	325 041
Natal	42 299	135 598
Orange Free State	110 171	33 438
South-West Africa	19 938	12 017
Total	850 459	775 878

A draft constitution was drawn up, which Saunders and Davenport point out 'bore little resemblance to a traditional Boer Republican constitution or to the draft of 1941'.[24] As they observe, the new constitution was almost a carbon copy of the South Africa Act it replaced – constitutionally speaking, Verwoerd achieved very little in this lengthy and divisive process. The only real change was simply that the head of state was to be a state president, replacing both the governor-general and the British monarch. And much like the latter, the president would not wield any significant political power – although he did get to dress up in a snappy little outfit featuring a top hat and satin sash directly modelled on those worn by Oom Paul.

Just what plans Verwoerd had for the future of South African democracy within this new republic are not entirely clear. Verwoerd's biographer J.J.J. Scholtz claimed that Verwoerd told him he planned to make South Africa an 'executive presidency', where the state president would have political control over Parliament. This certainly seems very much in line with not only his 1941 draft constitution, but also with what he had always openly desired.

This executive presidency never happened, but what the republic did bring was a closer relationship between the Nats and some of the English-speaking population. Many of those who feared the independence movements in Africa and who had resented Macmillan's speech now fell into the racist-loving arms of the National Party. Knowing that he needed their support if he was to further his political objectives, Verwoerd brought into his cabinet two English-speakers, Frank Waring and A.E. Trollip. As David Welsh puts it, 'The [referendum] victory, his apparent omniscience as a leader, and his miraculous survival of an assassination attempt on 9 April 1960, all contributed to virtual deification by his supporters, now including a growing number of English-speakers'.[25]

True to his word to these English supporters, Verwoerd did try to stay in the

The first republican cabinet: Same okes plus two *rooinekke* and one new sash

Commonwealth. On 13 March 1961, just two months before South Africa became a republic, he informed the other Commonwealth prime ministers in London of his wish to remain a member. Many African leaders, as well as those of India and Canada, were appalled by the prospect and raised serious objections. After some back and forth, it seemed like a solution to the impasse had been reached. However, as Thula Simpson reveals, 'several leaders objected that it was insufficient, with at least half vowing to raise apartheid at every future Commonwealth meeting. Following a short adjournment, Verwoerd returned and announced the withdrawal of the application.'[26]

Despite Verwoerd's defeat on the world stage, or maybe because of it (the arrogant and blinkered narrative of white South Africa against the rest of the world was fast developing), Verwoerd arrived back at Jan Smuts Airport to a hero's welcome.

When South Africa was declared a republic on 31 May 1961, Verwoerd had removed the final handbrake to putting into action his policies of grand apartheid.

The Long Fight for Freedom marches on

On 29 March 1961 three Supreme Court judges acquitted the remaining accused in the Treason Trial, because there was no evidence that their aim was to overthrow the state by violence. Later that year, Albert Luthuli won the Nobel Peace Prize for his commitment to non-violence. But the ANC was beginning to realise that it had run out of non-violent road. Sabotage targeting government buildings and installations (while taking care to avoid civilian casualties) was now being seriously considered. On 16 December 1961 (aka Dingane's Day), Umkhonto we Sizwe (MK) was officially launched. This provoked Vorster to put forward the Sabotage Act (1962), which made all sabotage a treasonable offence punishable by hanging.

The year after the Sabotage Act was passed, MK decided to move towards guerrilla activities rather than simply sabotage. But the operation, codenamed 'Mayibuye', came to an abrupt halt when security police raided a small farm named Liliesleaf in Rivonia on the afternoon of 11 July 1963. There they arrested many of the members of MK's high command. Mandela, who was already imprisoned, stood trial with ten others on counts of sabotage and several other offences. After an eighty-six-day trial, eight of the accused narrowly escaped the death sentence, instead receiving life imprisonment. Rusty Bernstein and James Kantor were acquitted due to a lack of evidence. Bob Hepple agreed to turn state witness, but once released he escaped the country with the help of Bram Fischer, the accuseds' lawyer.

As David Welsh puts it, the Rivonia Trial 'ripped the heart out of MK [and] marked the end of an era of resistance politics and the beginning of a new era in law enforcement'.[27]

ARMed and unready

On 4 July 1964, the Newlands flat of a young Liberal Party member named Adrian Leftwich was raided by security police. The raid seems to have been an act of simple-minded intimidation by the cops, with no real aim other than to put the wind up liberals. Although Leftwich believed his flat to be clean, while rifling through books the security police discovered pages that gave details of a clandestine bombing campaign.

Leftwich and his girlfriend, Lynette van der Riet, were arrested. Van der Riet was severely beaten and tortured. Leftwich broke after a few punches to the stomach, spilling the beans on the saboteur group calling themselves the African Resistance Movement (ARM). The list of names he provided included his best friend, Hugh Lewin, and around fifty others. Twenty-nine members of ARM were arrested in the following weeks, while around thirty managed to escape.

John Harris and his wife, Anne

One member who had not been identified by Leftwich was John Harris, a newish recruit to a cell group Leftwich knew little about. Desperate to show the apartheid government that ARM was still active, Harris planted a bomb in Johannesburg Central Railway Station on 24 July. This despite the fact that ARM had always refused to target installations where human casualties were possible. Harris called the railway station, the police and two newspapers, demanding that the station be cleared, but nothing was done. The bomb went off, injuring twenty-four people. One elderly lady later died of her burn wounds, and five were left badly scarred for life. Harris was tried and hanged; the only white man executed for anti-apartheid activities.

Of the twenty-nine arrested members of ARM, fourteen were given prison sentences. Whites were sent to Pretoria Central, while the only coloured member, Eddie Daniels, was sent to Robben Island for fifteen years. Leftwich, Van der Riet and another member, John Lloyd, acted as state witnesses against their friends and were later allowed to leave South Africa. Leftwich and Lloyd went on to have successful careers in the UK. During the trial, the judge famously stated that calling Leftwich 'a rat was hard on rats'.[28]

Cordoning off the road to freedom

By 1964 much of the leadership of anti-apartheid movements – from the ANC to the communists, the Liberals and the PAC – had been imprisoned, banned or had fled the country. Verwoerd and his NP *tjommies* would then pass the Criminal Procedure Amendment Bill, which introduced a clause that would effectively allow the state to hold people for 180 days without trial.

In the months leading up to the 1966 election, a staggering number of people of all races were imprisoned, on trial, detained or banned. These included the likes of Bram Fischer, Helen Joseph and Alex la Guma. Seemingly, the only people left relatively free in the anti-apartheid movement were Alan Paton, Margaret Ballinger and Edgar Brookes of the Liberal Party. In March of 1966, Brookes, writing in *Liberal Opinion*, stated:

> The Liberal Party in South Africa has reached its nadir. Repeated bannings have deprived us of the instructed manpower which we have built up and through which we were able to keep in touch with country branches. Never have there been so many of our members under restriction as at the present time. With the General Election only a few weeks away from us we have regretfully had to abandon the idea of putting up even one Liberal candidate for Parliament.[29]

The campaign of shame

The 1966 election was, in many ways, fought on two issues that had very little to do with reality in the country. Race would, of course, be at the centre of the election, but only tangentially. As Laurence Gandar, editor of the liberal *Rand Daily Mail*, said, there was something 'unreal', 'synthetic and unconvincing' about the debates of the campaign. His paper noted 'that the centre of gravity of politics had moved substantially farther to the Right' and made a truly disturbing observation: 'The middle ground formerly occupied by the United Party has been largely vacated for there are issues on which the United Party now stands to the Right of the Nationalist.'[30] The fact was that the United Party had hit an all-time low. A low that would have left even Smuts stuck on a spin cycle in his grave.

The UP's campaign decided to ignore the low-hanging fruit of apartheid oppression; instead, it and many of its English-speaking followers would lower themselves into the bucket of moral pigswill the Nats were bathing in. During the election, the UP decided to ignore the ever-increasing violence of Verwoerd's police state, as well as the fact that huge swathes of the population were living in enforced poverty, subjected to a dumbed-down education system. And it completely overlooked the hundreds if not thousands of people of all races living under banning orders or being imprisoned under the 180-day detention legislation. Instead, the election was fought on two issues: Rhodesia's illegal declaration of independence and the policy of Bantustans.

Rhodesia had, under Ian Smith, made a Unilateral Declaration of Independence on 11 November 1965, declaring the territory independent from Britain. In reality it was an attempt by Smith's racist regime to sidestep the possibility of Britain agreeing to a universal franchise, which would lead to black majority rule. This was, the UP seemed to believe, *the* hot topic of the election in South Africa. Assuming that supporting Ian Smith would be the clarion call to all English-speaking South Africans, De Villiers Graaff and his party declared itself decisively on the side of the (illegitimate) Smith regime.

Graaff believed that the English in South Africa saw themselves as indistinguishable from white Rhodesians. Interestingly, the NP had remained neutral on the issue, realising that supporting Smith publicly would only cause more trouble internationally for South Africa. As Kenneth Heard suggests, most voters seemed to understand the NP's position, seeing it as a reasonable approach to the problem.

The diminutive Progressive MP for Houghton, Helen Suzman, would refer to the UP's position as 'deeply dishonest'. But what it at least proved was that the UP believed that English-speakers had dropped their attachment to metropolitan Britain. No longer *souties*, the English-speakers were now fair game for both the Nats and the UP. And with Rhodesia's UDI topic simmering into insignificance, the UP turned its .22 pistol to target another mirage: Verwoerd's creation of the 'independent' Bantustans.

Trying to replicate NP politics, the UP attempted a *'swart en rooi gevaar'* campaign of their own. Graaff insisted that the NP, with its Bantustan policy, was the unconscious ally of the communists. He claimed that the Nats were creating 'little Cubas' within the sanctity of South Africa's borders. The UP's Afrikaans mouthpiece, *Ons Land*, went as far as claiming that the NP was engaged in 'K*****boetie politics'.[31]

The Star newspaper was dead on the money when they wrote that the concept of 'little Cubastans' was a non-issue for voters. People knew full well that real independence was never on the cards for the 'independent' Bantustans. As it happened, long after the creation of the homelands in the 1970s, the NP could not get even a single member of the international community to believe that independent Bantustans existed (possibly apart from the International Bowling Association, which admitted Transkei). They were, in real terms, a fiction. And the local South African voter was far savvier than the greybeards of the United Party. It was a scare tactic that the UP saw as the last throw of the dice.

The UP then took to their platforms to explain their own misty and inchoate version of racial segregation. And as for their other policies? Well, they were closer to bribes: they promised to introduce television and a state lottery. It was a sprinkle of spice to their otherwise bland *koshuis* serving.

The Nats swarm the country

Denying the allegation that they were involved in 'K*****boetie politics', the Nats came out firing. The deputy minister of Bantu administration and development, M.C. Botha, pointed out that since 1948, the NP had spent R4 million on non-white housing and R216 million on white housing. With this issue out of the way, the Nats placed front and centre the various straw men that sent the majority of whites into a cold sweat.

The NP ran their campaign on *'gevaar'*, plain and simple. All fears, real and imagined, were played on. The relative peace in the white areas of the country was presented as evidence that the NP's iron fist was working. Few would listen to the calls of Suzman, who argued that it was not the whites who were paying a high price for this 'peace'. Sadly, outside Houghton no politician really seemed to give the townships and the prison cells much thought.

The NP was making inroads into the English vote. In the provincial election of 1965, the NP had won an unprecedented eight out of twenty-five seats in the English heartland of Natal. Even the violently anti-English Broederbonder Dr Nico Diederichs was now talking of the English as part of the *volk*. He claimed that the election would be 'a national demonstration of the unity of our people'. As Verwoerd would state with a fair degree of truth, 'the English-speaking vote is, in ever increasing strength, and more and more openly, aligning itself with the Government policies'.[32]

United calamity

When voting went ahead, not a single paper or commentator got it wrong. The United Party was destroyed in the polls, winning only 23 per cent of the seats (39 out of 166). Although, again due to the skewed nature of the first-past-the-post system, they had in fact won 37 per cent of the vote. There were few positives for the opposition. One was that, to many people's surprise, Helen Suzman of the Progressive Party held on to her seat at Houghton, actually increasing her majority by a few hundred votes. However, the leader of the Progressives, Jan Steytler, was trounced in East London North, losing so badly that he had to forfeit his deposit. He retired to his farm in Queenstown, never to be heard of again. Another Progressive who was humiliatingly defeated was Colin Eglin in Sea Point, who lost to the very conservative UP politician Jack Basson by 4 055 votes.

The table below provides the details of the National Party's landslide:

	Seats won	Seats gained/lost	Popular vote	Percentage
NP	126	+21	759 331	58.31
UP	39	−10	476 815	36.62
Progressive	1	0	39 717	3.05

H.F. Verwoerd was now firmly entrenched as the leader of a country experiencing unprecedented economic growth, with little to no political agitation from any quarter. What was more, overseas confidence in South Africa's economic prospects was at an all-time high. And so it was that South Africa set sail for apartheid's Valhalla. There was only one small blip five months later, when a parliamentary messenger named Dimitri Tsafendas stabbed Verwoerd to death in the House of Assembly.

CHAPTER 10

BLACK CONSCIOUSNESS, WHITE DENIAL
1977

'Who can say that by word or deed I did not do my level best to create better relations between Afrikaans- and English-speakers?' – **B.J. Vorster**

Vorster 'salutes' the crowd at an election rally

FOR SEVERAL YEARS AFTER THE 1966 ELECTION, opposition to apartheid lay in tatters. Despite the assassination of Verwoerd, the NP under the new prime minister B.J. 'John' Vorster succeeded in creating a 'safe space' for whites. In reality they had simply created an echo chamber – all dissenting voices were either locked away or too petrified to speak up. Thanks to the Suppression of Communism Act and the Criminal Procedure Amendment Act, opposition politics did for a time remain silent too. But as the 1970s began, new voices began to emerge. The strongest of these answered to a new name – Black Consciousness.

1970 BC

Although Black Consciousness had some of its origins in the ANCYL Africanists' breakaway that formed the PAC, it now had a new theoretical background. Some of its force came from the theories of Frantz Fanon, a psychologist from Martinique who fought both for the French in World War II and against the French in colonial Algeria.

At the centre of the Black Consciousness Movement was a young medical student by the name of Stephen Bantu Biko. Biko was a man of many gifts. Good-looking, intelligent and articulate, he persuaded a generation of black youth that the problem they faced in apartheid South Africa was as much psychological as it was social.

Like Fanon, Biko focused as much on liberation as he did its psychological state. And both men were interested in Hegel's thesis vs. antithesis dialectic. As Biko explained, 'Since the thesis is white racism there can only be one valid antithesis

The conscious face of Steve Biko

i.e. a solid black unity to counterbalance the scale'. Although Black Consciousness never advocated violence, as Fanon's theories did, Biko awoke a movement whose actions would radically change the country. By the mid-1970s Black Consciousness had spread into schools, largely through young teachers who had been part of the protests at black universities from 1972. These teachers were members of the Black Consciousness–affiliated South African Students' Organisation (SASO).

These developments were now causing an undercurrent of tension unseen for nearly twelve years. When black schools in Soweto were told in 1975 that they had to teach mathematics and social sciences in Afrikaans, the wave broke. This policy was in direct opposition to the wishes of school boards and parents, both of whom wanted students to be taught in English. As Welsh puts it, the African Teachers' Association stated that English 'was an international language and the lingua franca of many African peoples (which was precisely why the Department [of Bantu Education] wanted its influence diluted)'.[1]

Uprising

In June 1976 the head of the Black Consciousness–aligned South African Students' Movement, Tsietsi Mashinini, called for a mass demonstration to protest these language policies and the overcrowding of schools in Soweto. The date was set as 16 June, and with this apartheid's fate was in many ways sealed. Mashinini demanded that the demonstration should be non-violent and disciplined and that students should not provoke the police. The idea was to form a mass column that would march to Orlando Stadium for a protest meeting.

On the 16th, 6 000 peaceful students marched along Vilakazi Street, where they encountered a contingent of forty black and eight white policemen under the command of Colonel Johannes Kleingeld. The colonel had been severely short-changed by not having been provided with a loudhailer. When Kleingeld called for the students to disperse, nothing happened – possibly because they did not hear him and/or realised that the police were hopelessly underprepared and woefully equipped.

When none of the tear-gas canisters the police fired went off, the crowd sensed the policemen's helplessness and continued on their way. The police, it seems, then panicked and fired without orders. By the end of the day, fifteen schoolchildren were dead. A photograph taken by Sam Nzima of a dying twelve-year-old boy, Hector Pieterson, being carried by Mbuyisa Makhubo was published in *The World*, a paper with a large black readership. It was soon distributed to the international press. In the eight months that followed, violence spread across South Africa, at the end of which around 700 people lay dead.

The murder of Steve Biko

Steve Biko was taken into custody on 18 August 1977 in the Eastern Cape after being caught breaking his banning order. During his interrogation he was subjected to a severe beating by security police in which he received what would ultimately prove to be a fatal head injury. The policemen, Harold Snyman, Gideon Nieuwoudt, Ruben Marx, Daantjie Siebert and Johan Beneke, all later admitted at the Truth and Reconciliation Commission (TRC) that they knew he had been concussed and yet they still chained him, naked, by both legs and arms to a metal grille. Snyman stated at the TRC 'that it was possible that we acted in an inhumane manner'.[2]

When a local district surgeon, Dr Ivor Lang, was called in to examine Biko on 7 September, the police lied to him, stating that Biko had either suffered a stroke or that he was faking symptoms. Lang found that Biko was incoherent, his speech slurred and his lips swollen. He nevertheless wrote the police a false exculpatory certificate, stating: 'I have found no evidence of any abnormality or pathology on the detainee.' The next day Lang and the chief district surgeon, Dr Benjamin Tucker, came to see Biko and found him lying naked under urine-soaked blankets on the floor of room 619 in the security police's offices in the Sanlam Building in Port Elizabeth. He was chained by one foot and handcuffed. He complained of pains in his head.

When the doctors took him to the local prison hospital, he was diagnosed with urinary incontinence, blood in the cerebrospinal fluid and early signs of brain damage. However, Lang wrote on the medical form that Biko showed 'no change in condition' and duly sent him back to the security police.

When the doctors arrived again to see him on 11 September, they finally admitted that Biko was in a very serious condition. Biko was then transported, naked and manacled, in the back of a bakkie to a prison hospital 1 000 kilometres away in Pretoria. On 12 September Biko died 'a miserable and lonely death on a mat on a stone floor in a prison cell'.[3] He was only thirty years old.

After the announcement of Biko's death, a grotesque and shameful attempted cover-up ensued. At first, justice minister Jimmy Kruger claimed at the National Party Conference that Biko had died 'following a hunger strike', but when challenged he would (famously) go on to say that Biko's death '*laat my koud*' ('leaves me cold', meaning that he didn't care one bit). In another statement symptomatic of the arrogance and depravity of the National Party system and its culture, Christoffel Venter, a Nat delegate from Springs, said that Kruger and the National Party had allowed detainees 'the democratic right to starve themselves to death'. As journalist Donald Woods relayed, after much sniggering and laughter, Kruger responded: 'Mr Venter is right. That is very democratic.'[4]

The true story of Biko's death was exposed in the pages of the *Rand Daily Mail* by a young, dedicated journalist by the name of Helen Zille. Kruger backed away from the hunger strike theory and then attempted to play an all-too-familiar semantic game, arguing that he had only said Biko died '*following* a hunger strike' not '*because* of a hunger strike'.

Due to pressure from journalists like Woods and Zille, as well as Biko's friends, student activists and certain members of the Progressive Federal Party, there was an inquest. As Woods describes in his book *Biko*, 'It took three weeks for the story of a killing to unfold. And during that time a strange sense of ordinariness overlaid the painful and shocking facts that came out.'[5]

Counterattack of the Nats

As Colin Eglin suggested somewhat sarcastically, in August 1977 Vorster and the NP launched their 'counter-attack' against the liberals by unveiling the government's plans for constitutional 'reform'. The government proposed three separate parliaments for whites, coloureds and Indians. Each of these would deal with issues specific to their race. Black representation was not considered. Vorster claimed that he had given blacks independence through the homelands 'to take, or to leave'. As he would go on, 'What we cannot offer the black man is co-participation with them in our parliament.'[6]

Despite the rejection of Vorster's policies by the vast majority of blacks, coloureds, Indians and the opposition parties, Vorster pressed on. When the minister of coloured affairs, Hennie Smit, met with coloured representatives, he added to the resistance against the proposed legislation by referring to coloureds as 'slow thinkers'. Coloured Representative Council members duly and ironically nicknamed him 'Flinkdink' ('quick thinker'). But sarcasm was hardly a sufficient response to the power the NP wielded over the country.

Bolzo Vorster

On 20 September 1977, Vorster surprised everyone by announcing a snap election for 30 November – a year and a half before one was constitutionally required. Vorster would deny that the announcement had anything to do with Steve Biko's death eight days earlier, claiming there were three more important reasons for calling an early election:

1. The electorate should be allowed to express its opposition to the mounting international interference in domestic affairs.
2. The electorate should be allowed to pass judgement on the new constitutional proposals.
3. Due to the breakup of the United Party into three factions, the voters should be given a chance to sort out for themselves the mess in which it had left Parliament.

Grumbles in the jumble

For many years the United Party wandered through Parliament like a bewildered wildebeest, not knowing from one minute to the next where its right hoof or left hoof was moving. Never had white opposition parties been in such a state of disarray as they were in 1977. The 'Old Guard' of the UP, under De Villiers Graaff, had for many years been uncertain of its policies, continually

De Villiers Graaff: Caught between a rock and a hard place

flirting with right-wing politics without having the stomach to go the whole warthog. But by the mid-seventies, the 'Young Turks' of the party led by Harry Schwarz wanted a more liberal approach to taking on the Nats.

Schwarz's group broke away from the UP to form the Reform Party. Shortly after that, they joined Suzman and Eglin's Progressives to form the Progressive Reform Party. When it was put forward that the UP should form an alliance with the Progressive Reform Party, six racist right-wing members broke away from the UP to form the South African Party. Then, with the handful of UP members left after the two breakaways, De Villiers Graaff formed the New Republic Party. Finally, the six remaining UP members who did not want to join Graaff joined the Progressive Reform Party, who then changed their name to the Progressive Federal Party or PFP. (We hope you're following this, because it took us a while to figure it out!)

Suffice to say, the opposition did not know its arse from a hole in the ground, or its elbow from the hell in a handbasket that was political irrelevance. In fact, when Vorster announced the election, most of the electorate did not even know the new names of the opposition parties. B.J. had chosen the perfect time to call an election!

Detention, deficit, disorder

Another underlying factor in South Africa at the time of the election was the economy. Not many whites seem to have felt it yet, but Vorster knew that serious capital flight after Soweto and ever-increasing sanctions did not bode well. That year, 1977, was the first in which output in South Africa had declined since the heady growth years of the 1960s. What's more, unlike South Korea, whose economy was similar to that of South Africa's in the 1970s, South Africa had not invested heavily (indeed, at all) in the education of its labour force.

Diversifying the economy and weaning off the addiction to mining and cheap labour was imperative. The policy hatched under Rhodes and Kruger of putting all the eggs in cheap labour's basket, added to the crimes of Bantu Education, was coming home to roost. It was perhaps better to get the elections out of the way before the inevitable confession that the goose laying the golden eggs was stuffed.

Almost exactly a month before the elections, one of the most controversial moments in South African history occurred. On 19 October, minister of justice Jimmy Kruger banned three publications: *The World*, *Weekend World* and *Pro Veritate*.

Percy Qoboza found out how unfree the press in South Africa really was

All three were associated with Black Consciousness. *The World*'s editor, Percy Qoboza, who had brought the details of the Soweto uprising to a broader audience, was arrested and held for six months without trial. The fact that he had only done his job did not seem to matter. Then came the arrest of seven members of Soweto's Committee of Ten, an organisation that had attempted to restore peace in the township.

The Christian Institute of South Africa (CISA) was also subjected to the Nats' wrath. *Pro Veritate*, which was run by Beyers Naudé and the CISA, had published in their last-ever edition an editorial on Steve Biko. It had made the argument that all people who voted for the apartheid government 'share the responsibility for the deaths it causes'. Naudé was punished for this and other 'offences', receiving a banning order for seven years. Also on the list of those banned was Steve Biko's friend and editor of the *Daily Dispatch*, Donald Woods. Along with them, eighteen organisations were banned, among them the Black People's Convention, SASO, the Black Parents' Association, the Christian Institute and the Soweto Students' Representative Council.

PFP candidate Kowie Marais compared Vorster to Hitler, claiming that South Africa was arising on 19 October to the dawn of Nazi rule. (And this was something Marais should have known at least something about – he had been an ardent supporter of Hitler in his youth and was a member of the OB along with Vorster.) Suzman came out swinging, saying that the bannings and imprisonments 'were a complete admission by the government that it was unable to govern without resorting to absolute despotism'.[7]

The Press down on freedom

Another pocket of turbulence for Vorster was created by the English-language press, which was still free(ish) but deeply worried about its future. *The Star* stated that what began on 19 October was 'one of the most shocking weeks in South Africa's recent history'. The *Rand Daily Mail* followed this with the statement, 'if anyone still had any doubts that South Africa was being led into an age of dictatorship in which the last lights of freedom and dissent are extinguished they must surely be removed now'. The article went on to say that the government's measures 'represent the most gravely authoritarian action this government has ever undertaken'.[8]

Vorster's move had even gone some way to scaring the Afrikaans press.

Rapport, which had the largest circulation of all Afrikaans papers, stated in its leading article:

> A newspaper does all its work in public. What it thinks and does, it publishes. Its faults and sins are thus displayed every day for all to read ... We gladly accept that the action of the Minister of Justice and the Security Police was in the best interests of the country. Nevertheless, we want to call on them to tell the country as soon as possible what it is all about. Democracy is best served in this way.[9]

Even *Die Transvaler*, once edited by H.F. Verwoerd, and *Die Burger*, formerly edited by D.F. Malan, questioned the government's actions. *Die Transvaler* asked for those who were arrested to be brought to trial timeously so that the government's claims that there was substantive evidence against them could be shared with the public. But the government flew through these criticisms without so much as turning on the fasten-your-seatbelt sign. They were, however, heading towards an international thunderstorm that would ultimately be one of their downfalls.

On 1 November the US House of Representatives condemned South Africa for 'suppression of political thought and violation of human rights'.[10] Three days later the United Nations declared a mandatory arms embargo against South Africa. It did this under Chapter Seven of the United Nations Charter, which is reserved for situations that threaten world peace. This was an unprecedented act against one of its member (and founder) states. But the UN felt that it needed to act in light of South Africa's domestic policies as well as the war it was waging in South West Africa and Angola.

But the UN was supposed to keep out of domestic affairs, and Vorster made hay with their embargo during the election. At an election meeting on 8 November, he angrily boomed:

> Those responsible for this embargo, what have they succeeded in doing? What they did was tantamount to an open invitation to certain misguided and militant nations saying to them that we are withholding arms from South Africa. And they must not be surprised that some foolish and misguided nations will take that as an invitation to attack South Africa. They must also not be surprised if certain irresponsible elements within South Africa take

that as an open invitation to create violence in South Africa. If that happens, then I say to you tonight, those nations responsible for the mandatory arms embargo, the responsibility is theirs and solely theirs.[11]

This was pure fearmongering. Of course, Vorster would not have admitted it, but the truth was that his security police were by far the most violent agents acting within the country. And far from other countries attacking South Africa, according to its own official reports, in 1977 South Africa had at the very least 2 000 troops stationed inside the borders of Angola. It also had troops operating inside both Rhodesia and Mozambique. Nevertheless, most of the white electorate was ready to swallow Vorster's claims and defend his fictions.

He then threw in some *rooi gevaar*. In Pietermaritzburg, Vorster would tell the English-speaking community that 'it is the grand strategy of the Soviets to ultimately control the southern tip of Africa'. To this red scare was added some vitriol against the US's new, stronger line against apartheid. And so the mood was set: South Africa was a lone island in a sea of communist desires and liberal lunacies.

Just what effect this kind of talk had on the election is difficult to say, but as Gordon Allport pointed out, overseas criticism of South Africa quite often had a galvanising effect – especially in Afrikaner communities. However, polling analysis after the election discovered that, if anything, these kinds of speeches by Vorster pushed a small number of mainly English-speaking voters – who, before the rhetoric and overseas pressure began, were quite happy to vote for either the NP or De Villiers Graaff's New Republic Party – towards the PFP.

It was Vorster's direct intention, however, to finally win over those pockets of English-speaking voters once and for all. In Vorster's final address before the election, he stated:

Perhaps if you had listened in at the time you would have heard me ... on 14 September 1966 saying that I dedicate myself to ... work for better relations between Afrikaans- and English-speakers in South Africa to bring the people of South Africa together as far as it is possible ... I make bold to say that they can say about me what they like, but there is no man in this audience or outside of this audience who can say that by word or deed I did not do my level best to create better relations between Afrikaans- and English-speakers? [Applause][12]

Ultimately, the minority of English-speaking voters who had turned against him because of international developments was only a tiny glitch in the NP campaign, and most of the gains for the PFP were made in what were already liberal constituencies. Van Zyl Slabbert, for example, increased his majority in Rondebosch by 2 305 votes. But while the PFP had held eighteen seats before the election (many of them belonging to old UP MPs),

The PFP's Colin Eglin,
Van Zyl Slabbert and Alex Boraine

by the end of the election they had only seventeen. The vast majority of the English-speaking community did not seem to care just how violent or dictatorial the NP was. The Nats, with their help, won not by a landslide but by an avalanche, winning 134 seats out of 165.[13]

	Seats won	Popular vote	Percentage
National Party	134	685 035	65.34
Progressive Federal Party	17	177 705	16.95
New Republic Party	10	127 335	12.15
Herstigte Nasionale Party	0	34 159	3.26
South African Party	3	17 915	1.71

Considering the number of uncontested seats in the 1977 election, Matthew Midlane roughly calculates that the NP won somewhere around 70 per cent of the (white) vote. As he goes on to state, 'the extent of the NP victory might be realised from the fact of their 17 gains, 12 were in seats which they had never won before and 7 in seats they had not considered it worthwhile to contest in 1974'.[14] English-speakers were voting for the Nats in their droves.

By the end of the election, the NP had the largest parliamentary majority in South African history. The cold reality was that there was little chance of the PFP (who were now the official opposition with their paltry seventeen seats) ever threatening it electorally. It became commonplace both locally and internationally to describe South Africa as a de facto one-party state.

Citizen Shame

One often-cited influence on the English-speaking voters in the 1977 election was *The Citizen* newspaper. It was in many ways the first of its kind – an English-language paper that took a pro-NP line. As William Hachten and Anthony Giffard state, '[it] read like an English translation of the pro-government Afrikaans newspapers. Its front page often featured official "leaks" that portrayed the government in a favourable light. It splashed no-holds-barred investigations of allegedly anti-South African organizations like the Rockefeller Foundation.'[15]

After Biko was killed, *The Citizen* reported that he had died as a result of a hunger strike. When the autopsy revealed that he had died of massive brain injuries, *The Citizen* claimed he had killed himself by banging his head against a wall. Its editorials were also vociferously pro Vorster's segregation policies.

However, almost a year to the day after the banning of *The World* and the imprisonment of its editor, it was revealed in the *Sunday Express* that *The Citizen* was a government front. In the end it was discovered that a R64-million 'propaganda package' of taxpayers' money had been spent on a project masterminded by the infamous head of the Department of Information, Eschel Rhoodie. After the election it became clear that Vorster, Connie Mulder and the malevolent head of state security 'Lang Hendrik' van den Bergh were also at the centre of what became known as the Information Scandal (much more about this in *Rogues' Gallery*).

The bannings, arrests, detentions without trial and deaths in detention were proof of that. The judicial system had become a farce: no real checks and balances to government power existed. This would be confirmed when, a mere twenty-four hours after the result of the election was declared, 'the magistrate at the Biko inquest ruled that no criminal offence had been committed against Biko and that no person could be held responsible for his death.'[16]

In an interview after the election, Vorster, sitting swollen-eyed and impassive, stated that the landslide victory would 'increase pressure' internationally, but that on the other hand people would take note of 'the resistance' of the white people of South Africa. When asked what would happen with the constitutional proposals regarding coloured and Indian representation, he stated that 'this constitutional plan will be implemented in the course of time.'[17] As we shall soon see ...

CHAPTER 11

TRICAMERAL ON FOR SIZE
1983 and 1984

'We must adapt or die.' – P.W. Botha, speaking to the National Party in 1980

A voter mulls her options ahead of the whites-only referendum

WHILE VORSTER WAS RIGHT in saying that the constitutional plan for coloured and Indian representation would be 'implemented in the course of time', he was wrong in assuming that he or his desired successor, Connie Mulder, would be leading the charge.

The fallout from the Information Scandal rippled outwards from the centre of the National Party from 1977 onwards. Vorster gamely clung on as prime minister for a few months, but the stress of trying to keep a dirty secret eventually became too much. At this point, Mulder – the party's powerful Transvaal leader – was still hopeful that he could nab the top job. But Cape leader P.W. Botha, who had on several occasions in the preceding years kicked up a fuss at being forced to allocate Defence Ministry budget to the Department of Information with no control over how it was spent, knew just enough to drag Mulder's name through the mud. When the NP parliamentary caucus was asked to choose between the men on 28 September 1978, Botha received ninety-eight votes to Mulder's seventy-four. He was sworn in as the eighth prime minister of South Africa eleven days later. Mulder was then redeployed and finally jumped ship, joining the Conservative Party.

Vorster was supposedly absolved of blame in the first report of the Erasmus Commission, which had been set up to investigate the Information Scandal. And Botha was happy to appoint him to the largely ceremonial role of state president. But on 29 May 1979, a second, supplementary report was released. This report stated that

(i) Mr Vorster knew everything about the basic financial arrangements for the department's funds;

(ii) he was consulted about the secret funds as well as the projects themselves;

(iii) and because he did not reveal the irregularities that came to his attention ... and delayed ... taking purposeful steps to put an end to this wrong state of affairs, he is jointly responsible for the fact that the irregularities continued.[1]

The grounds for the sudden about-turn were, at the very least, shaky. The first report, writes Brian Pottinger, accused BOSS boss 'Lang Hendrik' van den Bergh of 'openly disobeying an instruction from Vorster' and Mulder of being 'evasive' and unable to recall 'detail'.[2] But the second report relied on evidence from these two fine witnesses to twist the knife in Vorster's *boep*.

While Vorster almost certainly did know what was going on at the Department of Information, it seems unlikely that the supplementary report was motivated by a genuine desire to tell the whole truth and nothing but the truth.

Botha wanted State President Vorster and his gang out of the way, and – less than twenty-four hours after a tumultuous meeting at Tuynhuys on 3 June 1979 – he would have his wish. 'It was with a sense of shock that the House watched Botha rise after prayers ... and with an initially shaky but then firmer voice' announce that Vorster had resigned and that his replacement, Marais Viljoen, would be sworn in in less than four hours' time.[3]

Die Groot Krokodil

Looking back, it is hard to recall that Botha, the finger-wagging Groot Krokodil, was once seen as a reformist. But when he took the helm in the wake of the Soweto uprising and the Information Scandal, it was clear to many that something had to change. Of course, in the apartheid lexicon, the word 'change' did not always have positive connotations. While still defence minister (a position he had occupied since 1966), Botha had a vision for how South Africa should transform its foreign policy. As Allister Sparks noted, P.W. thought South Africa should

[s]top worrying about political unpopularity: it is respect for your physical power that counts in this hard world of *Realpolitik* ... As the brash young men at MI Headquarters liked to put it, 'If you've got them by the balls, their hearts and minds will follow.'[4]

But in the early seventies, Botha's vision was nothing more than a pipe dream. Connie Mulder seemed a shoo-in for next prime minister. And Mulder was certain to continue to rely on Lang Hendrik and the police force when it came to security strategy.

Once Connie was out of the way and Lang Hendrik had shuffled off to his chicken farm in Tweefontein, the road was paved for Botha's 'Total Strategy'.

Walking the political tightrope

The first five years of the Groot Krokodil's reign were occupied with what Pottinger describes memorably as 'the philosophical reconciliation of the promise to share power with the refusal to lose it'.[5] To veil their true intentions, Botha and his verbose minister of constitutional development, Chris Heunis, relied on endless jargon, committees, euphemisms and memoranda. So much so that Pottinger says that it was whispered in the Nat inner sanctum that if Heunis 'was

Heunis: Why say one word when a dozen will do?

run over by a bus nobody would know what was supposed to happen next'.[6]

The blueprint for NP strategy in this era was the party's Twelve-Point Plan, which the duo developed in 1979. To save a shameful wastage of ink, we won't reproduce the plan in full; suffice to say it was a masterclass in doublespeak. While 'an acceptance of multinationalism and of minorities' and 'the removal of unnecessary, hurtful discrimination' sounded grand, the subtext told a different story: continued segregation along 'cultural' (i.e. racial) lines, isolation and protectionism.[7]

Here's further clarification on Point 8, which pertained to a 'constellation of states', from P.W. himself:

In a constellation the constituent bodies have fixed positions vis-à-vis each other, unlike in a solar system in which planets revolve around a central point. In a constellation of states the countries therefore derive from their fixed proximity to each other a common interest while maintaining their individual sovereign status. This concept thus specifically excludes a satellite relationship among any of the constituents.[8]

Cosmic comedy aside, a few sections and phrases of the plan warrant serious inspection. Point 4 makes clear Botha's intention to allow the less 'threatening' minority groups (i.e. coloureds and Indians) some foothold in white South Africa, although it does not blatantly state which group will sit at the top of that pecking order. And Point 3 contains the (heavily veiled) admission that complete independence will not be possible for all black homelands and that citizens of these homelands would have to be accommodated in white South Africa somehow (but never given the vote). Perhaps most revealing of all is the promise, in Point 6, to remove 'unnecessary, hurtful forms of discrimination'. *Necessary discrimination*, it is clear, would remain a staple of Botha's government.

Total Strategy

The Groot Krokodil had long believed that there was 'a total onslaught on South Africa from both inside and outside the country'.[9] In 1970 he warned Parliament of an all-encompassing assault wrought by 'the forces of communism' that

> is operative in the economic sphere. It manifests itself in the form of incitement to boycotts and illegal strikes. It manifests itself in the sowing of confusion in government ranks, such as by means of student unrest, etc. It manifests itself, consciously or unconsciously, in the news media of the world. It manifests itself through subversion, infiltration and the sowing of disorder, and in terrorism in its various forms ... Today, virtually every sphere of life is part of that overall strategy and that total onslaught on the free world and the people of the West.[10]

To counteract this, he devised his infamous Total Strategy, an approach described by Padraig O'Malley as 'a two-handed strategy of reform accompanied by unprecedented repression'.[11] The idea had been formulated by a French general, André Beaufre, and was based on his experiences in both conventional (WWII) and unconventional (Algeria) warfare.

As James Selfe (now a Democratic Alliance MP) wrote in his MA thesis, Beaufre insisted that strategy should not be the domain of generals but of politicians

> who have at their disposal not only the resources of the armed forces, but of the whole state machinery. Beaufre [was] convinced that ... war was merely the extension of politics, but [that] the converse was also true – that in waging war, use had also to be made of political weapons.[12]

What Total Strategy meant, writes Sparks, 'was that any and every issue, domestic as well as foreign, local as well as national was potentially a security issue which justified the involvement of the military-security establishment in everything'.[13] The ANC's exiled leader Oliver Tambo pointed out that Botha's programme was 'based on the recognition that the apartheid system is immersed in a deep and permanent general crisis'.[14]

Under P.W., the defence force replaced the police force as the most important security apparatus in the land. Dubious of Vorster's police networks, as defence minister Botha had gathered around him a cabal he could trust. When he became prime minister, with the help of defence minister Magnus Malan and defence force chief Constand Viljoen, he oversaw what Sparks terms 'a massive militarization of the South African government, indeed of the whole country... The sheer size of the defence force... [gave] Pretoria the atmosphere of a capital city in war-time.'[15]

When in doubt, call in the army

Which is precisely what Pretoria was. Inordinate amounts of cash and effort were expended on suppressing all non-parliamentary opposition (i.e. killing black people), both at home and across southern Africa. Throughout the 1980s troops were deployed in the townships, and

[b]etween 1981 and 1983, the army was used to enforce compliance on every one of the country's neighbours. An undeclared war against Angola reduced a potentially oil-rich country to war-ravaged ruins, while a South African-sponsored conflict in Mozambique brought a poverty-stricken country to its knees. Nor was Botha averse to sending commando units across the borders into Botswana, Zimbabwe, Swaziland and Lesotho to attack and bomb South African refugees.[16]

Leonard Thompson has calculated that 'South Africa's destabilising tactics between 1980 and 1989 led to the deaths of one million people, made a further three million homeless and caused $35 billion worth of damage to the economies of neighbouring states.'[17]

Broader forces at play

But what probably worried P.W. even more than the *swart gevaar* was the fact that his enemies were not all black, communist or even English-speaking. After three decades of Nationalist rule, the Afrikaner revolution had lost some of its fervour. It was in many ways a victim of its own success, as the once downtrodden poor whites had prospered to the point of becoming a contented, largely urban bourgeoisie.

Among these Boere yuppies was a growing realisation that the pass laws (which resulted in around 200 000 arrests every year) and the policy of influx control (which aimed to keep the number of black people in white South Africa to a minimum) were not working. Some influential Afrikaners even started to realise that it had been a mistake all along. The 1978 editorial from *Die Vaderland* is quite something:

> An unskilled and unmotivated worker is also expensive because he is insufficiently productive. In practice this means that three of four people have to be employed to do the work of one. It also means that the white man is overburdened with the responsibility of providing skilled labour which places too great a demand on him ... Count up the cost of this and it should be evident that we have for many decades been running our economy with the handbrake on.[18]

Pride also came into it. Those white South Africans who were sufficiently wealthy (and inclined) to travel abroad were sick and tired of being treated like racist pariahs. 'So it was,' writes Sparks, 'that the adjustments required of the Regional Superpower strategy coincided with the changing needs and desires of a substantial sector of the Afrikaner community ... "Change" became a vogue word.'[19]

In 1979 P.W. converted some of this into action by removing 'job reservation in industry' (what was called the colour bar back in Smuts's and Hertzog's day) and recognising black trade unions. The irony, wrote Helen Suzman, 'was that few Black leaders were inclined to say a kind word when the Pass laws were finally abolished, although the lives of millions of South Africans would be materially improved'. This was because Botha had at the same time introduced two new security bills that resulted in a 'massive spate of detentions'.[20]

This was Total Strategy at play: give with the palm of one hand, while using the other fist (and both jackbooted feet) to take away.

Constitutional collywobbles

But let us leave the battlefield and return to the Union Buildings. Because when it came to Total Strategy, the red ink of constitutional reform was just as important as all the tear gas, landmines and R4s put together. In March 1980 Botha and Heunis began a process of constitutional reform, which was intended to open the door to coloureds and Indians while leaving black people out in the cold.

In May 1980 a Nat-dominated parliamentary commission recommended that the Senate be replaced by a President's Council made up of whites as well as coloured and Indian members nominated by government and wielding only advisory powers. PFP leader Frederik van Zyl Slabbert came out all guns blazing, stating that no member of his party would serve on the PC. (Serial fence-sitter Japie Basson promptly resigned from the PFP and returned to the Nationalist bosom, twenty-nine years and four political parties after first being elected as an MP.)

Not that any of this mattered to Botha. On 3 February 1981 the PC was inaugurated, and one of its first tasks was to come up with a new constitution. Before the PC had done any work, however, Botha (like Vorster before him) announced a snap election, some eighteen months before one was due. Colin Eglin wrote that he 'assumed that Botha wanted endorsement of the changes he had made and a mandate to take the process further'.[21] And this is precisely what he would get. The 1981 snap election – unlike those called by Smuts in 1924 and 1948 – would not yield any surprises. Despite being accused of running a 'k*****boetie government' (go figure!) by firebrand leader of the breakaway Herstigte Nasionale Party Jaap Marais, the Nats only lost three seats. The PFP managed to win an unprecedented twenty-six seats (gaining nine), but it was not enough to douse the flames of the Nats' constitutional dream.

After the election, a subcommittee of the PC chaired by Heunis continued to hammer out its ideas for a new constitution. Out was Verwoerd's grand apartheid ideal of totally separate development, and in was a hodgepodge of tweaks and tinkerings that attempted to appease the international community and gain traction among coloureds and Indians while still maintaining white supremacy.

At the core of these plans was the establishment of a new 'Tricameral' (literally 'three rooms') Parliament, comprising a white House of Assembly, a coloured House of Representatives and an Indian House of Delegates.

Black people who didn't relish living in the homelands would have to make do with Black Local Authorities (BLAs), a new form of black local government. These BLAs lacked both the credibility (their councillors were elected on extremely low turnouts) and the budget required to achieve any real progress. Which is presumably just what Botha wanted …

Central to the new Constitution was the concept of 'own affairs' versus 'general affairs'. 'Own affairs' were defined by the Constitution as '[m]atters which specially or differentially affect a population group in relation to the maintenance of its identity and the upholding and furtherance of its way of life, culture, traditions and customs'. Anything that wasn't an 'own affair' was considered a 'general affair'. As Ben Maclennan points out:

> This led to some interesting decisions: marriage officers became a white own affair, while *volkspele* or Afrikaner folk dances, became a general affair. The Afrikaans Language Monument in Paarl became a general affair, while the South African Cultural History Museum in Cape Town, in earlier days the black slave quarters, was a white own affair. Also defined as a white own affair was Botanical Research.[22]

Although the new legislation was at times farcical, Eglin notes that 'two facts remained dominant and crucial':

1. Black citizens were excluded from all of the constitutional structures. [There had been provision for an advisory black council constituted out of homeland formations, but it was soon scuppered, chiefly thanks to the opposition of Mangosuthu Buthelezi.]
2. Every decision on 'general affairs' at any joint meeting in the three Houses, or by the cabinet, the PC

Van Zyl Slabbert and Buthelezi:
My enemy's enemy is my friend

or the body electing the state president, would have a built-in majority of white representatives.

The old apartheid constitution had been based on domination by exclusion; the Tricameral constitution relied on domination by segregated structures.[23]

Suzman described it as 'the most important Bill to come before Parliament for a long time', and not in a good way: 'Athough the new Constitution was supposed to replace the Westminster system, it retained its worst features – the high degree of power and the "winner takes all" electoral system – and omitted the best – universal adult franchise under the rule of law.'[24]

In addition to these fundamental flaws, argued Van Zyl Slabbert, the Constitution had been steamrolled through Parliament with only '34 of the 103 clauses actually being debated'. Van Zyl Slabbert contended that 'the bungling began with the very process of creating the constitution [which] was unilaterally drawn up, unilaterally ratified and unilaterally tabled in Parliament'.[25]

Like moths to a flame

The proposed Constitution set off an unprecedented spate of political reformulations that saw old friends become bitter enemies – and vice versa. In January 1983,

Allan Hendrickse: Fringe benefits?

long before the bill came before Parliament, the coloureds-only Labour Party had voted overwhelmingly in favour of participating in elections for the Tricameral Parliament. This was odd as only five years earlier the Labour Party's leader, Allan Hendrickse, had stated his strong opposition to any laws that 'sought to ally whites, coloureds and Indians against Africans'. Since then, Hendrickse had been duped into believing that Botha had a genuine desire for reform, and he expressed his commitment to 'non-violent change ... through communication, consultation and negotiation'. While Hendrickse acknowledged that 'constitutional arrangements which did not include Africans could not be regarded as final', he also 'stressed that the Labour Party would not be intimidated by radical elements'.[26]

While the decision made Hendrickse many enemies, it represented a stunning coup for Heunis, who had spent countless hours and days trying to bring Hendrickse around to his way of thinking. A week later the South African Indian Council – which had started off as a government-sanctioned body but was now dominated by Amichand 'Bengal Tiger' Rajbansi's National People's Party – announced that it too would participate in the Tricameral elections. Which all goes to show what the promise of a little power can do to one's principles (assuming one has any). Not that Botha

Amichand 'Bengal Tiger' Rajbansi

was complaining – by hook or by crook (and it was mostly by crook) he had managed to apply a veneer of legitimacy to his plans.

The Prog P.W.

But Botha's smile would soon be wiped off his dial. At a regular NP parliamentary caucus meeting on Wednesday 24 February 1982, an argument that had been quietly simmering for years suddenly boiled over. It is only fitting that the straw that came closest to breaking the Krokodil's back was of the semantic variety.

When the NP romped to victory in 1977, they had euphemistically couched their reform plans as a matter of 'co-responsibility' – a term chosen, according to P.W., because 'it would not worry the [white] electorate'. But now, six years later, it turned out that even the Nats couldn't agree on what 'co-responsibility' actually meant.

On a stifling Cape Town day, the conservative faction of the NP, led by the popular Transvaal leader Andries Treurnicht, and the 'progressive' faction, helmed by Botha, almost came to blows over three letters: while Treurnicht and co. were all for *magsverdeling* (division of power), Heunis advocated *magsdeling* (sharing of power).[27]

Buried beneath the jargon

In opposition circles, notes Colin Eglin, the term 'Heunis-speak' had become synonymous with 'nonsense',[28] and we have certainly had a field day parodying both him and P.W. in this book. But Albert Grundlingh thinks there was more to it than this: 'By the 80s even the Nats could see that apartheid couldn't carry on as before. But they were afraid to admit it.' Instead of simply giving away state power (something that no regime that we're aware of has ever *willingly* done), they tried to choreograph a transition on their terms. Grundlingh feels that this at least partly explains why they came up with such convoluted reforms and couched them in layer upon layer of verbiage. 'You couldn't just admit that you'd misled people,' he says. 'Even if you had.'[29]

Fiery speeches made by Treurnicht (who stood up to speak on no fewer than four occasions) and his fellow rebels Willie van der Merwe and Daan van der Merwe (not related) prompted the Botha-loyalist Fanie Botha (also no relation) to propose a motion of confidence in the prime minister. As Pottinger has it, Treurnicht and co., 'seeing the abyss opening up before them, argued angrily that the matter was not a question of leadership but of policy'.[30] But by now there was no talking themselves out of the fight. The motion of confidence was carried, with 100 Nats voting for Botha and 22 against (there was also 1 abstention and 19 absentees).

On his way out of the meeting, Koos van der Merwe (also no relation!) broke the news to a row of unsuspecting journalists who'd been waiting in the lobby: '*Ek is klaar met die* Prog P.W. Botha.' (I'm done with the Progressive P.W. Botha). A few minutes later, Botha held a hasty press conference to say that twenty-two Nat MPs who had refused to support a motion of confidence in his leadership had been given time to reconsider. On a nearby bench, Pottinger notes, lay a copy of that day's *Citizen*, which proclaimed (fittingly, given that the rag had been established with a view to disseminating fake news): 'No Split Today.'[31]

While the results of the vote confirmed that Botha had most of the party behind him, things were far less certain in *die ou Transvaal*, as twenty-one of the twenty-two naysayers hailed from that province. The Treurnicht faction, (unlike the ultimately inconsequential breakaway led by Albert Hertzog in 1969), included big names like 'the angular, shock-haired animal husbandry expert' Ferdie Hartzenberg, Caspar Uys and deputy speaker Frank le Roux. Treurnicht had also taken with him the only female Nat, a true patriot by the name of Bessie

Scholtz who had, in Pottinger's words, 'borne the Republic ten children [she subsequently had an eleventh] and was a strong proponent of birth control for blacks'.[32]

But quick thinking by provincial vice-chairman F.W. de Klerk managed to prevent a Transvaal coup. A provincial motion of confidence held on 27 February saw Botha emerge victorious by 176 votes to 36 and De Klerk elected as acting head of the Transvaal NP. Three weeks later Treurnicht and the fifteen rebels who'd stuck with him (six had fallen by the wayside) formed the Conservative Party, which advocated a return to the strict segregation of the Verwoerd era. They even argued for the establishment of coloured and Indian

Treurnicht: Gatvol with P.W.'s 'liberal' ideas

homelands – while openly admitting that the idea might not be entirely practical.

Botha may have triumphed in the battle for control of his party, but the nationwide war was far from won. He had, according to Pottinger, lost 'up to 40 per cent of Afrikaners' nationwide.[33] Worse still was the fact that, in PFP MP Ken Andrew's estimation, many of the MPs who stuck with him did so because they saw no other option: 'Only Pik Botha and a few young Nats supported the reform strategy because they believed it was the right thing to do.'[34] Most of the others would seemingly have given their last koeksister for a return to the good old days of grand apartheid – if they could only find a way to make it happen.

Be careful what you wish for: The birth of the UDF

The great irony of Botha's Tricameral master plan was that instead of keeping the different races in their neat parliamentary 'rooms', it brought the opposition together like never before. When faced with his crackpot proposals, what had previously seemed like irreconcilable differences between whites and blacks, Muslims and Christians, communists and capitalists suddenly paled into insignificance. All that mattered now was to give P.W.'s plans the middle finger. (Jacob Zuma would create a similar situation by dividing the ANC and momentarily uniting the Freedom Front, the EFF and everyone in between in opposition to his corruption.)

In his annual January address on Radio Freedom, Oliver Tambo called 1983 'The Year of United Action' and told listeners 'we must organise the people into strong mass democratic organisations.'[35] A few weeks later, when Hendrickse's Labour Party expressed its intention to participate in the Tricameral Parliament, anti-apartheid churchman Allan Boesak said the decision 'reeked of opportunism' and accused Hendrickse and co. of being 'junior partners of apartheid.'[36]

The troubled times of Allan Aubrey Boesak

'Apartheid is a heresy'

Allan Boesak was born in Kakamas and grew up in Somerset West, where he served as an altar boy. As a coloured minister in the Dutch Reformed Church (*nogal*), he shot to fame at the August 1982 meeting of the World Alliance of Reformed Churches in Ottawa, Canada. Addressing representatives of 150 Calvinist churches from 76 countries, he tabled a resolution that declared apartheid 'a heresy contrary to the Gospel and inconsistent with Reformed Tradition'. When the resolution was passed, the white reformed churches 'were suspended from the World Alliance, and a Declaration on Racism was adopted.'[37] In a massive slap in the face to Pretoria, Boesak was then elected president of the alliance, making him the spiritual leader of all the Reformed Churches in the world.

While Boesak was one of the heroes of the anti-apartheid movement in the 1980s, the nineties were not nearly as kind to him. In 1990 he resigned from the DRC after his extramarital affair with SABC TV presenter Elna Botha was exposed. (Botha's husband, Colin Fluxman, who was also an SABC newsreader, memorably broke down on air while trying to read the news of his wife's infidelity.) In 1999, by which time Allan and Elna had married and had a kid, 'Boesak was convicted of stealing R1.3 million donated by American singer Paul Simon and various Scandinavian foundations to aid black children and voter education.'[38] He served one year of his three-year sentence and was later granted a presidential pardon by Thabo Mbeki in 2005.

Boesak, American senator Teddy Kennedy and UDF patron Bishop Desmond Tutu

In the months that followed the plans for a Tricameral Parliament, Boesak – seemingly without speaking to Tambo or the ANC – put it about that there 'is no reason why churches, civic associations, trade unions [and] student organisations should not unite on this issue, pool our resources, inform people of the fraud which is about to be perpetrated in their name, and on the day of the election expose the plans for what they are.'[39] After drumming up support for his idea from between 300 and 400 organisations, the United Democratic Front (UDF) was launched at a 'chaotic, crowded and euphoric' meeting at the Rocklands Community Centre in Mitchells Plain on a bitterly cold day in August 1983.

In the meeting's final speech, Boesak reminded the jubilant 15 000-strong crowd (according to some estimates) of 'three little words that I think we ought to hold on to as we continue the struggle':

You don't have to have a vast vocabulary to understand them. You do not need a philosophical bent to grasp them – they are just three little words ...

And the first word is the word all! We want all of our rights. Not just some rights, not just a few token handouts here and there that the government sees fit to give – we want all our rights ...

The second word is the word here! We want all of our rights and we want them here, in a united, undivided South Africa...

And the third word is the word now! We want all of our rights, and we want them here and we want them now...[40]

The referendum

Botha resolved to get popular (i.e. white) approval of his proposals via a referendum, and he was all for having a simple yes/no question on the ballot. Van Zyl Slabbert, the leader of the opposition, wanted 'a question with more options', including the possibility of black participation. Botha's proposed question – 'Are you in favour of the implementation of the Constitution Act, 1983, as approved by Parliament?' – was, according to Van Zyl Slabbert's biographer Albert Grundlingh,

> deliberately narrowed down to place the PFP in a predicament: opposing the new constitution with a 'no' vote would make them appear as boycotters of 'reasonable' change, and moreover would lump them together with the Conservative Party.[41]

This was a masterstroke by Botha. As Helen Suzman put it, 'We objected to the exclusion of Blacks, who were more than seventy per cent of the population, whereas the Conservative Party objected to the participation of Coloureds and Indians',[42] yet the parties found themselves hitting the hay together on a very uncomfortable straw mattress made for them by the Krokodil.

The beauty of Botha's binary question (from a Nat point of view) was that even in the unlikely event that the 'No' vote won, it would be impossible to ascertain whether the electorate was asking for an increase or a decrease in black rights. The meaning of a 'Yes' vote, however, would be unequivocal. As Van Zyl Slabbert recalled, when he pointed this idiosyncrasy out to Botha, the Groot Krokodil 'smiled and licked his lips in that familiar way of his. I could see he knew I was in for a beating. It was the kind of political contest he relished'.[43]

Despite some opposition within party ranks, veteran MP Harry Schwarz feared that campaigning for the 'No' vote would 'confuse' voters who were used to hearing PFP demands *for* change, not against it.[44] Van Zyl Slabbert, Suzman and Eglin were unequivocal. Regardless of how it made the party look, the PFP could not support Botha's proposals, and they campaigned vehemently for the 'No' vote. To do anything else would be to back the apartheid government's vision for the country.

The Nats ran a 'slick' campaign with loads of sympathetic newspaper and TV coverage and a really simple and effective slogan claiming that the proposals were 'A step in the right direction'.

The PFP, on the other hand, tried to expose what Eglin termed the 'glaring defects of the Tricameral constitution' with a pamphlet that proclaimed that '70 per cent of the population would say "no" if they were allowed to do so'. While this statement was almost certainly true (in fact 70 per cent seems an underestimate), it was a rather circuitous way of trying to convince white voters to reject the proposals.[45]

The PFP: Farting against thunder

They would probably have been better off building on this off-the-cuff comment made by Van Zyl Slabbert: 'Everybody likes a step in the right direction. When you are in a dark tunnel a step in the right direction towards the light can be very nice – except if that light is the light of an oncoming train.'[46]

Some liberal English papers, including the *Sunday Times* and the *Financial Mail*, swallowed hook, line and sinker the fetid redbait on the end of Botha's 'a step in the right direction' line and ended up urging their readers to vote 'Yes'. *The Star*, meanwhile, advised its readers to abstain from voting. One *Star* reporter expressed their frustration by sticking up a notice reading 'The Editor's Indecision is Final' in the newsroom.[47]

As the campaign drew on, it became clear that Botha's Machiavellian jostling had paid off. As Grundlingh puts it, 'Increasingly, the PFP was seen as a negative, boycotting party and the government as a trendsetter for change.' While Van Zyl Slabbert (rightly) dismissed this logic as 'thumbsucking and wishful thinking on a large scale',[48] the short-term consequences for the PFP were dire.

During apartheid, opinion polls were banned, so it was hard to know what to expect from the referendum. That being said, the general consensus was that Botha would scrape through with a 55 per cent 'Yes' vote. The reality was far grimmer.

On Wednesday 2 November 1983, 2 062 479 eligible South Africans (a whopping 76 per cent turnout) made their mark in the referendum. Once the dust settled, the extent of the bloodbath became clear: 65.95 per cent of whites had voted 'Yes', 33.53 per cent had voted no and 10 669 (readers of *The Star*?) had spoilt their ballots. To make matters worse for the liberal cause, closer inspection revealed that the majority of 'No' votes came from the Conservative Party, not the PFP.

The only polling area (out of fifteen) to record a win for the 'No' vote was the region surrounding Pietersburg in the northern Transvaal, and even there they only managed to convince 52.3 per cent of whites to opt for a return to Verwoerdian ideals. In the more liberal metropolitan areas, Botha *langarmed* his way to an easy victory: in Durban and Cape Town respectively, only 26.24 per cent and 24.2 per cent of voters put their cross in the 'No' column. South Africa's 'leading polling analyst', Lawrence Schlemmer, estimated that around a third of both the PFP's and the Conservative Party's traditional supporters had sided with Botha to vote 'Yes'.[49]

Botha was jubilant, as *The Times* reported:

Flushed with his greatest triumph since succeeding Mr John Vorster in 1978, Mr Botha told cheering supporters outside the Union Buildings here, where the votes were counted yesterday morning, that the outcome was a victory for evolutionary reform. He appealed to those who had voted 'No' to accept the decision. 'I see a new spirit of South African patriotism. Let us go forward together,' he said.[50]

He barely mentioned the blacks, coloureds and Indians who had not been able to vote.

Conservative leader Treurnicht said that he did not accept the result 'as the final choice of a people who want to maintain their freedom. The struggle to undo the new constitution begins today.' He argued that the new Constitution would open the door to eventual black majority rule. He also thought it was a formula for 'white suicide'.[51] The multiracial, non-parliamentary UDF rejected the result and turned its attention to persuading coloureds and Indians to boycott the upcoming election.

Van Zyl Slabbert was publicly more gracious, although he admitted in private to feeling 'politically dirty' about participating in a system that he viewed as a sham.[52] He had already begun to doubt whether the solution to South Africa's problems lay in Parliament and offered to resign as leader of the PFP. His colleagues persuaded him to stick it out a little longer (he finally went the extra-parliamentary route in 1986, shortly after publishing a book titled *The Last White Parliament*).

Botha may have won the battle, but for the first time in a while the real war was not being fought at the ballots. The extra-parliamentary movement for change was seriously gathering steam.

'The elephant has given birth to a mouse': Non-white reaction to the Tricameral Constitution

The UDF, with its crystal-clear slogan 'Apartheid divides, UDF unites', was emphatic in its repudiation of the proposals. And speaking after the referendum, ANC president Oliver Tambo (who was not a member of the UDF) also roundly rejected 'Botha's attempt to tamper with the constitution', explaining that it was

> an attempt on his part to get out of a crisis generated by the growing power of the oppressed masses and the democratic forces of our country. It became necessary for Botha to do something about the advancing forces of liberation; to divert them, to halt them, to delay them. He conceived of the idea of dividing these forces; recruiting from among them to strengthen the white minority numerically, to strengthen its repressive armed forces and to perpetuate the status quo.[53]

In *Long Walk to Freedom*, Nelson Mandela describes the supposed reforms as 'merely a "toy telephone"' (where have we heard that before?) 'as all

Oliver Tambo in the 1980s

parliamentary actions by Coloureds and Indians was subject to a white veto'.[54] Writing (clandestinely) on Robben Island in 1983, Govan Mbeki saw straight through Botha's supposed reforms: 'A new dispensation! Power-sharing! Words. Words. What is in them?' he asked, before going on to describe coloureds and Indians who participated in the elections as 'apartheid honey birds'.[55]

Mangosuthu Buthelezi, meanwhile, decreed cryptically that '[t]he elephant [Botha, presumably] has given birth to a mouse'.[56]

Say cheesy! P.W.'s last all-white cabinet

Fact or fiction? Nineteen Eighty-Four comes true in 1984

It is surely more than a coincidence that the Tricameral Parliament was voted in in 1984, the year in which George Orwell chose to set his magnum opus. Heunis and Botha were past masters of what Orwell defined as doublethink:

> To know and not to know, to be conscious of complete truthfulness while telling carefully constructed lies, to hold simultaneously two opinions which cancelled out, knowing them to be contradictory and believing in both of them, to use logic against logic, to repudiate morality while laying claim to it, to believe that democracy was impossible and that the Party was the guardian of democracy, to forget whatever it was necessary to forget, then to draw it back into memory again at the moment when it was needed, and then promptly to forget it again, and above all, to apply the same process to the process itself – that was the ultimate subtlety: consciously to induce unconsciousness, and then, once again, to become unconscious of the act of hypnosis you had just performed. Even to understand the word – doublethink – involved the use of doublethink.[57]

The vote (or lack thereof)

When Botha and Heunis first presented their new Constitution, they had suggested that after the white referendum, coloured and Indian voters would also be given a chance to accept or reject the proposals via a referendum. But the growing might of the UDF (which had swelled to include some 575 separate organisations) and the ever-loudening voice of the exiled ANC quickly put paid to that plan. We'll let Oliver Tambo explain why: 'Our people, the oppressed, made it abundantly clear to Botha that that referendum [for coloured and Indian voters] would return a resounding, definite "No" to the new constitution. He could see that. Therefore he evaded the referendum. He did not want to know the truth, and he opted instead for election.'[58]

Or to be precise, he opted for two elections: one for coloureds and one for Indians. (Whites had already expressed their adoration for the Groot Krokodil in the 1981 general election and the 1983 referendum, so there was no need to canvass their opinion again.)

On 17 August the United Nations Security Council 'rejected and declared null and void the new racist constitution of South Africa' and urged the international

As requested, coloured and Indian voters stayed away in their droves

community not to recognise the upcoming elections. Not one to be deterred by such pesky irritants as the UN, Botha sent the coloured community to the polls on 22 August. Allan Hendrickse's Labour Party cleaned up, persuading almost 75 per cent of the 267 377 voters to side with them. But herein lay the rub. Turnout for the election was a dismal 30.9 per cent; by staying away in their droves, coloureds had created a DIY referendum of their own, and the result was a resounding 'No'. The day was marked by nationwide protests and boycotts and 152 arrests.

Six days later, elections to the House of Delegates among the Indian community took place. While the contest was much closer – Rajbansi's NPP managed eighteen seats and the Solidarity party (whose wealthy leader J.N. Reddy enjoyed a cosy relationship with the Groot Krokodil) scooped seventeen – the turnout was even more damning than in the coloured community. A staggering 79.2 per cent of eligible Indian voters chose not to exercise their 'democratic' right!

On 30 August, Botha declared that he regarded the low turnout as a 'minor obstacle' that did not invalidate the revised constitution. 'I do not say that what we are entering into is perfect, nor is it the total solution to our problems. But, I ask, what is the alternative?' On the same day, police shot and killed one unarmed black youth and injured two more.[59]

Tambo's withering putdown of the whole sham deserves to be quoted here at length:

The people refused to participate in those elections by an overwhelming majority. They were therefore refusing to be divided; they were refusing to be recruited as an army against their own future, against a free South Africa. They were rejecting yet again the concept of white minority rule. If some 60 percent or more of the white favoured the new amendment, the blacks – and

I include all the blacks – must have rejected it by something like 90 percent –
90 percent allowing for a few who did vote. Allowing for the Allan Hendrickses
and so on. So the elections were a battlefield in which the enemy was soundly
defeated.[60]

Be that as it may, on 22 September 1984 the Tricameral Constitution came
into effect, and the position of prime minister fell away. The 178-member
(white) House of Assembly, 85-member (coloured) House of Representatives
and 45-member (Indian) House of Delegates usually met in separate buildings.
(Since 1994 the National Assembly has been housed in the chamber built for
joint sittings of the Tricameral Parliament.) After being voted in as executive
president by an electoral college comprising fifty whites, twenty-five coloureds
and thirteen Indians, P.W. repaid the favour by appointing Hendrickse, Rajbansi
and a couple of other non-whites to his cabinet.[61]

'Make the country ungovernable'

Tambo first enunciated the ANC's plan to take the struggle to the streets of South
Africa during the party's annual birthday address on 8 January 1984. Speaking
on Radio Freedom, he said, 'To march forward must mean that we advance
against the regime's organs of state-power, creating conditions in which the
country becomes increasingly ungovernable.'[62] Before long, writes Martha Evans,
'this directive [was] distilled into the popular slogans "Make apartheid unwork-
able" and "Make the country ungovernable".'[63]

Tambo would get his wish. On 3 September, the very day on which the
shiny new Constitution was inaugu-
rated, the Vaal Triangle became a war
zone. Protests against the Lekoa and
Evaton town councils' plans to raise
municipal tariffs resulted in clashes
with the police and left thirty people
dead. The marchers also looted shops,
set fire to houses and killed four councillors. By the end of the year almost
150 people had been killed in political
violence.[64]

Mourners in Duduza burn cars in
July 1985 after the funeral of eight activists
who had been killed by police

> ### By the numbers
> Cold, hard statistics shine a light on the heavy costs of the Tricameral system:
> * In October 1987 South Africa and its homelands boasted '11 presidents or prime ministers, 14 ministers of finance, 11 ministers of interior and 18 ministers of health.'[65]
> * The Bantustans, the Tricameral Parliament and the concept of 'own affairs' versus 'general affairs' meant that in 1986 no fewer than eighty-seven budgets passed through Parliament.
> * Between September 1984 and 24 January 1986, 955 people were killed in political violence incidents and 3 658 injured. In contrast, only twenty-five members of the security forces died.[66]

Crossing the Rubicon?

By the middle of 1985, even the Nats admitted that all was not well in the land. And so, on 2 August, senior members of the party met at Sterrewag in Pretoria to discuss the content of Botha's address to the annual party conference in Durban on the 15th. Botha received input from all his ministers, most notably Chris Heunis and Pik Botha. For some reason best known to him, Pik got it into his head that P.W. was in the mood for genuine reform. He went to the effort of writing an eleven-page draft speech detailing the exact substance of these reforms and got his press secretary to phone *Time* and *Newsweek* to say that 'a major policy announcement ... was on the cards'.[67]

The media were not to know that Pik was sniffing down the wrong hole. *The Times* of London wondered whether Mandela would be freed, and *Time* magazine told readers to 'expect the most important statement since Dutch settlers arrived in the Cape of Good Hope 300 years ago'.[68] For the first time in South Africa's history, international news networks came in their droves to cover the speech as it happened.

But on the day, instead of boldly crossing the Rubicon, the Krokodil lay on his side of the bank, snapping his jaws and refusing to even place his toe in the water. He began his speech with a warning:

Most of the media in South Africa have already informed you on what I was going to say tonight, or what I ought to say, according to their superior judgment.

Of all the tragedies in the world I think the greatest is the fact that our

electorate refrained so far to elect some of these gentlemen as their government. They have all the answers to all the problems.

Then, instead of promising to take South Africa forward, he clung to the past,
uttering an inordinately long and muddled string of excuses, justifications and
bald-faced lies. Here are some of the choicest pieces of Krokodil dung:

> But let me point out at once that since South Africa freed itself from colonialism,
> democracy has already been broadened and millions of people who never had
> a say in governmental affairs under the British Colonial system, have it today.
>
> ...
>
> We believe in the protection of minorities. Is there anybody in this hall
> who would get up and say he is not for the protection of minorities? Let me
> see how such a fool looks.
>
> ...
>
> I know for a fact that most leaders in their own right in South Africa and
> reasonable South Africans will not accept the principle of one-man-one-vote
> in a unitary system. That would lead to domination of one over the other and
> it would lead to chaos. Consequently, I reject it as a solution.

In his speech, Botha clung to the idea of homelands (with limited concessions),
rejected the idea of a fourth (black) chamber of Parliament, and took a moment
to 'remind the public of the reasons why Mr Mandela is in jail'. Still, he had the
audacity to end the speech by comparing his actions to Julius Caesar:

> The implementation of the principles I have stated today can have far-reaching
> effects on us all. I believe that we are today crossing the Rubicon. There can
> be no turning back. We now have a manifesto for the future of our country,
> and we must embark on a programme of positive action in the months and
> years that lie ahead.[69]

Nobody bought it. Dave Steward, who served as director-general of the South
African Communication Service from 1985 to 1992, described the speech as
'the worst political communication by any country at any time'.[70] Allister Sparks
called it a 'king-size damp squib' and a 'display of finger-wagging belligerence'.[71]
Pik Botha later referred to the press conference he gave after the speech as

'one of the most difficult tasks' of his life, saying: 'I tried to persuade the media that the [reformist] elements on which we all waited were hidden under all the aggression and *kragdadigheid* (forcefulness).'[72] Gerhard de Kock, governor of the Reserve Bank at the time, said, only half-jokingly, that 'the speech cost the country billions of rands – at a rate of a few million rand per word'.[73]

More recently, William Dicey has argued that the speech was actually quite reformist, as 'buried in the bellicosity was a quiet commitment to "shared citizen-ship" in a "multicultural society"', and that Botha's belligerent delivery was more problematic than the actual content.[74] We'll leave it to you to decide ...

'My father says'

The apartheid government had a long history of playing with reform in the form of disingenuous offerings. They first offered to release Mandela in 1973, but there was no way the ANC leader could possibly accept terms that required him to abandon politics and live out his days in K.D. Matanzima's Transkei. In 1985, a few months before the Rubicon speech, Botha made the government's sixth (but first public) offer to release Madiba, this time on condition that he 'reject violence as a political instrument'.

Botha believed he had painted his adversary into a corner, but, not for the last time, Mandela deftly assumed the moral high ground. After slipping his response to his wife Winnie during a prison visit, he arranged for his twenty-five-year-old daughter Zindzi (one of the few members of his family not subject to a banning order) to read it out at a UDF rally at Jabulani Stadium in Soweto on 10 February 1985. Zindzi, wearing a yellow UDF shirt, 'was ushered by Desmond Tutu and Allan Boesak through the jubilant crowd which then lifted her shoulder high to the platform'. The 'My father says' speech was the first time Mandela had addressed his people in twenty-two years:

> I am surprised by the conditions the government wants to impose on me. I am not a violent man. It was only when all other forms of resistance were no longer open to us that we turned to armed struggle. Let Botha show that he is different to Malan, Strijdom and Verwoerd. Let him renounce violence. I cherish my own freedom dearly but I care even more for yours.[75]

After the Rubicon speech, Padraig O'Malley noted 'a subtle shift became increasingly apparent: Botha was the prisoner, and he desperately needed Mandela to release him.'[76]

A blessing in disguise?

On the face of it, the implementation of the Tricameral Constitution, the ensuing police brutality and the massive let-down that was the Rubicon speech will be remembered as some of the lowest points in our nation's history. But with the benefit of hindsight, Botha's absurd war on reality – and the impassioned extra-parliamentary response it provoked – almost certainly helped to hasten the end of apartheid. In many ways Total Strategy was the Total Shakespearian Tragedy our country required. 'Caesar' did not cross the Rubicon, but instead he met his Brutus in the form of F.W. de Klerk.

In his 1986 annual address, Oliver Tambo summed up Botha's predicament perfectly:

> Realising that power is slipping out of its hands, the Botha regime [has] adopted new and more brutal ways of governing our country... Completely unable to deal with this enormous general crisis, Botha has increasingly lost contact with reality. Illusions are taking the place of facts. The hollow dreams of a tyrant appear to him to be the very essence of policy... [The Botha regime] has lost the strategic initiative. That initiative is now in our hands.[77]

Speaking after the train wreck, cabinet minister Gerrit Viljoen called the Tricameral Parliament 'the greatest miscalculation in the history of the National Party'.[78]

The last sitting of a whites-only parliament under the 1961 Constitution took place on 11 July 1984. Little did they know what the future had in store for them

PART FOUR
OVER THE RAINBOW

In 1994, a full 140 years after the Cape's first non-racial election,
South Africans of all races were at last able to make their mark.
Not for the first time in our history, the honeymoon would be short-lived.

CHAPTER 12

THE VIOLENT PANGS
OF A MIRACLE BIRTH
1994

'Making peace is like making love: no one can do it on your behalf.'
– Niël Barnard[1]

The long walk to freedom made just a little longer by the snaking queues to the polls

---

As VOTING QUEUES SNAKED ACROSS open fields and parking lots, onto pavements and into those holiest of places – polling booths – as men and women of all races stood together harmoniously, waiting patiently to make their cross on a ballot paper the length of an African python, the whole world marvelled at the peace and pleasantness of the first truly non-racial election in South African history.

Just how a country that had been at racial war with itself for hundreds of years could simply come together on four days in late April 1994 and decide on a leader was a *deus ex machina* moment. As Wellington said of the Battle of Waterloo, it was a near-run thing. And as this chapter reflects, 'battle' is precisely the word that best describes the violent carnage that bombarded the lead-up to the election.

No more *nog 'n pieps*

The birthday candle was blown out in 1989. The apartheid party was over. The Berlin Wall fell and the *rooi gevaar* ebbed. The Cold War, which had played such an important role in sustaining apartheid, was done and dusted. The trickle of support the apartheid regime was receiving from the West was about to be turned off. And P.W. Botha knew it.

Early in 1989, on the advice of the head of the National Intelligence Service, Niël Barnard, P.W. agreed to meet Mandela. He took some time to come around to the idea, but when he did, the apartheid regime secretly transported Mandela – in a new suit for the occasion – to Tuynhuys. Mandela, who had been pressing for such a meeting, had little idea of what to expect from the Groot Krokodil. Nor had Niël Barnard, who was sweating bullets over whether P.W. might unleash his infamous atomic warhead of a temper.

But the meeting went as well as could be expected. Both Mandela and Botha agreed that a negotiated settlement was by far the most sensible route for South Africa. And to Mandela's astonishment, Botha went as far as to pour him a cup of tea. As Mandela left under police guard, Botha suggested to him – as if he was strolling off to a house in Vredehoek – that he should keep in touch.

The Krokodil rocked

Botha had suffered a stroke a few months earlier, and when his weakness showed, his cabinet, who had grown weary of his autocratic attitude, pounced to unseat him. The man who would step into the breach was F.W. de Klerk.

Just what kind of a man De Klerk was is not easy to say. He was adamant during his time as leader that apartheid was simply a well-intentioned policy that had gone tragically wrong. In many ways this was a personal position as much as a political one. Admitting to the fundamental crime of apartheid would mean acknowledging that he, his father (a cabinet minister under Verwoerd) and his uncle J.G. Strijdom were criminals.

De Klerk was born with all the colours of apartheid coursing through his veins. Behind him in the laager stood his rifle-loading wife, Marike. After the 1983 referendum, F.W. had spoken at a public meeting about the need to extend political rights to black people. At this, Marike stood up in the crowd to berate her husband: 'If you had … witnessed the trauma of our people', she shouted at him, 'you wouldn't talk such nonsense'.[2] And sure enough, on being handed the tiller, F.W. ran a reactionary election campaign in 1989. His party faced stiff opposition from the right, and although the NP won, over 40 per cent of Afrikaners voted for the Conservative Party (CP).

Puppy dogs' tails

But whatever his love for segregation might have been, De Klerk was unique. As he said: 'If one has to cut off the tail of a dog, it is much better to do so with one clean and decisive stroke.'[3] This was a first in twentieth-century white South African history. It was the fundamental truth that the likes of Smuts and P.W. had not accepted. And on 2 February 1990, De Klerk took the dog by the tail and forded the Rubicon.

'My God, he's done it all,' Allister Sparks whispered to a fellow journalist as he watched F.W.'s speech in Parliament from an adjoining briefing room.[4] In one fell slice, De Klerk unbanned the ANC, SACP and PAC, lifted emergency regulations and media restrictions, and released Mandela. 'It is time for us to break out of the cycle of violence,' De Klerk stated, 'and break through to peace and reconciliation.'[5]

F.W. and Mandela
when he was still in prison

The first steps of freedom

Nine days later, on 11 February 1990, Nelson Mandela walked out of Victor Ver-
ster prison. He had gone to prison when the hand signal of the anti-apartheid
movement was the thumbs up. He exited jail (with his controversial wife, Winnie, at his side) raising the fist of black power. Then with Walter Sisulu beside
him and Cyril Ramaphosa holding the microphone, he spoke to the world for
the first time in twenty-seven years from the balcony of Cape Town City Hall,
overlooking the Grand Parade. 'Friends, comrades and fellow South Africans, I
greet you all in the name of peace, democracy and freedom for all,' he began. But
the peace was short-lived.

Sebokeng: Shooting people in the back

On 26 March 1990, an ANC protest ended in what would become an all-too-
familiar scene. When the sun set on the township south of Johannesburg, at
least eleven protestors lay dead and around 400 were injured. The massacre
occurred after a crowd of about 50 000 set out from Sebokeng to Vereeniging to
present a list of grievances. The police claimed that five stones had been thrown
at them during the march. The commanding officer, W. du Plooy, confirmed
that he had not ordered his men to fire on the crowd, but that five stones were
provocation enough. Many of the victims were shot in the back while attempting
to flee the scene. Mandela immediately called off a meeting with the government,
stating that De Klerk could not 'talk about negotiations on the one hand and
murder people on the other'.[6] De Klerk appointed Judge Richard Goldstone to
investigate the massacre.

ANCMKCOSATUUDF

De Klerk's 2 February speech had caught everybody by surprise, not least the
ANC. They were ideologically confused and unsettled as to how to approach
negotiations. Trained members of Umkhonto we Sizwe in exile, who were still
composing and practising martial songs about marching to Pretoria, were now
being issued South African travel documents and welcomed home by white
immigration officials.

Initially, there was a mixed bag of unhappiness, justified paranoia and utter
organisational chaos in the ANC. The recently released Sisulu was genuinely

shocked by the level of dissent and confusion that reigned among the rank and file in meetings in Lusaka. Adding to this confusion, the ANC began incorporating local UDF structures and established a political alliance with COSATU. Within this alphabet soup was not only every race and language group in South Africa, but a mixed muddle of exiles and 'inziles' (as domestic activists were termed) who had decidedly different political cultures. Just how they all managed to form a single political serving is perhaps one of the great South African miracles.

Conference calls

Even Mandela was partly hamstrung by the divisions. In July 1991, in Durban, the ANC held its first conference in South Africa in over thirty years. Jacob Zuma, with hair still covering the patch from which the showerhead would later emerge, welcomed the 2 224 delegates to his home province. Mandela stood unopposed for the position of president and was effectively handed the mantle from Oliver Tambo, who, clearly suffering from the side effects of a stroke, gave the opening address.

But the conference went directly against Madiba's wishes when it came to electing a secretary-general, rejecting the incumbent Alfred Nzo, who was his preferred candidate, in favour of a young COSATU leader named Cyril Ramaphosa. In fact, three men ran for the position. The third was Jacob Zuma, but Ramaphosa trounced them both.

The whole conference was filled with factious jostling. Chris Hani and Thabo Mbeki had both wanted to run for the position of deputy president, and both took some persuading not to by the party elders who felt that a head-to-head battle would weaken the party in the eyes of the country. Mbeki would have his long-time ally Zuma run for the position of secretary-general. When Zuma (and the Mbeki faction) lost humiliatingly to Ramaphosa, Zuma was obliged, in Anthony Butler's words, 'to retreat licking his wounds'.[7]

The conference also elected many UDF members into the National Executive Committee, 'inziles' who were largely unknown to Mandela and exiles like Mbeki and Zuma. In his closing remarks, outgoing secretary-general Nzo took time to tick off the party: the ANC lacked 'enterprise, creativity and initiative,' he commented. 'We appear very happy to remain pigeonholed within the confines of populist rhetoric.'[8] Not the most positive farewell message, but certainly the most honest.

A right mess

But if there were hidden divisions in the ANC, the divisions among the white right were apparent for all to see. When the leader of the CP, Andries Treurnicht, called for a mass meeting after *Rooivrydag* (Red Friday, the day of De Klerk's groundbreaking speech) at the Voortrekker monument, 60 000 Afrikaners arrived with horses, ox wagons and guns. There Treurnicht, despite being a 'long-standing proponent of nonviolence', promised 'a third freedom struggle' and a *Volkstaat* for the Afrikaner people.[9] And you only had to look at the flags being flown to register that something was rotten in the *Volkstaat* of Treurnicht's imagination: waving in the crowd flew the old ZAR Vierkleur, the flag of the Orange Free State and the three-armed swastika of the Afrikaner Weerstandsbeweging (AWB). Under this Nazi-like banner was the bearded visage of Eugène Terre'Blanche, a belligerent firebrand, vulgar racist and lifelong advocate of violence. ET wanted to fight 'like our forefathers fought' to call his home a *Volkstaat*, but the simple truth was that the right-wingers had no single vision. Some have estimated that at the time there were 186 right-wing organisations all claiming to speak in some way for the *volk*.

The AWB's campaign of murder

In 1990 over fifty acts of right-wing terror were committed. Of these, the most serious was near Durban in October 1990, when three AWB members opened fire on a bus killing seven black people and wounding twenty-seven. Between 1991 and 1993, at least forty similar shooting episodes took place.[10]

In 1991 the AWB also began a bombing campaign. The targets were generally either NP or ANC offices and left-wing Afrikaans newspapers. Hillview High School was bombed because it planned to admit black students, as was the war museum where the peace treaty that ended the Boer War had been signed. But their most murderous bombs were saved for the days before the election ...

The AWB were not only interested in murdering innocent black people. Almost on par with their hatred of other races was a passionate hatred for *volksverraiers* – Afrikaners seen to be betraying the *volk*. And *volksverraier* number one was F.W. de Klerk.

The Battle of Ventersdorp

On 9 August 1991 De Klerk was scheduled to give a speech in Ventersdorp, an ultra-right stronghold. That night Terre'Blanche called up around 2 000 AWB members to prevent De Klerk from speaking. This deployment of khaki-clad, swastika-emblazoned right-wingers came armed with rifles, pistols and tear gas, and the front line of men had their arms cast in plaster of Paris to fend off police dogs. They were met by around 1 500 armed policemen. Guns were fired, and a thirty-minute melee of hand-to-hand fighting broke out on Voortrekker Street. By the end of it, three AWB members lay dead and around forty were injured. Seven policemen were also wounded in the fighting, several being treated for gunshot wounds. The AWB then turned on members of the local black population, who had to be protected and rescued by the police. It was the first time since the Rand Revolt that police had opened fire on and killed white protestors.

I(ndia) F(oxtrot) Papa Zulu

Although many thought the white right would be the most troublesome road-block to the election process, this was not the case. As Martin Meredith states, the right's political and terror activities were soon 'overshadowed by a far greater danger emerging from the green rolling hills of Natal where a vicious struggle for power had developed. It centered on the controversial leader of the KwaZulu homeland, Mangosuthu Gatsha Buthelezi.'[11]

Gambling with lives

Mangosuthu Buthelezi is perhaps the most complex character in this book. Prime minister of KwaZulu and head of the Inkatha movement, he had always played a high-risk hand, gambling with both the apartheid regime and the anti-apartheid movements. But he never entirely came up trumps.

Buthelezi had once been a member of the ANC, which had encouraged him to form Inkatha. But he broke from the ANC in 1979 when they criticised him for advocating capitalism, opposing sanctions and presiding over an apartheid institution (the KwaZulu homeland). As Leonard Thompson puts it, Buthelezi then 'identified himself as a Zulu nationalist, in contrast to the broad South African nationalism of the ANC'.[12] In the 1980s Buthelezi went about building

Inkatha in opposition to the ANC proxies in the country, something that was encouraged by the apartheid regime. He was nevertheless at times a thorn in the side of the regime, and even Mandela acknowledged that he did play an important role in ending apartheid, above all by refusing independence.

Supported by conservative chiefs, Buthelezi began running KwaZulu as a one-party state 'with gross violations of human rights, while most urban and better-educated Zulus supported the ANC'.[13] The two sides fought for control of the KwaZulu–Natal area, and what were termed 'faction fights' were a regular phenomenon in the 1980s.

With the unbanning of the ANC and Inkatha becoming the Inkatha Freedom Party (IFP), there was an intensification of what were referred to as 'attacks'. IFP 'hit squads' and ANC 'self-defence units' (SDUs) fought each other in rival villages, killing men, women and children, burning homes and stealing cattle. One example was the so-called 'seven-day war' in March 1990 near Pietermaritzburg. Inkatha 'hit squads' were bussed in, and in the ensuing attacks over eighty people were killed and 20 000 left homeless.

Over 8 500 people would be killed in the KwaZulu–Natal area in political violence between 1989 and 1994.[14] Most of the victims of these kinds of attacks were ANC supporters, but a significant number of IFP supporters were also killed. As Thompson states, 'Mandela tried to calm the situation in KwaZulu but without success, largely because local ANC warlords prevented him from dealing directly with Buthelezi until it was too late to be effective.'[15]

Violence between the IFP and the ANC spread when Inkatha began a campaign in the Transvaal with a focus on recruiting miners living in hostels. As Meredith writes, 'hostels were a natural recruiting ground for Inkatha'[16] as they were occupied mainly by Zulu-speaking workers from KwaZulu–Natal areas.

On 22 July 1990, what became known as the 'Reef War' broke out across the Vaal Triangle. Hostels were turned into 'Zulu fortresses' when Zulu hostel-dwellers expelled Xhosa-speakers and other non-Zulu-speakers, while the ANC 'expelled Zulus – who were assumed to be Inkatha supporters – from the townships, forcing them to take shelter in workers' hostels'.[17] In August 1990 alone, over 500 people were killed in townships on the Rand as a result of ANC/IFP violence.

When addressing the issue of the 'Reef War' and the 'attacks' in KwaZulu-Natal in speeches, Mandela said that he believed they 'bore the hallmark of organised, covert government death-squads'.[18] This phenomenon would be named 'the Third Force'.

The Third Force was with us

A great deal of mystery surrounds the existence of the 'Third Force'. The idea was actively discussed by P.W. Botha as early as 1985, and there is little doubt that Botha's old structures were involved in the attempt to destabilise the country and the ANC.

As it turned out, the South African Defence Force (SADF) and police units had provided valuable financial and military assistance to the IFP in the form of money, training, weapons and personnel, and collaborated with the homeland government in covert activities against the ANC. Key Inkatha personnel were on the security forces' payroll.

The Truth and Reconciliation Commission later found that members of the SADF's special forces had collaborated with the IFP in planning massacres. Eugene de Kock aka 'Prime Evil', the infamous head of the Vlakplaas death squad, testified to having carried out attacks in the townships to destabilise them. It was also uncovered that in 1986 the SADF had trained an Inkatha paramilitary unit (or hit squad).

In July 1991 the *Weekly Mail* broke the story that South African security police in Natal had, with cabinet knowledge, provided R250 000 to Inkatha to help organise political rallies.

More direct evidence of third-force activities was exposed in November 1992, when the Goldstone Commission uncovered a 'dirty tricks' operation set up by military intelligence to discredit ANC politicians. Ferdi Barnard, a former criminal hitman who had been convicted of two murders, had been hired to implicate ANC politicians in criminal activity with a 'network of prostitutes, homosexuals, nightclub managers and criminal elements'.[19] (These days far less of an effort would be needed.)

The conventional approach

But as 1991 rolled on, the pressing question was when the negotiations for the transition would begin. Both Mandela and De Klerk were keen to get the ball rolling, but there was little forward movement until Cyril Ramaphosa telephoned the young NP minister Roelf Meyer. Their famous chemistry had an almost immediate reaction, and on 20 December 1991 various parties gathered in the glass-encased exhibition hall of the grandiosely named World Trade Centre in Kempton Park, near Joburg's Jan Smuts Airport.

Comprising nearly three hundred delegates of all races, including a large percentage of women, what became the Convention for a Democratic South Africa (CODESA) was a hugely different affair from the convention that had unified South Africa in 1910. There were delegations from the government, eight political parties and the ten homelands. And right from the start there was trouble. The PAC, the Azanian People's Organisation (AZAPO), and the Conservative Party and its *broeders* further to the right all refused to participate. And more importantly that great fly in the democratic muti, Buthelezi, declined to join the negotiations himself, although he did allow an IFP delegation to take part. Buthelezi's insistence on standing on the outside of the democratic tent and, as the saying goes, pissing into it, would become one of the main narratives of the negotiations. In hindsight, it did both him and his followers a great disservice.

Three future presidents at CODESA: Zuma, Mandela and Ramaphosa

But the IFP story took a bit of a back seat on the first day, when what was meant to be a meet-and-greet and exchange of pleasantries turned into a heated spat. Mandela had magnanimously agreed to allow De Klerk to speak last. F.W. took the opportunity to accuse the ANC of reneging on its promise to dismantle its military wing. Incensed by what he deemed to have been a trick, Mandela strode to the lectern and demanded a right to reply, stating:

> Although he wants these democratic changes, he has sometimes very little idea what democracy means and his statement here, many people will regard it as very harsh, where he is threatening us... He is forgetting that he cannot speak like a representative of a Government which has got legitimacy and which represents the majority of the population.

The normally unflappable De Klerk was visibly rattled.[20] And there was potentially more trouble brewing for the NP...

The 19 February by-election in Potchefstroom was touted as a barometer of white sentiment in the country. The pressure was on for De Klerk as he went to campaign personally in the constituency in the days leading up to the poll. But the CP won it with a swing of 11 per cent. F.W. was in trouble. Days later he announced that a whites-only referendum would take place on 17 March to decide if he had a mandate to continue the negotiations. He later stated: 'I decided to bite the bullet and to resign as leader if the referendum did not produce a positive result.'[21]

A yes/no question

The yes/no question put to voters was 'Do you support the continuation of the reform process that the state president started on 2 February 1990 and which is aimed at a new constitution through negotiations?'

De Klerk knew that he would have at least two allies: the Democratic Party (formed from the PFP) and the ANC. Mandela called on all whites to vote 'Yes' and warned that 'No' could only lead to civil war. And with South Africa playing World Cup cricket for the first time, many whites went to the polls thinking that the joy of international sport might end if they voted 'No'. Polls had predicted that 'Yes' would win 55 to 45 per cent, while De Klerk's own estimate was that he would win a troubling 53 per cent.

But De Klerk woke up on his birthday on the 18th and announced to the country: 'Today we have closed the book on apartheid.' In a huge voter turnout, 68.7 per cent of white South Africans had voted 'Yes'. In both Durban and Cape Town, the 'Yes' vote was as high as 85 per cent.

In the first week of
March 1992, eighty-three people
were killed in political violence

The result had a surprisingly negative effect at CODESA, where a fight broke out over the Constitution. Emboldened by the referendum, the NP insisted a 70 per cent majority should be required for decisions in the (elected) Constitution-making body, and a 75 per cent majority would be needed for decisions concerning the Bill of Rights, regions and the structure of government. The ANC demanded the international standard of a two-thirds majority on all issues. After a lot of pushing and pulling, the ANC briefly seemed to agree to a 70 per cent majority. But according to David Welsh, Ramaphosa engineered a deadlock in order to push the NP further into a corner. And when De Klerk refused to back down on the constitutional issue, CODESA broke down. The ANC subsequently called for a campaign of mass action, and violence once again broke out.

The massacres at Boipatong

The day after the mass action began, a group of Inkatha supporters unleashed mayhem on the township of Boipatong, south of Johannesburg. In what Sparks refers to as 'an orgy of slaughter', armed groups from the KwaMadala hostel rampaged through the township, murdering forty-five people and maiming twenty-two others.

Rumours circulated that the Zulu 'impi' had been brought in by police Casspirs and that police had escorted armed hostel-dwellers into the township. Another rumour (later verified) was that the police had received warning of an impending massacre and had dispersed ANC-aligned SDUs with birdshot and tear gas some two hours before the massacre took place.

The day after the massacre, Ramaphosa and Joe Slovo walked around the township talking to survivors. Ramaphosa told journalists covering the story: '[W]e charge President F.W. de Klerk and the government with complicity in this slaughter.'[22] De Klerk decided to visit Boipatong the next day, although it was made clear by the ANC that he would be unwelcome.

F.W. entered the township in an armoured Mercedes, accompanied by police in armoured Nyalas and a bus packed with press. As historian James Simpson says, 'a crowd of angry residents made good on the ANC's warning that De Klerk was not welcome in Boipatong, swarming his car and forcing him to take flight. Abandoning his plans to address residents, De Klerk's fleeing car hurtled over sidewalks, "scattering rubbish bins and sending chickens flying".'[23] In the ensuing mayhem of De Klerk's retreat, police shot and killed a young man. Sparks, who was there with his wife and eleven-year-old son, recalls:

> I saw the face of a man only two or three yards away disintegrate. Beyond, people were falling and rolling in the dust ... When the shooting stopped there was an eerie silence ... The police were still in a line ... one of them rose to his feet and began yelling in Afrikaans. 'Who told you to shoot?' he screamed at the policemen. 'I told you not to shoot without orders.' I walked among the fallen people counting them and trying to offer them what little help I could ... One man who I had seen hit, had his face shot away. A young woman press photographer was kneeling next to him, crying as she cradled his shattered head and tried to take his pulse. He groaned and died in her arms.[24]

Mandela visited Boipatong the next day. Speaking to residents on the soccer field where the shooting had happened, he said: 'I am convinced we are no longer dealing with human beings but animals ... We will not forget what Mr de Klerk, the National Party and the Inkatha Freedom Party have done to our people. I have never seen such cruelty.'[25]

A fisherman's tale

Mandela suspended all talks with the government. He and De Klerk were now barely on speaking terms, but one negotiating backchannel was still functioning. It had been set up when multimillionaire Sidney Frankel (later accused of paedophilia and whose name is now linked to a groundbreaking Constitutional Court judgment) invited Roelf Meyer and Cyril Ramaphosa to his trout farm.

As the story goes, Meyer's sons had begged their father to take them fishing but he lacked the skills. Ramaphosa, who was an experienced fly fisherman, stepped in and offered to teach them. When Meyer cast off, he got the hook caught deep in his left hand. According to Sparks, despite several attempts by both Ramaphosa

Cyril and Roelf: The two big fish
of the negotiation process

and his wife (a nurse) to remove it, they could not do so. 'There is only one way to do this,' Ramaphosa is claimed to have said. Getting some pliers, he took his opponent's hand and ripped out the hook. Blood spurted everywhere, but luckily Cyril's wife was at hand. From that moment on, trust is said to have grown between the two.

Several people have claimed that the story is either apocryphal or at the very least an exaggeration. Ramaphosa always denied that he and Roelf were friends in any conventional sense of the word, as they did not see each other socially. Nevertheless, the 'Cyril–Roelf' backchannel was created, and it played a critical role in keeping the subsequent negotiations on track. As Welsh puts it, 'Despite widely differing backgrounds, Meyer was in some respects Ramaphosa's counterpart in the NP. Both were relatively young and both were pragmatic as well as affable.'[26]

Meanwhile, the ANC continued to run their campaign of mass action. August 1992 was disrupted by strikes, and Mandela led around fifty thousand followers on a march through the streets of Pretoria. But the ANC also realised the need to place pressure on their foes running the homelands.

A murderous Oupa

As Chris Hani stated, Brigadier Oupa Gqozo's Ciskei was 'probably the worst example of tyranny in our country'.[27] In an interview in early September 1992, Gqozo said: 'I need some help to make the world realize that I am a very serious leader.'[28]

Ciskei was one of the heartlands of the ANC, and they believed that a rush and a push would reveal Gqozo to be a *not* 'very serious leader'. The plan was to cross the South African 'border' with a peaceful march on 7 September and occupy Bisho. The chief magistrate of Ciskei agreed to allow the marchers to assemble at Bisho stadium mere metres from the border, but stated that they should not go into the city itself. Ronnie Kasrils, one of the main organisers of the march, made it clear that he had no intention of heeding the ruling. Speaking to peace monitors over razor wire placed at the border to stop the march from entering Bisho, Kasrils stated that 'our intention is to come here and remain here'.[29]

Linking arms, Hani, Ramaphosa and Tokyo Sexwale initially led 70 000 to 80 000 people across the border and into the stadium without major incident.

But when a breakaway group of around 200 marchers directed by Kasrils exited the stadium and tried to enter Bisho through a gap in the razor wire, Ciskeian soldiers with itchy trigger fingers opened fire. Kasrils later recounted that the group 'instinctively' dove for 'mother earth' and lay there for 'an interminable time'.[30] Two two-minute bursts of machine-gun fire were pumped into the defenceless group. Twenty-nine people were killed.

Although the Ciskeian forces claimed that the ANC had started the shooting, the police memorandum stated that not one shot had been fired by the crowd. TV footage of the massacre shows Ramaphosa lying on the ground among the other marchers. He is then seen holding Sexwale's hand, visibly shocked, inspecting several of the dead. As Meredith states, the mood of South Africa at the time 'came ever closer to despair'.[31]

Concerning citizens

Once again South Africa was staring violence in the face. De Klerk and Mandela both concluded that it was essential to get the negotiations back on track. On 26 September they signed a Record of Understanding, agreeing that measures had to be put in place to stop the violence. Hostels would be fenced off and the carrying of traditional weapons banned.

The immediate effect of the Record of Understanding was to unite the ANC's enemies. Despite having hardly anything in common, on 6 October the Conservative Party, the Afrikaner Volksunie and the Afrikaner Vryheidstigting united with the homeland leaders Buthelezi, Gqozo and Lucas Mangope in what they called the Concerned South Africans Group (COSAG). COSAG not only shared a set of common goals but also, as Timothy Sisk puts it, 'an affinity for threats of violent resistance, or "war talk"'.[32]

Despite these concerning developments, negotiations between the ANC and NP hit a sweet spot. The process, now in full swing, was known as 'sufficient consensus'. It supposedly meant that if most parties agreed to something, they would move on. But as Ramaphosa described it, it really meant that 'if we and the National Party agree, everyone else can get stuffed'.[33] On 1 April 1993, a multiparty forum of twenty-six parties, including the IFP and CP, convened, and what became known as the Multiparty Negotiation Process (MPNP) – a streamlined, more effective version of CODESA – was formed. But then, disaster ...

The Polish assassin

Chris Hani was many things to many people. Often referred to as a 'hawk', he scared even some in the ANC. And his sabre-rattling was not simply talk. Unlike those who falsely claim MK 'veteranhood' in our current political environment, Hani was the genuine article.

As a high-ranking member of MK, he had led a group of ANC guerrilla fighters into Rhodesia in the late 1960s. He was captured and imprisoned for two years in Botswana for being caught entering the country with military weapons. Throughout his MK career, he had always promoted the idea of the intensification of the armed struggle and, controversially, even put forward the idea of targeting white civilians. This proposal was, however, rejected by the ANC.

After the Bisho massacre he began sounding a far more consolatory tone. As Sisk points out, in the weeks leading up to his assassination Hani 'had made repeated calls for peace and had denounced random attacks by the PAC's military wing on whites'. As Hani would say a few days before his death, 'I am now a combatant for peace.'[34]

On 10 April 1993, the anti-communist Polish immigrant and AWB member Janusz Waluś gunned Hani down in front of his home in Boksburg. Hani stumbled backwards against his garage door. Waluś then walked across the road and, standing over Hani's body, fired two more shots into the freedom fighter's head before leaping into his red Ford Laser and speeding off.

On hearing the commotion, Hani's white Afrikaner neighbour, Retha Harmse, went outside, took down the licence plate of the Ford – PBX231T – and phoned the police. Fifteen minutes later police arrested Waluś. The 9mm was still in his car. It would turn out that he was in league with Clive Derby-Lewis, a far-right MP and member of the CP. Waluś and Derby-Lewis were convicted of murder and sentenced to death (this was later commuted to life imprisonment).

As Sparks notes, 'anyone wanting to ignite an inferno of rage in the black community could not have chosen a better target'.[35] Riots broke out in several cities that led to the deaths of over seventy people. As the SACP's Jeremy Cronin put it, Hani's assassination came close to 'plunging South Africa into civil war'.[36]

The ANC realised that the country was on the brink of catastrophe. In the days that followed, they appealed for peace on television and radio. Mandela, who was on holiday in the Transkei at the time, rushed to Johannesburg to deliver a televised address to the nation. 'We must not permit ourselves to be provoked by those who seek to deny us the very freedom Chris Hani gave his life for,' he said.

Three days later, as the country lurched towards total insurrection, Mandela again appeared on television: 'Tonight I am reaching out to every single South African, black and white, from the very depths of my being. A white man, full of prejudice and hate, came to our country and committed a deed so foul that our whole nation now teeters on the brink of disaster. A white woman, of Afrikaner origin, risked her life so that we may know and bring to justice this assassin.'[37]

Hani's assassination cast a long shadow over South Africa

After this intervention the unrest subsided, and, with the National Party nowhere to be seen, Mandela took up the mantle of president-in-waiting.

The Joe Modise conspiracy theory

It is often claimed that Hani narrowly escaped being sentenced to death by the ANC in Zambia in 1969. He himself admitted that the majority of an ANC tribunal voted for him to receive 'the most severe punishment' for having put his name to what became known as the Hani Memorandum. The memorandum objected to the payment of salaries to senior ANC officials, most notably Joe Modise. It also objected to Modise's purchase of an expensive car and the 'double standards on health provision – senior leaders were sent abroad for medical treatment'. The people who signed the memorandum also accused Modise of consorting with 'dubious characters with shady political backgrounds'.[38]

Hani is alleged to have confronted Modise, some two weeks before his assassination, concerning the sale of a weapons cache worth $2.5 million. Years later, as minister of defence, Modise would be at the centre of another arms deal – one that would mar the post-apartheid political landscape for decades.

For these reasons some have speculated that elements within the ANC may have had a hand in Hani's assassination. The fact that Waluś and Derby-Lewis seem to have known that Hani's bodyguard had the day off on the day of the assassination raised a red flag. R.W. Johnson in particular has suggested that Zuma and Mbeki had much to gain by Hani's death. The matter is pure speculation, however.

The dry tinder that surrounded the date

The effect of Mandela's television appearances was that he was widely seen to be in control of the country. After Hani's funeral, Cyril Ramaphosa held a press conference at the World Trade Centre calling for negotiations to be sped up. In the month that followed, twenty-three of the twenty-six participating parties signed a declaration of intent, stating that elections would be held no later than April 1994. On 3 June 1993, the MPNP decided that South Africa's first truly multiracial election would take place on 27 April 1994.

Terrorist attack on the World Trade Centre

On 25 June a group of men adorned in khaki brought women, children, picnic hampers and braai-making equipment to the World Trade Centre. For the festivities they also brought along guns, hunting knives, AWB swastikas and a custard-coloured armoured car. As Sparks reported, the mood outside the WTC was festive as these people smashed up cars and abused journalists. After these fripperies, the horde surged to the front of the building, where former SADF general Constand Viljoen, the newly elected leader of the Afrikaner Volksfront, attempted to dissuade them from breaking into the building. But the AWB had other plans.

Closely followed by AWB foot soldiers shouting 'K*****, we are going to shoot you dead today', the armoured car smashed through the plate-glass doors of the WTC. They then took to wrecking the place, abusing people and urinating on the floors and furniture. Rumours spread throughout the building that the AWB had come to kill Cyril and Roelf, prompting the ANC and government delegates to lock themselves in offices under security protection. In one video, a woman in the building can be heard calling on the police to shoot the intruders, but although several policemen were injured in scuffles, they seem to have been less willing than usual to open fire when confronted by white men.

Once the AWB had put their penises back into their pants, there was time for a quick prayer, the singing of 'Die Stem' and a speech by Terre'Blanche. Sixty people were arrested, while the remainder went outside to light braais, drink beer and drunkenly march their extended bellies around the park.

The 6/25 attack on the World Trade Centre

Murder in the cathedral

Exactly a month after the storming of the WTC, members of the PAC's military wing, the Azanian People's Liberation Army (APLA), entered St James Church in Kenilworth, Cape Town, opening fire with AK-47s and throwing hand grenades into the congregation. Eleven people were killed, although the death toll may have been far worse if one of the congregants, Charl van Wyk, hadn't had his own firearm with him and fired back at the four APLA members, wounding one.

In the next six months, further APLA attacks took place at the King William's Town golf club and the Heidelberg Tavern in Observatory. In both massacres, four people were killed and many were wounded. APLA also carried out attacks at hotels in East London and Fort Beaufort. What was clear was that the PAC was not only refusing to suspend the armed struggle, but they were prepared to hit soft targets that had nothing to do with apartheid power structures.

Of course, you could always count on the Nats to make a bad situation worse. The intelligence services believed that APLA was operating from bases in the Transkei, and on 8 October 1993 SADF commandos entered the homeland to kill APLA operatives. The mission proved an utter fiasco. While storming a house in Umtata, the soldiers opened fire and killed five youths, including a twelve-year-old who was thought to be reaching for a gun. The weapons cache believed to be at the house was not found, and it was never proved to be an APLA 'safe house'.

A healthy constitution

But the violence could not now distract the political process. The MPNP delegates got the bit between their teeth and began to bash out the Interim Constitution. They agreed that

- a two-thirds majority in a joint sitting of both houses of Parliament would be enough to change the Constitution;
- a Constitutional Court should be formed to arbitrate over the constitutionality of laws and government actions;
- South Africa would be divided into nine provinces, and the homelands would be incorporated into these provinces. Federal powers, although considerable, would stop short of US federalism; and
- proportional representation would replace the first-past-the-post voting system that had led to a minority of the minority white electorate controlling the country in 1948 (although this would come with its own set of issues).

The Interim Constitution also contained a mix of 'capitalist' and 'socialist' rights. Several people wondered just how some of these rights – like the right to water and the right to child nutrition and basic health services – could be substantively upheld in a court of law. These rights were in many senses aspirational and a blueprint for the imagined ethical and political future of the country. Just what did happen to these rights is a question well worth asking.

Far more controversial were the rights to property and land. This was a matter on which both the NP and the DP remained firm. The Interim Constitution stated that '[e]very person shall have the right to acquire and hold rights in property' but that property rights could be expropriated for public purposes and 'the payment of such compensation ... may be determined by a court of law as just and equitable, taking into account all relevant factors, including, in the case of compensation, the use to which the property is being put, [and] the history of its acquisition.'[39]

The Interim Constitution, which would create an important foundation for the Final Constitution, was the result of a negotiated settlement on the part of the NP and the ANC. The ANC would be handed 'unfettered majority rule' via the proportional representation system, but this would be subject to some constraints on its powers within the economy. But most people seem to forget that Ramaphosa ran circles around the Nats and achieved most of the ANC's goals. The NP in comparison achieved very few. Minority rights, entrenched power-sharing, a formal federal system and a 75 per cent constitutional amendment clause all fell by the wayside as Cyril and his team, with carrots and sticks, urged and forced the apartheid regime ever onwards. As Welsh puts it, 'numbers, increasing mobilisation and support, the capacity for mass action, including strikes, and command of the moral high ground in much of the international community, inexorably shifted the balance of influence in [the ANC's] favour.'[40]

Sunset on the GNU

It was agreed that there would be a form of compulsory power-sharing until 1999 – what Joe Slovo famously called the 'sunset clause'. This was a strange-looking beast that was rather aptly called the GNU (Government of National Unity). All minority parties that won 20 per cent of the vote were allowed a deputy president, and all parties that won 5 per cent of the vote would be given a place in the cabinet. However, after 1999 the sun would set on this South African invention, and the country would go back to the democratic practice of majority rule.

The deadline for registering to participate in the election was set for 12 February 1994. But the CP, IFP, PAC, AZAPO and the ruling parties in the Ciskei and Bophuthatswana all failed to do so. The date was then extended to 4 March. Constand Viljoen, for one, saw sense and, announcing the creation of the new Freedom Front party, registered a few moments before midnight on the due date.

The Alien White Boer (AWB) invasion of Bop

It had been decided in the negotiations that Bophuthatswana, like all the other homelands, would be absorbed into South Africa on election day. But one man was having absolutely none of this.

Lucas Mangope had hoped to maintain Bop under his control in some form of federal system. The Nats had warned him this was decidedly unlikely, but he was nevertheless determined to hold on. South Africa's ambassador to Bop, Tjaart van der Walt, stated: 'I love him dearly but he is living in another world.' When Mandela tried appealing to the homeland leader, he said the experience was rather like 'talking to a stone'.[41]

Things began to unravel when Bop's civil servants, who had grown anxious about their futures, went on strike. Students and ordinary citizens joined in the protests, which led to extensive looting, particularly of the Mega City shopping mall in Mmabatho. As the situation got worse, Mangope turned to another set of stones.

The homeland leader contacted Constand Viljoen (a member of the so-called 'Freedom Alliance' – a pressure group comprising the Afrikaner Volksfront, Inkatha and the CP, among others), requesting he send a force to bolster the Bop army, but making clear that the AWB would not be welcome. Viljoen mobilised 1500 right-wingers from the paramilitary Boere Krisis Aksie, who entered Bop to await orders. Off his own bat, the extraterrestrial Terre'Blanche then organised 600 members of the AWB's Ystergarde (Iron Guard) to enter Bop's territory. These 'delightful' human beings then went on what one of them referred to as 'K*****skietpiekniek' – indiscriminately firing at black civilians.

Incited by the AWB's murderous actions, the Bophuthatswana Defence Force mutinied and went on a hunting party of their own. Shouting ANC slogans, soldiers chased down the AWB rabble, who put their tails between their legs and fled, continuing to shoot at civilians as they went. Around sixty people were killed in this manner, including a nurse on her way to work. One convoy of these savages met a police and army roadblock, on which they opened fire. The army returned fire, and the last car in the convoy, an old light-blue Mercedes-Benz, came to a halt. Three bearded khaki-clad men slumped out into the dust. The driver was clearly dead.

The surviving men, who had been shooting at civilians and journalists minutes before, begged for help as the press swarmed around them. A policeman asked: 'What are you doing here?' The men looked bemused. Suddenly, another policeman armed with an assault rifle walked up to them and, as Judge Kriegler put it, 'shot them like dogs in the glaring publicity of television'.[42]

The SADF, who were awaiting developments nearby, moved in and took control. The battle for Bop was over, although this needed to be conveyed to the homeland's leader. Pik Botha and the ANC's Mac Maharaj were helicoptered to Mangope's palatial private residence. As Pik later related, he told Mangope: 'Look, Mr President, it's over.'[43]

The Zulu war

It may have been over for Lucas, but Buthelezi still did not yield. Mandela had gone to Durban on 1 March to meet him. 'I will go down on my knees,' Mandela said, 'to beg those who want to drag our country into bloodshed' and to persuade them not to do so.[44] De Klerk, too, held meetings with Buthelezi, but he would not budge. Henry Kissinger also arrived on a mission to change Buthelezi's mind, but none of his famous 'Machiavellian schemes' Monty Python had sung about could shift the IFP head. On departing, Kissinger said: 'I have never been on such a catastrophic mission and its failure now has cataclysmic consequences for South Africa.'[45]

Monday, bloody Monday

The reason for the march into central Johannesburg on 28 March by tens of thousands of Zulus bearing 'traditional weapons' and guns was said to have been to demand that KwaZulu be transformed from a homeland into a sovereign Zulu kingdom. The IFP claimed that the march was organised by Zulu indunas. But it was later revealed that several high-ranking members of Inkatha were behind the march, and the event application stated that it was 'for the purpose of launching a campaign by the IFP against the holding of the election'.[46] Themba Khoza, a leading IFP member who had been on the Vlakplaas payroll as a police informer, was instrumental in its planning.[47]

As the crowds of armed protestors began to make their way to the city, rumours were rife within the ANC security structures that their headquarters at Shell House would be attacked. What was more, reports of violence and

Pouring petrol on the flames: The march to Shell House

vandalism by the marchers were spreading across the city. As the crowds gathered, shooting began. In one incident the marchers dragged a truck driver from his vehicle and killed him. There were also reports that ANC security guards had opened fire on marchers and killed one person at the ANC offices at Lancet Hall.

Then, some of the marchers en route to the rally at Library Gardens found themselves outside Shell House, which the police had not deemed necessary to protect or cordon off, despite the fact that the ANC had specifically requested the marchers be kept away.

Tensions heightened. Believing they were under attack, ANC security guards at Shell House opened fire on the crowd, killing eight people. There is no evidence that the marchers had attacked (although there had been a great deal of provocation), and many were shot in the back.

As the day unfolded, another nine people were shot in and around central Johannesburg. Police were involved in some of these shootings, while others may have been killed by snipers on the roofs of buildings. Such was the chaos that armed marchers, ANC security guards and police all discharged weapons as if in the Wild West. By the end of the day around fifty people were dead.

Pre-Natal decisions

Despite the deaths of IFP supporters at the hands of ANC security guards, few people locally or internationally had much sympathy for Buthelezi. In what was termed a *deus ex machina* moment, Buthelezi's old friend, the Kenyan diplomat Washington Okumu, finally managed to get through to him and he agreed to participate in the election with only days to spare. For the Independent Electoral Commission, the IFP's late entry became a logistical nightmare, and stickers with the IFP logo had to be hand-stuck to the bottom of millions of ballot papers. But as the miracle of the election unfolded, the deed was somehow done.

Still, there was one group that was not going to let the election proceed without murder and mayhem.

The bombs of an unstable AWB

In the days leading up to the election, the AWB put into action a bombing campaign that rocked many parts of the Rand. A massive ninety-kilogram car bomb was detonated close to the ANC headquarters at Shell House on Sunday the 24th. Among the nine people killed were a pavement fruit seller and the ANC's Johannesburg secretary-general, Susan Keane.

The next day a 100-kilogram bomb (the biggest terrorist bomb ever detonated in South Africa) was placed in a trailer allegedly belonging to Eugène Terre'Blanche. The trailer was driven to Germiston where it was unhitched at a taxi rank. The explosion killed ten people and injured over a hundred.

Another bomb blast on the same day rocked the taxi rank near the Randfontein station, and an explosive device was thrown at minibus taxis parked under a bridge near Westonaria. Nobody was injured in either incident. Then, at 8.30 p.m., a pipe bomb exploded at a restaurant on the corner of the aptly named Bloed Street in Pretoria, killing three and injuring four.

On the first day the public went to the polls, on 27 April, a car bomb was detonated in Johannesburg's Jan Smuts Airport in front of the international departures terminal. The blast shattered plate-glass windows, blew a hole in the roof and sent debris raining down into the airport. Eighteen people were injured, two of them seriously.

In total, thirty-one people were killed in bomb blasts in April. Forty members of the AWB were arrested for these crimes, many of them receiving lengthy prison sentences. Several polling stations were also set on fire and destroyed in further attempts to kibosh the freedom and fairness of the election.

The cost of a 'peacefully' negotiated settlement in South Africa was not insignificant:

Deaths due to political violence from 1989 to 1994[48]

Year	KZN	Total
1989	1279	1403
1990	1811	3699
1991	1057	2706
1992	1427	3347
1993	1489	3794
1994	1464	2476
Total	8527	17425

Awaking to an election

Despite the AWB bombs, the fact that KwaZulu and Natal only had one week to prepare, and the lack of a sufficient voters' roll, the election proceeded. Enemies,

Mandela voting in KZN, with Jacob Zuma lurking in the background

racists and xenophobes (as well as peace-loving South Africans) all stood together, waiting to place two pieces of paper into a box. Under the banner headline 'Vote, the beloved country', *The Star* newspaper reported that the queues 'were long and friendly'.

Sparks suggests it was for many a joyous moment, but not one of great celebration: 'It was I believe a sense of personal liberation – for blacks, liberation from oppression; for whites, liberation from guilt.'[49] One black man in the queue said to him: 'Now I am a human being.'

The days of voting were followed by days of counting, none of which were free from disorder, confusion and chaos. But whatever the inconsistencies of the election, it was largely considered free and a fair representation of the people's will.

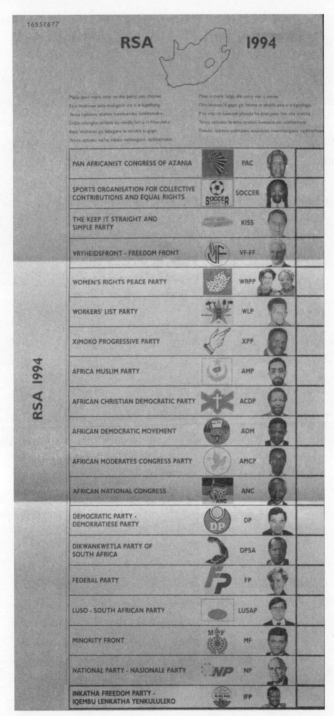

The long ballot of freedom, with the IFP stuck at the bottom

On 2 May, with the counting far from complete, F.W. conceded defeat, stating in a speech:

> Mandela has walked a long road and now stands at the top of the hill. A traveller would sit down and admire the view. But a man of destiny knows that beyond this hill lies another and another. The journey is never complete. As he contemplates the next hill, I hold out my hand in friendship and in cooperation.[50]

On the same day, at a party organised at the Carlton Hotel, Mandela told the nation:

> I stand here before you filled with deep pride and joy – pride in the ordinary, humble people of this country. You have shown such a calm, patient determination to reclaim this country as your own. And joy that we can loudly proclaim from the rooftops – free at last! ... I promise that I will do my best to be worthy of the faith and confidence you have placed in me and my organisation, the African National Congress. Let us build the future together, and toast a better life for all South Africans.[51]

When the dust settled and the scores were tallied from a far from perfect electoral system, the Independent Electoral Commission declared the results as follows:[52]

Party	Votes	Per cent	Seats
ANC	12 237 655	62.65	252
NP	3 983 690	20.39	82
IFP	2 058 294	10.54	43
Freedom Front	424 555	2.17	9
Democratic Party	338 426	1.73	7
PAC	243 478	1.25	5
African Christian Democratic Party	88 104	0.45	2

Mbeki, Mandela and De Klerk inaugurating a new South Africa

The miracle birth

The new South Africa was delivered tired, unhealthy and gasping for breath, but it was nevertheless a miracle birth. The recovery would certainly be long, and as we see today it is far from complete.

Although proportional representation and the party-list system was the answer to one of the problems that had previously plagued South African politics, it contained its own issue: a lack of direct accountability to the people. And as this partially unaccountable child grew up, it developed some distinctly anti-social(ist) behaviours. Greed, corruption and a totally unacceptable accumulation of wealth at the expense of the poor gripped many of the former fighters for social justice. And if Jacob Zuma is to be believed, it will take another miracle birth in the form of the Second Coming of Jesus Christ before the ANC falls from power. Which is not to say the ANC has not had some internal growing pains of its own ...

CHAPTER 13

THE MULTIPLYING CONSEQUENCES OF LONG DIVISION: POLOKWANE AND NASREC
2007 and 2017

'I am deeply hurt [by the divisions in the ANC] where a sister is attacking a sister and comrades are at each other's throats.' – Winnie Madikizela-Mandela, 2007[1]

Zapiro hit the nail on the showerhead with this 2006 prediction

S INCE 1994 THE FUTURE OF SOUTH AFRICA has been decided not at the national polls but at the ANC's elective conferences, where a few thousand delegates from the ANC's branches choose the president of the party – and therefore of the country. Two of these contests stand out.

'You could see his power leaving him'

The atmosphere in the inner precinct of the Expo Centre in the Johannesburg suburb of Nasrec on the evening of 18 December 2017 was electric – even if it was difficult to hear oneself think as throngs of singing, dancing, shouting dele-gates cheered on their chosen candidates. When it was finally time to announce the new leader of the ANC, journalist Nickolaus Bauer had long since given up trying to keep track of what was happening on the main stage. He was too far from the action to be able to do much more than drink in the atmosphere of what promised to be a seminal moment in our young democracy's history.

Then Bauer turned around and found himself face to face with none other than ... Jacob Zuma. 'It was a complete fluke,' he remembers with a laugh. 'And one of the highlights of my career.' After composing himself, he whipped out his iPhone and started recording. 'I had no idea which way the vote would go,' he says. 'But I realised I had a unique opportunity to capture JZ's reaction to it. Come what may.'[2]

Zuma had gone to Nasrec knowing that it would be his last party conference as ANC president. With national elections due a year and a half later, he had probably also accepted (despite rumours that he was plotting an unprecedented third term) that he'd soon have to relinquish his role as president of the country. But with the threat of commissions of inquiry and criminal charges swirling, he was determined not to let the conference mark the end of his political career. For Zuma and his corrupt cronies, the Guptas, to cling to power in some form, it was vital that his ex-wife Nkosazana Dlamini Zuma defeat Cyril Ramaphosa for the ANC presidency.

The twenty-five-second video – which is all over the internet – is worth watching. 'It's almost like the guy has an out-of-body experience,' says Bauer:

When the numbers were announced, I could see him trying to make sense of what they meant. For a second our eyes caught. And then I could just see the 'Oh shit moment' when he realised NDZ had lost ... A few days later [veteran political analyst and broadcaster] Stephen Grootes pointed out to me that you could actually *see the power leaving him*. Looking back that's exactly what I was witnessing. In barely a second his power just seeped away, starting from his face and rippling its way down through his chest and his stomach ...[3]

Nasrec marked the end of what many have termed South Africa's 'lost decade' under Zuma. And the beginning of what just as many hoped would be a new dawn under Ramaphosa.

But let's go back to the beginning ...

JZ at the moment he realised that CR had beaten NDZ

A child of apartheid[4]

Matamela Cyril Ramaphosa was born in Western Native Township, near Sophiatown, on 17 November 1952, to policeman Samuel and community activist/ entrepreneur Erdmuthe. He wasn't just a lot younger than most ANC leaders of his era, he also had the distinction of having lived his entire life in South Africa.

As a young boy, Cyril and his family of devout Lutheran Vendas lived among coloureds, Zulus and Sothos, and he went to a Tswana school. That all changed in 1962 when, under the Group Areas Act, Western Native Township was declared 'coloured' (and under renamed Westbury). The Ramaphosas were shunted off to 'grim and unappealing' Tshiawelo (Verwoerd and co. had the audacity to choose a Venda name that meant 'place of rest'), a remote new part of Soweto for Vendas only.

When he was sixteen, Cyril went back to his Venda roots, enrolling as a boarder at Mphaphuli High School near Louis Trichardt. Cyril claims the decision was his, but it's likely his parents wanted to get him away from the activist friends he'd started making in Soweto. If this was their plan, it didn't work. At Mphaphuli, Cyril immersed himself in community activism and empowerment. Within days of his arrival, this 'special student' was elected chair of the Student Christian Movement, which, under his leadership, did loads to improve the lives of local families who were among the most marginalised and maligned souls in a country that specialised in marginalisation and malignment.

At Mphaphuli Cyril met Tshenuwani Farisani, a Black Consciousness activist and Lutheran minister-in-training who was to have a lasting impact on his protégé. As Ramaphosa's biographer Anthony Butler explains,

> The Lutheran Church of Cyril's parents proclaimed that God had created earthly government – even in South Africa – and that God's creations were respected by all men. Farisani, however, emphasised that even if God had created government, the system of apartheid which was driving this authority in an evil direction was the creation of men. These men could rightly be castigated as selfish, bigoted and racist.[5]

Cyril's connection with the Black Consciousness movement deepened at Turfloop (one of the 'bush colleges' that were the apogee of Bantu Education; now the University of Limpopo), where he quickly rose in activist circles. In 1974 he spent eleven months in solitary confinement, and following the Soweto uprising he was jailed for a further six months for assisting student protestors including his younger brother, Douglas, who was arrested shortly afterwards.

After his release in February 1977, he found a job as an articled clerk with Henry Dolowitz, and he was admitted as an attorney in 1981. During the same period, he was also elected to the board of the Urban Foundation, an organisation set up by 'liberal' mine owners, including Harry Oppenheimer, with the purpose of finding a way out of South Africa's problems while still retaining control of the mines. Here, Cyril struck up an unlikely friendship with Clive Menell, the CEO of Anglovaal. Cyril would stay at the Menells' home regularly. Quite something considering his next gig...

'It's Ramaphosa all the way'

Almost everyone who's had dealings with Ramaphosa remarks on his incredible ability to master situations, as Butler's biography attests:

- As a legal clerk for Henry Dolowitz in the late 1970s, Ramaphosa made a point of taking the 'Whites Only' lift up to his offices every morning. As Dolowitz recalls, 'The superintendent used to give me hell all the time about it ... But he never said a word to Cyril.'[6]

- When Ramaphosa was arrested during a dispute at a Phalaborwa mine in the mid-1980s, National Union of Mineworkers (NUM) lawyer Clive Thompson spent the whole day fighting to get him released. When Thompson eventually went to collect him from the cells, 'he emerged barefoot and dusty, but essentially unmoved by everything around him ... No great indignation over his incarceration, no great jubilation or appreciation upon his liberation. No sense of martyrdom either. He was just doing the necessary and wearing the consequences.'[7]

- Reflecting on the CODESA negotiations, F.W. de Klerk observed that Cyril's 'relaxed manner and congenial expression were contradicted by coldly calculating eyes, which seemed to be searching continuously for the softest spot in the defences of his opponents. His silver tongue and honeyed phrases lulled potential victims while his arguments relentlessly tightened around them.' Tertius Delport, one of the main Nat negotiators, meanwhile, was almost in awe of Ramaphosa: 'Oh he has impressed me for sure. Angered me ... I respect him for his ability, oh yes, I respect him for his ability. I think Ramaphosa ... is the outstanding personality in the ANC. He is superior by far to Mbeki, for instance, in terms of the sheer force of personality, the sheer presence. It's Ramaphosa all the way.'[8]

Cyril entered the world of work a couple of years later and made a beeline for the black trade unions, which had been effectively unbanned (the white communist mineworkers of the Rand Revolt must have been turning in their graves). In 1982, at the age of twenty-nine, he was set the seemingly impossible task of establishing the nationwide all-black National Union of Mineworkers.

Others would have run a mile from the impregnable hostels and their antediluvian white mine managers who had no time for the changes in the law, but not our Cyril. He jumped in his car and started visiting mines, and in the NUM's first two years he managed to sign up a quarter of a million members! In 1987 he led the biggest mine strike in South Africa's history, with 340 000 coal and gold miners downing tools on 9 August. While the strike was ultimately defeated and the mine owners took the opportunity to 'improve efficiency' (i.e. fire people) in the decade that followed, it was a massive moment in the political history of both South Africa and Cyril Ramaphosa.

A Negotiating Cyril (ANC)

Cyril first came into contact with the still-banned ANC in about 1983, and he enjoyed a truly meteoric rise within the organisation. He used his legendary negotiating skills to help to secure the release of the Robben Island prisoners on the ANC's terms, and from February 1990 he was constantly seen at Mandela's side. As we have seen, only five years after joining the ANC, he was elected its secretary-general.

At one point, Cyril's star was so bright that he seemed destined to succeed Mandela as president of the country. But once it became clear that the older and supposedly wiser Thabo Mbeki had outmanoeuvred him, Cyril made other plans. At the urging of Mandela and Dr Nthato Motlana (an older Soweto businessman and former leader of the ANCYL), he was persuaded to join Motlana's black empowerment company, NAIL. And nail it he did, becoming one of South Africa's richest businessmen.

Ramaphosa was apparently not at all amused when Motlana told him that upon his return to politics, 'You will have enough money to be incorruptible.'[9]

Opening Pandora's box at Polokwane

Mbeki duly succeeded Mandela as president of both party and country. By the time the ANC's 52nd national elective conference in Polokwane rolled around in 2007 he was well into his second term. Political scientist and ANC expert Susan Booysen believes that 'Polokwane 2007 was the opening of the ANC's Pandora's box'.[10] As Winnie Madikizela-Mandela said,

I have been a member of the ANC for more than 50 years and there have been many contestations in the past, but never has it been characterised by such a high level of acrimony, personal attacks, accusations and counter-accusations and a total disregard for the ANC and what it stands for by both sides.[11]

Ever since Polokwane, writes Booysen, the ANC has been plagued by rampant factionalism, 'free-for-alls in mobilisation to secure enclaves of power in the party and in the state, and rejection of the idea of movement elders being supreme in wisdom and authority... It was a cathartic event for the ANC, changing the movement permanently.'[12]

Polokwane also established the 'slate' system whereby opposing factions each proposed a slate of names to occupy the top six positions in the party. This was in many ways similar to the shift towards party politics that took place in the 1890s, first in the ZAR and then in the Cape Colony – except it was happening within the party, not on the national stage. As Stephen Grootes explained to us, 'before slates, the idea was that every quarter of the party would be represented', as the candidates who received the most votes would make it into the top six. The change to the slate system, and the idea that only one slate would prevail, meant that as much as 49 per cent of the party could feel aggrieved at the result of an election.[13]

The reasons for this cataclysmic rift were at once exceedingly complex and dreadfully simple. While Mbeki has mainly been remembered for his catastrophic AIDS policy, this doesn't seem to have had too much to do with his failure to hang on to the ANC reins. Despite the fallout from the corruption accusations surrounding the Arms Deal (more on this soon), the Zuma camp was emboldened by three factors:

1. The growth of the ANC in KwaZulu-Natal and the under-representation of Zulus in top leadership.
2. The fact that Mbeki was seeking a third term as the ANC's leader. 'A third term would allow him to control government from Luthuli House and to install a puppet leader as state president,' says Butler, adding: 'A third term often turns into a life presidency.'[14]
3. Mbeki's increasingly erratic and paranoid leadership.

'People forget what he was like,' says Grootes. 'He was incredibly difficult, prickly, ignored the point, inaccessible, and impossible on AIDS. At the time many people felt that Zuma couldn't possibly be worse than Mbeki.'[15]

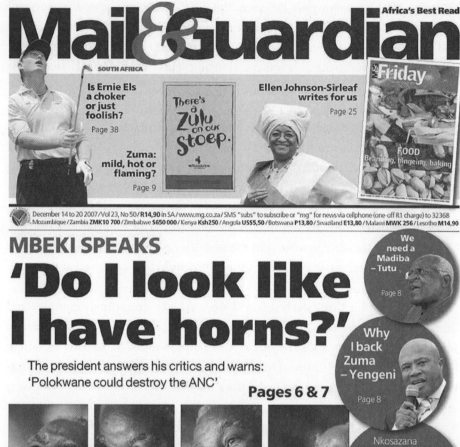

Mail&Guardian

SOUTH AFRICA

Africa's Best Read

Is Ernie Els a choker or just foolish?
Page 38

Zuma: mild, hot or flaming?
Page 9

There's a Zulu on our Stoep.

Ellen Johnson-Sirleaf writes for us
Page 25

Friday

FOOD
Branding, bingeing, baking

December 14 to 20 2007 / Vol 23, No 50 / **R14,90** in SA / www.mg.co.za / SMS "subs" to subscribe or "mg" for news via cellphone (one-off R1 charge) to 32368
Mozambique / Zambia **ZMK10 700** / Zimbabwe **$650 000** / Kenya **Ksh250** / Angola **US$5,50** / Botswana **P13,80** / Swaziland **E13,80** / Malawi **MWK 256** / Lesotho **M14,90**

MBEKI SPEAKS

'Do I look like I have horns?'

The president answers his critics and warns:
'Polokwane could destroy the ANC'

Pages 6 & 7

We need a Madiba – Tutu
Page 8

Why I back Zuma – Yengeni
Page 8

Nkosazana Dlamini-Zuma on the run-up to Polokwane
Page 4

ARMS DEAL

Ministers got millions

Pages 2 & 3

Trevor Manuel on the future
Page 4

PLUS
Manuel speaks about the ANC's ethos of service
Page 21

Mbeki got one thing right: Polokwane did go a long way towards destroying the ANC

The deal about the arms

When, in 1999, PAC MP Patricia de Lille lifted the lid on the rancid cauldron of corruption that was the Arms Deal, she precipitated a rift in the ANC that in many ways persists. In the very early days, remembers ANC whistle-blower Andrew Feinstein, it was Mbeki who pressured the Standing Committee on Public Accounts to drop their investigations. But this all changed when it emerged that the French arms manufacturer Thomson-CSF had agreed, via 'encrypted fax' (those were the days!), to pay Zuma R500 000 a year to 'protect their interests in South Africa'. Suddenly, Mbeki was claiming that the law should take its course and Zuma was 'trying every trick in the book to avoid his day in court'.[16] (*That* never-ending story!)

Attention soon turned to the relationship between Zuma and his financial advisor, Schabir Shaik, who was charged with 'gratuitously [making] some 238 separate payments of money, either directly to or for the benefit of Mr Jacob Zuma'.[17] Bulelani Ngcuka, the head of the National Prosecuting Authority (NPA), said that despite there being a *prima facie* case against Zuma, the deputy president would not be charged alongside Shaik as the case against JZ 'could not be won'. When Shaik was eventually found guilty on 2 June 2005, Judge Squires said there was 'overwhelming' evidence of a corrupt relationship between him and Zuma.[18] This set off one of the more convoluted and memorable legal chain reactions in our country's muddled jurisprudential history.

Twelve days after Shaik's conviction, Mbeki 'released' Zuma as deputy president of South Africa, appointing none other than Ngcuka's wife, Phumzile Mlambo-Ngcuka, as his replacement. A week later, new NPA boss (the organisation was engaged in what seemed like an endless round of musical chairs at the time) Vusi Pikoli announced that Zuma would be charged on two counts of corruption. But the rot didn't stop there. In December 2005, Zuma was charged with raping the daughter of a family friend – a woman who became known to the press as Khwezi. Despite knowing Khwezi was HIV-positive, Zuma testified that he did not use a condom because there was little chance of men contracting the disease. He also said that he took a shower after having sex with her because 'it was one of the things that would minimise contact with the disease'.[19] And so the showerhead was born.

Throughout the trial, Zuma enjoyed the vociferous support of Julius Malema and the ANCYL, who gathered outside the courthouse to sing 'Umshini wami' ('Bring me my machine gun') and other struggle songs. Zuma was acquitted of rape in May 2006.

Juju back in his ANCYL days

In September 2006, Zuma's corruption case was struck from the roll (but, importantly, not completely dismissed) because the state had taken too long to prepare its case. But this technical glitch was never going to be the end of the matter. In the lead-up to the ANC conference at Polokwane, writes Grootes, 'there was a great deal of speculation about how and when the NPA would charge Zuma. That he *would* be charged was more or less a foregone conclusion; the conviction of Schabir Shaik for paying him money corruptly compelled Zuma to be charged for receiving that money. What was not known was the timing.'[20] Would it happen before or after Polokwane?

Making a mountain out of a Browse Mole(hill)

But Zuma was not the only one who felt the world was out to get him. Mbeki became increasingly paranoid as his presidency wore on, and he made a habit of firing or redeploying anyone who was seen to be against him. Rather predictably, these aggrieved souls eventually came together in a 'coalition of the wounded', which would back Zuma's bid for the ANC presidency at Polokwane.

As Mbeki's biographer Mark Gevisser writes, 'it was not unusual in the parallel universe that was the presidency between 2000 and 2002, to hear otherwise reasonable people saying, in absolute seriousness that the Americans might engineer "regime change" to get rid of a president'.[21]

In 2001 Mbeki allegedly got minister of safety and security Steve Tshwete to announce that high-profile ANC figures Mathews Phosa, Tokyo Sexwale and Cyril Ramaphosa were being investigated for plotting to overthrow Mbeki. Tshwete claimed, without proof, that the trio had accused Mbeki of being involved in the murder of Chris Hani. Recognising this tale as the nonsense it surely was, Mandela came out in support of the three musketeers. (When a judge exonerated them, Mbeki also did an about-turn – on this particular conspiracy theory, at least.)

In 2006 Mbeki told an NEC meeting that a group of people had conspired to oust him as president of both party and country. His only evidence? The fact that there had been some recent 'pro-Zuma demonstrations and media columns'.[22] But he saved the best for last, Booysen writes, with the leak in 2007 of

> the 'top secret' *Special Browse Mole Consolidated Report* about an alleged plot by Zuma, his left allies and former Umkhonto we Sizwe (MK) leaders, who allegedly conspired with President José Eduardo dos Santos of Angola and Libyan leader Muammar Gaddafi to 'overthrow' Mbeki ... The document provided evidence that Zuma's 'presidential ambitions are fuelled and sustained by a conspiracy playing out both inside South Africa and on the African continental stage'.[23]

Unfortunately, none of the allegations held up to scrutiny. The author of the report, senior Scorpions investigator Ivor Powell (a respected investigative journalist), admitted that he 'had compiled the report on instruction from Scorpions boss Leonard McCarthy'. Powell then explained, rather worryingly, that he had been 'required to use certain phrases and McCarthy did the conclusions and recommendations'.[24]

After reading the report, Vusi Pikoli, who was momentarily enjoying his time in charge of the NPA hamster wheel, was not convinced. He passed it on to the SA Secret Service and the National Intelligence Agency, and they reached 'consensus that there were huge question marks about some of the information ... in the report'.[25] Pikoli said he had never approved the Scorpions' investigation, and in February 2008 (i.e. after Zuma had won at Polokwane) the report was found to have been produced illegally.

As Zuma-friendly journalist Ranjeni Munusamy (who later became a fierce Zuma critic at the *Daily Maverick* and has subsequently been accused of corruption at the Zondo Commission) noted, the irony of it all was that *Browse Mole* actually 'opened Zuma's path to the ANC presidency ... Had the NPA and its political masters not run their malicious, two-pronged media-prosecutorial operation against Zuma, the Polokwane revolt would probably not have happened'.[26]

Which brings us neatly to said revolt ...

Jacob's ladder

In truth, *Browse Mole* was only one of the reasons Mbeki was toppled. Booysen explains that Mbeki 'precipitated Polokwane' because he mistakenly believed that

his 'loyalists and performance record in government, rather than ANC endorsement, would carry him and his circle into another term.'[27] By stacking the NEC
with yes-men and ignoring the rest of the ANC, Mbeki erected the gallows that
would be used to hang him. Publicly expressing his desire to be a three-term ANC
president who would 'save South Africa from Jacob Zuma' only tightened the noose.
(Butler feels that Mbeki might have 'supported Zuma to be his deputy in 2002 not
just because of Zuma's power in KZN but also because Zuma was vulnerable to
prosecution. This suggests Mbeki was already thinking about his third term.'[28])

Mbeki probably assumed that Zuma's many legal troubles would be the end of
his presidential bid. But JZ proved to be made of a mixture of Teflon and cunning.
As ANC stalwart Pallo Jordan once stated, '[Zuma] has great native intelligence, and
that is shown in part by the fact that he is wise enough to be conscious of his own
limitations.'[29] Case in point: his decision to leave it to veteran anti-apartheid activist
(and fellow Schabir Shaik acquaintance) Mac Maharaj to mastermind his campaign for the party presidency. JZ and Mac needed plenty of 'native intelligence' to
wrest control of the ANC from the ground up. The ANC's leaders had technically
always been elected by paid-up party members, but in the ninety-odd years prior to
Polokwane the real power had almost always been exerted from the top. Mac
changed that by mobilising vast numbers of ordinary members to vote for JZ.[30]

'The carpetbagger in the Presidency'

Jordan's use of the term 'native intelligence' was probably a reference to Ronald
Suresh Roberts's book *Fit to Govern: The Native Intelligence of Thabo Mbeki*.
Suresh Roberts was so close to Mbeki that the *Sunday Times* described him as
'the carpetbagger in the Presidency', for which he took them to court. Acting
Judge Leslie Weinkove ruled that this description did not amount to defamation.
In his written judgment, Weinkove explained why: 'Mr Roberts, you were
obsessive … and also haughty, arrogant, self-important, a name-dropper,
excessive, outlandish, vindictive, venomous, relentless, evasive, argumentative,
opportunistic, unconvincing and untruthful.'[31]

Mbeki had always favoured a smaller ANC, often quoting Lenin's phrase 'better
fewer, but better'; i.e. 'having a smaller number of higher quality members was
better for party and country'.[32] While this stance appears to have been born out
of genuine concern for the party, it would come back to bite Thabo.

Zuma took advantage of the many enemies Mbeki had made during his presidency to secure the support of several provincial party leaders and the leadership of the party's Youth and Women's Leagues. It goes without saying that the bonds that held this 'coalition of the wounded' together had far more to do with a mutual loathing for Mbeki than they did with a love for Zuma. Either way, when the provinces nominated their slates a couple of months before the conference, Zuma was preferred by KZN, Mpumalanga, Gauteng, the Northern Cape and Free State, not to mention both aforementioned leagues. Despite Mbeki's support in the Xhosa heartland of the Eastern Cape (whose 153 000 members made it the largest ANC province at the time), Zuma still seemed assured of victory. What once had been termed 'the Xhosa Nostra' was slowly losing its grip on the ANC.

There were two ways in which the Mbeki camp might have been able to overcome what the *Mail & Guardian* referred to as the 'Zunami'. One, given that conference delegates vote individually and in secret, they could attempt to persuade delegates to vote against the wishes of their provinces. And, two, they could seek to have pro-Zuma delegates barred from attending the conference due to various voter irregularities. These included, writes Ferial Haffajee, widespread accusations of vote-buying – 'backyard branches [and] "ghost" members whose ID numbers are used by rent-seekers to buy membership in order to create branches to buy votes and secure executive positions for themselves'.[33]

Just before the conference, twenty-nine Free State branches were instructed to elect new delegates, and 100 Gauteng delegates were barred from even attending. But this seems to have been the tip of the iceberg. At the time, Zuma's choice for deputy president, Kgalema Motlanthe, conceded that vote-buying was 'rampant and pronounced'.[34]

The Polokwane conference in December 2007 was unlike any in the ANC's history. Pro-Mbeki voices were drowned out by raucous renditions of 'Umshini wami' and other pro-Zuma songs. The soccer hand signal for substitution featured prominently. And the Youth League demanded that votes be counted manually – computers, they argued, simply couldn't be trusted.

By the end of the first day, a rumour was doing the rounds that, having seen the writing on the wall, Mbeki would withdraw. He ended up sticking it out, but less than twenty-four hours later his gut feel would be confirmed. Zuma – and, tellingly, everyone else on his top-six slate – had the support of more than 60 per cent of the party.[35]

Province	Zuma votes	Mbeki votes
KwaZulu-Natal	580	9
Free State	287	76
Mpumalanga	263	37
Gauteng	262	94
Northern Cape	137	106
Eastern Cape	322	520
Limpopo	210	224
Western Cape	87	142
North West	88	186
TOTAL	2236 (62%)	1394 (38%)

If you are in any doubt of the scale of Zuma's victory, compare his performance in KZN to Mbeki's in the Eastern Cape. The Zulu populist JZ nabbed a staggering 98.5 per cent of the votes in his home province, while out-of-touch Mbeki only managed 61 per cent in the Xhosa heartland of the Eastern Cape, the traditional epicentre of the party. It was a decisive moment in the simmering Zulu–Xhosa rivalry that had bubbled just under the party's surface ever since the faction fighting of the 1980s and '90s.

As Booysen notes, Zuma toppled the incumbent by bringing together a motley crew of

> rebellious youth leaders [including Julius Malema], diehard nationalists, reformed and subjugated Mbeki-ists, conventional ANC leaders of moderate nationalist and non-socialist persuasion, those who had been hurt or aggrieved in the course of Mbeki's long tenure, irrespective of ideological inclination, and unionists and socialists who saw in the Mbeki fallout the opportunity to enter and influence the ANC from within.[36]

Many would say that this sort of organisational schizophrenia has plagued the ANC ever since, and that Ramaphosa (or anyone else for that matter) will never be able to prevent the inevitable sinking of the ship. Only time will tell.

Of lame ducks, spy tapes and COPEing mechanisms

While the party had voted against him, Mbeki was still the president of the country, and he was hellbent on using his position to keep Zuma out of the top job. Just ten days after his victory at Polokwane, corruption charges against Zuma were reinstated. At the same time, it emerged that tapes had been made of conversations between former NPA boss Ngcuka and Scorpions head Leonard McCarthy in which the two were said to be discussing when the most politically damaging time to charge Zuma would be.

The precise contents of the so-called 'spy tapes' would only be revealed in September 2014, when the Supreme Court of Appeal ruled that the Democratic Alliance could access transcripts of the thirty-six conversations. But just knowing that they existed was sufficient fodder for the Zuma camp. While Ngcuka no longer held any official sway, the fact that his wife had taken over from JZ as deputy president gave the spy tapes a decidedly fishy odour. It was hard not to jump to the conclusion that Mbeki might have pressured the NPA to prosecute Zuma. This is certainly the conclusion Judge Chris Nicholson reached when he found that the charges were most likely politically motivated and should be withdrawn:

> The timing of the indictment by Mr Mpshe [the new acting head of the NPA] on December 28 2007, after the president [Mbeki] suffered a political defeat at Polokwane was most unfortunate. This factor, together with the suspension of Mr [Vusi] Pikoli [the previous NPA head], who was supposed to be independent and immune from executive interference, persuade me that the most plausible inference is that the baleful political influence was continuing.[37]

The 'Nicholson obiter' was seized upon by Zuma as evidence of a conspiracy against him and was used as a pretext to get rid of Mbeki. After a heated meeting at Esselen Park (named after Louis, Smuts's sidekick during the Rand Revolt), the ANC's NEC voted to recall him. And on Sunday 21 September 2008, Mbeki announced his resignation in a televised address to the nation. Kgalema Motlanthe – number two on the Zuma slate at Polokwane – would hold the fort until the 2009 elections.

After a few days of confusion, it was confirmed on 24 September that six Mbeki loyalists (including Mlambo-Ngcuka) had resigned from cabinet. The following day Motlanthe was sworn in as president. And a day after that it was confirmed that a breakaway party would be launched in due course. After only fourteen years in power, was this the moment of truth for the ANC?

While many in the media and the opposition thought it might be, Jacob Zuma was unperturbed. As he said:

One thing that we know from decades of experience [is that] anyone who has left the ANC, for whatever reason, has failed to shine. The ANC is simply bigger than the individuals in it.[38]

On 1 November 2008, the Congress of the People (COPE, inspired by the name of the 1955 gathering that adopted the Freedom Charter) was launched by Mosiuoa Lekota, Mbhazima Shilowa and Mluleki George. The ANC immediately applied to the Pretoria High Court to prevent the party from using the name. But COPE's lawyers 'told the court that the ANC was simply "running scared" of the new movement and denied that the name would confuse the electorate'. The court dismissed the ANC's application with costs.[39]

On 12 January 2009, the Supreme Court of Appeal set Nicholson's judgment aside, but by then it was too late. Zuma had long since been confirmed as the ANC's candidate for state president. On 6 April, just sixteen days before the general election, the charges against Zuma were once again dropped.

On 22 April Zuma romped his way to the presidency with 65.90 per cent of the vote. COPE could only muster 7.42 per cent, putting them in third place behind the DA. (Five years later COPE's share had shrunk to 0.67 per cent, fulfilling Zuma's prophecy.)

Malema, Marikana and Mangaung
No sooner had JZ been elected president than South Africa's economy went into recession for the first time in seventeen years. And for once it wasn't even Zuma's fault. Like Hertzog in 1929, the South African president was forced to deal with the impact of a global economic downturn precipitated by events in the United States. Unlike Hertzog, Zuma did precious little to improve the lot of the people who'd voted for him.

July 2009 saw the start of service delivery protests, which have continued pretty much unabated ever since. The country's problems were temporarily forgotten in 2010 when we hosted the FIFA World Cup. But just weeks after the last vuvuzela had sounded, some of Zuma's COSATU allies started to turn against

Mazibuko, De Lille and Zille: The DA's vision
of a multiracial, female leadership didn't last long

him. First, general secretary Zwelinzima Vavi (who had been a Zuma stalwart at Polokwane) accused JZ of leading 'a powerful, corrupt and demagogic elite of political hyenas'.[40] Vavi then led a nationwide strike of nurses, teachers and other public servants. These factors contributed to a poor showing for the ANC in the 2011 municipal elections (62 per cent of the vote compared to 65.9 per cent in 2009) and the DA jumping from 16 per cent to 24 per cent.

Chastened, the ANC's various factions turned their attention to the party's centenary conference, which was to be held in December 2012 in Mangaung. Vavi doubled down on his corruption allegations, and Julius Malema, who had once said he would 'kill' for Zuma, abruptly switched sides, describing Mbeki as 'the best president the country ever had' and publicly rueing his decision to back the 'domkop' Zuma.[41] (It should be noted that there was no love lost between Vavi and Malema. Just a few months prior, Juju had said that Vavi was doing Helen Zille's job as leader of the opposition for her.) Vavi and Malema stole the headlines, but Zuma also had less-vocal opponents within the ANC: by this point many prominent members were muttering about his 'Zulufication' of the ANC and his improper 'friendship' with the Guptas.

Just not cricket

As keen supporters of Western Province cricket, the authors of this book were not best pleased when, in 2004, our beloved home ground was renamed Sahara Park Newlands. Our objections, however, were broadly anti-corporate and had nothing to do with the exact nature of the sponsor's business – the Sahara computer group seemed innocuous enough.

Little did we know. Since setting up shop in SA in 1993, brothers Ajay, Atul and Rajesh (also known as Tony) Gupta from the Indian state of Uttar Pradesh established a sprawling business empire based on an octopoid patronage network whose tentacles reached to the very highest levels of government. While the Guptas wangled their way into the lives (and wallets) of many in Mbeki's inner circle, they took things to the next level with Zuma. Several members of Zuma's immediate family worked for Gupta-owned companies and over the years, numerous Zuma weddings, homes and holidays were bankrolled by the Guptas. The Guptas' newspaper *The New Age* and news channel ANN7 were both fiercely pro-Zuma.

Of course, there's no such thing as a free lunch. During the Zuma years,

Gupta companies were awarded state contracts with alarming regularity (Tegeta Resources' nabbing of the Eskom coal contract was a real high point), and several accusations emerged of them effectively hiring and firing government ministers. Before a family wedding in 2013, they were also, infamously, allowed to land a private plane at the Waterkloof Air Base near Pretoria.

Free breakfast: JZ and Atul Gupta at the launch of *The New Age*

In an attempt to shore up support ahead of Mangaung, Zuma fired two ministers who had been accused of corruption (the irony) and did nothing to stop Malema from being suspended from the ANC for five years for utterances 'which sought to portray the ANC government and its leadership under President Zuma in a negative light'.[42] (Early in 2012, none other than Cyril Ramaphosa presided over the committee that rejected Malema's appeal against the decision.) Zuma also attempted to appease the left-leaning side of the party by bringing SACP leader Blade Nzimande into his cabinet.

Zuma hoped that these measures would result in him being elected to the party leadership unopposed. But Motlanthe, his second-in-command, had other ideas. As Butler writes, 'he expressed his disdain for the direction Zuma was taking the ANC and the country [and] decided he would not serve as a fig leaf for Zuma's erratic and corrupt leadership'.[43] Motlanthe had also got it into his head that the position of party president must be contested, but much like Slim Piet Joubert he did not want to openly campaign for the position.

Kgalema's cunning plan?

Butler suggests that Motlanthe's decision to run against Zuma might have been part of a plan hatched by him and Gwede Mantashe to pave the way for an eventual Ramaphosa presidency:

> Kgalema is an enigmatic and complex politician. He was aware that the deputy presidency was valuable only as a stepping stone to the presidency and that he himself would not be able to take this step. He described speculation that he played a key role in the rise of Ramaphosa to the deputy presidency as 'implausible'. But that doesn't mean that it isn't accurate.[44]

Zuma's long-term strategy was to get either his ex-wife Nkosazana or KZN premier Zweli Mkhize to succeed him as party president in five years. But he could not risk going to Nasrec with a Zulu number two. Better to let them work on their CVs and come back with a bang in 2017. To this end, Zuma controversially managed to land his ex-wife the position of chair of the African Union Commission. (She reputedly burst into tears when she heard she was being shipped off to Addis Ababa but warmed to the idea once he'd explained the logic behind it. Mkhize, meanwhile, would run for and easily win the position of ANC treasurer-general on Zuma's slate.)

Motlanthe was still Zuma's first choice for a deputy. But by March 2012, it was reported that JZ was on the lookout for an alternative running mate if Kgalema refused to play ball. Oddly, Cyril Ramaphosa's name was the one most loudly whispered. As Butler notes, 'there was no love lost between Zuma and Ramaphosa', who had pipped Zuma to the position of secretary-general way back in 1991. But politics is seldom about friendship. Zuma wanted Ramaphosa for several reasons: he had strong ties with the NUM and COSATU; he would provide ethnic balance to the top six; and his name would be well received by investors and middle-class, mostly urban voters. But 'above all, Cyril was an attractive number two because his prospects of succeeding Zuma seemed to be so slight'.[45]

These prospects sank even lower when, in August 2012, the Marikana massacre rocked the country. After a week-long build-up of tension between striking miners and security forces that saw around ten people (including two policemen and two security guards) lose their lives, tragedy struck on 16 August when thirty-four miners were shot dead by police. Marikana was the deadliest use of force by the South African state in the democratic era.

In the legal inquest that followed, George Bizos, who was representing the victims, drew a line all the way back to another massacre in which most victims had been shot in the back:

> Since Sharpeville there has been a stratagem on police violence against people of not appointing anybody to be in control ... This will help them to say we were under attack and we shot in self-defence. In this case [Marikana] there may have been the same stratagem.[46]

Marikana was a tragedy. Protesting, poor, underpaid black workers were not supposed to be gunned down in the new South Africa. And to make matters worse, Ramaphosa – who has been a lifelong activist for miners' rights and was imprisoned in the wake of the 1976 uprising – now sat on the other side of the ~~machine gun~~ table. As one of the board members of Lonmin, Ramaphosa could have interceded on the miners' behalf. Instead, a chain of emails sent to the Farlam Commission of Inquiry showed that he had done precisely the opposite. Before the massacre, he wrote to the rest of the board saying:

> The terrible events that have unfolded cannot be described as a labour dispute. They are plainly dastardly criminal and must be characterised as such ... There needs to be concomitant action to address this situation.[47]

'In a twist of logic,' writes Butler, 'the shadow of Marikana also made the case for Ramaphosa stronger.'[48] Zuma assumed that Ramaphosa would never be able to challenge for the top job with this stain on his reputation. Here, JZ was writing himself into a long history of South African leaders underestimating their rivals. A history that goes all the way back to the Zulu kingdom, and one which Zuma himself had been part of – in the 2000s very few people had thought he would ever bounce back from his corruption and rape trials.

So, when Motlanthe declared that he would run against JZ at Mangaung, Cyril slipped seamlessly onto the Zuma slate in the number two spot. While there was talk before the conference that the vote might be a close-run thing, this ignored the massive increase in ANC members in provinces that supported Zuma and/or his cronies. Between 2010 and 2012, the number of ANC members in KZN jumped from 192 618 to 331 820, in Mpumalanga they increased from 46 405 to 132 729 and in the Free State they leapt from 41 627 to 121 074.[49] If Zuma's victory at Polokwane was evidence that the ANC leadership could be won via the branches, Mangaung was the smoking gun. Despite the inner sanctum of the party being very much divided over Zuma's leadership, he won by a landslide, beating Motlanthe by 2 978 votes to 991. Everyone else on his slate won by a simi-lar margin, with the exception of Jessie Duarte, who was re-elected unopposed.

All smiles

Of chicken runs and cabinet reshuffles

A lot had changed by the time the ANC's Nasrec conference rolled around in December 2017.

On 5 December 2013, the death of Nelson Mandela had provided temporary respite to Zuma, who, barely a week earlier, had been dealing with the *Mail & Guardian*'s leak of Public Protector Thuli Madonsela's preliminary report (titled 'Opulence on a Grand Scale') into R246 million worth of irregular spending on the president's Nkandla homestead.

After a stirring and seemingly heartfelt address to the nation in which Zuma described Mandela as South Africa's 'greatest son', political author William Gumede was quoted as saying,

> Mandela's death has rescued Zuma politically. He was getting to a tipping point with Nkandla and other crises ... The ANC might get some temporary relief. Its own polls had said the highest they could get in the [2014 general] election was 55% and the lowest 45%. But now they might get 60% again because people who'd decided they weren't going to vote may now give them one more chance.[50]

As it turned out, Zuma was booed by sections of the crowd at the memorial for Mandela at the FNB Stadium on 10 December. But the ANC managed 62.15 per cent in the elections, which took place on 7 May the following year. Zuma was sworn in for a second term and Ramaphosa slipped quietly into the deputy president's chair. Helen Zille's DA jumped more than 5 per cent, to 16.66 per cent (read into all those sixes what you will), and Julius Malema's much-talked-about Economic Freedom Fighters (EFF) managed only 6.35 per cent, an even worse showing than COPE's debut in 2009. (Unlike COPE, which has faded into insignificance, the EFF has increased its share of the vote in almost every subsequent election.)

After the elections, Zuma challenged Madonsela's final report into Nkandla (which had been retitled 'Secure in Comfort' but reiterated all the most damning allegations) in the courts. And he asked his police minister, Nkosinathi Nhleko, to prepare a report of his own. Astonishingly, Nhleko found that the infamous 'fire pool', the cattle kraal, chicken run, visitors' centre and amphitheatre were all 'necessary' security features and concluded that Zuma did not owe South African taxpayers a cent. The report was adopted by the National Assembly on 18 August 2015.

The source of JZ's discomfort

That year also saw Zuma and the Guptas' hollowing out of Eskom (and other state-owned enterprises) really hit home. Between January and September, the country experienced ninety-nine days of load-shedding, 'causing a decrease in manufacturing and mining output, dragging down economic growth'[51] and forcing us all to braai midweek. Then, to rub salt into the *tjops* wounds, Eskom coal scientists Mark van der Riet and Charlotte Ramavhona were suspended for expressing concerns about the quality of coal Eskom was being forced to buy from Gupta-owned Tegeta Exploration and Resources.

Things came to a head on 9 December 2015 when Zuma summarily replaced his competent finance minister Nhlanhla Nene with ANC back-bencher Des van Rooyen, an obscure former mayor from the West Rand. Nene had fallen out of favour with Zuma for taking on South African Airways chairwoman Dudu Myeni, who had been widely accused of corruption, and because he opposed a nuclear deal with Russia. In a single day, the rand lost 5.4 per cent against the US dollar and the JSE dropped 18.54 per cent.

Four days after his appointment, Zuma was forced to replace Van Rooyen with former finance minister and SARS commissioner Pravin Gordhan. But by then the people had had enough. December 16th – a very significant date in South Africa's history – marked the first #ZumaMustFall protests, with thousands of South Africans from all walks of life demanding the president's recall. One woman in her fifties told the BBC that it was the first protest she had attended 'since she saw friends and family killed during the 1976 Soweto uprising'.[52]

On 31 March 2016, after a drawn-out legal battle, the Constitutional Court found against Zuma in a unanimous ruling on the Nkandla affair. The court stated that Madonsela's 'Secure in Comfort' report on Nkandla was binding and ordered Zuma to pay back (some of) the money. Zuma duly obtained a loan for R7.8 million from VBS Mutual Bank, the preferred lender of EFF BFFs, which would be liquidated in 2018 after having defrauded customers out of over R1.8 billion.[53]

In the August 2016 municipal elections, the ANC limped to the worst electoral performance in its history, mustering *only* 61.95 per cent of the national vote and notably losing control of three major metros: Nelson Mandela Bay, Tshwane and Johannesburg.

By 2017, the year of the Nasrec conference, Zuma's position had become even more awkward. On 7 April tens of thousands of people gathered in all major towns and cities in the largest #ZumaMustFall protests yet. And in October the Supreme Court of Appeal ruled that he must face eighteen counts of corruption, fraud, racketeering and money laundering.

Under Mmusi Maimane the DA did manage to
win Tshwane, pipping the ANC by four seats

Ramaphosa, meanwhile, had been largely keeping his head down as deputy
president. By now Marikana was, for many people, an unfortunate but forgiv-
able blot on his copybook. In any normal country he would have been a shoo-in
to replace JZ when his second term came to an end. But the crazy thing was that
within the starkly divided ANC, Zuma still had a fifty-fifty chance of clinging on
to power via his proxy, Nkosazana Dlamini Zuma.

Honourable members

The stakes at Nasrec were extremely high for Zuma and his cabal of cadres,
ministers and friends with benefits. If Ramaphosa was able to wrest control of
first the ANC and then the country, there was a very real chance that many of the
individuals embroiled in his state of capture would have to deal with significantly
straitened personal circumstances. For some key individuals, including Zuma
and ANC secretary-general Ace Magashule, jail time was a distinct possibility.

It was only natural that those who had benefited most during the Zuma
administration would coalesce around the idea of an NDZ presidency, which
would keep the NPA in check and allow state capture and the influence of the

Guptas to continue unabated. Meanwhile, Ramaphosa and his slate of chosen leaders had campaigned on an anti-corruption ticket – even if some of their number, not least tainted former housing and finance MEC Paul Mashatile, had deeply dubious track records.

'I am unity and unity is me'

'Membership figures shed instant light on the health of an organization,' writes Booysen, '[and] the ANC's membership showed far-reaching declines in the period after 2012.'[54] Overall membership of the party dropped from 1.22 million in its centenary year to 989 000 in 2017. Twenty-three years into the democratic project, the party was in a severely weakened state.

But within this wider trend there were provincial winners and losers. The decline was most sharply felt in Zuma's KZN home base, where numbers dropped from a (falsely inflated?) Mangaung high of 331 000 to 181 000 in 2017. The Eastern Cape's importance continued to slip (from 24.7 per cent in 2007 to 14.2 per cent a decade later). But, in what seemed like a good omen for Zuma, the two biggest winners in the five years between Mangaung and Nasrec were North West (which had 6.2 per cent of ANC members in 2012 and almost double that five years later) and Mpumalanga (which leapt from having a 10.9 per cent share of the vote in 2012 to 16 per cent at Nasrec). And it was Mpumalanga that would prove the Nasrec kingmaker.

DD Mabuza: 'If Paul dies, I also die.'

In the lead-up to Nasrec, former Zuma-phile David 'DD' Mabuza and Paul Mashatile (long-time friends who happened to be on technically opposing slates) seem to have decided that an NDZ victory would be disastrous for the party's prospects at the national polls. Suddenly, they were prevailing on anyone who would listen (and many would) to opt for an alternative to the damaging, factional slate system. This they called 'unity', and it involved getting their supporters to vote for one another. ('If Paul dies, I also die' was the way Mabuza explained it.[55])

In her book *Balance of Power*, Qaanitah Hunter attempts to understand what was meant by 'unity':

> On 1 December 2017, I travelled to Nelspruit in Mpumalanga where Mabuza called the final meeting of ANC branches in his province. Bizarrely, 223 branches nominated 'unity' to become president, 123 voted for Dlamini Zuma and 117 voted for Ramaphosa ... Later, in a hilarious encounter, I asked Mabuza ... who 'unity' was, and he responded, 'I am unity and unity is me'.[56]

As Hunter goes on to note, 'All three groupings [CR17, NDZ and Unity] were unanimous in agreeing on two positions: that the deputy president should be David Mabuza and the treasurer-general should be Paul Mashatile'.[57]

Mabuza, a staunch supporter of Zuma at Polokwane and Mangaung, had been rewarded with the premiership of Mpumalanga in 2009. A year later he'd done so well for himself that thieves were allegedly able to steal R14 million in cash from his farm.[58] (He later claimed it was *only* R4 million.) And in 2015, after an alleged poisoning incident, he was allegedly flown in the Guptas' private jet to Moscow for medical treatment.

But that was then and this was now. The moment Nasrec hinged on was when Mabuza invited his supporters to 'vote with your conscience' just minutes before voting began. Quite a change from his promise to Zuma twenty-four hours earlier that he would deliver the 2500 votes needed to ensure an NDZ victory. (As the *Sunday Times* later reported, 'Mabuza did get the 2,500 votes, but only for himself.'[59])

This vote of 'conscience' seems to have pushed Ramaphosa over the line ahead of NDZ by a hair's breadth. Ramaphosa snuck it, and he knew it.[60]

	Ramaphosa slate		NDZ slate	
President	Cyril Ramaphosa	2440 (52%)	Nkosazana Dlamini Zuma	2261 (48%)
Deputy president	Lindiwe Sisulu	2159 (46%)	David Mabuza	2538 (54%)
National chairperson	Gwede Mantashe	2418 (52%)	Nathi Mthethwa	2269 (48%)
Secretary-general	Senzo Mchunu	2336 (49.7%)	Ace Magashule	2360 (50.3%)
Deputy SG	Zingiswa Losi	2213 (47%)	Jessie Duarte	2474 (53%)
Treasurer-general	Paul Mashatile	2517 (54%)	Maite Nkoana-Mashabane	2178 (46%)

After the vote, Cyril snapped a selfie
indicating the narrow margin of his victory

When the dust had settled, both camps had secured three spots in the top six and 'unity' – whatever that really meant – was the only clear winner. While Ramaphosa, NDZ and the party itself had all dismissed the possibility of a 'third way' in the lead-up to the conference, they now decided to embrace it. There had been talk among political commentators of a possible legal challenge to Magashule's victory (voting irregularities are common at ANC conferences, and with such a slim margin there was every possibility of it being overturned), but Ramaphosa put this to bed in his closing remarks to the delegates:

> In the months and weeks before this Conference, speculation was rife that this 54th National Conference would either not be held or that it would collapse.
>
> There were some who even suggested that Nasrec would represent the end of the ANC as we would emerge from here divided. We are still here. Standing almost 106 years later. United.
>
> Nasrec 2017 has not only united us. It has strengthened us. It has galvanised us and rejuvenated us. We continue to confound our critics.[61]

Ace to win

The battle for secretary-general was the closest of the night. As Bauer remembers it, the room descended into 'utter chaos' when CR stalwart Senzo Mchunu was hoisted atop the shoulders of his supporters and carried towards the podium in the false belief that he'd been elected SG. As it turned out, NDZ ally and captor of the Free State Ace Magashule had controversially beaten him to it by a measly twenty-four votes. 'Magashule's win was the moment when we all realised that we could forget about slates,' recalls Bauer, 'that anything was possible.'[62]

Ace doing a spot of laundering

President versus president

Ramaphosa was now the leader of the ANC, but according to the Constitution Zuma would remain the president of the country until the next elections in 2019. Just like Zuma had done in 2008, Ramaphosa set about trying to consolidate his grip on the country. Given all his talk of unity, he tried to allow Zuma a dignified exit. But Zuma, believing (rightly as it turns out) that his freedom depended on him remaining president, stubbornly clung on, ignoring repeated calls from his own party to step aside.

The end of the Zuma affair, when it came on Valentine's Day 2018, was as swift as it was brutal. Before dawn, police raided the Guptas' infamous Saxonwold shebeen. At noon, the ANC announced plans for a vote of no confidence in Zuma (a trick opposition parties had tried on at least eight occasions). That night Zuma announced his resignation. In his televised address to the nation, he remained defiant. After joking with the press (whom he accused of looking 'serious'), Zuma said: 'No life should be lost in my name and also the ANC should never be divided in my name. I have therefore come to the decision to resign as president of the republic with immediate effect,' before adding, unconvincingly: 'even though I disagree with the decision of the leadership of my organisation, I have always been a disciplined member of the ANC.'[63]

At last Ramaphosa had what he wanted. Or did he? As Booysen notes:

> The ANC had hoped for a Polokwane-style outcome [while] Nasrec delivered a presidential winner but also a bi-slate victory board without definitive margins which came to haunt the ANC even if the Ramaphosa victory had brought organisational reprieve and electoral success. The battle of Nasrec continued far beyond the moment of the conference nationally and in the provinces.[64]

At the time of writing, in late 2021, it remains too early to tell who really won at Nasrec. Will Cyril eventually get what he wants? Or will Mabuza, Magashule, Mashatile or someone else have the last laugh?

EPILOGUE:
A RETURN TO
MINORITY RULE?

2021

O N 1 NOVEMBER 2021, as this book was being readied for print, South Africans went to the polls in local government elections (LGEs). Or at least some did: only twenty-six million of almost thirty-nine million eligible voters registered,[1] and a measly twelve million (30.7 per cent of eligible voters) bothered to make their marks.

While the turnout didn't quite reach Tricameral levels, it was pretty damned poor. In an op-ed published in the *Daily Maverick* the day after the election, human rights activist Mark Heywood described the low turnout as 'a return to minority rule'.[2]

How did we get here?

After Nasrec, and even after Zuma's resignation, Ramaphosa's grip on the ANC remained tenuous. In the 2019 general elections, he led the ANC to a disappointing 57.5 per cent majority. Perhaps as a result, he once again demurred from making sweeping changes to his cabinet or party.

When COVID-19 struck in early 2020, he was forced to confront an even more pressing crisis. (In hindsight, he handled COVID far better than many world leaders.) Embarrassingly, the personal protective equipment (PPE) corruption scandal that broke in July 2020 centred around his spokesperson, Khusela Diko, and her husband. While this was not ideal for the image of the so-called 'clean ANC', it did set in motion a process that would eventually see Cyril push through a rule that compels members of the ANC who stand accused of a crime to step aside from party duties until they're found innocent.

The rule would soon be applied to those associated with Zuma. In November 2020, Cyril stood by smiling as Ace Magashule (who had refused to obey the step-aside rule) was arrested on charges of corruption, theft, fraud and money laundering. And the following year, health minister Zweli Mkhize – Zuma's plan B after NDZ – did step aside after he was implicated in COVID-related corruption.

By far the biggest moment in the battle for the ANC (and the country) came in June 2021, when Zuma was sentenced to fifteen months in jail for refusing to appear before the Zondo Commission of Inquiry into Allegations of State Capture. When he eventually reported to prison on 7 July, it was hailed as proof that South Africa's justice system was finding its feet under Ramaphosa. (As an aside, Zuma was the first figure on the cover of *Rogues' Gallery*, our book about 350 years of corrupt South African leaders, to spend even a night in jail on corruption-related charges.)

The euphoria was short-lived. On 9 July, when the courts upheld Zuma's sentence, KZN erupted in violence. Trucks were torched, shopping malls ransacked and ordinary citizens rendered prisoners in their own homes. The unrest soon spread to Gauteng. By 18 July, when the worst was over, more than 340 people had been killed and R50 billion worth of damage caused. It soon became an open secret that the violence had been incited by key Zuma allies. As early as 13 July, state security minister Ayanda Dlodlo said that the SSA was investigating whether 'senior former agents in the agency and senior ANC members aligned to former president Jacob Zuma [were] responsible for igniting the recent violence'.[3]

On 20 July, former deputy chief justice Dikgang Moseneke released the final report of his 'Inquiry into Ensuring Free and Fair Elections during COVID-19'. Both the IEC and the ANC embraced Moseneke's recommendation that the elections be postponed until early 2022. But Moseneke had been tasked with investigating the risks of holding an election during the COVID pandemic; his report did not take into account the unrest. Based on these legal parameters, the report was dismissed by the Constitutional Court, which ruled that elections must take place by 1 November.

At one point it looked like the ANC would be forced *not* to contest 93 of the country's 278 municipalities, as they had failed to submit candidate lists in time. While the IEC subsequently reopened the submissions window, the ANC was also struggling to pay staff salaries, their electoral machinery was in disarray and the unrest had brought Zulu factionalism within the party back to the fore. Not since 1994 had an election been anticipated with more trepidation.

Winners and losers

While the turnout was abysmal, the elections were declared free and fair and there was no significant violence on the day. It soon became clear that the ANC was the biggest loser. Although LGEs should not be compared with general elections, it was impossible to ignore that the ANC's nationwide support had dipped below 50 per cent for the first time, hitting a barely believable 46.05 per cent. The party lost control of thirty-nine councils, and the number of hung councils nationwide leapt from twenty-seven to sixty-six.

As Anthony Butler noted in the *Financial Mail*, 'the ANC has been drinking in the last-chance electoral saloon for almost a decade'.[4] The party's 54 per cent in Gauteng in the 2014 general elections was the first clear evidence of its urban decline, and we've already discussed its disastrous performance in the 2016 LGEs. Strong performances in KZN during JZ's reign provided a convenient bulge in the party balloon, but its flaccid overall state was revealed spectacularly in 2021.

Against this backdrop you might expect the second-biggest party in the country to do really well. But across the country the DA secured only 1 400 seats – a full 400 fewer than it managed in 2016.

The biggest nationwide winner was probably the largely Afrikaans FF+, which more than trebled its support, jumping from 67 seats in 2016 to 220. The predominantly coloured Patriotic Alliance did even better: a mere five seats in 2016 jumped to seventy-four in 2021. While the EFF didn't shoot the lights out, it must have been fairly content with an increase of over 200 seats.[5]

There were massive regional winners too. Former DA mayor of Jozi Herman Mashaba's ActionSA scooped 18.1 per cent of the proportional representation vote in Johannesburg and 9.3 per cent in Tshwane. And, in an apparent rejection of the ANC's role in the July riots, KZN voters rewarded the IFP, which gained more than 100 seats (419 to 527). Other super-regional parties also did comparatively well: Dr Ruben Richards's seven-week-old party, Cederberg Eerste, toppled the DA in the Cederberg municipality, and the Cape Coloured Congress got 2.76 per cent in Cape Town.[6] Around the country, voters were expressing their dismay with the ANC and DA, asserting instead that local is lekker.

Post-mortem

The ANC could likely have done even worse. Ever since taking charge, Ramaphosa has been far more popular than his party (an IRR poll in October found that 62 per cent of voters favoured the president, compared to 50 per cent the ANC), and his smiling face and aura of competence probably encouraged a few voters who had become *gatvol* with the ANC's corruption and mismanagement to come out and vote for the party one more time.[7]

The DA, on the other hand, appears to have been hamstrung by the attitudes and complexion of some of its leaders. If voters were only worried about potholes, rubbish collection and clean audits, the DA should have cleaned up: a *News24* analysis shortly before the election found that the six best non-metro municipalities in the country were all DA-run; the worst non-metro municipalities in the country were all run by the ANC or the IFP.[8] But in a country with a history such as ours, the replacement of black leader Mmusi Maimane after the party's poor showing in 2019 with the pale male Steenhuisen was delusional in the extreme. An ill-judged poster campaign in the largely Indian suburb of Phoenix, KwaZulu-Natal, the site of vigilante killings of black people by neighbourhood watch groups during the July unrest, was another own goal. The posters, reading 'THE ANC CALLED YOU RACISTS. THE DA CALLS YOU HEROES', were taken down following media backlash. The campaign disturbed many, even within the DA. However, the party went on to win all five wards in the suburb – read into that what you will![9]

Looking ahead to 2024

At the end of the previous chapter, we asked whether Ramaphosa would survive the ANC's 55th elective conference in December 2022. And this is a question many in the RET faction are still asking, despite widespread agreement that the party would have done even worse without him at the helm. Although Cyril is the clear favourite, this doesn't mean that he is assured of victory when the party meets in 2022. Does Magashule have an ace up his sleeve? Will Mabuza 'The Cat' shake the rumours of ill health and ever-present corruption allegations to creep into power? Or could KZN darling Mkhize sanitise himself of the Digital Vibes corruption scandal to capitalise on recently remobilised Zulu support? Curiouser still, might NDZ become the party's first female leader?

Fascinating though these questions may be, for the first time in democratic South Africa's history, the identity of the next ANC leader might not be the most important issue hanging over the country. If the ANC's slide at the polls continues, there's a very real chance that we could be entering coalition country after the general elections in 2024. When analyst Dawie Scholtz crunched the numbers, he got the following simulated result for 2024: ANC 48.2%, DA 20.5%, EFF 11.2%, IFP 5.2%. But, Scholtz adds, if ActionSA competes nationally in 2023 (as everyone expects them to), 'it could be worse for the ANC, DA and EFF'.[10]

The ANC dropping below 50 per cent in a general election would be a massive deal. But both Butler and Stephen Grootes reckon that it's too soon to start writing obituaries for the party. As Grootes writes, 'Instead of a "Big Bang" moment when coalitions enter national government and the ANC exits in one move, it may be that coalitions enter national government more slowly and that the ANC exits national government more gradually.'[11] And while many South

Africans hope that such an event would result in a coming together of the DA and the Ramaphosa faction of the ANC, Butler sees three possible futures for the country: First, we should not 'rule out the possibility of authoritarian rule,' he writes, explaining that 'many in the ANC find more inspiration in the Chinese party-state than in the liberal and social democracies of Europe, Asia and the Americas'. Second, we should remember that dominant parties in middle-income countries 'typically survive, and sometimes they thrive, in more competitive party systems'. Third, the ANC might well 'embrace the return of the EFF to the mother body after a national election defeat'.[12] (Imagine the power Julius Malema would wield in such a scenario!) This theory was put temporarily on ice when, on 22 and 23 November, EFF councillors helped to vote in DA mayors in Johannesburg, Tshwane and Ekurhuleni.

While it's too early to tell what any of this means, quotes from an EFF insider suggest that the DA's road ahead will be filled with Mashaba- and Malema-shaped potholes: 'We ... don't want Helen [Zille]'s permission. We are

voting for her by force ... [W]e don't want an impression that we will want something from her or anyone.'[13] For his part, Mashaba stated that ActionSA's vote for the DA was 'not a gift'.[14]

While the 2022 ANC conference is sure to provide fascinating theatre, there's a very real feeling that for the first time in a long while it might only be a curtain-raiser to the main event a year later.

Will the (late) mother of the ANC soon have reason to smile again?

ACKNOWLEDGEMENTS

Spoilt Ballots wouldn't have been half as fascinating to research (and, hopefully, to read) without the often despicable actions of our forebears. Thanking them is not appropriate, but they do deserve some kind of nod. And we hope to have done their ill-gotten reputations a grave disservice.

Writing a book is always a team effort, but this has been particularly true of *Spoilt Ballots*. Dealing with such a large swathe of history, and wanting to allow as many voices as possible to be heard for each of the elections in question, meant that we had to rely heavily on the feedback of the experts who so kindly agreed to read one or more chapters. The book has been improved immeasurably by their input. We list them here in order of the chapter(s) they dealt with: John Laband (who has been involved in the chapter on Shaka Zulu from its conception), Tembeka Ngcukaitobi, Carolyn Hamilton, Kirsten McKenzie, Herman van Niekerk, Carel van der Merwe, Nicol Stassen, William Beinart, Robert Edgar (whose fingerprints are all over Part 2), Richard Steyn, Henry Dee, Milton Shain, Roger Southall (whose elections knowledge spans centuries), Albert Grundlingh, Ken Andrew, Thula Simpson (whose insight, knowledge and speed of reading we are truly envious of and very grateful for), Nickolaus Bauer, Anthony Butler and Stephen Grootes.

Writing this book was neither easy nor quick, and we leaned heavily on the wonderful team at Penguin every step of the way. Managing editor Robert Plummer has been a reassuring beacon of wisdom throughout, and his insights into both South African history and book publishing have improved this book immeasurably. Alice Inggs proved herself, once again, to be a shrewd and sensitive editor, and Dane Wallace's eagle-eyed proofreading was a revelation. Monique Cleghorn has outdone herself with the cover design, and Monique van den Berg and Ryan Africa have worked wonders with the layout and typesetting. The behind-the-scenes efforts of indexer Sanet le Roux are also much appreciated. Finally, our publisher, Marlene Fryer, and our marketing man, Ian Dennewill, have never been anything but super enthusiastic about our writing.

Spoilt Ballots contains almost 150 archival images, and we could not have sourced these without the help of Penguin picture editor Colette Stott and a small army of archivists in all corners of South Africa: Zabeth Botha, Nazim Gani, Marita Buys, Lila Komnick, Robert Dolby, Erika le Roux, Melanie Geustyn and Sewela Mamphiswana all deserve kudos.

In addition to going through their relevant sections with a fine-tooth comb, some of the experts mentioned above read the entire book. Nickolaus, Roger and Thula all deserve a second thank you. As does Mandy Wiener, who provided such glowing feedback in record time. The readers and reviewers who were so positive about *Rogues' Gallery* also deserve a special mention. Without your comments and encouragement, it is doubtful we would have embarked on this project, let alone so soon after completing our first book.

A final thanks is due to those closest to us, who had to put up with our presence (or lack thereof) throughout the writing process.

*To Shelly and the kids: I owe you one, and I promise I won't write another book for a while. To my family – extended and immediate – apologies for finding a way to turn every conversation into a history lesson, and thanks for at least feigning interest. And to Matthew, thank you for more than holding up your side of the bargain; I think we both underestimated the scale of this project, and I'm very glad I didn't have to go it alone. – **Nick Dall***

*Thank you to Sally, Michael, Emma and my ever-present companion Morgan. To my friends Grant Quixley and Chad Rossouw who are always a source of great support. And to Nick, who can work faster, find better pictures and email publishers at a rate I could only dream of, I owe you a great deal. I would also like to remember my first friend in Cape Town and my inside centre through junior school, Richard O'Kill, who was killed in the St James Church massacre. – **Matthew Blackman***

NOTES

CHAPTER 1: DINGANE HAS HIS DAY | 1828

1. John Laband, *The Assassination of King Shaka: Zulu History's Dramatic Moment* (Cape Town: Jonathan Ball, 2017), p. 154.
2. Colin de B. Webb and John B. Wright (eds), *The James Stuart Archive of Recorded Oral Evidence Relating to the History of the Zulu and Neighbouring Peoples: Volume 4* (Pietermaritzburg: University of Natal Press, 1976), p. 80.
3. John Laband, *The Eight Zulu Kings: From Shaka to Goodwill Zwelithini* (Cape Town: Jonathan Ball, 2018), p. 87.
4. Carolyn Anne Hamilton, '"The Character and Objects of Chaka": A Reconsideration of the Making of Shaka as "Mfecane" Motor', *The Journal of African History*, Vol. 33 (1992), p. 60.
5. Email correspondence with Carolyn Hamilton, 28 July 2021.
6. This sidebar is drawn almost entirely from Hamilton, '"The Character and Objects of Chaka"', pp. 37–63.
7. D.K. Rycroft and A.B. Ngcobo, *The Praises of Dingana: Izibongo zikaDingana* (Durban: Killie Campbell Africana Library Publications, 1988), p. 71.
8. Laband, *The Assassination of King Shaka*, p. 136.
9. Ibid., p. 138.
10. Charles Rawden Maclean in Stephen Gray (ed.), *The Natal Papers of 'John Ross'* (Durban: Killie Campbell Africana Library Publications, 1992), pp. 109–10.
11. Maclean in Gray (ed.), *The Natal Papers of 'John Ross'*, p. 111.
12. Laband, *The Assassination of King Shaka*, p. 139.
13. Webb and Wright (eds.), *James Stuart Archive: Volume 1* (Pietermaritzburg: University of KwaZulu-Natal Press and Killie Campbell Africana Library, 1976), p. 187.
14. Laband, *The Assassination of King Shaka*, p. 140.
15. Ibid.
16. Laband, *The Eight Zulu Kings*, p. 16.
17. Laband, *The Assassination of King Shaka*, p. 35.
18. Laband, *The Eight Zulu Kings*, p. 17.
19. Laband, *The Assassination of King Shaka*, p. 56.
20. Ibid.
21. Ibid., p. 25.
22. Stephen Taylor, *Shaka's Children: A History of the Zulu People* (London: HarperCollins, 1994), p. 49.
23. Webb and Wright (eds.), 'Jantshi' in *James Stuart Archive: Volume 1*, pp. 182–3.
24. Maclean, *The Natal Papers of 'John Ross'*, p. 76.
25. Maclean, *The Natal Papers of 'John Ross'*, p. 55.
26. Laband, *The Eight Zulu Kings*, p. 63.

27. Author's interview with Tembeka Ngcukaitobi, 13 June 2021.

28. Laband, *The Eight Zulu Kings*, p. 63.

29. Henry Francis Fynn in James Stuart and D. McK. Malcolm (eds.), *The Diary of Henry Francis Fynn* (Pietermaritzburg: Shuter and Shooter, 1950), p. 83.

30. Laband, *The Eight Zulu Kings*, p. 65.

31. Sifiso Mxolisi Ndlovu, '"He Did What Any Other Person in his Position Would Have Done to Fight the Forces of Invasion and Disruption": Africans, the Land and Contending Images of King Dingane ("the Patriot") in the Twentieth Century, 1916–1950s', *South African Historical Journal*, Vol. 38 (May 1998), p. 102.

32. Ibid., p. 103.

33. Office Holidays, 'Day of Reconciliation in South Africa in 2021', available at https://www.officeholidays.com/holidays/south-africa/day-of-reconciliation (last accessed 3 October 2021).

34. Rycroft and Ngcobo, *The Praises of Dingana*, p. 87.

35. Laband, *The Assassination of King Shaka*, p. 142.

36. Laband, *The Eight Zulu Kings*, p. 54.

37. Laband, *The Assassination of King Shaka*, pp. 142–4.

38. Ibid., pp. 148–9.

39. Ibid., p. 150.

40. Webb and Wright, *James Stuart Archive: Volume 4*, p. 346.

41. Ndlovu, '"He Did What Any Other Person in his Position Would Have Done to Fight the Forces of Invasion and Disruption"', p. 106.

42. Jason Porath, 'Mkabayi kaJama (c.1750–c.1843) Power Behind the Zulu Throne', *Rejected Princesses*, available at https://www.rejectedprincesses.com/princesses/mkabayi -kajama (last accessed 6 August 2021).

43. Heinrich Filter and S. Bourquin, *Paulina Dlamini: Servant of Two Kings* (Durban: Killie Campbell Africana Library Publications, 1986), p. 35.

44. Rycroft and Ngcobo, *The Praises of Dingana*, p. 71.

45. Ndlovu, '"He Did What Any Other Person in his Position Would Have Done to Fight the Forces of Invasion and Disruption"', p. 104.

46. Ibid., p. 130.

47. Colin de B. Webb and John B. Wright, *A Zulu King Speaks: Statements Made by Cetshwayo kaMpande on the History and Customs of his People* (Pietermaritzburg: University of KwaZulu-Natal Press and Killie Campbell Africana Library Publications, 1986), p. 98.

48. Rycroft and Ngcobo, *The Praises of Dingana*, p. 87.

49. Ndlovu, '"He Did What Any Other Person in his Position Would Have Done to Fight the Forces of Invasion and Disruption"', p. 104.

50. Rycroft and Ngcobo, *The Praises of Dingana*, p. 73.

51. Author's interview with Tembeka Ngcukaitobi, 13 June 2021.

52. Ndlovu, '"He Did What Any Other Person in his Position Would Have Done to Fight the Forces of Invasion and Disruption"', pp. 99–143.

53. Rycroft and Ngcobo, *The Praises of Dingana*, p. 126.

54. Ndlovu, '"He Did What Any Other Person in his Position Would Have Done to Fight the Forces of Invasion and Disruption"', p. 104.

55. Ibid., p. 111.
56. Ibid.
57. Author's interview with John Laband, 18 November 2020.
58. Ibid.
59. Laband, *The Assassination of King Shaka*, pp. 43–4.

CHAPTER 2: THE MOTHER OF ALL ELECTIONS | 1854

1. Phyllis Lewsen, 'The Cape Liberal Tradition – Myth or Reality?', *Race*, Vol. 13, No. 1 (1971), p. 71.
2. Ralph Kilpin, *The Romance of a Colonial Parliament* (London: Longmans, Green & Co., 1930), p. 47.
3. Kirsten McKenzie, '"Franklins of the Cape": The *South African Commercial Advertiser* and the Creation of a Colonial Public Sphere, 1824–1854', *Kronos*, No. 25 (1998), p. 89. Available at http://www.jstor.org/stable/41056429 (last accessed 29 April 2021).
4. Andrew Bank, 'The Great Debate and the Origins of South African Historiography', *The Journal of African History*, Vol. 38, No. 2 (1997), pp. 261–81. Available at http://www.jstor.org/stable/182824 (last accessed 14 June 2021).
5. H.C. Botha, *Fairbairn in South Africa* (South Africa: Historical Publication Society, 1984), p. 69.
6. Dr John Philip quoted in Bank, 'The Great Debate and the Origins of South African Historiography', p. 263.
7. McKenzie, '"Franklins of the Cape"', p. 89.
8. Bank, 'The Great Debate and the Origins of South African Historiography', p. 278.
9. Ralph Kilpin, *The Romance of a Colonial Parliament*, p. 56.
10. Ibid., pp. 59–60.
11. J.L. McCracken, *New Light at the Cape of Good Hope: William Porter, the Father of Cape Liberalism* (Belfast: The Ulster Historical Foundation, 1993), p. 80.
12. Ibid., p. 69.
13. Ibid., p. 71.
14. Kilpin, *The Romance of a Colonial Parliament*, p. 60.
15. Ralph Kilpin, *The Old Cape House: Being Pages from the History of a Legislative Assembly* (Cape Town: T. Maskew Miller, n.d.), p. 9.
16. George McCall Theal, *History of South Africa Since September 1795, Vol. 3: The Cape Colony from 1846 to 1860, Natal from 1847 to 1857, British Kaffraria from 1847 to 1860, and the Orange River Sovereignty and the Transvaal Republic from 1847 to 1854* (Cambridge: Cambridge University Press, 2010), p. 119.
17. Noël Mostert, *Frontiers: The Epic of South Africa's Creation and the Tragedy of the Xhosa People* (New York: Knopf, 1992), p. 688.
18. John Milton, *The Edges of War: A History of Frontier Wars (1702–1878)* (Cape Town: Juta & Co. Ltd, 1983), p. 136.
19. Quoted in McCracken, *New Light at the Cape of Good Hope*, p. 105.
20. Sir George Cory, *The Rise of South Africa: A History of the Origin of South African Colonisation and of Its Development Towards the East from the Earliest Times to 1857, Volume V* (London: Longmans, Green, and Co., 1930), p. 183.

21. William Francis Patrick Napier, *The Life and Opinions of General Sir Charles James Napier, G.C.B.* (Cambridge: Cambridge University Press, 1857), p. 327.

22. Cory, *The Rise of South Africa*, p. 185.

23. Kilpin, *The Romance of a Colonial Parliament*, p. 69.

24. Cory, *The Rise of South Africa, Vol. V*, p. 191.

25. Susan Blackbeard, 'Kat River Revisited' (PhD thesis, University of Cape Town, 2018).

26. Botha, *Fairbairn in South Africa*, p. 208.

27. Cory, *The Rise of South Africa, Vol. V*, p. 196.

28. Ibid., p. 198.

29. Botha, *Fairbairn in South Africa*, p. 210.

30. Kilpin, *The Romance of a Colonial Parliament*, p. 73.

31. Cory, *The Rise of South Africa, Vol. V*, p. 207.

32. Kilpin, *The Romance of a Colonial Parliament*, pp. 74–5.

33. Cory, *The Rise of South Africa, Vol. V*, p. 208.

34. Botha, *Fairbairn in South Africa*, p. 218.

35. Cory, *The Rise of South Africa, Vol. V*, p. 185.

36. J.L. McCracken, *The Cape Parliament, 1854–1910* (Oxford: Clarendon P., 1967), p. 13.

37. Cory, *The Rise of South Africa, Vol. V*, p. 245.

38. Ibid., p. 247.

39. Mostert, *Frontiers*, p. 364.

40. Ibid., p. 995.

41. J.L. Dracopoli, *Sir Andries Stockenström, 1792–1864: The Origins of the Racial Conflict in South Africa* (Cape Town: A.A. Balkema, 1969), p. 9.

42. Robert Ross, *The Borders of Race in Colonial South Africa: The Kat River Settlement, 1829–1856* (Cambridge: Cambridge University Press, 2013), p. 275.

43. Cory, *The Rise of South Africa, Volume V*, p. 249.

44. Ibid.

45. Ibid., p. 250.

46. Kilpin, *The Romance of a Colonial Parliament*, p. 77.

47. Eric Anderson Walker (ed.), *The Cambridge History of the British Empire, Vol. 1* (Cambridge: Cambridge University Press, 1936), p. 381.

48. Kilpin, *The Romance of a Colonial Parliament*, p. 78.

49. Great Britain House of Commons, Accounts and Papers: Colonies, Volume 7, p. 92.

50. Cory, *The Rise of South Africa, Volume V*, p. 258.

51. Robert Ross, *Status and Respectability in the Cape Colony, 1750–1870: A Tragedy of Manners* (Cambridge: Cambridge University Press, 2004), p. 171.

52. Lewsen, 'The Cape Liberal Tradition – Myth or Reality?', p. 71.

53. Ibid., p. 50.

54. Ibid.

55. Stanley Trapido, 'The Origins of the Cape Franchise Qualifications of 1853', *The Journal of African History*, Vol. 5, No. 1 (1964), p. 52. Available at http://www.jstor.org/stable/179767 (last accessed 12 December 2020).

56. Quoted in Botha, *Fairbairn in South Africa*, p. 281.

57. Botha, *Fairbairn in South Africa*, p. 259.

58. Ibid., p. 265.
59. Ibid., p. 289.
60. Ibid.
61. Trapido, 'The Origins of the Cape Franchise Qualifications of 1853', p. 53.
62. Theal, *History of South Africa Since September 1795, Vol. 3*, pp. 134–5.
63. Ibid.
64. Botha, *Fairbairn in South Africa*, p. 291.
65. Cory, *The Rise of South Africa, Volume V*, p. 284.
66. Theal, *History of South Africa Since September 1795, Vol. 3*, p. 138.
67. Naomi Parkinson, 'Elections in the Mid-Nineteenth Century British Empire' (PhD thesis, Cambridge University, 2017), pp. 49, 135.
68. Footnote 1 in Cory, *The Rise of South Africa, Volume V*, p. 286.
69. Parkinson, 'Elections in the Mid-Nineteenth Century British Empire', p. 118.
70. Ross, *The Borders of Race in Colonial South Africa*, p. 283.
71. McKenzie, '"Franklins of the Cape"', p. 102.

CHAPTER 3: THE BATTLE OF THE BEARDS | 1893

1. Paul Kruger, *The Memoirs of Paul Kruger: Four Times President of the South African Republic* (Toronto: George A. Morang & Company, 1902), p. 209.
2. Ibid.
3. Author's email correspondence with Herman van Niekerk, 11 May 2021.
4. C.T. Gordon, *The Growth of Boer Opposition to Kruger (1890–1895)* (Cape Town: Oxford University Press, 1970), p. 207.
5. Matthew Blackman and Nick Dall, *Rogues' Gallery: 350 Years of Corruption in South Africa* (Cape Town: Penguin Books, 2021), p. 96.
6. D.W. Krüger, *The Age of the Generals* (Johannesburg: Dagbreek Book Store, 1958), pp. 15–16.
7. Charles van Onselen, *The Cowboy Capitalist: John Hays Hammond, the American West & the Jameson Raid* (Cape Town: Jonathan Ball, 2017), p. 17.
8. Kathy Munro, 'Census 1896 – The Making of Johannesburg', *The Heritage Portal*, 22 September 2020. Available at http://www.theheritageportal.co.za/article/census-1896 -making-johannesburg (last accessed 11 August 2021).
9. Gordon, *The Growth of Boer Opposition to Kruger*, pp. 139–40.
10. J. Scott Keltie, 'South African Republic' in *The Statesman's Yearbook*. Available at https://link.springer.com/chapter/10.1057%2F9780230253216_50 (last accessed 11 August 2021).
11. Van Onselen, *The Cowboy Capitalist*, p. 26.
12. Ibid., p. 21.
13. Hermann Giliomee, *The Afrikaners: Biography of a People* (Cape Town: Tafelberg, 2003), p. 187.
14. 'William Robinson', *Historia Junior*, January 1958. Available at https://www.afrikanerge skiedenis.co.za/?p=13075 (last accessed 11 August 2021).
15. Herman van Niekerk (tr. Heini Kotzè), *Eugène Marais: New Facts and New Insights* (Kindle edition, 2020).
16. Gordon, *The Growth of Boer Opposition to Kruger (1890–1895)*, p. ix.

17. Ibid., pp. 29–31.
18. Heinie Heydenrych, 'Paul Kruger en die Pers in die ZAR, 1890–1895', *LitNet*, 19 January 2016. Available at https://www.litnet.co.za/paul-kruger-en-die-pers-in-die-zar-1890-1895/ (last accessed 11 August 2021).
19. Gordon, *The Growth of Boer Opposition to Kruger* (1890–1895), pp. 86–7.
20. Ibid., pp. 111–13.
21. Ibid., p. 126.
22. J.S. Marais, *The Fall of Kruger's Republic* (Oxford: The Clarendon Press, 1961), pp. 16–17.
23. Gordon, *The Growth of Boer Opposition to Kruger* (1890–1895), p. 139.
24. Marais, *The Fall of Kruger's Republic*, pp. 14–15.
25. Ibid., p. 17.
26. Ibid., p. 16.
27. Ibid., p. 11.
28. Van Onselen, *The Cowboy Capitalist*, p. 230.
29. J.P. FitzPatrick, *The Transvaal from Within: A Private Record of Public Affairs* (London: William Heinemann, 1899), p. 88.
30. Gordon, *The Growth of Boer Opposition to Kruger*, pp. 250–1.
31. Van Onselen, *The Cowboy Capitalist*, p. 230.
32. FitzPatrick, *The Transvaal from Within*, p. 86.
33. Gordon, *The Growth of Boer Opposition to Kruger*, pp. 205–6.
34. Blackman and Dall, *Rogues' Gallery*, p. 109.
35. Most of the information in this sidebar is from Van Niekerk, *Eugène Marais*.
36. Van Niekerk, *Eugène Marais*, p. 40.
37. Sandra Swart, '"An Irritating Pebble in Kruger's Shoe" – Eugène Marais and *Land en Volk* in the ZAR, 1891–1896', *Historia*, Vol. 48, No. 2 (November 2003), pp. 66–87.
38. Ibid., pp. 66–87.
39. Gordon, *The Growth of Boer Opposition to Kruger*, pp. 198–9.
40. Ibid., p. 205.
41. Leon Rousseau, *The Dark Stream: The Story of Eugène N Marais* (Cape Town: Jonathan Ball, 1982), pp. 73–4.
42. Gordon, *The Growth of Boer Opposition to Kruger*, p. 212.
43. Ibid., pp. 209–10.
44. Ibid., p. 210.
45. Ibid., p. 214.
46. Ibid., pp. 215–16.
47. Rousseau, *The Dark Stream*, p. 78.
48. Gordon, *The Growth of Boer Opposition to Kruger*, p. 218.
49. Ibid., p. 219.
50. Ibid., p. 223.
51. Ibid.
52. Ibid., p. 220.
53. Ibid., p. 225.

54. Kruger, *The Memoirs of Paul Kruger*, pp. 213–14.
55. Gordon, *The Growth of Boer Opposition to Kruger*, p. 231.
56. Ibid., p. 241.

CHAPTER 4: RHODES: PAVING THE CAPE WITH BAD INTENTIONS | 1898

1. Robert I. Rotberg, *The Founder: Cecil Rhodes and the Pursuit of Power* (Oxford: Oxford University Press, 1988), p. 364.
2. B.A. Tindall (ed.), *James Rose Innes, Chief Justice of South Africa, 1914–27: Autobiography* (Cape Town: Oxford University Press, 1949), p. 87.
3. Antony Thomas, *Rhodes: The Race for Africa* (Johannesburg: Jonathan Ball, 1997), p. 83.
4. Hannah Arendt, *The Origins of Totalitarianism* (New York: Penguin Modern Classics, 2017), p. 266.
5. Olive Schreiner and C.S. Cronwright-Schreiner, *The Political Situation* (London: T. Fisher Unwin, 1896), p. 109.
6. Rodney Davenport, 'The Cape Liberal Tradition to 1910' in J. Butler et al. (eds.), *Democratic Liberalism in South Africa: Its History and Prospect* (Cape Town: David Philip, 1987), p. 32.
7. J.L. McCracken, *The Cape Parliament, 1854–1910* (Oxford: Clarendon Press), p. 114.
8. Phyllis Lewsen, *John X. Merriman: Paradoxical South African Statesman* (Johannesburg: AD Donker, 1982), p. 98.
9. Rotberg, *The Founder*, p. 224.
10. Ibid., p. 341.
11. Ibid., p. 343.
12. Mordechai Tamarkin, *Cecil Rhodes and the Cape Afrikaners: The Imperial Colossus and the Colonial Parish Pump* (London: Frank Cass, 1996), p. 140.
13. Ibid.
14. Rotberg, *The Founder*, p. 344.
15. Ibid.
16. Ibid., p. 364.
17. Thomas, *Rhodes*, p. 268.
18. T.R.H. Davenport and Christopher Saunders, *South Africa: A Modern History* (London: Macmillan Press, 2000), p. 65.
19. André Odendaal, *The Founders: The Origins of the ANC and the Struggle for Democracy in South Africa* (Johannesburg: Jacana, 2012), p. 144.
20. Arendt, *The Origins of Totalitarianism*, p. 160.
21. Tamarkin, *Cecil Rhodes and the Cape Afrikaners*, p. 245.
22. Ibid., p. 250.
23. Alan Smith, 'General Election in the Cape Colony 1898–1908' (Unpublished thesis, University of Cape Town, 1980), p. 9.
24. Lewsen, *John X. Merriman*, p. 196.
25. Harrison M. Wright, *Sir James Rose Innes: Selected Correspondence (1884–1902)* (Cape Town: National Commercial Printers Ltd, 1972), p. 247.
26. Wright, *Sir James Rose Innes*, p. 245.
27. Odendaal, *The Founders*, p. 147.

28. Gerald Shaw, *Some Beginnings: The Cape Times 1876–1910* (Cape Town: Oxford University Press, 1975), appendix.

29. Phyllis Lewsen (ed.), *Selections from the Correspondence of John X. Merriman 1890–98* (Cape Town: Van Riebeeck Society, 1963), p. 306.

30. T.R.H. Davenport, *The Afrikaner Bond: The History of a South African Political Party, 1880–1911* (New York: Oxford University Press, 1966), p. 184.

31. William Plomer, *Cecil Rhodes* (London: Peter Davies Ltd, 1933), p. 132.

32. Eric A. Walker, *W.P. Schreiner: A South African* (London: Oxford University Press, 1937), p. 113.

33. Tamarkin, *Cecil Rhodes and the Cape Afrikaners*, p. 279.

34. Thomas, *Rhodes: The Race for Africa*, pp. 331–32.

35. Rotberg, *The Founder*, p. 608.

36. Vivian Solomon (ed.), *Selections from the Correspondence of Percy Alport Molteno, 1892–1914* (Cape Town: Van Riebeeck Society, 1981), p. 70.

37. B.A. Tindall (ed.), *Rose Innes: Autobiography* (London: Oxford University Press, 1949), p. 170.

38. Lewsen, *John X. Merriman*, p. 198.

39. Lewsen, *Selections from the Correspondence of John X. Merriman 1890–98*, p. 314.

40. Odendaal, *The Founders*, p. 150.

41. Rotberg, *The Founder*, p. 608.

42. Quoted in Rotberg, *The Founder*, p. 608.

43. F.S. Crafford, *Jan Smuts: A Biography* (New York: Doubleday, Doran & Co., Inc., 1943), p. 49.

44. Liz Stanley and Andrea Salter (eds.), *The World's Great Question: Olive Schreiner's South African Letters 1889–1920* (Cape Town: Van Riebeeck Society, 2014), p. 68.

45. Thomas, *Rhodes*, p. 310.

46. Stanley and Salter, *The World's Great Question*, p. 90.

47. Quotes can be found in Western Cape Archives, KAB, CSC2/1/1/355/14 in evidence under Examination of the Honourable Cecil John Rhodes, M.L.A., pp. 1–12.

48. Walker, *W.P. Schreiner*, p. 114.

49. *Decisions of the Supreme Court of the Cape of Good Hope Vol. XVI During the Year 1899* (Cape Town, J.C. Juta and Co., 1901), p. 89.

50. Lewsen, *John X. Merriman*, p. 200.

51. Olive Schreiner, *An English-South African's View of the Situation: Words in Season* (London: Hodder & Stoughton, 1899), p. 109.

52. Arendt, *The Origins of Totalitarianism*, p. 265.

CHAPTER 5: WEDDING BELLS FOR A DIVIDED UNION | 1910

1. Martin Plaut, *Dr Abdullah Abdurahman: South Africa's First Elected Black Politician* (Johannesburg: Jacana, 2020), p. 74.

2. Deneys Reitz, *Commando: A Boer Journal of the Boer War* (London: Faber & Faber, 1950), p. 320.

3. Leonard Thompson, *A History of South Africa* (Johannesburg: Jonathan Ball, 2006), p. 143.

4. Leonard Thompson, *The Unification of South Africa: 1902–1910* (Oxford: Clarendon Press, 1961), p. 10.
5. Ibid., p. 11.
6. Ibid.
7. Ibid.
8. Saul Dubow, 'Colonial Nationalism, the Milner Kindergarten and the Rise of "South Africanism", 1902–10', *History Workshop Journal*, No. 43 (1997), p. 56. Available at http://www.jstor.org/stable/4289491 (last accessed 20 June 2021).
9. Thompson, *A History of South Africa*, p. 147.
10. Thompson, *The Unification of South Africa*, p. 32.
11. Quoted in Thompson, *The Unification of South Africa*, p. 183.
12. Ian Loveland, *By Due Process of Law? Racial Discrimination and the Right to Vote in South Africa 1855–1960* (Oxford: Hart Publishing, 1999), p. 104.
13. Quoted in T.R.H. Davenport and Christopher Saunders, *South Africa: A Modern History* (London: Macmillan Press, 2000), p. 258.
14. Olive Schreiner, *Closer Union: A Letter on South African Union and the Principles of Government* (London: A.C. Fifield, 1909).
15. Thompson, *A History of South Africa*, p. 147.
16. Thompson, *The Unification of South Africa*, p. 132.
17. Monica Wilson and Leonard Thompson (eds.), *The Oxford History of South Africa, Volume II: South Africa 1870–1966* (Oxford: Clarendon Press, 1971), p. 361.
18. Davenport and Saunders, *South Africa*, p. 249.
19. Thompson, *The Unification of South Africa*, p. 111.
20. Eric A. Walker, *W.P. Schreiner: A South African* (London: Oxford University Press, 1937), pp. 291–2.
21. Plaut, *Dr Abdullah Abdurahman*, p. 52.
22. Thompson, *The Unification of South Africa*, p. 215.
23. André Odendaal, *The Founders: The Origins of the ANC and the Struggle for Democracy in South Africa* (Johannesburg: Jacana, 2012), p. 377.
24. Ibid.
25. Ibid., p. 378.
26. Plaut, *Dr Abdullah Abdurahman*, p. 59.
27. Walker, *W.P. Schreiner*, p. 319.
28. Odendaal, *The Founders*, p. 393.
29. Ibid., p. 395.
30. Ibid., p. 399.
31. Ibid., p. 404.
32. BC16/Box4/Fold2/1909/20, Letter by Olive Schreiner to William Philip Schreiner, 9 April 1909. Available at https://www.oliveschreiner.org/vre?view=collections&colid =101&letterid=20 (last accessed 3 October 2021).
33. Walker, *W.P. Schreiner*, p. 323.
34. Ibid., p. 322.
35. Ibid., p. 325.
36. Euzhan Palcy (dir.), *A Dry White Season* (MGM, 1989).

37. Odendaal, *The Founders*, p. 433.
38. Plaut, *Dr Abdullah Abdurahman*, p. 67.
39. Quoted in Plaut, *Dr Abdullah Abdurahman*, p. 74.
40. Wilson and Thompson (eds.), *The Oxford History of South Africa, Volume II*, p. 358.
41. Quoted in Louis Fischer, *Gandhi: His Life and Message for the World* (New York: Signet Classics, 1982), p. 25.
42. Odendaal, *The Founders*, p. 423.
43. Quoted in Plaut, *Dr Abdullah Abdurahman*, p. 79.
44. Thompson, *The Unification of South Africa*, p. 453.
45. Ibid., p. 456.
46. Ibid.
47. Ibid., p. 468.
48. Ibid., p. 469.
49. Ibid., p. 462.
50. Percy FitzPatrick, *South African Memories* (Cape Town: AD Donker, 1979), p. 255.
51. Timothy Stapleton, 'Mpilo Walter Benson Rubusana: South Africa's First Black Parliamentarian' in Josep M. Fradera, José María Portillo and Teresa Segura-Garcia (eds.), *Unexpected Voices in Imperial Parliaments* (London: Bloomsbury Academic, 2021). Available at https://www.perlego.com/book/2632335/unexpected-voices-in-imperial -parliaments-pdf (last accessed 30 July 2021).

CHAPTER 6: PACT LUNCH: BOEREWORS AND MASH | 1924

1. J.C. Smuts, *Jan Christian Smuts by His Son* (Johannesburg: Heinemann & Cassell, 1952), p. 415.
2. Oswald Pirow, *James Barry Munnik Hertzog* (Cape Town: Howard Timmins, 1958), pp. 97–8.
3. W.K. Hancock, *Smuts: Volume 2: Fields of Force, 1919–1950* (Cambridge: Cambridge University Press, 1968), p. 161.
4. Pirow, *James Barry Munnik Hertzog*, p. 98.
5. Richard Steyn, *Jan Smuts: Unafraid of Greatness* (Cape Town: Jonathan Ball, 2015), pp. 10–11.
6. Terry Eksteen, *The Statesmen* (Cape Town: Don Nelson, 1978), p. 55.
7. D.W. Krüger, *The Age of the Generals* (Johannesburg: Dagbreek Book Store, 1958), p. 133.
8. Eksteen, *The Statesmen*, p. 55.
9. Krüger, *The Age of the Generals*, p. 134.
10. Pirow, *James Barry Munnik Hertzog*, p. 97.
11. Krüger, *The Age of the Generals*, p. 111.
12. Ibid.
13. Emilia Potenza, 'All that Glitters – The glitter of gold', *South African History Online*. Available at https://www.sahistory.org.za/archive/all-glitters-glitter-gold-emilia-potenza (last accessed 2 September 2021).
14. Krüger, *The Age of the Generals*, p. 120.
15. Email correspondence with Richard Steyn, 14 July 2021.

16. 'Rand Rebellion 1922', *South African History Online*. Available at https://www.sahistory .org.za/article/rand-rebellion-1922 (last accessed 28 September 2021).

17. Krüger, *The Age of the Generals*, pp. 120–1.

18. Ibid., p. 121.

19. Ibid., p. 122.

20. Jeremy Krikler, *White Rising: The 1922 Insurrection and Racial Killing in South Africa* (Manchester: Manchester University Press, 2005), p. 108.

21. J.P. Brits, *Tielman Roos – Political Prophet or Opportunist?* (Pretoria: Unisa, 1987), pp. 86–7.

22. S.J. de Klerk, 'Tracing the 1922 Strike', *The Heritage Portal*, 14 July 2019. Available at http://www.theheritageportal.co.za/article/tracing-1922-strike (last accessed 2 September 2021).

23. Krüger, *The Age of the Generals*, p. 123.

24. Krikler, *White Rising*, pp. 82–3.

25. De Klerk, 'Tracing the 1922 Strike'.

26. Ibid.

27. This timeline was compiled from a number of sources, most importantly Jeremy Krikler's *White Rising* and De Klerk's 'Tracing the 1922 Strike'.

28. Krikler, *White Rising*, p. 12.

29. Ibid., p. 201.

30. De Klerk, 'Tracing the 1922 Strike'.

31. Krikler, *White Rising*, p. 189.

32. Smuts, *Jan Christian Smuts by His Son*, p. 412.

33. Krikler, *White Rising*, p. 267.

34. Ibid.

35. Ibid., p. 285.

36. J.P. Brits and Burridge Spies, 'A turbulent decade', in Hermann Giliomee and Bernard Mbenga (eds), *New History of South Africa* (Cape Town: Tafelberg, 2007), p. 247.

37. Ibid.

38. Quoted in Joseph Lelyveld, *Move Your Shadow: South Africa, Black and White* (Johannesburg: Jonathan Ball, 1986), p. 63.

39. Author's interview with Tembeka Ngcukaitobi, 20 May 2021.

40. Robert R. Edgar, *The Finger of God: Enoch Mgijima, the Israelites, and the Bulhoek Massacre in South Africa* (Charlottesville: University of Virginia Press, 2018), Google eBook.

41. Ibid.

42. Gavin Llewellyn Mackenzie Lewis, 'The Bondelswarts Rebellion of 1922' (MA thesis, Rhodes University, 1977), pp. 48–50.

43. Ibid., p. 50.

44. Ibid., p. 104.

45. Ibid., p. 113.

46. Smuts, *Jan Christian Smuts by His Son*, p. 415.

47. Hancock, *Smuts*, p. 109.

48. F.S. Crafford, *Jan Smuts: A Biography* (New York: Doubleday, Doran & Co., 1943), p. 223.

49. Pirow, *James Barry Munnik Hertzog*, p. 96.

50. J. Steinmeyer, 'Political Coalitions in the Union of South Africa', South African Institute of Race Relations, 11 December 1950, p. 4. Available at http://wwwhistoricalpa pers.wits.ac.za/inventories/inv_pdf0/AD1715/AD1715-22-3-3-001-jpeg.pdf (last accessed 6 October 2021).

51. Pirow, *James Barry Munnik Hertzog*, p. 96.

52. Wikipedia, '1922 Southern Rhodesian government referendum'. Available at https://en .wikipedia.org/wiki/1922_Southern_Rhodesian_government_referendum (last accessed 2 September 2021).

53. Eric A. Walker, *A History of Southern Africa*, p. 596.

54. Donal Lowry, '"White woman's country": Ethel Tawse Jollie and the making of White Rhodesia.' *Journal of Southern African Studies*, Vol.23, No.2 (1997), p. 261.

55. Steyn, *Jan Smuts*, p. 227.

56. Jeremy Seekings, '"Not a Single White Person Should Be Allowed to Go Under": Swartgevaar and the Origins of South Africa's Welfare State, 1924–1929', *The Journal of African History*, Vol. 48, No. 3 (2007), p. 380.

57. Hancock, *Smuts*, p. 150.

58. Thula Simpson, *History of South Africa: From 1902 to the Present* (Cape Town: Penguin Books, 2021), p. 78.

59. Seekings, '"Not a Single White Person Should Be Allowed to Go Under"', p. 381.

60. Ibid., p. 382.

61. Pirow, *James Barry Munnik Hertzog*, p. 194.

62. Giliomee, *The Afrikaners*, p. 337.

63. Clements Kadalie, *My Life and the ICU: The autobiography of a black trade unionist in South Africa* (London: Frank Cass, 1970), p. 58.

64. Sylvia Neame, *The Congress Movement* (Cape Town: HSRC Press, 2015), p. 360.

65. Ibid.

66. 'Polling in South Africa: Gen. Smuts's Prospects', *The Times*, 17 June 1924.

67. Ibid.

68. 'Polling in South Africa: Rand Views', *The Times*, 17 June 1924.

69. Hancock, *Smuts*, p. 161.

70. Ibid., p. 164.

71. Seekings, '"Not a Single White Person Should Be Allowed to Go Under"', p. 382.

72. Neame, *The Congress Movement*, p. 370.

73. Ibid., p. 369.

74. Brits and Spies, 'A turbulent decade', p. 253.

75. Seekings, '"Not a Single White Person Should Be Allowed to Go Under"', p. 383.

76. Steyn, *Jan Smuts*, pp. 112–3.

77. Hancock, *Smuts*, p. 100.

78. James Morris, *Farewell the Trumpets: An Imperial Retreat* (London: Penguin, 1979), p. 397.

CHAPTER 7: *SWART GEVAAR* AND THE CONFUSION OF FUSION | 1929 AND 1933

1. Krüger, *The Age of the Generals*, p. 161.

2. List adapted from Krüger, *The Age of the Generals*, pp. 160–1, and Pirow, *JBM Hertzog*, pp. 156–7.

3. Krüger, *The Age of the Generals*, p. 161.

4. William Keith Hancock, *Smuts: The Fields of Force, 1919–1950* (Cambridge: Cambridge University Press, 1962), p. 199.

5. Email correspondence with Chris Saunders, 4 September 2021.

6. Gwendolyn M. Carter and Thomas Karis, *From Protest to Challenge, Vol. 1: A Documentary History of African Politics in South Africa, 1882–1964: Protest and Hope, 1882–1934* (Stanford: Hoover Institution Press, 1972), Kindle edition.

7. Tembeka Ngcukaitobi, *The Land Is Ours* (Cape Town: Penguin Books, 2018), p. 252.

8. Giliomee and Mbenga, *New History of South Africa*, pp. 285–6.

9. Act No. 5 of 1927. Available at https://disa.ukzn.ac.za/sites/default/files/pdf_files/leg1927 0327.028.020.005.pdf (last accessed 29 January 2021).

10. Walker, *A History of Southern Africa*, p. 623.

11. Ngcukaitobi, *The Land Is Ours*, p. 147.

12. Ibid., p. 149.

13. Act 38 of 1927. Available at https://www.gov.za/sites/default/files/gcis_document/201505 /act38of1927.pdf (last accessed 21 January 2021).

14. Hancock, *Smuts*, p. 199.

15. 'The Prince in South Africa', *The Times*, 24 July 1925.

16. Hilary Sapire, 'The Prince and Afrikaners: The Royal Visit of 1925', *Royal Studies Journal*, Vol. 5, No. 1 (2018), pp. 123–4.

17. Krüger, *The Age of the Generals*, p. 144.

18. H.C. Armstrong, *Grey Steel: A Study in Arrogance* (London: Arthur Barker, 1937), p. 369.

19. Armstrong, *Grey Steel*, p. 370.

20. Krüger, *The Age of the Generals*, p. 145.

21. Armstrong, *Grey Steel*, p. 370.

22. Hancock, *Smuts*, p. 200.

23. Ibid.

24. Krüger, *The Age of the Generals*, p. 143.

25. Hancock, *Smuts*, p. 203.

26. Govan Mbeki, *The Prison Writings of Govan Mbeki* (Cape Town: David Philip, 1991), p. 18.

27. Hancock, *Smuts*, p. 218.

28. South African National Archives, Pretoria, NTS 2076 166/280 'Influx of Nyasaland Natives into the Union', letter to Secretary for Native Affairs, 07/02/1929.

29. Jonathan Crush, Alan Jeeves and David Yudelman, *South Africa's Labor Empire: A History of Black Migrancy to the Gold Mines* (Boulder: Westview Press, 1995), pp. 234–5.

30. Hancock, *Smuts*, p. 218.

31. Ibid.

32. Email correspondence with Robert Edgar, 1 September 2021.

33. 'Germiston: Communist Party Enters the Field with a Native Candidate', *Umsebenzi*, 1 October 1932.

34. Giliomee, *The Afrikaners*, p. 392.

35. Giliomee and Mbenga, *New History of South Africa*, p. 265.

36. Ibid.

37. Patricia van der Spuy, 'Not only "the younger daughter of Dr Abdurahman": A feminist exploration of early influences on the political development of Cissie Gool' (PhD thesis, University of Cape Town, 2002), pp. 181–2.

38. Ibid., pp. 180–1.

39. Gairoonisa Paleker, '"She Was Certainly Not a Rosa Luxemborg": A Biography of Cissie Gool in Images and Words' (MA thesis, University of Cape Town, 2002), pp. 36–7.

40. Van der Spuy, 'Not only "the younger daughter of Dr Abdurahman"', Abstract.

41. Paleker, '"She Was Certainly Not a Rosa Luxemborg"', p. 29.

42. All senators' quotes are taken from 'Women's Vote Bill in the Senate', *The Star*, 8 May 1930.

43. 'Women's Votes at Last', *Cape Times*, 15 May 1930.

44. All senators' quotes are taken from 'Women's Vote Bill in the Senate', *The Star*, 8 May 1930.

45. Vic Alhadeff, *A Newspaper History of South Africa* (Cape Town: Don Nelson, 1979), p. 42.

46. Ibid., p. 41.

47. 'The Bertha Behind the Bill that Changed Women's Lives', *South African Jewish Report*, 8 August 2019. Available at https://www.sajr.co.za/the-bertha-behind-the-bill-that-changed -women-s-lives/ (last accessed 9 September 2021).

48. Ibid.

49. Act No. 37 of 1953. Available at https://www.gov.za/sites/default/files/gcis_document/ 201505/act-37-1953.pdf (last accessed 2 February 2021).

50. Frank Füredi, *The Silent War: Imperialism and the Changing Perception of Race* (New Brunswick: Rutgers University Press, 1998), pp. 66–7.

51. Giliomee and Mbenga, *New History of South Africa*, pp. 280–2.

52. Ibid.

53. Armstrong, *Grey Steel*, pp. 379–80.

54. Ibid., pp. 380–1.

55. Ibid., p. 381.

56. Krüger, *The Age of the Generals*, p. 157.

57. F.S. Crafford, *Jan Smuts: A Biography* (New York: Doubleday, Doran & Co, 1943), p. 237.

58. Steyn, *Smuts*, p. 122.

59. Krüger, *The Age of the Generals*, p. 159.

60. Pirow, *James Barry Munnik Hertzog*, p. 156.

61. Steyn, *Smuts*, p. 122.

62. *Cape Times*, 17 May 1933.

63. *Cape Argus*, 17 May 1933.

64. Ibid., 15 May 1933.

65. *The Times*, 18 May 1933.

66. Crafford, *Jan Smuts*, pp. 237–8.

67. Table based on information from Wikipedia, '1929 South African general election' and '1933 South African general election'. Available at https://en.wikipedia.org/wiki/1929 _South_African_general_election and https://en.wikipedia.org/wiki/1933_South_African _general_election (last accessed 3 October 2021).

68. Lindie Korf, 'D.F. Malan: A political biography' (PhD thesis, University of Stellenbosch, 2010), p. 311.

69. *The Times*, 19 May 1933.

70. Alhadeff, *A Newspaper History of South Africa*, p. 47.

71. Armstrong, *Grey Steel*, p. 385.

72. Giliomee, *The Afrikaners*, p. 408.

73. Krüger, *The Age of the Generals*, p. 165.

74. Charles Bloomberg, *Christian-Nationalism and the Rise of the Afrikaner Broederbond in South Africa, 1918–48* (London: Macmillan Press, 1990), p. 89.

75. Giliomee, *The Afrikaners*, p. 408.

76. Ibid., p. 407.

77. 'Kanonkop Paul Sauer 2015 Tops Tim Atkin Report with First 100 Point Rating for South African Wine', Kanonkop Wine Estate. Available at https://www.kanonkop.co.za/paul -sauer-2015-gets-100-point-rating/ (last accessed 9 September 2021).

CHAPTER 8: ELECTING FOR APARTHEID | 1948

1. Krüger, *The Age of the Generals*, p. 225.

2. Vic Alhadeff, *A Newspaper History of South Africa* (Cape Town: D. Nelson, 1985), p. 73.

3. James Rose Innes, *James Rose Innes, Chief Justice of South Africa, 1914–27: Autobiography* (Cape Town: Oxford University Press, 1949), p. 322.

4. D.D.T. Jabavu, 'The Findings of the All African Convention (Pamphlet Three)', December 1935. Available at http://www.historicalpapers.wits.ac.za/inventories/inv_pdfo/AD1715/ AD1715-23-1-1-001-jpeg.pdf (last accessed 14 September 2021).

5. Loveland, *By Due Process of Law? Racial Discrimination and the Right to Vote in South Africa 1855–1960*, p. 201.

6. Krüger, *The Age of the Generals*, p. 200.

7. Richard Steyn, *Seven Votes: How WWII Changed South Africa Forever* (Johannesburg: Jonathan Ball, 2020), p. 69.

8. Newell M. Stultz, *The Nationalists in Opposition, 1934–1948* (Cape Town: Human & Rousseau, 1974), p. 75.

9. Charles Bloomberg and Saul Dubow (ed.), *Christian Nationalism and the Rise of the Afrikaner Broederbond in South Africa, 1918–48* (London: Macmillan, 1990), p. 160.

10. Patrick J. Furlong, *Between Crown and Swastika: The Impact of the Radical Right on the Afrikaner Nationalist Movement in the Fascist Era* (Johannesburg: Wits University Press, 1991), pp. 154–55.

11. Stultz, *The Nationalists in Opposition*, p. 77.

12. Bloomberg and Dubow, *Christian Nationalism and the Rise of the Afrikaner Broederbond in South Africa*, p. 170.

13. Dan O'Meara, *Volkskapitalisme: Class, Capital, and Ideology in the Development of Afrikaner Nationalism, 1934–1948* (Cambridge: Cambridge University Press, 2009), p. 202.

14. David Harrison, *The White Tribe of Africa: South Africa in Perspective* (Johannesburg: Macmillan South Africa, 1986), p. 136.

15. Steyn, *Seven Votes: How WWII Changed South Africa Forever*, p. 85.

16. Furlong, *Between Crown and Swastika: The Impact of the Radical Right on the Afrikaner Nationalist Movement in the Fascist Era* (Johnnesburg: Witwatersrand University Press, 1991), p. 160.

17. Quoted in Bloomberg and Dubow, *Christian Nationalism and the Rise of the Afrikaner Broederbond in South Africa*, p. 169.
18. Wikipedia, '1943 South African general election'. Available at https://en.wikipedia.org/wiki/1943_South_African_general_election (last accessed 27 October 2021).
19. Krüger, *The Age of the Generals*, p. 223.
20. David Welsh, *The Rise and Fall of Apartheid* (Johannesburg: Jonathan Ball, 2009), p. 25.
21. René de Villiers, 'Afrikaner Nationalism' in Wilson and Thompson, *The Oxford History of South Africa*, p. 395.
22. J.H.P. Serfontein, *Brotherhood of Power: An Expose of the Secret Afrikaner Broederbond* (London: Rex Collings, 1978), p. 31.
23. Quoted in Bloomberg and Dubow, *Christian Nationalism and the Rise of the Afrikaner Broederbond in South Africa*, p. 191.
24. Bloomberg and Dubow, *Christian Nationalism and the Rise of the Afrikaner Broederbond in South Africa*, p. 192.
25. Ibid., p. 200.
26. David Harrison, *The White Tribe of Africa: South Africa in Perspective* (California: University of California Press, 1983), p. 135.
27. Z.K. Matthews, *Freedom for My People* (Cape Town: David Philip, 1983), pp. 144–5.
28. Peter Dickens, 'Job Maseko; one very remarkable South African war hero'. Available at https://samilhistory.com/2015/12/26/a-true-south-african-hero-job-maseko/ (last accessed 22 March 2021).
29. Matthews, *Freedom for My People*, p. 142.
30. Dan O'Meara, 'The 1946 African Mine Workers' Strike and the Political Economy of South Africa', *The Journal of Commonwealth & Comparative Politics*, Vol. 13, No. 2 (1975), p. 168.
31. T. Dunbar Moodie, 'The Moral Economy of the Black Miners' Strike of 1946', *Journal of Southern African Studies*, Vol. 13, No. 1 (1986), p. 20. Available at http://www.jstor.org/stable/2636674 (last accessed 22 March 2021).
32. Ibid., p. 28.
33. From the *Rand Daily Mail*, 13 August 1946, quoted in Moodie, 'The Moral Economy of the Black Miners' Strike of 1946', p. 29.
34. O'Meara, 'The 1946 African Mine Workers' Strike and the Political Economy of South Africa', p. 161.
35. Matthews, *Freedom for My People*, p. 147.
36. Ibid., p. 150.
37. Furlong, *Between Crown and Swastika*, p. 157.
38. Stultz, *The Nationalists in Opposition*, p. 125.
39. Ibid., p. 124.
40. Alan Paton, *South African Tragedy: The Life and Times of Jan Hofmeyr* (New York: Charles Scribner's Sons, 1965), p. 344.
41. Krüger, *The Age of the Generals*, p. 225.
42. Saul Dubow, *Apartheid, 1948–1994* (Oxford: Oxford University Press, 2014), p. 10.
43. Martha Evans, *Speeches that Shaped South Africa: From Malan to Malema* (Cape Town: Penguin Books, 2017), p. 5.

44. Stultz, *The Nationalists in Opposition*, p. 136.
45. Kenneth A. Heard, *General Elections in South Africa, 1943–1970* (Oxford: Oxford University Press, 1974), p. 33.
46. Stultz, *The Nationalists in Opposition*, p. 138.
47. Welsh, *The Rise and Fall of Apartheid*, p. 19.
48. Evans, *Speeches that Shaped South Africa*, p. 2.
49. Ibid., p. 3.
50. Heard, *General Elections in South Africa*, p. 34.
51. Ibid.
52. Ivor Wilkins and Hans Strydom, *The Super-Afrikaners: Inside the Afrikaner Broederbond* (Johannesburg: Jonathan Ball, 2012), p. 93.
53. Stultz, *The Nationalists in Opposition*, p. 145.
54. Roger Southall, *Whites and Democracy in South Africa* (unpublished manuscript).
55. Wikipedia, '1948 South African general election'. Available at https://en.wikipedia.org/wiki/1948_South_African_general_election (last accessed 5 October 2021).
56. Thompson, *A History of South Africa*, p. 186.

CHAPTER 9: THE REPUBLIC OF VERWOERD | 1960 AND 1966

1. Joanna Strangwayes-Booth, *A Cricket in the Thorn Tree: Helen Suzman and the Progressive Party of South Africa* (Johannesburg: Hutchison of South Africa, 1976), p. 220.
2. William Beinart, *Twentieth-Century South Africa* (Oxford: Oxford University Press, 2001), p. 143.
3. Dennis Davis and Michelle le Roux, *Lawfare: Judging Politics in South Africa* (Johannesburg: Jonathan Ball, 2019), p. 57.
4. Ian Loveland, *By Due Process of Law? Racial Discrimination and the Right to Vote in South Africa 1855–1960* (Oxford: Hart Publishing, 1999), p. 359.
5. Beinart, *Twentieth-Century South Africa*, p. 160.
6. Edgar Brookes, *A South African Pilgrimage* (Johannesburg: Ravan Press, 1977), p. 56.
7. Davenport and Saunders, *South Africa*, p. 406.
8. Saul Dubow, *Apartheid 1948–1994* (Oxford: Oxford University Press, 2014), p. 70.
9. Henry Kenney, *Verwoerd: Architect of Apartheid* (Johannesburg: Jonathan Ball, 1980), p. 57.
10. Quoted in Brian Bunting, *The Rise of the South African Reich* (London: International Defence and Aid Fund for South Africa, 1986), pp. 107–109.
11. Ibid., p. 110.
12. Davenport and Saunders, *South Africa*, p. 416.
13. Address by Harold Macmillan to Members of both Houses of the Parliament of the Union of South Africa, Cape Town, 3 February 1960. Available at https://web-archives.univ-pau.fr/english/TD2doc1.pdf (last accessed 8 November 2021).
14. Muriel Horrell, *A Survey of Race Relations in South Africa: 1959–1960* (Johannesburg: South African Institute of Race Relations, 1961), p. 6.
15. Thompson, *A History of South Africa*, p. 188.
16. Strangwayes-Booth, *A Cricket in the Thorn Tree*, p. 156.

17. D.M. Scher, 'Teaching and Making History: The Remarkable Career of Margaret Ballinger', *Kleio*, Vol. 13, No. 1–2 (1981), p. 34.
18. Ibid., p. 36.
19. F.A. Mouton, 'Margaret Ballinger, Opponent of Apartheid or Collaborator?', *South African Historical Journal*, Vol. 26, No. 1 (1992), p. 145.
20. Randolph Vigne, *Liberals Against Apartheid: A History of the Liberal Party of South Africa* (London: MacMillan Press, 1997), p. 35.
21. Horrell, *A Survey of Race Relations in South Africa: 1959–1960*, p. 5.
22. David Harrison, *The White Tribe of Africa: South Africa in Perspective* (Johannesburg: Southern Book Publishers, 1987), p. 165.
23. Horrell, *A Survey of Race Relations in South Africa: 1959–1960*, p. 107.
24. Davenport and Saunders, *South Africa*, p. 417.
25. Welsh, *The Rise and Fall of Apartheid*, p. 67.
26. Thula Simpson, *History of South Africa: From 1902 to the Present* (Cape Town: Penguin, 2021), p. 172.
27. Welsh, *The Rise and Fall of Apartheid*, p. 129.
28. Adrian Leftwich, 'I gave the names', *Granta*, 2002. Available at https://granta.com/i-gave-the-names/ (last accessed 17 September 2021).
29. *Liberal Opinion*, Vol. 4, No. 4 (March 1966).
30. Heard, *General Elections in South Africa, 1943–1970*, p. 156.
31. Ibid., p. 160.
32. Strangwayes-Booth, *A Cricket in the Thorn Tree*, p. 220.

CHAPTER 10: BLACK CONSCIOUSNESS, WHITE DENIAL | 1977

1. Welsh, *The Rise and Fall of Apartheid*, p. 154.
2. SABC (uploaded 2011), *TRC Episode 65, Part 02* [Video] https://www.youtube.com/watch?v=oxNQV9CbUW4&t=637s (last accessed 8 October 2021).
3. Quoted in Xolela Mangcu, *Biko: A Biography* (Cape Town: Tafelberg, 2012), p. 262.
4. Donald Woods, *Biko* (Penguin, 1987), p. 214.
5. Ibid., p. 227.
6. Colin Eglin, *Crossing the Borders of Power: The Memoirs of Colin Eglin* (Johannesburg: Jonathan Ball, 2007), p. 168.
7. Henry Lever, 'South African General Election, 1977', *Social Science*, Vol. 56, No. 4 (1981), p. 214. Available at http://www.jstor.org/stable/41886697 (last accessed 18 July 2021).
8. Ibid., p. 214.
9. Ibid.
10. Matthew Midlane, 'The South African General Election of 1977', *African Affairs*, Vol. 78, No. 312 (1979), p. 378. Available at http://www.jstor.org/stable/722147 (last accessed 18 July 2021).
11. AP Archive (1977), *SYND 10 11 77 President Vorster Addresses Election Meeting* [Video] https://www.youtube.com/watch?v=TFMH1bDrb1I (last accessed 17 September 2021).
12. AP Archive (1977), *UPITN 30 11 77 Vorster At Final Rally Before Election* [Video] https://www.youtube.com/watch?v=uRORuVwM608 (last accessed 17 September 2021).

13. Wikipedia, '1977 South African general election'. Available at https://en.wikipedia.org/ wiki/1977_South_African_general_election (last accessed 8 October 2021).

14. Midlane, 'The South African General Election of 1977', p. 384.

15. William A. Hachten and C. Anthony Giffard, *The Press and Apartheid: Repression and Propaganda in South Africa* (London: Palgrave Macmillan, 1984), p. 241.

16. Midlane, 'The South African General Election of 1977', p. 384.

17. AP Archive (1977), *SYND 1 12 77 Vorster Election Victory Interview* [Video] https://www .youtube.com/watch?v=3RaDrMz4GLo (last accessed 17 September 2021).

CHAPTER 11: TRICAMERAL ON FOR SIZE | 1983 AND 1984

1. RP 113/1978, 'Report of the Supplementary Commission of Inquiry into Alleged Irregularities in the Former Department of Information', Para 10.337.

2. Brian Pottinger, *The Imperial Presidency: P.W. Botha, the First 10 Years* (Johannesburg: Southern Book Publishers, 1988), p. 24.

3. Pottinger, *The Imperial Presidency*, p. 25.

4. Allister Sparks, *The Mind of South Africa: The Story of the Rise and Fall of Apartheid* (London: William Heineman Ltd, 1990), p. 307.

5. Pottinger, *The Imperial Presidency*, p. 121.

6. Ibid.

7. Alan Emery, 'The Insurgent Origins of Democratization in South Africa', paper presented to the First Annual Graduate Student Conference for Comparative Research, 8–9 May 1999. Available at https://omalley.nelsonmandela.org/omalley/cis/omalley/OMalleyWeb/03lvo 2424/04lvo3370/05lvo3401.htm (last accessed 11 October 2021).

8. Pottinger, *The Imperial Presidency*, p. 122.

9. Padraig O'Malley, 'South Africa – Total Strategy', O'Malley Archives. Available at https://omalley.nelsonmandela.org/omalley/index.php/site/q/03lvo2424/04lvo2730/05lv 02918/06lvo2972.htm (last accessed 11 October 2021).

10. James Selfe, 'The Total Onslaught and the Total Strategy: Adaptations to the Security Intelligence Decision-Making Strategy Under PW Botha's Administration' (MA thesis, University of Cape Town, 1987), p. 45.

11. O'Malley, 'South Africa – Total Strategy'.

12. Selfe, 'The Total Onslaught and the Total Strategy', p. 115.

13. Sparks, *The Mind of South Africa*, p. 310.

14. Oliver Tambo, '"Year of the Woman" Address', 8 January 1984.

15. Sparks, *The Mind of South Africa*, pp. 308–9.

16. O'Malley, 'South Africa – Total Strategy'.

17. William Dicey, *1986* (Cape Town: Umuzi, 2021), p. 39.

18. Sparks, *The Mind of South Africa*, p. 317.

19. Ibid., pp. 317–18.

20. Helen Suzman, *In No Uncertain Terms: Memoirs* (Johannesburg: Jonathan Ball, 1993), pp. 253–4.

21. Colin Eglin, *Crossing the Borders of Power* (Johannesburg: Jonathan Ball, 2007), p. 197.

22. Ben Maclennan, *Apartheid: The Lighter Side* (Cape Town: Chameleon Press, 1990), p. 65.

23. Eglin, *Crossing the Borders of Power*, pp. 198–9.
24. Suzman, *In No Uncertain Terms*, pp. 238–9.
25. Albert Grundlingh, *Slabbert: Man on a Mission* (Johannesburg: Jonathan Ball, 2021), pp. 96–7.
26. Shelagh Gastrow, *Who's Who in South African Politics: Number 4* (Johannesburg: Ravan Press, 1992), pp. 99–100.
27. Pottinger, *The Imperial Presidency*, p. 140.
28. Eglin, *Crossing the Borders of Power*, p. 198.
29. Author's interview with Albert Grundlingh, 29 September 2021.
30. Pottinger, *The Imperial Presidency*, p. 141.
31. Ibid., pp. 140–1.
32. Ibid., p. 142.
33. Ibid., p. 147.
34. Author's interview with Ken Andrew, 8 March 2021.
35. Evans, *Speeches that Shaped South Africa*, p. 152.
36. Ibid., p. 151.
37. Gastrow, *Who's Who in South African Politics*, pp. 11–12.
38. Blackman and Dall, *Rogues' Gallery*, p. 287.
39. Evans, *Speeches that Shaped South Africa*, pp. 151–2.
40. Ibid., p. 156.
41. Grundlingh, *Slabbert*, pp. 97–8.
42. Suzman, *In No Uncertain Terms*, p. 238.
43. Grundlingh, *Slabbert*, p. 98.
44. Ibid., p. 99.
45. Ibid., pp. 99–101.
46. Ibid., p. 100.
47. Suzman, *In No Uncertain Terms*, p. 239.
48. Grundlingh, *Slabbert*, p. 100.
49. Allister Sparks, 'S. Africa Whites Back Wider Vote in Referendum', *Washington Post*, 4 November 1983. Available at https://www.washingtonpost.com/archive/politics/1983/11/04/s-africa-whites-back-wider-vote-in-referendum/3b12a4c5-0d9a-4bf5-a1ea-b3d27103dfob/ (last accessed 11 October 2021).
50. Michael Hornsby, 'Botha Hails Referendum Result as Victory for Evolutionary Reform', *The Times*, 4 November 1983.
51. Sparks, 'S. Africa Whites Back Wider Vote in Referendum'.
52. Grundlingh, *Slabbert*, p. 101.
53. 'Interview with Oliver Tambo by Mayibuye on the Current Situation in South Africa and Southern Africa in General, 01 March 1984', South African History Online. Available at https://www.sahistory.org.za/archive/interview-oliver-tambo-mayibuye-current-situation-south-africa-and-southern-africa-general (last accessed 11 October 2021).
54. Nelson Mandela, *Long Walk to Freedom* (London: Abacus, 1995), p. 618.
55. Govan Mbeki, *The Prison Writings of Govan Mbeki* (Cape Town: David Philip, 1991), pp. 48–63.
56. Evans, *Speeches that Shaped South Africa*, p. 151.

57. George Orwell, *1984* (New York: New American Library, 1950), p. 35.
58. 'Interview with Oliver Tambo by Mayibuye', South African History Online.
59. Michael Hornsby, 'Botha Not Dismayed by Low Turnout', *The Times*, 31 August 1984.
60. 'Interview with Oliver Tambo by Mayibuye', South African History Online.
61. Wikipedia, 'Tricameral Parliament'. Available at https://en.wikipedia.org/wiki/Tricameral _Parliament (last accessed 29 November 2021).
62. Tambo, '"Year of the Woman" Address'.
63. Evans, *Speeches that Shaped South Africa*, p. 170.
64. 'Township Uprising, 1984–1985', South African History Online. Available at https://www.sahistory.org.za/article/township-uprising-1984-1985 (last accessed 11 October 2021).
65. Maclennan, *Apartheid*, p. 65.
66. Padraig O'Malley, '1984', O'Malley Archives. Available at https://omalley.nelsonmandela .org/omalley/index.php/site/q/03lv01538/04lv01539/05lv01573/06lv01578.htm (last accessed 11 October 2021).
67. Fanie Cloete, 'Resolving P.W. Botha's 1985 Rubicon Riddle', *Historia* [online], Vol. 64, No. 2 (2019). Available at http://www.scielo.org.za/scielo.php?script=sci_arttext&pid=S 0018-229X2019000200006 (last accessed 11 October 2021).
68. Evans, *Speeches that Shaped South Africa*, p. 180.
69. All quotes from the Rubicon speech are taken from Evans, *Speeches that Shaped South Africa*, pp. 179–90.
70. Dave Steward, 'From the Rubicon to February 2nd 1990', *Politicsweb*, 11 February 2010. Available at https://www.politicsweb.co.za/opinion/from-the-rubicon-to-february-2nd -1990 (last accessed 11 October 2021).
71. Sparks, *The Mind of South Africa*, p. 350.
72. Hermann Giliomee, 'The Rubicon revisited', *Politicsweb*, 20 August 2008. Available at https://www.politicsweb.co.za/news-and-analysis/the-rubicon-revisited (last accessed 11 October 2021).
73. Ibid.
74. Dicey, *1986*, p. 45.
75. Both the quote from the speech and the explanation preceding it come from Evans, *Speeches that Shaped South Africa*, pp. 173–8.
76. O'Malley, 'South Africa – Total Strategy'.
77. '"Attack, Advance, Give the Enemy No Quarter!" by O.R. Tambo, Message of the National Executive Committee of the ANC on the 74th Anniversary of the ANC, 8 January 1986', South African History Online. Available at https://www.sahistory.org.za/ archive/attack-advance-give-enemy-no-quarter-o-r-tambo-message-national-executive -committee-anc (last accessed 11 October 2021).
78. Dicey, *1986*, p. 79.

CHAPTER 12: THE VIOLENT PANGS OF A MIRACLE BIRTH | 1994

1. Anthony Butler, *Cyril Ramaphosa* (Johannesburg: Jacana, 2008), p. 289.
2. Allister Sparks, *Tomorrow Is Another Country: The Inside Story of South Africa's Road to Change* (Cape Town: Struik, 1994), p. 93.

3. Quoted in David Welsh, *The Rise and Fall of Apartheid*, p. 384.
4. Sparks, *Tomorrow Is Another Country*, p. 107.
5. Martin Meredith, *South Africa's New Era: The 1994 Election* (London: Mandarin, 1994), p. 18.
6. Quoted in David Ottaway, *Chained Together: Mandela, De Klerk, and the Struggle to Remake South Africa* (New York: Crown, 1993), p. 105.
7. Butler, *Cyril Ramaphosa*, p. 254.
8. Welsh, *The Rise and Fall of Apartheid*, p. 431.
9. Timothy Sisk, *Democratization in South Africa: The Elusive Social Contract* (Princeton: Princeton University Press, 1995), p. 229.
10. David Welsh, 'Right-wing Terrorism in South Africa', *Terrorism and Political Violence*, Vol. 7, No. 1 (1995). Available at http://www.tandfonline.com/loi/ftpv20 (last accessed 20 October 2021).
11. Meredith, *South Africa's New Era*, p. 28.
12. Thompson, *A History of South Africa*, p. 249.
13. Ibid., p. 449.
14. Stuart J. Kaufman, 'South Africa's Civil War, 1985–1995', *South African Journal of International Affairs*, Vol. 24, No. 4 (2017), p. 509.
15. Thompson, *A History of South Africa*, p. 250.
16. Meredith, *South Africa's New Era*, p. 33.
17. Kaufman, 'South Africa's Civil War', p. 508.
18. Stephen Ellis, 'The Historical Significance of South Africa's Third Force', *Journal of Southern African Studies*, Vol. 24, No. 2 (1998), p. 261.
19. Sparks, *Tomorrow Is Another Country*, p. 173.
20. Ibid., p. 132.
21. Welsh, *The Rise and Fall of Apartheid*, p. 439.
22. John Carlin, 'Rampage through township', *The Independent*, 19 June 1992.
23. James G.R. Simpson, 'Boipatong: The Politics of a Massacre and the South African Transition', *Journal of Southern African Studies*, Vol. 38, No. 3 (2012), p. 635.
24. Sparks, *Tomorrow Is Another Country*, pp. 142–3.
25. Quoted in Simpson, 'Boipatong', pp. 635–6.
26. Welsh, *The Rise and Fall of Apartheid*, p. 432.
27. SABC (uploaded 2011), *TRC Episode 19, Part 03* [Video]. Available at https://www.youtube.com/watch?v=yYL4QqiUzDU&t=726s (last accessed 4 October 2021).
28. Bill Keller, 'Democracy vs. Dictator in Apartheid "Homeland"', *New York Times*, 10 September 1992.
29. SABC (uploaded 2011), *TRC Episode 19, Part 03* [Video].
30. Ibid.
31. Meredith, *South Africa's New Era*, p. 54.
32. Sisk, *Democratization in South Africa*, p. 229.
33. Welsh, *The Rise and Fall of Apartheid*, p. 482.
34. Quoted in Meredith, *South Africa's New Era*, p. 62.
35. Sparks, *Tomorrow Is Another Country*, p. 188.
36. SAPA, 'Hani Killers Almost Succeeded in Their Aims, TRC Hears', 4 December 1997.

Available at https://www.justice.gov.za/trc/media/1997/9712/s971204s.htm (last accessed 4 October 2021).

37. BBC Newsnight (2013), *How Mandela Responded to the Assassination of Chris Hani* [Video]. Available at https://www.youtube.com/watch?v=lOn24d9xwYQ (last accessed 4 October 2021).

38. Hugh Macmillan, *A Biography of a South African Martyr: Chris Hani* (Athens: Ohio University Press, 2021). Available at https://www.perlego.com/book/2101960/chris-hani -pdf (last accessed 11 October 2021).

39. Welsh, *The Rise and Fall of Apartheid*, p. 527.

40. Ibid., p. 488.

41. Quoted in Meredith, *South Africa's New Era*, pp. 79–80.

42. Stephen Clarke, Mick Gold and Stewart Lansley (dirs.), 'The Whites' Last Stand' (ep. 3), *Death of Apartheid* (BBC, 1995). Available at https://www.youtube.com/watch?v=PPvu AVO2-NI (last accessed 13 October 2021).

43. Ibid.

44. Welsh, *The Rise and Fall of Apartheid*, p. 511.

45. Ibid., p. 515.

46. Judge R.W. Nugent, 'Shell House Massacre March 28 1994: The Inquest Findings', 28 March 2014. Available at https://www.politicsweb.co.za/documents/shell-house-mas sacre-march-28-1994-the-inquest-fin (last accessed 4 October 2021).

47. Nugent, 'Shell House Massacre March 28 1994' and Stephen Ellis, 'The Historical Significance of South Africa's Third Force', p. 284.

48. Kaufman, 'South Africa's Civil War, 1985–1995', p. 509.

49. Sparks, *Tomorrow Is Another Country*, p. 227.

50. Reuter, 'De Klerk: "My Political Task Is Just Beginning"', *Washington Post*, 3 May 1994.

51. 'Speech by Nelson Mandela announcing the ANC election victory' [audio recording]. Available at http://db.nelsonmandela.org/speeches/pub_view.asp?pg=item&ItemID=N MS174&txtstr=Carlton%20Hotel (last accessed 11 October 2021).

52. Wikipedia, '1994 South African general election'. Available at https://en.wikipedia.org/ wiki/1994_South_African_general_election (last accessed 5 October 2021).

CHAPTER 13: THE MULTIPLYING CONSEQUENCES OF LONG DIVISION: POLOKWANE AND NASREC | 2007 AND 2017

1. *News24*, 'We haven't heard from Winnie', 9 December 2007.

2. Author's interview with Nickolaus Bauer, 1 June 2021.

3. Ibid.

4. This section is based on Anthony Butler, *Cyril Ramaphosa: The Road to Presidential Power* (Auckland Park: Jacana, 2019).

5. Butler, *Cyril Ramaphosa*, pp. 43–4.

6. Ibid., pp. 93–4.

7. Ibid., p. 199.

8. Ibid., p. 324.

9. Ibid., p. 368.

10. Susan Booysen, *The African National Congress and the Regeneration of Political Power* (Johannesburg: Wits University Press, 2011), p. 33.
11. Ibid., p. 41.
12. Ibid.
13. Author's interview with Stephen Grootes, 7 May 2021.
14. Email correspondence with Anthony Butler, 27 September 2021.
15. Author's interview with Stephen Grootes, 7 May 2021.
16. Author's interview with Andrew Feinstein, 21 June 2021.
17. *S v Shaik and Others*, Case No.: CC27/04, 'Judgment'. Available at https://omalley.nelson mandela.org/omalley/index.php/site/q/03lv03445/04lv04015/05lv04148/06lv04149.htm (last accessed 4 October 2021).
18. Ibid.
19. 'Zuma says he showered to reduce risk of HIV', *Irish Times*, 5 April 2006.
20. Stephen Grootes, 'Mokotedi Mpshe's Zuma tapes affidavit: It's all about Leonard McCarthy', *Daily Maverick*, 1 July 2015.
21. Mark Gevisser, *Thabo Mbeki: The Dream Deferred* (Johannesburg: Jonathan Ball, 2013), Kindle edition.
22. Booysen, *The African National Congress and the Regeneration of Political Power*, p. 47.
23. Ibid., p. 48.
24. Ibid.
25. Staff reporter, 'Mbeki: Browse Mole was right', *Mail & Guardian*, 16 May 2008.
26. Booysen, *The African National Congress and the Regeneration of Political Power*, p. 48.
27. Ibid., p. 42.
28. Email correspondence with Anthony Butler, 27 September 2021.
29. In Booysen, *The African National Congress and the Regeneration of Political Power*, p. 43.
30. Ibid., p. 65.
31. John Yeld, 'Judge also finds biographer "unlikeable"', *IOL*, 9 January 2007.
32. Ferial Haffajee, 'Ace boosts ANC membership to 1.4-million – highest ever', *Daily Maverick*, 4 December 2020.
33. Ibid.
34. Booysen, *The African National Congress and the Regeneration of Political Power*, p. 63.
35. Table adapted from Booysen, *The African National Congress and the Regeneration of Political Power*, p. 65.
36. Booysen, *The African National Congress and the Regeneration of Political Power*, pp. 66–7.
37. Alicestine October, 'I stand by my judgment – judge who threw out Zuma corruption case', *City Press*, 16 February 2016.
38. Booysen, *The African National Congress and the Regeneration of Political Power*, p. 70.
39. Sapa, 'Cope wins name battle', *The Times*, 12 December 2008.
40. *News24*, 'Political hyenas in feeding frenzy – Vavi', 26 August 2010.
41. *New African*, 'The Malema Dilemma', 14 November 2011. Available at https://newafrican magazine.com/2743/ (last accessed 4 October 2021).
42. African National Congress, 'Public Announcement on the Disciplinary hearings of:

Floyd Shivambu, Julius Malema and Sindiso Magaqa', Luthuli House, Johannesburg, 29 February 2012. Available at https://web.archive.org/web/20130818022140/http://images.businessday.co.za/Discipline.pdf (last accessed 4 October 2021).

43. Butler, *Cyril Ramaphosa*, p. 468.
44. Ibid.
45. Ibid., pp. 460–3.
46. Jonisayi Maromo, 'Marikana strategy "same as Sharpeville"', *IOL*, 26 March 2014.
47. Nick Dawes, 'Marikana massacre: the untold story of the strike leader who died for workers' rights', *The Guardian*, 19 May 2015.
48. Butler, *Cyril Ramaphosa*, p. 463.
49. Raymond Suttner, 'ANC membership numbers: What is the significance?', *Daily Maverick*, 20 October 2015.
50. David Smith, 'Mandela's death gives respite for Jacob Zuma and the ANC – but for how long?', *The Guardian*, 9 December 2013.
51. Tehillah Niselow, 'Sunday Read: Load shedding through the years and how Eskom has struggled to keep the lights on', *fin24*, 24 March 2019.
52. BBC, '#ZumaMustFall: South Africans march against Jacob Zuma', 16 December 2015.
53. SARB media release, 'VBS Mutual Bank investigators report to the Prudential Authority', 10 October 2018. Available at https://www.resbank.co.za/en/home/publications/publication-detail-pages/media-releases/2018/8830 (last accessed 4 October 2021).
54. Susan Booysen, *Precarious Power: Compliance and Discontent under Ramaphosa's ANC* (Johannesburg: Wits University Press, 2021), p. 26.
55. Qaanitah Hunter, *Balance of Power: Ramaphosa and the future of South Africa* (Cape Town: Kwela Books, 2019), Kindle edition.
56. Ibid.
57. Ibid.
58. Charles Molele and Mzilikazi wa Afrika, 'R14m theft of cash from home of premier', *TimesLive*, 28 March 2010.
59. Qaanitah Hunter, 'How David Mabuza outplayed the NDZ camp', *TimesLive*, 22 December 2017.
60. Table adapted from Booysen, *Precarious Power*, p. 31.
61. 'Closing Address by ANC President Cyril Ramaphosa', ANC 54th National Conference, Nasrec, 20 December 2017. Available at https://www.news24.com/news24/Columnists/GuestColumn/ramaphosas-first-address-as-anc-president-read-the-full-speech-20171221 (last accessed 4 October 2021).
62. Author's interview with Nickolaus Bauer, 1 June 2021.
63. BBC, 'South Africa's Jacob Zuma resigns after pressure from party', 15 February 2018.
64. Booysen, *Precarious Power*, pp. 27–30.

EPILOGUE: A RETURN TO MINORITY RULE? | 2021

1. Voter registration statistics: Registered voters as at 16 October 2021, IEC. Available at https://www.elections.org.za/pw/StatsData/Voter-Registration-Statistics (last accessed 22 November 2021).
2. Marc Heywood, 'The great no-vote: South Africa's return to minority rule', *Daily Maverick*,

2 November 2021. Available at https://www.dailymaverick.co.za/article/2021-11-02-the-gr eat-no-vote-south-africas-return-to-minority-rule/ (last accessed 22 November 2021).

3. Liela Magnus, 'Senior ex-intelligence agents and ANC members under probe for allegedly igniting Zuma riots', SABC News, 13 July 2021. Available at https://www.sabcnews.com/ sabcnews/some-ex-intelligence-agents-and-anc-members-under-probe-for-alleged-invol vement-in-igniting-zuma-riots/ (last accessed 22 November 2021).

4. Anthony Butler, '2024 And All That', *Financial Mail*, 11–17 November 2021.

5. 'Municipal Elections', *News24*. Available at https://www.news24.com/news24/elections/ map/lge?year=2021&level=country (last accessed 29 November 2021).

6. Rebecca Davis, 'The biggest winners and losers of South Africa's local government polls', *Daily Maverick*, 6 November 2021. Available at https://www.dailymaverick.co.za/article/ 2021-11-06-the-biggest-winners-and-losers-of-south-africas-local-government-polls/ (last accessed 22 November 2021).

7. Dawie Boonzaaier, 'Ramaphosa way more popular than ANC', *City Press*, 10 October 2021. Available at https://www.news24.com/citypress/politics/ramaphosa-way-more-popular -than-anc-20211009 (last accessed 22 November 2021).

8. 'Warning signs in the Out of Order Index', *News24*. Available at https://outoforder.news24 .com/ (last accessed 22 November 2021).

9. Des Erasmus, 'DA wins all wards in Phoenix, site of contentious election posters', *Daily Maverick*, 3 November 2021. Available at https://www.dailymaverick.co.za/ article/2021-11-03-da-wins-all-wards-in-phoenix-site-of-contentious-election-posters/ (last accessed 24 November 2021).

10. Dawie Scholtz, 'Thoughts on 2024', Twitter. Available at https://twitter.com/DawieScholtz/ status/1458659805258784770 (last accessed 29 November 2021).

11. Stephen Grootes, 'The ANC will remain in power for many years after 2024 – here's why', *Daily Maverick*, 1 December 2021. Available at https://www.dailymaverick.co.za/article/ 2021-12-01-the-anc-will-remain-in-power-for-many-years-after-2024-heres-why/ (last accessed 8 December 2021).

12. Butler, '2024 And All That', *Financial Mail*, 11–17 November 2021.

13. Andisiwe Makinana, Kgothatso Madisa and Zimasa Matiwane, '"We are playing our political game": DA scores as ANC gets EFFed up in the metros', *Sunday Times*, 22 November 2021. Available at https://www.timeslive.co.za/sunday-times-daily/politics/ 2021-11-22-we-are-playing-our-political-game-da-scores-as-anc-gets-effed-up-in-the -metros/ (last accessed 24 November 2021).

14. Isaac Mahlangu, 'DA should understand our vote for them is not a gift – Mashaba', *Sowetan Live*, 23 November 2021. Available at https://www.sowetanlive.co.za/news/ south-africa/2021-11-23-da-should-understand-our-vote-for-them-is-not-a-gift-mashaba/ (last accessed 24 November 2021).

PICTURE CREDITS

p. 5: Allen Francis Gardiner, Public domain, via Wikimedia Commons

p. 9: Supplied, public domain

p. 13: James King, Public domain, via Wikimedia Commons

p. 15: National Museum Bloemfontein

p. 17: JRamatsui, CC BY-SA 3.0, via Wikimedia Commons

p. 19: Cornelius H. (Cornelius Howard), 1860–1939, Public domain, via Wikimedia Commons

p. 23: Internet Archive Book Images, via Wikimedia Commons

p. 24: Artist unknown, Public domain, via Wikimedia Commons

p. 27: Western Cape Archives and Records Service

p. 29: Western Cape Archives and Records Service

p. 30: Western Cape Archives and Records Service

p. 31: Western Cape Archives and Records Service

p. 33: Western Cape Archives and Records Service

p. 34: Western Cape Archives and Records Service

p. 37: Collection of Parliament of South Africa, ref. no. 26239

p. 41: Western Cape Archives and Records Service

p. 45: Collection of Parliament of South Africa, ref. no. 32404

p. 53 left: Western Cape Archives and Records Service; right: National Archives of South Africa, Pretoria / Zabeth Botha

p. 55: From *The Schröder Art Memento* (Pretoria: 'The Press' Printing and Publishing Work, 1894)

p. 58: Offenberg Photographie, Damstraat, Amsterdam, Public domain, via Wikimedia Commons

p. 61: Joseph Morewood Staniforth (1863–1921), Public domain, via Wikimedia Commons

p. 62: Jan Veth, Public domain, via Wikimedia Commons

p. 63: Public domain, via Wikimedia Commons

p. 65: Elliott & Fry, Public domain, via Wikimedia Commons

p. 67: National Archives of South Africa, Pretoria / Zabeth Botha

p. 74: National Archives of South Africa, Pretoria / Zabeth Botha

p. 77: Western Cape Archives and Records Service

p. 80: National Library of Norway, Public domain, via Wikimedia Commons

p. 81 left: E, Peters, 1914, Collection of Parliament of South Africa, 27403; middle and right: Western Cape Archives and Records Service

p. 83: Photographer unknown, Public domain, via Wikimedia Commons

p. 86: Supplied / From Eric A. Walker, *W.P. Schreiner: A South African* (London: Oxford University Press, 1937), credit not given

p. 89: Supplied by Historical Publications Southern Africa

p. 96: Amazwi South African Museum of Literature / NELM

p. 98: Western Cape Archives and Records Service

p. 105: Artw. 080 National Convention 1909–1910 by E. Roworth. Collection of Parliament of South Africa

p. 110: Supplied, private collection

p. 111: Bower Studio, 1098. Collection of Parliament of South Africa

p. 117: The Heritage Portal, Public domain

p. 122: SAL. Anon., Public domain, via Wikimedia Commons

p. 124: Alan Paton Centre and Struggle Archives

p. 126: SA government, Public domain, via Wikimedia Commons

p. 129: Supplied by Brian Willan

p. 131: Prof. W.A. Kleynhans Poster Collection (KPC). UNISA Library, Archives and Special Collections

p. 134: Photographer unknown, Public domain, via Wikimedia Commons

p. 136: Watson, Public domain, via Wikimedia Commons

p. 137: Work by employee of the South African government over fifty years ago, Public domain, via Wikimedia Commons

p. 138: Collection of Parliament of South Africa, ref. no. 40894

p. 140: Historical Papers Research Archive, University of the Witwatersrand, South Africa

p. 141: Johannesburg Heritage Foundation, CC BY-SA 4.0, via Wikimedia Commons

p. 143: Historical Papers Research Archive, University of the Witwatersrand, South Africa

p. 146: Supplied by Robert Edgar

p. 147: Western Cape Archives and Records Service

p. 151: SAP Election flyer, Public domain

p. 152: From W.K. Hancock, *Smuts: The Fields of Force*, (Cambridge University Press, 1968), p. 150

p. 157: Photo of First National Party Cabinet, 1924, *Erfenisstigting* Archives, Pretoria

p. 159: *Cape Times*, Public domain, via Wikimedia Commons

p. 160: Brenthurst Library

p. 162: Supplied by Henry Dee

p. 163: Supplied by Henry Dee

p. 169: Photographer unknown, Public domain, via Wikimedia Commons

p. 171: Supplied by National Library of South Africa

p. 174: Desmond Louw / DNA Photographers

p. 176: City of Cape Town

p. 178: Public domain, via Wikimedia Commons

p. 181 left: Western Cape Archives and Records Service; right: Tielman Roos by D.C. Boonzaier c.1922, Collection of Parliament of South Africa, ref. no. 20534 07

p. 184: Western Cape Archives and Records Service

p. 186: Public domain, via Wikimedia Commons

p. 188: Die Triomf van Nasionalisme in Suid-Afrika 1910–1953, Public domain, via Wikimedia Commons

p. 191: *Erfenisstigting* Archives, Pretoria

p. 196: South African National Library
p. 198: South African National Library
p. 199: Malherbe Papers / Campbell Collection
p. 201: Malherbe Papers / Campbell Collection
p. 203: National Archives of South Africa, Pretoria / Zabeth Botha
p. 205: The Ditsong National Museum of Military History
p. 209: South African History Online, Public domain
p. 211: National Archives of South Africa, Pretoria / Zabeth Botha
p. 212: Artw.038 N.C. Havenga by Edward Roworth 1950. Collection of Parliament of
    South Africa
p. 216: Artw.082 Smuts by Frank Wiles 1953. Collection of Parliament of South Africa
p. 217: Photographer unknown, Public domain, via Wikimedia Commons
p. 219: Snikkers / Anefo, CCo, via Wikimedia Commons
p. 225: Public domain, via Wikimedia Commons
p. 226: Still from news reel / Supplied. https://www.youtube.com/watch?v=lJBChGJDGJs
p. 230: Photographer unknown, Public domain, via Wikimedia Commons
p. 231: *An Illustrated History of South Africa* (Africana-museum), Public domain, via
    Wikimedia Commons
p. 232: Prof. W.A. Kleynhans Poster Collection (KPC). UNISA Library, Archives and
    Special Collections
p. 233: Government of South Africa, Public domain, via Wikimedia Commons
p. 234: Western Cape Archives and Records Service
p. 236: Source unknown
p. 241: National Archives of South Africa, Pretoria / Zabeth Botha
p. 242: Unknown photographer, CC BY-SA 4.0, via Wikimedia Commons
p. 245: National Archives of South Africa, Pretoria / Zabeth Botha
p. 246: National Archives of South Africa, Pretoria / Zabeth Botha
p. 247: Arena Holdings Archive
p. 251: With permission of the Boraine family
p. 253: *Erfenisstigting* Archives, Pretoria
p. 254: National Archives of South Africa, Pretoria / Zabeth Botha
p. 256: National Archives of South Africa, Pretoria / Zabeth Botha
p. 258: Alan Paton Centre and Struggle Archives
p. 261: Stellenbosch University Library
p. 262: National Archives of South Africa, Pretoria / Zabeth Botha
p. 263: Artw.939 Mr Amichand Rajbansi MP. Library of Parliament
p. 265: *Erfenisstigting* Archives, Pretoria
p. 266: Rob C. Croes / Anefo, CC BY-SA 3.0 NL, via Wikimedia Commons
p. 267: Alan Paton Centre and Struggle Archives
p. 269: Prof. W.A. Kleynhans Poster Collection (KPC). UNISA Library, Archives and
    Special Collections
p. 271: Rob C. Croes / Anefo, CC BY-SA 3.0 NL, via Wikimedia Commons
p. 272–3: Artw.528 P.W. Botha's Cabinet by Fleur Ferri, 1982. Collection of Parliament of
    South Africa

INDEX